SOLARIS

Solaris Administration:
A Beginner's Guide

ABOUT THE AUTHOR

Paul A. Watters, M.Phil. (Cambridge), B.A.(Hons.)(Tasmania), B.A.(Newcastle) recently submitted his doctorate for the Ph.D. degree in computer science at Macquarie University, Australia, in the area of artificial neural networks. The software he developed as part of his doctoral studies runs on high-end Solaris servers, providing simulation results through a WWW interface. In addition, he has eight years of systems management and application development experience in commercial and R&D organizations. He specializes in building e-commerce and internet information systems, based on Solaris, Java, and open standards like CORBA, through Cassowary Computing Pty Ltd. He has published many scientific articles on computer science in leading international journals, such as *Applied Signal Processing*, *Internet Research*, and *International Journal of Systems Science*. He is also a columnist for the trade journal *Inside Solaris*, and is the author of *Solaris 8: The Complete Reference*, published by Osborne/McGraw-Hill.

ABOUT THE TECHNICAL REVIEWERS

Tim Gibbs is an independent UNIX System Administrator and RDBMS Consultant, living and working in Sydney, Australia. He works with Fortune 500 companies to provide them with solutions in the area of IT Infrastructure. He has extensive experience with Solaris, Linux and Major Relational Databases and has written a number of articles and books on these subjects. He always welcomes comments and can be contacted via email on tim@timgibbs.com.

Nalneesh Gaur is a Technical Solutions Engineer with Digital Island in Dallas, Texas. He works with Fortune 500 companies to provide them with solutions in the area of content delivery and web hosting. He has extensive experience with UNIX and Windows NT systems administration, eCommerce architectures, UNIX/NT integration, eCommerce security, and web application development. He is SUN Enterprise certified and a Microsoft Certified Systems Engineer (MCSE).

SOLARIS

Solaris Administration:
A Beginner's Guide

PAUL A. **WATTERS**

Osborne/**McGraw-Hill**

New York   Chicago   San Francisco
Lisbon   London   Madrid   Mexico City
Milan   New Delhi   San Juan
Seoul   Singapore   Sydney   Toronto

Osborne/**McGraw-Hill**
2600 Tenth Street
Berkeley, California 94710
U.S.A.

To arrange bulk purchase discounts for sales promotions, premiums, or fundraisers, please contact Osborne/**McGraw-Hill** at the above address. For information on translations or book distributors outside the U.S.A., please see the International Contact Information page immediately following the index of this book.

Solaris Administration: A Beginner's Guide

234567890 CUS CUS 01987654321

ISBN 0-07-213155-1

Publisher	**Proofreader**
Brandon A. Nordin	Linda Medoff
Vice President and	**Indexer**
Associate Publisher	Jack Lewis
Scott Rogers	**Computer Designers**
Acquisitions Editor	Gary Corrigan
Jane Brownlow	Lucie Ericksen
Project Editor	Lauren McCarthy
Elizabeth Seymour	**Illustrators**
Acquisitions Coordinator	Beth E. Young
Ross Doll	Lyssa Sieben-Wald
Technical Editor	Michael Mueller
Tim Gibbs	**Cover Design**
Nalneesh Gaur	Amparo Del Rio
Copy Editor	**Series Design**
Karyn DiCastri	Peter F. Hancik

This book was composed with Corel VENTURA™ Publisher.

For Natashia Herewane—a very special sister

AT A GLANCE

CONTENTS

Part I
Installation

Part II

Single Host Administration

Part III

Managing Internet Services

Part IV

Managing Intranet Services

FOREWORD

As the creator of the sunfreeware.com project which provides free software for the Solaris operating system, I constantly receive e-mail with questions from the users (and potential users) of Solaris.

Since my work does not generally extend to Solaris support (beyond helping with freeware), I like to point people to reference works that I respect, for information. In the past year, the book I have recommended most has been *Solaris 8: The Complete Reference* by Paul Watters with Sriranga Veeraraghavan (Osborne/McGraw-Hill, 2000). In fact, that book is the first place I look to get answers to my own questions!

The many first-time users of Solaris who contact me are new not only to Solaris, but to UNIX as well. There is, therefore, a need for books that assume very little knowledge of UNIX system administration on the part of the reader. Paul's new book, *Solaris Administration: A Beginner's Guide*, provides users of Solaris with an easily comprehended guide for instructions on how to install and set up Solaris. The book is also a valuable resource for learning how to best employ Solaris's many features. And it points Solaris users to numerous resources that will treat questions not covered in this book.

Every new— and even a seasoned—user of Solaris will find a wealth of practical knowledge in *Solaris Administration: A Beginner's Guide*. I recommend that all of them study it—and enjoy it.

—Steve Christensen
Founder, sunfreeware.com

ACKNOWLEDGMENTS

Special thanks to my wife Maya for her love and patience, and to Moppet and Miki. I would also like to acknowledge my parents, Walter and Judith Watters, and Cliff and Florenica Herewane, and my grandparents, Ray and Irene Watters. Cheers to Chris Watters, Joy Paculba, Adonis Espinosa, Michael Espinosa, and Arlene Nagy. A big thank you to Matthew and Shanice.

I would like to acknowledge the great work of the team at Osborne/McGraw-Hill, especially Jane Brownlow, Scott Rogers, Ross Doll, and Elizabeth Seymour. Their professionalism, attention to detail and persistence with a challenging title will ensure that this text is readable and relevant to the information technology industry. Technical Editors Tim Gibbs and Nalneesh Guar provided expert advice and tips on all aspects of Solaris.

My agency team at Studio B—Neil Salkind, David and Sherry Rogelberg, Kristen Pickens, Craig Wiley and Stacey Barone—provided much-needed support and encouragement during the conception and execution of this project. Their high expectations and welcome assurances make writing a pleasure.

I would like to thank my business partners, Graham Gulliver, Brad Matthews, and Sukhdev Singh, for their patience when I've missed meetings to meet writing deadlines. Thanks also to Matt Langford for many inspirational discussions about the Internet, and what technologies we'll all be using by 2020.

In technical terms, I'd like to thank Firaz Osman, Tony Kol and Muhammad Mugal for their assistance and insight into solving difficult problems. Thanks also to the yum cha crew: Helen Lee, Lay Chin Tay, Ken Yang, Sheng-Lung "Steve" Chiang and Po Yee "Sania" Chan. Keep those chicken feet coming, guys!

INTRODUCTION

So, you've picked up this book because your boss has told you to skill up on Solaris, or because you've seen the salaries for Solaris administrators and thought "I'd like to earn that." Maybe you're dissatisfied with your current operating systems, or perhaps you just have a thirst for knowledge. Whatever the reason, I hope that you find *Solaris Administration: A Beginner's Guide* a useful introduction to the Solaris operating environment.

This book is targeted at experienced administrators who have developed skills in Microsoft Windows, Linux or some other flavor of UNIX. The good news for experienced administrators is that Solaris is not that difficult to learn—if you're used to managing systems through the Windows desktop using control panels and service managers, you'll be pleased to know that Solaris provides many GUI tools to make it easy for you to learn the environment.

For Linux users, many of the commands will have the same names that you're used to, even if some options have a different format, or if System V startup and configuration options are new to you. The great challenge for Windows administrators will be to learn how to use the shell effectively to perform tasks programmatically. Linux administrators will have a steep learning curve with Solaris package management and services like the SunScreen firewall.

I hope this book will make it easy to learn the things you don't yet know, and reassure you about the things you already know. For example, both Microsoft Windows and Linux have support for TCP/IP networking and SMB filesharing—so does Solaris. All three operating systems support the Apache webserver. Even where the specific form of service is different, prior training can always help in learning new concepts. For example, Microsoft Windows administrators know about hierarchical directory services because they've used Active Directory—Solaris uses NIS+ to achieve similar goals. Linux administrators may have used plain old NIS, and will approve of the secure enhancements made in the Solaris version.

Each of the 20 chapters in the book is meant to provide concise introductions to the topics at hand. Worked examples are provided throughout, as painting a picture saves one thousand words (or at least, saves you from one thousand words of verbose text). Typically, we aim to cover introductory material, which explains why a service is required, before discussing how the service is implemented in Solaris. After demonstrating installation and configuration, we look at run-time and troubleshooting issues. Typically, we also provide pointers to more advanced material.

This book is not a reference book, so you won't always see every option to a command covered, or every service in Solaris discussed. This book is strictly introductory—there is much more to Solaris than we can cover in 20 chapters, but you will be equipped to work comfortably and confidently with Solaris after covering all of the material in this book. If you need a reference book for Solaris, I would recommend my other Osborne/McGraw Hill title: *Solaris 8: The Complete Reference*.

PART I

Installation

CHAPTER 1

Introduction to Solaris

This book is about the Solaris operating environment, developed and distributed by Sun Microsystems. In Part I, we will give the reader all the information required to install and configure a Solaris system. In this chapter, we will briefly cover the history of the Solaris operating system and the distinguishing features of Sun SPARC (Scalable Processor Architecture) hardware, and we will highlight the improvements introduced with the latest release (Solaris 8).

In addition, we will introduce the common features that Solaris shares with other network operating systems, such as Transmission Control Protocol/Internet Protocol (TCP/IP) networking, and highlight key advantages over its competitors, such as multiuser logins, multiprocessing, and lightweight processes. We also provide a comprehensive review of resources on the Internet, such as the World Wide Web (WWW), File Transfer Program (FTP), and USENET, which can be useful complements to professional support services.

OVERVIEW OF SOLARIS

Solaris is an enterprise-level operating environment that encompasses the multiprocess, multiuser Sun Operating System (SunOS). It is a network operating system that runs on Intel-based PC systems, as well as systems built around the SPARC CPU architecture. These systems can have up to 64 CPUs operating concurrently in the E10000 server system. Thus, when administrators speak of Sun, they could be referring to SPARC-based computer systems, or the Solaris operating environment.

As an experienced administrator of Linux and/or Microsoft Windows, you might be wondering what Solaris can do, where it came from, and why you should (or shouldn't) use it. Some administrators may be concerned about the use of proprietary hardware or the often-reported statistic that 80 percent of the world's computers run a Microsoft operating system. Since the average Solaris system can support Graphical User Interface (GUI) logins for hundreds of users, making comparisons with single-user operating systems, such as some versions of Microsoft Windows, is quite meaningless. Different scenarios may well justify the expense of purchasing an E10000 in some organizations; but if you just need domain support and/or centralized file system management, then Microsoft Windows might be more appropriate.

Solaris is the dominant UNIX-like operating system on the market today. Sun's systems are the hardware of choice for high-availability applications, such as database systems, Web servers, and computationally intensive tasks such as modeling and simulation. These systems are widely deployed in commercial and research and development (R&D) organizations. They also integrate well into heterogeneous networks composed of Linux and Microsoft Windows systems, particularly as reliable fileservers.

For example, Linux clients are supported by the Network File System (NFS) and the Network Information Service (NIS), while Microsoft Windows clients are supported with Session Message Block (SMB) networking and Samba-based primary domain control. Since Solaris operates largely on a client/server model, clients from multiple operating systems are usually supported.

Sun recently released Solaris 8, which is the latest in a long line of releases that have delivered increased functionality and reliability at each stage. Recent innovations in Solaris include support for 64-bit kernels; high-availability full moon clustering; and the adoption of the Common Desktop Environment (CDE), which is the standard X11-based desktop deployed by most UNIX vendors in recent years.

Solaris and Other Operating Systems

You may be wondering at this point exactly how different Solaris is to your existing operating system. If you're from a Microsoft Windows background, you're probably used to a GUI desktop like the one shown in Figure 1-1. You'll be pleased to know that the CDE desktop, shown in Figure 1-2, has many similar features, including icons, workspaces, menus, and tool tips. Just like Microsoft Windows, all of these features can be customized to an individual user's preferences, or they can be mandated sitewide if there is an organization policy governing the appearance of desktops.

If you're a Microsoft Windows administrator, you no doubt write batch files that can be executed at various intervals using the at command. A sample batch file and command

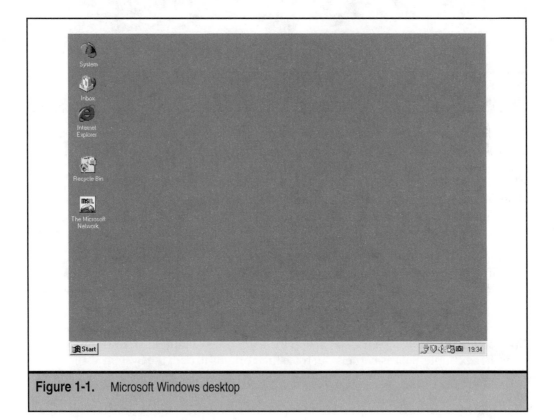

Figure 1-1.   Microsoft Windows desktop

Figure 1-2.   Solaris CDE desktop

prompt interface is shown in Figure 1-3. Here, commands may be issued interactively, such as the command for a directory listing, dir.

Similarly, when a user shell is spawned by the initialization of a CDE terminal window, various commands can be issued on the command line, which are then interpreted by a command interpreter, as shown in Figure 1-4.

Although these examples may seem trivial, they illustrate a very important point: a lot of operating systems share a set of core features that are differentiated by presentation but not necessarily in functionality. For example, Microsoft Windows, Linux, and Solaris are all process-based operating systems: that is, independent activities can be carried out in discrete processes, which can be managed by process tools. Processes can be prioritized, stopped, or started by using a GUI interface or command-line tools.

Some of the major differences between UNIX and UNIX-like platforms, and the Microsoft platforms can be traced back to the early days of multiuser, multiprocess systems. For example, Solaris kernels can trace their origins to both the System V and Berke-

Figure 1-3.   Executing commands with a Windows command prompt

ley Software Distribution (BSD) variants of UNIX, while Microsoft NT was based on the VMS kernel originally developed for the high-end VAX systems. There are many similarities; however, in Windows 2000, Microsoft introduces a new service called Active Directory (AD) that is reminiscent of Sun's hierarchical Network Information Service (NIS/NIS+), which is used to manage user, system, and domain data on large networks.

The benefits of using Solaris over other operating systems typically become apparent in a symmetrical multiprocessing (SMP) and/or multiuser environment. Although Microsoft Windows does support multiple CPU support, Solaris supports up to 64 CPUs operating concurrently with almost linear scaling of performance. Some other operating systems appear to devote most of the processing capacity of a second, third, or fourth CPU to scheduling rather than operations. In addition, Solaris is particularly suited to supporting hundreds of interactive users on a single system: that is, every user can be logged in using a desktop that is being executed on a central server.

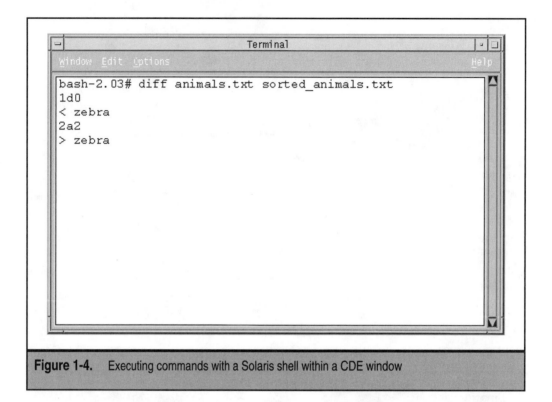

Figure 1-4.   Executing commands with a Solaris shell within a CDE window

Although Microsoft Windows features great products, such as pcAnywhere, that allow users to run a desktop remotely, these products typically only allow a single user to run a session at any one time. There are few hard constraints placed on Solaris systems in terms of support for concurrently logged-in users. This is one major reason why Solaris systems are favored at the enterprise level.

Often, I hear administrators saying that Linux does all of this and more. It's true that Linux has SMP support, and it's also true that Linux is a multiuser system. However, you have to consider the investment that a company makes in both hardware and software to really understand the main benefits of Solaris as a platform.

Solaris is 100 percent owned and managed by Sun Microsystems; Linux is developed by Linus Torvalds, and commercial support is provided by a number of different vendors, including Red Hat (http://www.redhat.com) and SuSE (http://www.suse.com). Although you can pay support fees to Red Hat and SuSE, just like you can pay them to Sun, Red Hat and SuSE do not own the source code to the operating system they support, while Sun does. In this sense, Solaris has more in common with Microsoft Windows: it is a proprietary platform that is 100 percent owned and supported by its managing organization.

However, Sun does support the notion that operating system software should be free for educational purposes and for developers. This is why they have binary and source license programs for Solaris, where users can receive several CDs full of Solaris software for around $75 (this amount pays for shipping and handling).

This is not an evaluation version: this is the same version of the software that an enterprise system user will be installing and using on his or her E10000. Taking advantage of the "free" Solaris program has lured many administrators away from the uncertainties of Linux to the advantages of a Sun-supported and -developed product.

Sun has also begun attracting Linux administrators because of its support of the Intel platform for Solaris. There have been several releases of Solaris for Intel, and Sun is committed to supporting the platform in the future. Indeed, Microsoft Windows administrators who have shied away from using UNIX in the past because of concerns over proprietary hardware can now install Solaris on their favorite PCs. In addition, Solaris fully supports dual-booting on these platforms, meaning that a boot manager like LILO or Boot Magic can be used to launch Solaris and/or Microsoft Windows and/or Linux from the same system.

Another feather in Sun's cap has been the specification and development of the Java programming language, which has rapidly grown to capture around 10 percent of the world marketplace in software engineering. This is a phenomenal rise, since Java has only been released in full production for around five years.

The basic idea behind Java is that the choice of operating systems should be a separate issue from software design and implementation. That is, good object-oriented development principles should not be sacrificed because a particular language is not available in a standard format on a particular platform. Thus, Java aims to compile and execute on any platform.

Binaries generated on a Microsoft Windows development system, for example, can be shipped across to a Solaris deployment server without having to be recompiled, thanks to the cross-platform bytecode developed by Sun. Java also incorporates cross-platform networking and GUI development methods, meaning that a network monitoring tool written on Solaris should execute exactly the same on a Microsoft Windows or Linux system. This means that the choice of deployment platform can be governed by performance studies and objective testing, rather than irrational and subjective arguments about which operating system is the best.

In summary, Solaris shares some key features with other operating systems, but it excels in the support of SMP systems, cross-platform OSs, and developer support; it also excels because it controls its operating system, while making it available to educational users and developers. The adoption of the Intel hardware platform is one key attraction for existing Microsoft Windows and Linux administrators.

Another recent advantage was the acquisition of Star Division's StarOffice suite. This product is competitive with Microsoft's Office suite. However, it is completely free for commercial and noncommercial use; it provides an integrated environment for word processing, spreadsheets, presentations, and database applications; and it is available in several different European languages—which means that SPARC system users can share data seamlessly with users on the Microsoft Windows and Linux platforms, as StarOffice is available on all three.

Why Learn Solaris?

Learning Solaris is just like learning any new operating environment: there is a fairly steep learning curve to begin with, which will eventually flatten out as you develop Solaris-specific skills. For example, Microsoft Windows administrators will have to learn about managing users and groups, and the differences between AD and NIS+ domains. Linux administrators will have to learn to refer to Solaris device names for disks that are much more complicated than what they are used to.

For example, a Linux hard disk partition might be called /dev/hda1, which refers to the first partition on the first Integrated Device Electronics (IDE) hard disk. A similar partition on a Solaris system might be called /dev/dsk/c0t0d0s1. If you're ever confused about the devices that have been detected on a system, you can use the prtconf command to display their configuration details:

```
bash-2.03# prtconf
System Configuration:  Sun Microsystems   sun4u
Memory size: 128 Megabytes
System Peripherals (Software Nodes):

SUNW,Ultra-5_10
    packages (driver not attached)
        terminal-emulator (driver not attached)
        deblocker (driver not attached)
        obp-tftp (driver not attached)
        disk-label (driver not attached)
        SUNW,builtin-drivers (driver not attached)
        sun-keyboard (driver not attached)
        ufs-file-system (driver not attached)
    chosen (driver not attached)
    openprom (driver not attached)
        client-services (driver not attached)
    options, instance #0
    aliases (driver not attached)
    memory (driver not attached)
    virtual-memory (driver not attached)
    pci, instance #0
        pci, instance #0
            ebus, instance #0
                auxio (driver not attached)
                power, instance #0
                SUNW,pll (driver not attached)
                se, instance #0
                su, instance #0
                su, instance #1
```

```
        ecpp (driver not attached)
        fdthree, instance #0
        eeprom (driver not attached)
        flashprom (driver not attached)
        SUNW,CS4231 (driver not attached)
    network, instance #0
    SUNW,m64B (driver not attached)
    ide, instance #0
        disk (driver not attached)
        cdrom (driver not attached)
        dad, instance #0
        sd, instance #30
pci, instance #1
    scsi, instance #0
        disk (driver not attached)
        tape (driver not attached)
        sd, instance #0 (driver not attached)
        sd, instance #1 (driver not attached)
        sd, instance #2 (driver not attached)
        sd, instance #3
        sd, instance #4 (driver not attached)
        sd, instance #5 (driver not attached)
        sd, instance #6 (driver not attached)
        sd, instance #7 (driver not attached)
        sd, instance #8 (driver not attached)
        sd, instance #9 (driver not attached)
        sd, instance #10 (driver not attached)
        sd, instance #11 (driver not attached)
        sd, instance #12 (driver not attached)
        sd, instance #13 (driver not attached)
        sd, instance #14 (driver not attached)
    scsi, instance #1
        disk (driver not attached)
        tape (driver not attached)
        sd, instance #15 (driver not attached)
        sd, instance #16 (driver not attached)
        sd, instance #17 (driver not attached)
        sd, instance #18 (driver not attached)
        sd, instance #19 (driver not attached)
        sd, instance #20 (driver not attached)
        sd, instance #21 (driver not attached)
        sd, instance #22 (driver not attached)
        sd, instance #23 (driver not attached)
        sd, instance #24 (driver not attached)
```

```
            sd, instance #25 (driver not attached)
            sd, instance #26 (driver not attached)
            sd, instance #27 (driver not attached)
            sd, instance #28 (driver not attached)
            sd, instance #29 (driver not attached)
    SUNW,UltraSPARC-IIi (driver not attached)
    SUNW,ffb, instance #0
    pseudo, instance #0
```

This book aims to introduce Solaris to administrators who have experience with either Windows NT/2000 and/or Linux to Solaris system administration. We will cover the administration of both the Intel and SPARC versions of Solaris, based on the current Solaris release (version 8); however, many of the skills that are developed for Solaris are equally applicable to earlier (and future) versions of the operating system.

By building on the reader's experience with Intel hardware, we will introduce the major features of the Sun product line. Since the introduction of the Solaris binary and source license program for the Intel platform, many readers will be evaluating Solaris as a server system for mail, news, and Web services, as well as for managing printers and shared filesystems. They may well discover that their Microsoft Windows or Linux system can no longer cope with the volume of data being transferred or that uptimes are not to their satisfaction. By the way, you can tell how long a Solaris system has been up by using the following command:

```
emu# w | grep "up"
  9:25am  up 288 day(s), 13:50,   39 users,   load average: 1.32, 1.45,
1.48
```

The last time the system was rebooted was during the upgrade from Solaris 7 to Solaris 8. Reliability is one of the great attractions of Solaris.

This book is focused on providing practical solutions rather than an academic discussion of operating systems: for example, we won't discuss process scheduling models, but we will examine how to manage processes. We don't just provide a list of commands, but we present the expected output from different commands under several different conditions. This book provides many worked examples of configuration files and the installation of third-party software packages, without the assumption that the reader is a Solaris guru.

This book aims to help you transfer the lessons of both practical experience and skill development required to understand the impact of new services and new software products on existing server systems. We do not cover so-called historical services, like UNIX-to-UNIX Copy Program (UUCP), which can easily fill chapters, but focus on applications that are not commonly found in today's production environments. If it's not relevant or not widely used, you won't find it covered in this book.

The target audience for this book is administrators who already use Linux or Microsoft Windows NT/2000. These readers may be evaluating Solaris as a network server, or they may need a technical basis upon which to set up Solaris as a replacement for other operating systems, covering key issues in terminology with which they are familiar. Readers will be expected to have knowledge and experience of a networked environment. An existing network administrator who is trained on legacy network systems, such as Novell, or has completed NT certification will, in this book, find the technical detail required to install and configure basic Solaris network services.

Solaris and related products like Java are rapidly becoming known as the most reliable and scalable solution on which to build reliable systems and networks. One of the problems that potential users face is finding out more information about what Solaris offers: they want to know how much technical work is involved in migrating to Solaris, and what kind of philosophy Solaris is based on.

Unfortunately, there are very few books available on Solaris, other than those published by Sun (Amazon.com lists 71 books with Solaris in the title, and only a few of these specifically cover Solaris 8). While Sun's own system manuals are very good, users will be looking for third-party, independent titles that not only praise Solaris, but are critical and realistic in their appraisal. For an independent reference book, administrators can also read *Solaris 8: The Complete Reference*, published by Osborne McGraw Hill. *Solaris 8: The Complete Reference* is a reference for Solaris 8, but it does not specifically introduce Solaris concepts to administrators trained in other operating systems.

Reading this book will help you determine when and why to deploy Solaris, and how to provide networked services to the enterprise in a secure and scalable environment.

HISTORY AND FEATURES OF SOLARIS

The SunOS operating system is a variant of the UNIX operating system, which was originally produced by Ken Thompson at Bell Laboratories in 1969—an era when mainframes were dominant, and smaller, leaner systems (such as the DEC PDP-7) were a novelty. Most kernels during the 1960s were written using assembly language or machine (binary) code, so the development of a high-level language for writing kernels (the C language) was one of the founding ideas of UNIX. This level of abstraction from hardware meant that kernels could be ported to other hardware platforms without having to be completely rewritten.

The tradition of writing kernels in C continues today; for example, the Linux kernel is written in C. Obviously, a kernel alone is not a complete operating environment; so many additional applications, such as the visual editor (vi), were added to what UNIX users would recognize as the suite of standard UNIX tools. In later years, tools such as the Practical Extraction and Reporting Language (perl) and the GNU GCC compiler were added to this toolkit.

There are two main variants of UNIX systems: the commercial version (System V, produced by AT&T) and the BSD. The split occurred after universities (such as the University of California) were granted source licenses for the UNIX operating system, which they then used as the basis for further development and innovation. After realizing that UNIX may well have some valuable intellectual property, AT&T restricted the terms of the license and began charging fees.

The BSD group responded by completely rewriting the operating system so that it contained no proprietary code, and contained key innovations such as virtual memory and fast filesystems. However, as the two codebases further diverged, some differences in coding style and command options led to many shell scripts being unportable from one system to the next without major revisions. While the BSD products are still available in the forms of NetBSD and FreeBSD, most commercial UNIX systems are based on AT&T UNIX.

The one exception to this rule is Solaris, which began life as a BSD-style UNIX, but has slowly migrated to the System V standard. This is because some of the founding fathers at Sun, including Bill Joy, were instrumental in the development of the BSD. It is also one of the reasons that Sun garnered more support in the early years, since they were perceived to be more in touch with their developers and their platform growth was essentially developer driven.

In later years, Sun has attempted to make Solaris more compatible with other UNIX systems, adopting the CDE over its OpenWindows product, and working toward a Common Open Software Environment (COSE) with IBM, Hewlett-Packard (HP), and other enterprise market players.

Sun Microsystems distinguished itself early on by providing a complete end-to-end service, based on the high-end SPARC CPU architecture that was specifically designed to work with Solaris, for their Solaris systems SPARC. Other hardware innovations included the development of the OpenBoot monitor and integrated power management, which far exceeds the capabilities of a PC BIOS. In addition, early versions of Solaris introduced SMP support and implemented the NFS and the OpenWindows graphical user environment, which was based on the X11 graphics system.

More recently, Solaris has led the way for the UNIX industry by complying with relevant standards (such as UNIX 95 and UNIX 98), improving NFS, developing high-availability and clustering solutions, and developing enhanced volume management. In addition, the introduction of 64-bit kernels, Java, JumpStart installations, and integration of Kerberos authentication into its security architecture have greatly benefited Solaris users and administrators. Solaris now features a number of standard tools, such as package, patch, and storage management, that are supported by a Portable Operating System Interface for Computer Environments (POSIX)–compliant development environment.

THE SOLARIS WAY

We've looked in broad terms at the key features of Solaris, as well as some of the similarities and differences between Solaris and other network operating systems. In this section, we will look at one aspect of Solaris in depth so that you can get a feel for what could be termed the "Solaris way."

The way that Solaris boots from disk is quite different from other operating systems, and the differences are at the software and hardware levels. SPARC systems have a boot monitor application known as the OpenBoot monitor, which can be used to boot the system with the boot command, but actually has a Forth language interpreter built in, as well as a number of diagnostic tools. Thus, it is possible to build small programs to perform a wide variety of standard tests using firmware, which are independent of the operating system. So, even if you decide to install Linux on your SPARC system, you will still need to understand the OpenBoot monitor and how it operates.

In a PC's BIOS, you can typically autodetect disks and perform several system configuration tasks. You can do all this and more using the OpenBoot monitor. You can also boot using a local hard disk, tape, or CD-ROM, or you can boot through the network. Traffic from any of the Ethernet interfaces can also be captured and examined by using the watch-net command.

In terms of software, Solaris has some similarities to Microsoft Windows and Linux. Although it doesn't have an AUTOEXEC.BAT or CONFIG.SYS file, Solaris does have a number of script files that are executed in a specific order to start services. These scripts are typically created in the /etc/init.d directory as Bourne shell (sh) scripts and are then symbolically linked into the run-level directories. Just as Microsoft Windows has safe modes, Solaris supports a number of different modes of operation, from restricted single-user modes to full multiuser run levels.

The complete set of run levels, with their respective run control script directories, is displayed in Table 1-1.

Run Level	Description	User Status	Run Control Script Directory
0	Hardware maintenance mode	Console Access	/etc/rc0.d
1	Administrative state; only root filesystem is available	Single User	/etc/rc1.d
2	First multiuser state; NFS resources unavailable	MultiUser	/etc/rc2.d
3	NFS resources available	MultiUser	/etc/rc3.d
4	User-defined state	Not Specified	N/A
5	Power-down firmware state	Console Access	/etc/rc5.d
6	Operating system halted	Single User	/etc/rc6.d
S	Administrative tasks and repair of corrupted filesystems	Console Access	/etc/rcS.d

Table 1-1.   Solaris Run Levels and Their Functions

When a Solaris system starts, the init process, which is responsible for managing processes and the transitions between run levels, is spawned. You can switch manually between run levels yourself by using the init command. To halt the operating system (run level 6), you can simply type the following command:

```
bash-2.03# init 6
```

Every Solaris init state (such as init state 6) has its own run-level script directory (for example, /etc/rc6.d). This contains a set of symbolic links (like shortcuts in Microsoft Windows) that are associated with the service startup files in the /etc/init.d directory. Each linked script starts with the letter *S* (start) or the letter *K* (kill) and are used to start or kill processes. When a system is booted, processes are started. When a system is shut down, processes are killed. The start and kill links are typically made to the same script file, which interprets two parameters: start and stop.

The scripts are executed in numerical order, so a script like /etc/rc3.d/ S20dhcp is executed before /etc/rc3.d/ S21sshd. If you're curious about what kind of scripts are started or killed in Solaris during startup and shutdown, Table 1-2 shows the startup scripts in /etc/rc2.d, while Table 1-3 shows the kill scripts found in /etc/rc0.d. It's important to realize that these will change from system to system.

Script	Description
S05RMTMPFILES	Removes temporary files in the /tmp directory
S20sysetup	Establishes system setup requirements, and checks /var/crash to determine whether the system is recovering from a crash
S21perf	Enables system accounting using /usr/lib/sa/sadc and /var/adm/sa/sa
S30sysid.net	Executes /usr/sbin/sysidnet, /usr/sbin/sysidconfig, and /sbin/ifconfig, which are responsible for configuring network services
S69inet	Initiates second phase of TCP/IP configuration, following on from the basic services established during single-user mode (rcS); setting up Internet Protocol (IP) routing (if /etc/defaultrouter exists), performing TCP/IP parameter tuning (using ndd), and setting the NIS domain name (if required) all performed here
S70uucp	Initializes the UUCP by removing locks and other unnecessary files

Table 1-2.   Typical Multiuser Startup Scripts Under Solaris 8

Script	Description
S71sysid.sys	Executes /usr/sbin/sysidsys and /usr/sbin/sysidroot
S72autoinstall	Executes JumpStart installation if appropriate
S72inetsvc	Final network configuration using /usr/sbin/ifconfig after NIS/NIS+ have been initialized; also initializes Internet Domain Name Service (DNS) if appropriate
S80PRESERVE	Preserves editing files by executing /usr/lib/expreserve
S91leoconfig	Configuration for ZX graphics cards (if installed)
S92rtvc-config	Configuration for SunVideo cards (if installed)
S92volmgt	Starts volume management for removable media using /usr/sbin/vold

Table 1-2.   Typical Multiuser Startup Scripts Under Solaris 8 *(continued)*

Script	Description
K00ANNOUNCE	Announces that System services are now being stopped
K10dtlogin	Initializes tasks for the CDE, including killing the dtlogin process
K20lp	Stops printing services using /usr/lib/lpshut
K22acct	Terminates process accounting using /usr/lib/acct/shutacct
K42audit	Kills the auditing daemon (/usr/sbin/audit)
K47asppp	Stops the asynchronous Point-to-Point Protocol (PPP) daemon (/usr/sbin/aspppd)
K50utmpd	Kills the utmp daemon (/usr/lib/utmpd)
K55syslog	Terminates the system logging service (/usr/sbin/syslogd)
K57sendmail	Halts the sendmail mail service (/usr/lib/sendmail)
K66nfs.server	Kills all processes required for the NFS server (/usr/lib/nfs/nfsd)

Table 1-3.   Typical Single-User Kill Scripts Under Solaris 8

Script	Description
K69autofs	Stops the automounter (/usr/sbin/automount)
K70cron	Terminates the cron daemon (/usr/bin/cron)
K75nfs.client	Disables client NFS
K76nscd	Kills the name service cache daemon (/usr/sbin/nscd)
K85rpc	Disables Remote Procedure Call (RPC) (rpc) services (/usr/sbin/rpcbind)

Table 1-3. Typical Single-User Kill Scripts Under Solaris 8 *(continued)*

BOOK OUTLINE

This book is divided into four parts. Part I gives readers all the information that they require to install and configure a Solaris system. Part II looks at how to use and manage a Solaris system: we begin by examining how to use the shell, which is the application that is used to issue commands, and manage jobs and processes. Part III focuses solely on providing scalable and reliable Internet services, which is one of the major reasons that administrators may choose Solaris over Linux or Windows NT/2000. Part IV covers the services that Solaris provides for managing intranets and local area networks. These four parts provide coverage of the areas commonly used in day-to-day administration of Solaris systems.

As we have seen, Chapter 1 gives the history of the Solaris operating system, covers the features of Sun SPARC hardware, and highlights the improvements introduced with the latest release (Solaris 8). The reader will learn about the features that Solaris shares with other network operating systems (for example, TCP/IP networking), and determine key advantages over its competitors (for example, multiuser logins, multiprocessing, and lightweight processes). We also provide a comprehensive review of resources on the Internet, such as WWW, FTP, and USENET, which can be useful complements to professional support services.

One of the main differences between Solaris and its competitors (Windows NT/2000 and Linux) is the SPARC hardware on which the operating system was originally designed to run. Although Windows and Linux run on many different platforms, Solaris runs best on the SPARC architecture, which is proprietary to Sun. While this is seen as a disadvantage by some critics, the performance of Sun workstations is legendary: the low CPU speeds of older systems are not reflective of the high-throughput I/O performance achieved by the workstation bus. In Chapter 2, the reader will go through the installation and basic configuration of Solaris for Sun SPARC.

Recently, Sun introduced the Solaris x86 platform, which is designed to run on Intel-based hardware. This makes Solaris very accessible for users who already own Intel systems running Linux and/or Windows NT/2000. In Chapter 3, the reader will learn how to install and configure a bare x86 system with Solaris. We will examine the major hardware components supported by Solaris and identify the differences in installation between the SPARC and Intel editions.

Once Solaris is installed, the CDE will be configured as the default window manager running under X11. The CDE supersedes Sun's own OpenWindows platform and is commonly found on HP-UX, Linux, and other UNIX systems. Before learning about Solaris, it's important to master the CDE, particularly if ex-Windows users want to avoid command-line usage. In Chapter 4, the reader will learn how to use the CDE effectively and to launch applications, edit text files, send e-mail, and use the File Manager. We will also examine how to localize and configure the CDE to your requirements.

In Chapter 5, the reader will learn how to execute commands, use standard UNIX utilities, list files and directories, set and access environment variables, use pipes, and get help with the man system. In Chapter 6, we review the concepts of file ownership, processes, and signals, and examine how these are different from Linux and Windows NT/2000. We also examine how to create shell scripts.

The concept of the user is central to Solaris: all processes and files on a Solaris system are owned by a particular user and are assigned to a specific user group. In Chapter 7, the reader will learn how to add users to the system, select an appropriate shell, and add and modify groups. We also examine the key user databases, including the password, shadow password, and group files. Finally, we introduce the admintool, which is a GUI-based user administration tool that may be easier for Windows NT/2000 administrators to adjust to.

In Chapter 8, we introduce the related concepts of process, system file system, CPU, and memory resources management. The reader will learn how to interpret process displays, trace system calls for processes that are resident in memory, and send signals to processes. In addition, we examine tools such as top, which can be used for online monitoring of process activity.

Package management is a key concept in managing Solaris systems effectively. In Chapter 9, the reader will learn how to install software, using pkgadd, and how to build and compile software from source using Makefiles and the C compiler. We also focus on how to build and distribute software packages using standard Solaris tools.

Chapter 10 introduces the concepts involved in transferring electronic mail between hosts. The standard UNIX mail transport agent (sendmail) is reviewed in detail, including configuration of mail delivery rules and troubleshooting. The reader will also learn how to configure Post Office Protocol (POP) services for enabling remote delivery of mail to PC- and Linux-based clients.

The Internet depends on a distributed network and host-naming system known as the DNS. In Chapter 11, readers will learn how to name a network's hosts and configure a DNS server using standard Solaris tools. In addition, we will examine third-party configuration systems that can be used to simplify the process of DNS administration.

Standard Solaris TCP/IP services are provided through an Internet super daemon (inetd), which supports FTP, telnet (remote access), talk (terminal communication), finger (check logged-in users), and a wide variety of other services. In Chapter 12, we cover the configuration of the Internet daemon and associated software, such as TCP wrappers, which can be used to improve the security of inetd. The reader will learn how to enable and disable Internet services, interpret activity log files, set up anonymous FTP, and manage the services database.

Following on in Chapter 13, we extend coverage of network services to include optional and third-party remote access tools, including anonymous FTP. Other tools include more secure alternatives to telnet, testing services and preventing packet sniffing of usernames and passwords.

The WWW has become one of the most dominant Internet services provided by organizations and individuals worldwide. Everyone has a home page that they wish to share with the rest of the world; alternatively, many companies offer goods and services through the Internet. In Chapter 14, the reader will learn how to install and configure the popular Apache Web server and write simple Common Gateway Interface (CGI) applications using Perl. In addition, we will examine how to use the Apache JServ Java servlet runner to deploy server-side Java applications to the WWW.

Having examined how to install and configure a wide range of Internet services, we devote Chapter 15 to securing a Solaris system. The reader will learn how to implement effective password strategies, how to evaluate security risks by using the SAINT program, and how to filter network traffic by configuring a firewall, to prevent denial-of-service attacks. In addition, we will examine how to enable and disable TCP and User Datagram Protocol (UDP) ports.

In Chapter 16, we begin by examining the Samba software suite. Samba is used to share Solaris filesystems and printers with any client that supports SMB networking (including Windows, Linux, and MacOS). This means that Solaris can be used as a reliable, centralized fileserver, replacing unreliable servers running other operating systems. The reader will learn how to export filesystems, share printers, and share filesystems between Samba servers.

In Chapter 17, we examine the Dynamic Host Configuration Protocol (DHCP), which is an easy way to dynamically manage IP addresses in Class A, Class B, and Class C networks. Since at any one time, only a few IP addresses on a network may be in use, it makes sense to ration their allocation, rather than statically assigning them to individual hosts. This is particularly important for expanding Class C networks, where only a few hundred addresses are available. Readers will learn how to install a Solaris DHCP server and how to configure DHCP clients on different platforms (including Windows and Linux).

In Chapter 18, we examine Sun's own NFS. Although NFS is similar to Samba in concept (file system sharing), NFS features high-data throughput because of dedicated kernel support. The reader will learn how to set up and install an NFS server and an NFS client, and how to export file systems. In addition, we examine how to set up the automounter so that a user's home directory across all machines on an intranet is automatically shared and available, irrespective of their login host.

NIS+, which provides hierarchical domain management services to local area networks, is another Sun-specific service. Authentication can be distributed and accessed through a series of virtual tables, and user configuration data (such as passwords) are available to all local hosts. In addition, the newer NIS+ system provides improved security, including Data Encryption Standard (DES) encryption. In Chapter 19, readers will learn how to set up namespaces with up to 10,000 hosts; enable resource authorization lists; and manage server addresses, time zones, and network services.

Managing print services is an important function of Solaris services. In addition to supporting both BSD- and System V-style print services, Solaris also provides a wide variety of text processing tools that can be used to render material suitable for printing. In Chapter 20, readers will learn to install and configure printing services and use Solaris text-processing tools like StarOffice.

RESOURCES

The first place to learn more about Solaris is from the Sun Microsystems home page for Solaris (http://www.sun.com). Some key documents within the Sun site for Solaris include the following:

- ▼ Solaris overview (http://www.sun.com/software/solaris/ds/ds-sol8oe)
- ■ Solaris downloads (http://www.sun.com/software/solaris/downloads.html)
- ■ Solaris support (http://www.sun.com/software/solaris/support.html)
- ■ Solaris education (http://www.sun.com/software/solaris/education.html)
- ■ Solaris clustering (http://www.sun.com/software/fullmoon)
- ▲ Solaris Intel platform (http://www.sun.com/software/intel)

Possibly the most important link on the Sun site is the documentation (http://docs.sun.com). Here, you can interactively search or browse all of the Sun documentation and/or download entire manuals in Portable Document Format (PDF) format. These manuals include the following:

- ▼ 64-bit developer's guide
- ■ Binary compatibility guide
- ■ CDE transition guide
- ■ CDE user guide
- ■ Device drivers guide

- Internationalization guide
- JumpStart guide
- Mail server guide
- Naming services guide
- NFS administration guide
- NIS+ guide
- OpenWindows user guide
- Power management user guide
- Source compatibility guide
- SPARC assembly language guide
- STREAMS guide
- SunShield security guide
- System administration guides
- TCP/IP guide
- Troubleshooting guides
- ▲ WebNFS developer's guide

Many packages for Solaris come in source form, which you are expected to build yourself. One example is the GNU C Compiler (GCC): Solaris no longer comes with a free compiler, so you must either buy one from Sun or use GCC. Of course, you may be wondering how you can download and compile a compiler without having a compiler in the first place! The answer is that Steve Christensen runs a great site called Sun Freeware (http://www.sunfreeware.com). This site contains many prebuilt packages for Solaris (SPARC and Intel) that can be downloaded and installed using the package tools described in Chapter 9. Packages are available for the platforms for Solaris 2.5 and above.

If you're interested in buying Sun hardware, the Sun Solutions Catalog is available online at http://store.sun.com. This page allows you to build a SPARC system and obtain a quote in real time. For example, an entry-level Ultra 5 system with a 400MHz CPU, 128MB of RAM, a 9Gb hard drive, and a CD-ROM now costs under $2,000.

USENET can also be a great source of information about Solaris. The web sites comp.unix.solaris and alt.solaris.x86 are inhabited by many talented and experienced administrators who share information and experiences with each other. There are two FAQs for Solaris available at http://www.wins.uva.nl/pub/solaris/solaris2 and http://sun.pmbc.com/faq for Solaris SPARC and Solaris Intel, respectively. If you prefer a mailing list format to USENET, then you should definitely join the Sun Manager's List at ftp://ftp.cs.toronto.edu/pub/jdd/sun-managers/faq.

SUMMARY

In this chapter, we have examined what differentiates Solaris from its competitors—Microsoft Windows and Linux. Although there are many similarities among all of these operating systems, Solaris distinguishes itself by providing support for high-performance hardware, including 64-CPU systems, as well as advanced, System V–compliant tools and services.

Solaris is derived from both major variations of UNIX, taking the best features of each, including a flexible booting system, virtual memory support, and the various shells that now form a powerful command-line interface for users. In addition, modern GUI interfaces have been based on the industry-standard CDE desktop environment, meaning that Solaris users can easily transfer their skills to other UNIX platforms.

CHAPTER 2

Installing Solaris SPARC (Scalable Processor Architecture)

Ons of the main differences between Solaris and its competitors (such as Windows NT/2000 and Linux) is the SPARC hardware on which the operating system was originally designed to run. Although Windows and Linux run on many different platforms, Solaris runs best on the SPARC architecture, which is managed by the SPARC architecture group (http://www.SPARC.org). While vendor-specific hardware is often viewed as a disadvantage by some administrators, the performance of Sun workstations is legendary: the low CPU speeds of older systems are not reflective of the high-throughput I/O performance achieved by the Sun workstation bus. In this chapter, the reader will be walked through the installation and basic configuration of Solaris for Sun SPARC.

OBTAINING SOLARIS

The Solaris operating environment is typically not available in your local computer store—it must be obtained directly from Sun or through an authorized reseller. The good news is that if your SPARC system has 8 CPUs or less, you may now obtain a Solaris license free of charge by applying directly to Sun; the catch is that you must pay for postage and handling, which Sun calculates to be $75 per package. This is an increase of the shipping and handling charges associated with previous editions of the free Solaris program; however, the new package has a number of value-added extras, including the Oracle database server. It is also possible to obtain the source code to Solaris at http://www.sun.com/software/solaris/source.

The free Solaris license program is targeted at home users who wish to take advantage of the stability of the Solaris platform for using StarOffice and other productivity applications, as well as Solaris developers who wish to deploy on the Solaris platform. More information is available from http://www.sun.com/software/solaris/binaries.

The Solaris 8 media pack comes with several CDs, including the following:

▼ Web Start Installation CD, which is used to install the Solaris operating environment

■ Two Solaris Software CDs, which contain all of the standard Solaris packages

■ Solaris documentation CDs, which contain all of the Solaris documentation in AnswerBook format

■ Languages CD, which contains local customizations for nine different languages

■ StarOffice 5.2 productivity suite

■ Forth for Java integrated development environment

■ GNU software CD

■ iPlanet software suite, which provides a Web server, directory server, certificate manager, sun screen firewall, and application server

■ Oracle database server

▲ Supplemental software CD, including support for OpenGL; Java 3D; and advanced networking support, including, SunATM, SunFDDI, and Sun GigabitEthernet

SPARC HARDWARE

Sun has developed a wide range of hardware systems over the past few years, much of which is still supported by Solaris 8. These systems are based on SPARC, which is managed by a SPARC member organization (http://www.SPARC.org). In addition to Sun Microsystems, Fujitsu (http://www.fujitsu.com) and T. Sqware (http://www.tsqware.com) also build SPARC-compliant CPU systems.

System vendors who sell systems based on SPARC CPUs include Amdahl Corporation (http://www.amdahl.com), Tatung (http://www.tatung.com), Tadpole (http://www.tadpole.com), and Toshiba (http://www.toshiba.com). Vendors of system boards and peripherals for SPARC CPU–based systems include Hitachi (http://www.hitachi.com), Seagate (http://www.seagate.com), and Kingston Technology (http://www.kingston.com).

Although media critics and competitors often paint Sun's SPARC systems as stand-alone, vendor-specific traps for the unwary, the reality is that a large number of hardware vendors also support the SPARC platform. It should also be noted that software vendors, such as Red Hat, also support SPARC versions of Linux, meaning that Solaris is not the only operating system that powers the SPARC platform. The SPARC standards can be downloaded free of charge from http://www.SPARC.org/standards.html.

Often, administrators of Linux and Microsoft Windows systems, who are used to PC hardware, are incredulous to discover that some supported systems (such as the SPARCclassic) have CPUs that run at sub-100MHz. This must seem a very slow CPU speed in the age of Intel CPUs and their clones reaching the 1GHz mark. However, CPU speed is only one component that contributes to the overall performance of a system—SPARC systems are renowned for their high-speed buses and very fast I/O performance.

In addition, many SPARC systems were designed for continuous operation; it is not unheard of for systems to have several years of uptime, compared to several days for other operating systems. The many impressive features of the Solaris operating system were developed with the SPARC hardware platform as a target, and these systems naturally have the best performance.

However, Sun has not ignored hardware developments and emerging standard—in recent years, they have created the Ultra series of workstations and servers that feature a Peripheral Component Interconnect (PCI) bus and compatibility with Super Video Graphics Array (SVGA) multisync monitors commonly sold with PC systems.

Of course, SPARC systems have always supported the Small Computer System Interface (SCSI) standard, and all SCSI devices will work with Solaris. At the same time, Sun has proceeded with innovations such as the 64-CPU Enterprise 10000 (E10000) system, which can operate as a single system with massively parallel computational abilities, or it can be logically partitioned to act as up to 64 different systems.

Imagine being able to control an entire Application Service Provider (ASP), with no apparent shared hosting to the client, and all hosting being serviced by only a single physical system. Although the up-front cost of an E10000 far exceeds that required for 64 systems running Linux or Microsoft Windows, only one administrator is required to manage an E10000, while 64 different systems might require more than one administrator.

Supported Platforms

The following SPARC systems are supported under Solaris 8:

▼ SPARCclassic

■ SPARCstation LX

■ SPARCstation 4

■ SPARCstation 5

■ SPARCstation 10

■ SPARCstation 20

■ Ultra 1 (including Creator and Creator 3D models)

■ Enterprise 1

■ Ultra 2 (including Creator and Creator 3D models)

■ Ultra 5

■ Ultra 10

■ Ultra 30

■ Ultra 60

■ Ultra 450

■ Enterprise 2

■ Enterprise 150

■ Enterprise 250

■ Enterprise 450

■ Enterprise 3000

■ Enterprise 3500

■ Enterprise 4000

■ Enterprise 4500

■ Enterprise 5000

■ Enterprise 5500

■ Enterprise 6000

- Enterprise 10000
- SPARCserver 1000
- ▲ SPARCcenter 2000

Some popular systems are no longer supported, such as the SPARCstation 1 and SPARCstation 2. Often, these can be upgraded with a firmware or CPU change to be compatible with Solaris 8. In addition, a minimum of 64MB RAM is required to install Solaris 8: the installer will not let you proceed unless it can detect this amount of physical RAM, so be sure to check that your system meets the basic requirements before attempting to install Solaris 8.

OpenBoot PROM Monitor

One of the main hardware differences between SPARC systems that run Solaris and PC systems that run Linux or Microsoft Windows is that SPARC systems have an OpenBoot PROM monitor program, which can be used to modify firmware settings prior to booting. It is based on the Forth programming language and can be used to run Forth programs that perform the following functions:

- ▼ Booting the system by using the boot command
- Performing diagnostics on hardware devices by using the diag command
- ▲ Testing network connectivity by using the watch-net command

The output from the watch-net program looks like this:

```
Internal Loopback test - succeeded
External Loopback test - succeeded
Looking for Ethernet packets.
'.' is a good packet. 'X' is a bad packet.
Type any key to stop
......X.........XXXX.........XX............
```

When you run a command in the OpenBoot monitor, you can pass a number of options to each command to modify its behavior. For example, the boot command takes a number of different options, including which device should be booted. To boot from the default boot device (usually the primary hard drive), you would type

```
ok boot
```

However, it is also possible to boot using the CD-ROM by using the command

```
ok boot cdrom
```

The system may be booted from a host on the network by using the command

```
ok boot net
```

Alternatively, if you have a boot floppy, the following command may be used:

```
ok boot floppy
```

As many early Solaris distributions were made on magnetic tape, it's also possible to boot using a tape drive with the following command:

```
ok boot tape
```

In addition to the watch-net command, the OpenBoot monitor can perform a number of other diagnostic tests. The probe-scsi command displays all of the SCSI devices attached to the system. The following is a sample output:

```
ok probe-scsi
Target 1
Unit 0 Disk SUN0104 Copyright (C) 1995 Sun Microsystems All rights reserved
Target 1
Unit 0 Disk SUN0207 Copyright (C) 1995 Sun Microsystems All rights reserved
```

The test command is used to test specific hardware devices, such as the loopback network device. This device could be tested by using the command

```
ok test net
Internal Loopback test - (OK)
External Loopback test - (OK)
```

The watch-clock command is used to test the clock device.

```
ok watch-clock
Watching the 'seconds' register of the real time clock chip.
 It should be ticking once a second.
 Type any key to stop.
1
2
3
```

To view the OpenBoot release information for your firmware, use the command

```
ok banner
SPARCstation 20, Type 5 Keyboard
ROM Rev. 2.4, 256 MB memory installed, Serial #456543
Ethernet address 5:2:12:c:ee:5a HostID 456543
```

If you have modified your hardware configuration, and you want the new devices to be recognized, you should always reboot by using the command

```
boot -r
```

Device References

Some of the most challenging aspects of understanding Solaris hardware are the device names and references used by Solaris to manage devices. Solaris uses a very specific set of naming conventions to associate physical devices with instance names on the operating system. For Linux and Microsoft Windows administrators, this can be incredibly confusing. In addition, devices can also be referred to by their device name, which is associated with a device file created in the /dev directory after configuration.

For example, a hard disk may have the physical device name /pci@1f,0/pci@1,1/ide@3/dad@0,0, which is associated with the device file /dev/dsk/c0t0d0. In Microsoft Windows, disks are simply labeled by their drive letter (C:, D:, E: and so on); while in Linux, device files are much simplified (for example, /dev/had for an integrated development environment [IDE] hard disk).

The benefit of the more complex Solaris device names and physical device references is that it is easy to interpret the characteristics of each device by looking at its name. Using the same disk example just given, /pci@1f,0/pci@1,1/ide@3/dad@0,0, we can see that the IDE hard drive is located on a PCI bus at target 0. When we view the amount of free disk space on the system, it is easy to identify slices on the same disk by looking at the device name:

```
bash-2.03# df -k
Filesystem              kbytes     used    avail capacity  Mounted on
/proc                        0        0        0     0%    /proc
/dev/dsk/c0t0d0s0      1982988   615991  1307508    33%    /
fd                           0        0        0     0%    /dev/fd
/dev/dsk/c0t0d0s3      1487119   357511  1070124    26%    /usr
swap                    182040      416   181624     1%    /tmp
```

In the preceding code, we can see that /dev/dsk/c0t0d0s0 and /dev/dsk/c0t0d0s3 are slice 0 and slice 3 of the disk /dev/dsk/c0t0d0.

If you're ever unsure of which physical disk is associated with a specific disk device name, the format command will tell you:

```
bash-2.03# format
Searching for disks...done
AVAILABLE DISK SELECTIONS:
0. c1t3d0 <SUN2.1G cyl 2733 alt 2 hd 19 sec 80>
          /pci@1f,0/pci@1/scsi@1/sd@3,0
```

In the preceding code, we can see that physical device /pci@1f,0/pci@1/scsi@1/sd@3,0 is matched with the disk device /dev/dsk/c1t3d0.

In addition, a list of mappings between physical devices to instance names is always kept in the /etc/path_to_inst file:

```
"/sbus@1f,0" 0 "sbus"
"/sbus@1f,0/sbusmem@2,0" 2 "sbusmem"
"/sbus@1f,0/sbusmem@3,0" 3 "sbusmem"
"/sbus@1f,0/sbusmem@0,0" 0 "sbusmem"
"/sbus@1f,0/sbusmem@1,0" 1 "sbusmem"
"/sbus@1f,0/SUNW,fas@2,8800000" 1 "fas"
"/sbus@1f,0/SUNW,fas@2,8800000/ses@f,0" 1 "ses"
"/sbus@1f,0/SUNW,fas@2,8800000/sd@1,0" 16 "sd"
"/sbus@1f,0/SUNW,fas@2,8800000/sd@0,0" 15 "sd"
"/sbus@1f,0/SUNW,fas@2,8800000/sd@3,0" 18 "sd"
"/sbus@1f,0/SUNW,fas@2,8800000/sd@2,0" 17 "sd"
"/sbus@1f,0/SUNW,fas@2,8800000/sd@5,0" 20 "sd"
"/sbus@1f,0/SUNW,fas@2,8800000/sd@4,0" 19 "sd"
"/sbus@1f,0/SUNW,fas@2,8800000/sd@6,0" 21 "sd"
"/sbus@1f,0/SUNW,fas@2,8800000/sd@9,0" 23 "sd"
"/sbus@1f,0/SUNW,fas@2,8800000/sd@8,0" 22 "sd"
"/sbus@1f,0/SUNW,fas@2,8800000/sd@a,0" 24 "sd"
"/sbus@1f,0/SUNW,fas@2,8800000/st@1,0" 8 "st"
"/sbus@1f,0/SUNW,fas@2,8800000/st@0,0" 7 "st"
"/sbus@1f,0/SUNW,fas@2,8800000/sd@c,0" 26 "sd"
"/sbus@1f,0/SUNW,fas@2,8800000/st@3,0" 10 "st"
"/sbus@1f,0/SUNW,fas@2,8800000/sd@b,0" 25 "sd"
"/sbus@1f,0/SUNW,fas@2,8800000/st@2,0" 9 "st"
"/sbus@1f,0/SUNW,fas@2,8800000/sd@e,0" 28 "sd"
"/sbus@1f,0/SUNW,fas@2,8800000/st@5,0" 12 "st"
"/sbus@1f,0/SUNW,fas@2,8800000/sd@d,0" 27 "sd"
"/sbus@1f,0/SUNW,fas@2,8800000/st@4,0" 11 "st"
"/sbus@1f,0/SUNW,fas@2,8800000/sd@f,0" 29 "sd"
"/sbus@1f,0/SUNW,fas@2,8800000/st@6,0" 13 "st"
"/sbus@1f,0/SUNW,CS4231@d,c000000" 0 "audiocs"
"/sbus@1f,0/dma@0,81000" 0 "dma"
"/sbus@1f,0/dma@0,81000/esp@0,80000" 0 "esp"
"/sbus@1f,0/dma@0,81000/esp@0,80000/sd@0,0" 30 "sd"
"/sbus@1f,0/dma@0,81000/esp@0,80000/sd@1,0" 31 "sd"
"/sbus@1f,0/dma@0,81000/esp@0,80000/sd@2,0" 32 "sd"
"/sbus@1f,0/dma@0,81000/esp@0,80000/sd@3,0" 33 "sd"
"/sbus@1f,0/dma@0,81000/esp@0,80000/sd@4,0" 34 "sd"
"/sbus@1f,0/dma@0,81000/esp@0,80000/sd@5,0" 35 "sd"
"/sbus@1f,0/dma@0,81000/esp@0,80000/sd@6,0" 36 "sd"
"/sbus@1f,0/dma@0,81000/esp@0,80000/st@0,0" 14 "st"
"/sbus@1f,0/dma@0,81000/esp@0,80000/st@1,0" 15 "st"
"/sbus@1f,0/dma@0,81000/esp@0,80000/st@2,0" 16 "st"
"/sbus@1f,0/dma@0,81000/esp@0,80000/st@3,0" 17 "st"
"/sbus@1f,0/dma@0,81000/esp@0,80000/st@4,0" 18 "st"
```

```
"/sbus@1f,0/dma@0,81000/esp@0,80000/st@5,0" 19 "st"
"/sbus@1f,0/dma@0,81000/esp@0,80000/st@6,0" 20 "st"
"/sbus@1f,0/sbusmem@f,0" 15 "sbusmem"
"/sbus@1f,0/sbusmem@d,0" 13 "sbusmem"
"/sbus@1f,0/sbusmem@e,0" 14 "sbusmem"
"/sbus@1f,0/cgthree@1,0" 0 "cgthree"
"/sbus@1f,0/SUNW,hme@e,8c00000" 0 "hme"
"/sbus@1f,0/zs@f,1000000" 1 "zs"
"/sbus@1f,0/zs@f,1100000" 0 "zs"
"/sbus@1f,0/SUNW,bpp@e,c800000" 0 "bpp"
"/sbus@1f,0/lebuffer@0,40000" 0 "lebuffer"
"/sbus@1f,0/lebuffer@0,40000/le@0,60000" 0 "le"
"/sbus@1f,0/SUNW,hme@2,8c00000" 1 "hme"
"/sbus@1f,0/SUNW,fdtwo@f,1400000" 0 "fd"
"/options" 0 "options"
"/pseudo" 0 "pseudo"
```

In the preceding code, we can see entries for the network interface, /sbus@1f,0/ SUNW,hme@2,8c00000, as well as the floppy disk /sbus@1f,0/SUNW,fdtwo@f,1400000 and the SBUS sbus@1f,0.

PREINSTALLATION TASKS

Before installing your system, you will need the following information from your network administrator:

▼ **Hostname (for example, www)**   This is the name that you wish to give your host to identify it uniquely on the local area network.

■ **Internet Protocol (IP) address (for example, 204.58.32.46)**   The IP address is used by the transport layer to locate a specific host on the worldwide Internet.

■ **Domain name (for example, cassowary.net)**   The domain name is the organization to which your host belongs. All hosts on the Internet must belong to a domain.

■ **Domain Name Service (DNS) Server (for example, ns)**   The DNS server maps IP addresses to domain names, and domain names to IP addresses.

▲ **Subnet Mask (for example, 255.255.255.0)**   The mask is used to locate hosts that form part of the same subnet on the local area network.

You will also need to decide which language you wish to use when installing Solaris. The following languages are supported for performing the installation process:

▼ English
■ French

- German
- Italian
- Japanese
- Korean
- Simplified Chinese
- Spanish
- Swedish
- ▲ Traditional Chinese

There are four primary configurations that have been developed for Solaris Intel, and they are shown along with their approximate installed size in Table 2-1.

If the system has never had Solaris installed, you can simply insert the CD-ROM into its caddy and/or CD-ROM drive, and the Web Start installer will start. Alternatively, once the system has started booting, you can click Stop; press the A key; and when you get the ok prompt, you can simply type the following:

```
ok boot cdrom
```

Distribution	Approximate Size
Entire Distribution Plus Original Equipment Manufacturer (OEM) Support	2.4Gb
Entire Distribution Without OEM Support	2.3Gb
Developer System Support	1.9Gb
End User System Support	1.6Gb

Table 2-1.   Size of Different Solaris Distributions

You will then see output similar to the following:

```
Boot device: /sbus/espdma@e,8400000/esp@e,8800000/sd@6,0:f File and args:
SunOS Release 5.8 Version Generic 32-bit
Copyright 1983-2000 Sun Microsystems, Inc. All rights reserved.
Configuring /dev and /devices
Using RPC Bootparams for network configuration information.
Solaris Web Start 3.0 installer
English has been selected as the language in which to perform the install.
Starting the Web Start 3.0 Solaris installer
Solaris installer is searching the system's hard disks for a
location to place the Solaris installer software.
Your system appears to be upgradeable.
Do you want to do an Initial Install or Upgrade?
1) Initial Install
2) Upgrade
Please Enter 1 or 2 >
```

If the following message appeared in the boot messages, then you may elect to perform an
upgrade of the existing Solaris installation. However, most administrators would back up
their existing software, perform a fresh install, and then restore their data and applications
once their system is operational. In this case, we will choose to perform an initial install,
which will overwrite the existing operating system.

After you enter **1**, and press ENTER, you will see a message like this:

```
The default root disk is /dev/dsk/c0t0d0.
The Solaris installer needs to format
/dev/dsk/c0t0d0 to install Solaris.
WARNING: ALL INFORMATION ON THE DISK WILL BE ERASED!
Do you want to format /dev/dsk/c0t0d0? [y,n,?,q]
```

Formatting the hard drive will overwrite all existing data on the drive—you must ensure
that, if you had previously installed an operating system on the target drive (c0t0d0), you
have backed up all data that you will need in the future. This includes both user directories
and application installations.

After pressing Y, the following screen will appear:

```
Enter a swap slice size between 384MB and 2027MB, default = 512MB [?]
```

NOTE: The swap size cannot be changed during filesystem layout.

Press the ENTER key to accept the default on 512MB if your system has 256MB physical RAM, as the sample system has. However, as a general rule, you should only allocate twice the amount of physical RAM as swap space; otherwise, system performance will be impaired. The swap partition should be placed at the beginning of the drive, as the following message indicates, so that other slices are not dependent on its physical location:

```
The Installer prefers that the swap slice is at the beginning of the
disk. This will allow the most flexible filesystem partitioning later in the
installation.
Can the swap slice start at the beginning of the disk [y,n,?,q]
```

After answering Y to this question, you will be asked to confirm the formatting settings:

```
You have selected the following to be used by the Solaris installer:
Disk Slice : /dev/dsk/c0t0d0
Size : 1024 MB
Start Cyl. : 0
WARNING: ALL INFORMATION ON THE DISK WILL BE ERASED!
Is this OK [y,n,?,q]
```

If you answer Y, then the disk will be formatted and the miniroot file system will be copied to the disk, after which the system will be rebooted and the Web Start Wizard installation process can begin:

```
The Solaris installer will use disk slice, /dev/dsk/c0t0d0s1.
After files are copied, the system will automatically reboot, and
installation will continue.
Please Wait...
Copying mini-root to local disk....done.
Copying platform specific files....done.
Preparing to reboot and continue installation.
Rebooting to continue the installation.
Syncing file systems... 41 done
rebooting...
Resetting ...
SPARCstation 20 (1 X 390Z50), Keyboard Present
ROM Rev. 2.4, 256 MB memory installed, Serial #456543
Ethernet address 5:2:12:c:ee:5a HostID 456543
Rebooting with command: boot /sbus@1f,0/espdma@e,8400000/esp@e,8800000/sd@0,0:b
Boot device: /sbus@1f,0/espdma@e,8400000/esp@e,8800000/sd@0,0:b File and args:
SunOS Release 5.8 Version Generic 32-bit
```

```
Copyright 1983-2000 Sun Microsystems, Inc. All rights reserved.
Configuring /dev and /devices
Using RPC Bootparams for network configuration information.
```

WEB START WIZARD INSTALLATION

Using the Web Start Wizard is the easiest way to install and configure Solaris. Although it is possible to use the Solaris Interactive installer supplied with previous Solaris versions, the Web Start Wizard allows users to install entire distributions or groups of packages, and automatically size, lay out, and create slices on the file system. It also configures the boot disk and other disks that are installed locally.

However, if you wish to install individual packages or change the size of the swap file, then you will not be able to use the Web Start Wizard. Users from a Microsoft Windows background, or those who have only installed Linux using a Graphical User Interface (GUI)–based installation package, like SuSE's YaST2 (Sun Systems Environment's Yet Another Sysadmin Tool 2), are advised to use the Web Start Wizard.

Network

The first section of the wizard involves setting up the network. The Network Connectivity screen gives users the option to select a networked or nonnetworked system. If you don't need to install network support, you will still need a unique hostname, and this must then be entered. Network users will have to enter a hostname, but they must first identify how their system obtains IP support.

One possibility is that the system will use Dynamic Host Configuration Protocol (DHCP), which is useful because IP addresses are becoming scarce on Class C networks. DHCP allows individual systems to be allocated only for the period during which they are up. Thus, if a client machine is only operated between 9 A.M. and 5 P.M. every day, it is only leased an IP address for that period of time. When an IP address is not leased to a specific host, it can be reused by another host. Solaris DHCP servers can service Solaris clients, as well as Microsoft Windows and Linux clients. Chapter 17 provides more information about DHCP services under Solaris.

Next, you need to indicate whether Internet Protocol version 6 (IPv6) needs to be supported by this system. The decision to use or not to use DHCP will depend on whether your network is part of the mbone, the IPv6-enabled version of the Internet. As proposed in Request for Comments (RFC) 2471, IPv6 will replace Internet Protocol version 4 (IPv4) in the years to come, as it provides for many more IP addresses than IPv4. Once IPv6 is adopted worldwide, there will be less reliance on stop-gap measures like DHCP.

However, IPv6 also incorporates a number of innovations above and beyond the addition of more IP addresses for the Internet: enhanced security provided by authenticating header information, for example, will reduce the risk of IP spoofing and denial of service attacks succeeding. Since IPv6 support does not interfere with existing IPv4 support, most administrators will want to support it.

Finally, you need to enter the IP address assigned to this system by the network administrator. It is important not to use an IP address that is currently being used by another host, since packets may be misrouted. You will also need to enter the netmask for the system, which will be 255.0.0.0 (Class A), 255.255.0.0 (Class B), or 255.255.255.0 (Class C). If you're not sure of the netmask for your system, ask your network administrator.

Name Service

A name service allows your system to find other hosts on the Internet or on the local-area network. Solaris supports several different naming servers, including the Network Information Service (NIS/NIS+), and the DNS, or file-based name resolution. NIS/NIS+ is used to manage large domains by creating maps of hosts, services, and resources that are shared among hosts and can be centrally managed.

The DNS, on the other hand, only stores maps of IP addresses and hostnames. Solaris supports the concurrent operation of different naming services, so it's possible to select NIS/NIS+ at this point and set up DNS manually later. However, since most hosts are now connected to the Internet, it may be more appropriate to install DNS first and install NIS/NIS+ after installation.

If you select DNS or NIS/NIS+, you will be asked to enter a domain name for the local system. This should be the fully qualified domain name (FQDN) (for example, cassowary.net). If you selected DNS, you will either need to search the local subnet for a DNS server, or enter the IP address of the primary DNS server that is authoritative for your domain.

You may also enter up to two secondary DNS servers that have records of your domain. This can be a useful backup if your primary DNS server goes down. It is also possible that, when searching for hosts with a hostname rather than a FQDN, you would want to search multiple local domains. For example, the host www.finance.cassowary.net belongs to the finance.cassowary.net domain.

However, your users may wish to locate other hosts within the broader cassowary.net domain by using the simple hostname. In order to facilitate them, you can add the cassowary.net domain to a list of domains to be searched for hosts.

Date and Time

The next section requires that you enter your time zone as specified by geographic region, the number of hours beyond or before Greenwich Mean Time (GMT), or by time zone file. Using the geographic region is the easiest method, although if you already know the GMT offset and/or the name of the time zone file, you may enter that instead. Next, you are required to enter the current time and date, with a four-digit year, month, day, hour, and minute.

Root Password

The most important stage of the installation procedure occurs next: the selection of the root password. The root user has the same powers as the root user on Linux or the Administrator account on Windows NT. If an intruder gains root access, he or she is free to roam the system, deleting or stealing data, removing or adding user accounts, or installing Trojan horses that transparently modify the way that your system operates.

One way to protect against an unauthorized user gaining root access is to use a difficult-to-guess root password. This makes it hard for a cracker to use a password-cracking program and be successful. The optimal password is a completely random string of alphanumeric and punctuation characters. There are some applications, discussed in Chapter 15, that can be used to generate passwords that are easy to remember, but which contain almost random combinations of characters.

In addition, the root password should never be written down, unless it is locked in the company safe or told to anyone who doesn't need to know it. If users require levels of access that are typically privileged (such as mounting CD-ROMs), it is better to use the pseudo utility to limit the access of each user to specific applications for execution as the superuser, rather than giving out the root password to everyone who asks for it.

The root password must be entered twice in case you should happen to make a typographical error, as the characters that you type are masked on the screen.

Power Management

Do you want your system to switch off automatically after 30 minutes of inactivity? If you can honestly answer yes to this question (for example, because you have a workstation that does not run services), then you should enable power management, as it can save costly power bills. However, if you're administering a server, then you'll definitely want to TURN POWER MANAGEMENT OFF. Once your server has shut down in the middle of the night and your clients cannot access data, then you'll remember reading this section and the message TURN POWER MANAGEMENT OFF, and you'll disable power management.

Proxy Server

A proxy server acts as a buffer between hosts on a local network and the rest of the Internet. A proxy server passes connections back and forth between local hosts and any other host on the Internet. It usually acts in conjunction with a firewall to block access to internal systems, thereby protecting sensitive data. One of the most popular firewalls is squid, which also acts as a caching server.

To enable access to the Internet through a proxy server, you need to enter the hostname of the proxy server and the port on which the proxy operates.

KIOSK

After all of the configuration settings have been entered, the following message will be seen on the screen:

```
Please wait while the system is configured with your settings. . .
```

The installation Kiosk will then appear on the screen. The Kiosk is primarily used to select the type of installation that you wish to perform. To begin the software selection process, you need to eject the Web Start CD-ROM and insert the Software (1) CD-ROM. Next, you have the option of installing all Solaris software using the default options or customizing your selection before copying the files from the CD-ROM.

If you have a lot of disk space and a fast system, you may prefer to install the entire distribution and delete packages after installation that you no longer require. This is definitely the fastest method. Alternatively, you can elect to perform a customized installation.

You are then presented with a screen of all the available software groups. Here, you may select or deselect individual package groups or package clusters, depending on your requirements. For example, you may decide to install the Netscape Navigator software, but not install the NIS/NIS+ server for Solaris. After choosing the packages that you wish to install, you are then required to enter your locale based on geographic region (the United States entry is selected by default).

You may also elect to install third-party software during the Solaris installation process—for example, this is particularly useful if you have a standard operating environment that consists of using the Oracle database server in conjunction with the Solaris operating environment. You need to insert the product CD-ROM at this point so that it can be identified.

After selecting your software, you will need to lay out the disks. This involves defining disk slices that will store the different kinds of data on your system. The fastest configuration option involves selecting the boot disk and allowing the installer to automatically lay out the partitions according to the software selection that you have chosen. For example, you may wish to expand the size of the /var partition to allow for large print jobs to be spooled or Web servers logs to be recorded.

Finally, you will be asked to confirm your software selections and proceed with installation. All of the packages will then be installed to your system. A progress bar displayed on the screen indicates which packages have been installed at any particular point and how many remain to be installed. After you have installed all of the software, you will have to reboot the system. After restarting, your system should boot directly into Solaris unless you have a dual-booting system, in which case you will need to select the Solaris boot partition from the Solaris boot manager.

After installation, the system will reboot and display a status message when starting up, which is printed on the console. The following is a sample console displayed during booting:

```
ok boot
Resetting ...
SPARCstation 20 (1 X 390Z50), Keyboard Present
ROM Rev. 2.4, 256 MB memory installed, Serial #456543
Ethernet address 5:2:12:c:ee:5a HostID 456543
Boot device: /iommu/sbus/espdma@f,400000/esp@f,800000/sd@1,0
File and args:
SunOS Release 5.8 Version generic [UNIX(R) System V Release 4.0]
Copyright (c) 1983-2000, Sun Microsystems, Inc.
configuring network interfaces: le0.
Hostname: server
The system is coming up. Please wait.
add net default: gateway 204.58.62.33
NIS domainname is paulwatters.net
starting rpc services: rpcbind keyserv ypbind done.
Setting netmask of le0 to 255.255.255.0
Setting default interface for multicast: add net 224.0.0.0: gateway emu
syslog service starting.
Print services started.
volume management starting.
The system is ready.
emu console login:
```

By default, the Common Desktop Environment (CDE) login screen is then displayed. Using the CDE interface is covered in Chapter 4.

SUMMARY

In this chapter, we have examined the procedure for installing Solaris on the SPARC platform, including using the OpenBoot PROM monitor and the Web Star Wizard installer. We have also reviewed the various kinds of Sun hardware on which Solaris can be installed. Traditionally, most organizations have used SPARC hardware. However, in Chapter 3, we examine how to install Solaris onto an Intel-based system, since Solaris for the Intel platform is increasing in popularity.

CHAPTER 3

Installing Solaris Intel

Recently, Sun introduced Solaris x86, which is designed to run on Intel-based hardware. This makes Solaris accessible for users who already own Intel systems running Linux and/or Windows NT/2000. In Chapter 3, you will learn how to install and configure a bare x86 system with Solaris. We examine the major hardware components supported by Solaris and identify the differences in installation between the Sparc and Intel editions. And, since many Windows NT/2000 and Linux systems will want to dual boot Solaris, we review several methods for enabling dual booting and for transitioning from existing operating systems to Solaris.

CHOOSING HARDWARE

The Hardware Compatibility List (HCL), which is available at http://soldc.sun.com/support/drivers/hcl/index.html, is the definitive guide to all hardware devices that are supported by the Solaris-Intel platform. If a device does not appear in the HCL, then it is unlikely that it will be supported under Solaris Intel. There are some exceptions: motherboards, for example, often follow fairly loose standards, with clone boards often working correctly under Solaris if they don't appear in the HCL. The most common compatibility issue occurs with video cards—many are not supported at all, or if they are, their full feature set is unsupported. For example, some video cards have hardware support for receiving TV signals; but while their graphical rendering ability will be supported, the TV functions will generally not work with Solaris.

Fortunately, if your video card is not supported, it is possible to replace the X server provided by Solaris with the XFree-86 X server (http://www.xfree.org). This server is functionally equivalent to any other server that supports the X11R6 standard, meaning that Commn Desktop Environment (CDE) and all other Solaris Graphical User Interface (GUI) applications will run if you have XFree-86 X installed. The main advantage of using XFree-86 X is that it supports a much larger array of hardware devices than the Solaris X server.

In this section, we will review some of the families of devices supported under Solaris Intel (we don't list every device that is supported under Solaris—check the HCL for complete details), and we will review examples of products that Solaris Intel is likely to support.

Motherboards

Most common motherboards are supported, including those developed by Acer, ASUS, EpoX, and Intel. Some examples are

▼ Acer M9N MP
■ ASUS A7V
■ EPoX EP-MVP3G
▲ Intel JN440BX

In addition, motherboard support has been established for many prebuilt systems, including the following models (one from each manufacturer supported):

▼   Acer AcerAcros T7000 MT

■   Bull Information Systems Express 5800-HX4500

■   Compaq Deskpro EN 6400

■   Dell OptiPlex G1

■   Fujitsu FMV-5166D9K

■   Hitachi HA8000/150

■   HP NetServer LHII

■   IBM IntelliStation E Pro 6893

■   IBM Netfinity 3500 8644-21U

■   Intel SKA4

■   Motorola CPV5000 Single-Board Computer

■   NCR 3271

■   NEC Express 5800-HX4500

■   Siemens AG PRIMERGY 170

■   Toshiba Magnia 3000

▲   Zenith Data Systems Express 5800-ES1200

Video Cards

Video cards from many different manufacturers are supported, including those operating from ISA, PCI, or AGP buses. Five display resolutions are supported:

▼ 800×600 pixels

■ $1,024 \times 768$ pixels

■ $1,152 \times 900$ pixels

■ $1,280 \times 1,024$ pixels

▲ $1,600 \times 1,200$ pixels

Both 8- and 24-bit color are supported in all of these modes, depending on the chipset and onboard memory. The following cards are supported:

▼   ATI 3D RAGE

■   Boca Voyager 64

■   Chips & Technology 65540

■   Cirrus Logic 5420

■   Creative Labs 3D Blaster RIVA TNT2

■   Diamond Fire GL 1000 Pro

- ELSA Victory 3D
- Everex FIC 864P
- Hercules Dynamite 128/Video
- Intergraph G95
- Matrox Millennium
- ▲ NVIDIA TNT2

Monitors

All multisync monitors are supported. Fixed-sync monitors should work as long as their frequency is supported by the video card at the resolution you require.

Mice

Serial, bus, and PS/2 mouse devices are supported under Solaris. In addition, the following third-party pointing devices are supported:

- ▼ MicroSpeed MicroTRAC trackball
- LogiTech MouseMan cordless
- Kraft Systems MicroTrack
- ▲ InterLink PortAPoint

Symmetric MultiProcessing (SMP)

Many SMP-capable motherboards are supported. No special configuration is required to support SMP devices, and they are plug and play. Some popular models include

- ▼ Acer AcerAltos 21000
- Bull Information Systems Express 5800-HX4500
- Compaq Professional Workstation 8000
- Dell PowerEdge 6300
- Fujitsu TeamSERVER-T890i
- Gateway 8400
- Hitachi VisionBase 8880R UWRAID (with 8 CPUs)
- HP Kayak XU 6-300 PC Workstation
- ▲ Intel SPM8

SCSI Host Adapters

Both standard and ultrawide Small Computer System Interface (SCSI) support is included for the most popular host adapters, including the following:

- ▼ Adaptec AHA-2940/2940W
- ■ AMD PcSCSI
- ■ Compaq 32-bit Fast-Wide SCSI-2
- ■ DPT PM2024
- ■ DTC DTC-3130
- ■ Hitachi PC-CS7210
- ■ Intel PcISCSI
- ■ LSI Logic NCR 53C810
- ▲ QLogic QLA510

Zip/Jaz Devices

Many Iomega devices are supported under Solaris, including the SCSI devices 2250S Zip drive (250MB), the V2008I Jaz drive (2GB), as well as the ATAPI and IDE Z100A Zip (100MB) drives.

Network Adapters

Many different types of network adapters are supported, including 10Mbps and 100Mbps data transfer rates. The following adapters are representative of those supported:

- ▼ 3Com EtherLink III PCI Bus Master
- ■ Adaptec ANA-6901
- ■ AMD PCnet-PCI
- ■ CNet CN970EBT
- ■ Cogent EM110 T4
- ■ Compaq Deskpro 4000 NetFlex-3
- ■ DEC EtherWORKS
- ■ D-Link DE-530CT
- ■ HP PC LAN NC/16 TP
- ■ Intel EtherExpress PRO/10+
- ■ Kingston KNE40BT
- ■ Linksys LNE100TX
- ■ Samsung SEB-3000C
- ▲ SMC EtherPower SMC8432BT

PCMCIA Devices

Personal Computer Memory card International Association (PCMCIA) devices for laptops are also largely supported, including both modems and network adapters. Some PCMCIA devices that are supported are

▼ ATI Technologies 14400 ETC-EXPRESS

■ Compaq SpeedPaq 192

■ Hayes 5361US

■ Intel 110-US

■ Kingston DataRex 87G9851

▲ US Robotics Sun/USR WorldPort

PREINSTALLATION CONFIGURATION

Before installing your system, you will need the following information from your network administrator:

▼ **Hostname (for example, www)**   This is the name that you wish to give your host to identify it uniquely on the local area network.

■ **Internet Protocol (IP) address (for example, 204.58.32.46)**   The IP address is used by the transport layer to locate a specific host on the worldwide Internet.

■ **Domain name (for example, cassowary.net)**   The domain name is the organization to which your host belongs. All hosts on the Internet must belong to a domain.

■ **Domain Name Service (DNS) Server (for example, ns)**   The DNS server maps IP addresses to domain names, and domain names to IP addresses.

▲ **Subnet Mask (for example, 255.255.255.0)**   The mask that is used to locate hosts that form part of the same subnet on the local area network.

You will also need to decide which language you wish to use when installing Solaris. The following languages are supported to perform the installation process:

▼ English

■ French

■ German

■ Italian

- Japanese
- Korean
- Simplified Chinese
- Spanish
- Swedish
▲ Traditional Chinese

There are four primary configurations that have been developed for Solaris Intel, and they are shown along with their approximate installed sizes in Table 3-1.

To install Solaris Intel, the first step is to switch on the system and insert the Solaris 8 installation CD-ROM into the drive. After the BIOS messages have been displayed, you will be shown the following message:

```
SunOS Secondary Boot version 3.00
Solaris Intel Platform Edition Booting System
Running Configuration Assistant
```

The configuration assistant will then be initialized. At the opening screen, simply press F2 to proceed with the installation, unless you are performing an upgrade.

Device Configuration Assistant

The first task performed by the configuration assistant is determining the bus types supported by your system, and collecting data about the devices installed in your system. During this process, the following message will be displayed on your screen:

```
Determining bus types and gathering hardware configuration data
```

Configuration	Approximate Size
Entire distribution plus OEM support	2.4GB
Entire distribution without OEM support	2.3GB
Developer system support	1.9GB
End user system support	1.6GB

Table 3-1. Size of Different Solaris Configurations

After all of the devices have been discovered by scanning, a list of identified devices is printed on the screen:

```
The following devices have been identified on this system. To identify
devices not on this list or to modify device characteristics, choose
Device Task. Platform types may be included in this list.

    ISA: Floppy disk controller
    ISA: IDE controller
    ISA: IDE controller
    ISA: Motherboard
    ISA: PS/2 Mouse
    ISA: PnP bios: 16550-compatible serial controller
    ISA: PnP bios: 8514-compatible display controller
    ISA: PnP bios: Audio device
    ISA: System keyboard (US-English)
```

If you are satisfied that the devices required for installation have been correctly detected (for example, video card and RAM size), then you may press F2 to proceed with booting. Alternatively, you may perform several other tasks on this screen, including

▼ Viewing and editing devices

■ Setting the keyboard type

■ Saving the current configuration

■ Deleting a saved configuration

▲ Setting the default console device

If your system does not already have a UNIX File System (UFS) file system installed, or if it is a completely new system, you will need to use fdisk to create new partitions at this point, so that your system may be installed. However, if you have an existing Linux that you wish to dual boot with Solaris, you must ensure that the Linux swap partition is not confused with a Solaris UFS device, since they have the same type within fdisk. You should be able to distinguish Linux swap partitions by their maximum size (127MB). The following page will be displayed during booting and prior to the execution of fdisk:

```
<<< Current Boot Parameters >>>
Boot path: /pci@1,0/pci-ide@6,1/ide@2/sd@1,0:a
Boot args: kernel/unix
SunOS Release 5.8 Version Generic 32-bit
Copyright 1983-2000 Sun Microsystems, Inc. All rights reserved.
Configuring /dev and /devices
Using RPC Bootparams for network configuration information.
Solaris Web Start 3.0 installer
English has been selected as the language in which to perform the install.
```

```
Starting the Web Start 3.0 Solaris installer
Solaris installer is searching the system's hard disks for a
location to place the Solaris installer software.
No suitable Solaris fdisk partition was found.
Solaris Installer needs to create a Solaris fdisk partition
on your root disk, c0d0, that is at least 395 MB.
WARNING: All information on the disk will be lost.
May the Solaris Installer create a Solaris fdisk [y,n,?]
```

You should heed the warning that all data will be lost if you choose to overwrite it with fdisk.

fdisk

If you consent to using fdisk, you will see a screen similar to the following:

```
Total disk size is 2048 cylinders
Cylinder size is 4032 (512 byte) blocks
Cylinders
Partition  Status  Type  Start  End   Length  %
=========  ======  ====  =====  ====  ======  ===
1                  UNIX  0      1023  1024    50
2                  DOS   1024   2047  1024    50
SELECT ONE OF THE FOLLOWING:
1. Create a partition
2. Specify the active partition
3. Delete a partition
4. Exit (update disk configuration and exit)
5. Cancel (exit without updating disk configuration)
Enter Selection:
```

In this example, we can see that there are two existing partitions occupying 1,204 cylinders each. Partition 1 is a UNIX partition (perhaps from SCO UNIX), and Partition 2 is a MSDOS partition. If we want to use the entire disk for Solaris, we would need to select option 3 on this menu twice, to delete each existing partition in turn. Alternatively, if we wish to retain the UNIX partition, but delete the MS-DOS partition, we would use option 3 only once, and select partition 2 for deletion.

After you have freed up space (if necessary), you will be required to select option 1 to create a partition. You will then be required to select option A from the following menu to create a Solaris partition:

```
Select the partition type to create:
1=SOLARIS 2=UNIX 3=PCIXOS 4=Other
5=DOS12 6=DOS16 7=DOSEXT 8=DOSBIG
A=x86 Boot B=Diagnostic 0=Exit?
```

Note that it is not possible to run Solaris from a non-UFS partition; however, it is possible to mount non-Solaris file systems after the system has been installed. Next, you need to specify the size of the partition, in either the number of cylinders or the percentage of the disk to be used. In this example, we would enter either 100% or 2048 cylinders:

```
Specify the percentage of disk to use for this partition
(or type "c" to specify the size in cylinders)
```

Next, you will need to indicate whether or not the target partition is going to be activated. This means that the system will attempt to boot the default operating system loader from this partition. If you are going to use the Solaris boot manager, then you may activate this partition. However, if you are using Boot Magic or LILO to manage existing Microsoft Windows or Linux partitions, and you wish to continue using either of these systems, then you should answer no.

After you have created the partition, the fdisk menu will be updated and displayed as follows:

```
2 Active x86 Boot 8 16 9 1
Total disk size is 2048 cylinders
Cylinder size is 4032 (512 byte) blocks
Cylinders
Partition  Status  Type        Start  End   Length  %
=========  ======  =========   =====  ====  ======  ===
2          Active  x86 Boot    0      2047  2048    100
SELECT ONE OF THE FOLLOWING:
1. Create a partition
2. Specify the active partition
3. Delete a partition
4. Exit (update disk configuration and exit)
5. Cancel (exit without updating disk configuration)
Enter Selection:
```

At this point, you should select option 4. You will then be prompted with the following message:

```
No suitable Solaris fdisk partition was found.
Solaris Installer needs to create a Solaris fdisk partition
on your root disk, c0d0, that is at least 395 MB.
WARNING: All information on the disk will be lost.
May the Solaris Installer create a Solaris fdisk [y,n,?]
```

Since you've just created the appropriate partition using fdisk, you should type **n** here. You will then see this message:

```
To restart the installation, run /sbin/cd0_install.
```

After restarting the Installer, you will see the formatting display shown in the next section.

Formatting and Swap

If your system already has a UFS partition, or if you have just created one, you will see a screen similar to the following:

```
<<< Current Boot Parameters >>>
Boot path: /pci@1,0/pci-ide@6,1/ide@2/sd@1,0:a
Boot args: kernel/unix
<<< Starting Installation >>>
SunOS Release 5.8 Version Generic 32-bit
Copyright 1983-2000 Sun Microsystems, Inc. All rights reserved.
Configuring /dev and /devices
Using RPC Bootparams for network configuration information.
Solaris Web Start 3.0 installer
English has been selected as the language in which to perform the install.
Starting the Web Start 3.0 Solaris installer
Solaris installer is searching the system's hard disks for a
location to place the Solaris installer software.
The default root disk is /dev/dsk/c0d0.
The Solaris installer needs to format
/dev/dsk/c0d0 to install Solaris.
WARNING: ALL INFORMATION ON THE DISK WILL BE ERASED!
Do you want to format /dev/dsk/c0d0? [y,n,?,q]
```

At this point, you simply reply **y**, and the disk will be formatted as required, so that new partitions may be created. You will then be prompted to enter the size of the swap partition:

```
NOTE: The swap size cannot be changed during filesystem layout.
Enter a swap partition size between 384MB and 1865MB, default = 512MB [?]
```

You will the be asked to confirm that the swap slice can be installed at the beginning of the partition:

```
The Installer prefers that the swap slice is at the beginning of the
disk. This will allow the most flexible filesystem partitioning later in the installation.
Can the swap slice start at the beginning of the disk [y,n,?,q]
```

After creating the swap partition, the other slices can be created on the target disk, since the installation program requires a UFS file system to install correctly; however, the system must first be rebooted to perform the layout.

```
The Solaris installer will use disk slice, /dev/dsk/c0d0s1.
After files are copied, the system will automatically reboot, and
installation will continue.
Please Wait
```

```
Copying mini-root to local disk....done.
Copying platform specific files....done
Preparing to reboot and continue installation
Need to reboot to continue the installation
Please remove the boot media (floppy or cdrom) and press Enter
Note: If the boot media is cdrom, you must wait for the system
to reset in order to eject.
```

After you press the ENTER key, you will see the standard Solaris shutdown messages, including

```
Syncing file systems... 49 done
rebooting
```

kdmconfig

After ejecting the installation CD-ROM from your drive, you will see the standard Solaris boot manager menu.

```
SunOS - Intel Platform Edition Primary Boot Subsystem, vsn 2.0
Current Disk Partition Information
Part#   Status  Type        Start   Length
=========================================
1       Active  X86 BOOT  0       2048
Please select the partition you wish to boot:
```

After you enter **1** and press the ENTER key, you will see the following message:

```
SunOS Secondary Boot version 3.00
Solaris Intel Platform Edition Booting System
Running Configuration Assistant
Autobooting from boot path: /pci@1,0/pci-ide@6,1/ide@2/sd@1,0:a
If the system hardware has changed, or to boot from a different
device, interrupt the autoboot process by pressing E FILENAME 15503f.docSC
```

A few seconds later, the boot interpreter is initialized:

```
Initializing system
Please wait
<<< Current Boot Parameters >>>
Boot path: /pci@0,0/pci-ide@7,1/ata@1/cmdk@0,0:b
Boot args:
Type b [file-name] [boot-flags] <ENTER> to boot with options
or i <ENTER> to enter boot interpreter
or <ENTER> to boot with defaults
<<< timeout in 5 seconds >>>
Select (b)oot or (i)nterpreter:
SunOS Release 5.8 Version Generic 32-bit
Copyright 1983-2000 Sun Microsystems, Inc. All rights reserved.
Configuring /dev and /devices
Using RPC Bootparams for network configuration information.
```

Next, you will need to use kdmconfig to set up your graphics card and monitor, so that the Web Start Wizard can display its windows correctly. To start kdmconfig, press F2, after which you will be taken to the kdmconfig introduction screen. After pressing F2 again, you will be asked to perform the kdmconfig view/edit system configuration window. Here, you can make changes to the settings detected for your system. If your system is listed on the HCL, you won't have any problems with hardware detection. After pressing F2, the display settings will be tested, and if all of the colors appear OK and you can move the mouse, the Installer begins.

WEB START WIZARD INSTALLATION

Using the Web Start Wizard is the easiest way to install and configure Solaris. Although it is possible to use the Solaris Interactive Installer supplied with previous Solaris versions, the Web Start Wizard allows users to install entire distributions or groups of packages, and automatically size, lay out, and create slices on the file system. It also configures the boot disk and other disks that are installed locally. However, if you wish to install individual packages, or change the size of the swap file, then you will not be able to use the Web Start Wizard. Users from a Microsoft Windows background, or who have only installed Linux using a GUI-based installation package (like SuSE's YaST2), are advised to use the Web Start Wizard.

Network

The first section of the Web Start Wizard involves setting up the network. The Network Connectivity screen gives users the option to select a networked or nonnetworked system. If you don't need to install network support, you will still need a unique hostname, and this must then be entered. Network users will have to enter a hostname, but must first identify how their system obtains IP support. One possibility is that the system will use Dynamic Host Configuration Protocol (DHCP), which is useful because IP addresses are becoming scarce on a Class C network. DHCP allows individual systems to be allocated only for the period during which they are up; thus, if a client machine is only operated between 9 A.M. and 5 P.M. every day, it is only leased an IP address for that period of time. When an IP address is not leased to a specific host, it can be reused by another host. Solaris DHCP servers can service Solaris clients, as well as Microsoft Windows and Linux clients. Chapter 17 provides more information about DHCP services under Solaris.

Next, you need to indicate whether Internet Protocol version 6 (IPv6) needs to be supported by this system. The decision to use or not to use DHCP will depend on whether your network is part of the mbone, the IP-v6-enabled version of the Internet. As proposed in RFC 2471, IPv6 will replace Internet Protocol version 4 (IPv4) in the years to come, as it provides for many more IP addresses than IPv4. Once IPv6 is adopted worldwide, there will be less reliance on stop-gap measures like DHCP. IPv6 also incorporates a number of innovations above and beyond the addition of more IP addresses for the Internet: for example, enhanced security provided by authenticating header information will reduce the success of IP spoofing and denial-of-service attacks. Since IPv6 support does not interfere with existing IPv4 support, most administrators will want to support it.

Finally, you need to enter the IP address assigned to this system by the network administrator. It is important not to use an IP address that is currently being used by another host, since packets may be misrouted. You will also need to enter the netmask for the system, which will be 255.0.0.0 (Class A), 255.255.0.0 (Class B), or 255.255.255.0 (Class C). If you're not sure, ask your network administrator.

Name Service

A name service allows your system to find other hosts on the Internet or on the local-area network. Solaris supports several different naming servers, including the Network Information Service (NIS/NIS+) and the DNS or file-based name resolution. NIS/NIS+ is used to manage large domains by creating maps of hosts, services, and resources that are shared between hosts and can be centrally managed. The DNS, on the other hand, only stores maps of IP addresses and hostnames. Solaris supports the concurrent operation of different naming services, so it's possible to select NIS/NIS+ at this point and set up DNS manually later; however, since most hosts are now connected to the Internet, it may be more appropriate to install DNS first and install NIS/NIS+ after.

If you select DNS or NIS/NIS+, you will be asked to enter a domain name for the local system. This should be the fully qualified domain name (for example, cassowary.net). If you selected DNS, then you will either need to search the local subnet for a DNS server or enter the IP address of the primary DNS server that is authoritative for your domain. You may also enter up to two secondary DNS servers that have records of your domain. This can be a useful backup if your primary DNS server goes down. When searching for hosts with a hostname rather than a fully qualified domain name, you should search multiple local domains. For example, the host www.finance.cassowary.net belongs to the finance.cassowary.net domain; however, your users may wish to locate other hosts within the broader cassowary.net domain by using the simple hostname, in which case, you can add the cassowary.net domain to a list of domains to be searched for hosts.

Date and Time

The next section requires that you enter your time zone, as specified by geographic region, the number of hours beyond or before Greenwich Mean Time (GMT), or time zone file. Using the geographic region is the easiest method, although if you already know the GMT offset and/or the name of the time zone file, you may enter that instead. Next, you are required to enter the current time and date, with a four-digit year and a month, day, hour, and minute.

Root Password

The most important stage of the installation procedure occurs next: the selection of the root password. The Solaris root user has the same powers as the root user on Linux or the Administrator account on Windows NT/2000. If an intruder gains root access, he or she is free to roam the system, deleting or stealing data, removing or adding user accounts, or installing Trojan horses that transparently modify the way that your system operates.

One way to protect against an authorized user gaining root access is to use a difficult-to-guess root password. This makes it difficult for a cracker to use a password-cracking program to guess your password. The optimal password is a completely random string of alphanumeric and punctuation characters. There are some applications, discussed in Chapter 15, which can be used to generate passwords that are easy to remember, but which contain almost random combinations of characters.

In addition, the root password should never be written down, unless it is locked in the company safe, or told to anyone who doesn't need to know it. If users require levels of access that are typically privileged (such as mounting CD-ROMs), it is better to use the pseudo-utility to limit the access of each user to specific applications for execution as the superuser, rather than give out the root password to everyone who asks for it.

The root password must be entered twice—just in case you should happen to make a typographical error, as the characters that you type are masked on the screen.

Power Management

Do you want your system to switch off automatically after 30 minutes of inactivity? If you can honestly answer yes to this question (for example, because you have a workstation that does not run services), then you should enable power management, as it can save costly power bills. However, if you're administering a server, then you'll definitely want to turn power management off. Once your server has shut down in the middle of the night, and your clients cannot access data, then you'll remember reading this section and the message turn power management off, and disable power management.

Proxy Server

A proxy server acts as a buffer between hosts on a local network and the rest of the Internet. A proxy server passes connections back and forth between local hosts and any other host on the Internet. It usually acts in conjunction with a firewall, to block access to internal systems, thereby protecting sensitive data. One of the most popular firewalls is Squid, which also acts as a caching server.

To enable access to the Internet through a proxy server, you need to enter the hostname of the proxy server and the port on which the proxy operates.

KIOSK

After all of the configuration settings have been entered, the following message will be seen on the screen:

```
Please wait while the system is configured with your settings
```

The installation Kiosk will then appear on the screen. The Kiosk is primarily used to select the type of installation that you wish to perform. To begin the software selection process, you need to eject the Web Start CD-ROM and insert the Software (1) CD-ROM.

Next, you have the option of installing all Solaris software using the default options or customizing your selection before copying the files from the CD-ROM. Obviously, if you have a lot of disk space, and a fast system, you may prefer to install the entire distribution, then delete the packages that you no longer require after installation. This is definitely the fastest method. Alternatively, you can elect to perform a customized installation.

You are then presented with a screen of all the available software groups. Here, you may select or deselect individual package groups or package clusters, depending on your requirements. For example, you may decide to install the Netscape Navigator software, but not install the NIS/NIS+ server for Solaris. After choosing the packages that you wish to install, you are then required to enter your locale based on geographic region (the United States entry is selected by default). You may also elect to install third-party software during the Solaris installation process. This is particularly useful, for example, if you have a standard operating environment that consists of using the Oracle database server in conjunction with the Solaris operating environment. To install the third-party software, you need to insert the product CD-ROM at this point so that it can be identified.

After selecting your software, you will need to lay out the disks. This involves defining disk slices that will store the different kinds of data on your system. The fastest configuration option involves selecting the boot disk and allowing the Installer to automatically lay out the partitions according to the software selection that you have chosen. For example, you may wish to expand the size of the /var partition to allow for large print jobs to be spooled or for Web server logs to be recorded.

Finally, you will be asked to confirm your software selections and proceed with installation. All of the packages will then be installed on your system. A progress bar displayed on the screen indicates which packages have been installed at any particular point and how many remain to be installed. After you have installed all of the software, you will have to reboot the system. After restarting, your system should boot directly into Solaris unless you have a dual-booting system, in which case, you will need to select the Solaris boot partition from the Solaris boot manager. After displaying the startup messages, you will arrive at the CDE login screen. You can then begin using your system as described in Chapter 4.

SUMMARY

In this chapter, we have examined how to install and configure Solaris for the Intel platform. By accepting most of the default options, the installation process should take about one hour; however, if you need to lay out your own disks or select individual software packages, then installation will take longer.

CHAPTER 4

Using the Common Desktop Environment (CDE)

O nce Solaris is installed, the CDE will be installed as the default window manager running under X11. The CDE supersedes Sun Microsystems' OpenWindows platform and is commonly found on Hewlett-Packard/UNIX (HP/UX), Linux, and other UNIX systems. CDE is an initiative of the Common Open Software Environment (COSE), which aims to standardize UNIX operations across platforms. Before learning about Solaris, it's important to master the CDE, particularly if Microsoft Windows administrators wish to avoid using the command line as much as possible. In Chapter 4, the reader will learn how to use the CDE effectively, launch applications, edit text files, send e-mail, and use File Manager.

USING CDE

The CDE is best learned by experience: you will quickly become competent at logging in, running applications, configuring your own workspace, and customizing applications. In the following sections, we examine how to run the most popular applications, as well as navigate around the workspace and run the CDE terminal application (dtterm), to spawn a user's default shell.

dtlogin

After your system has been installed, you will be presented with the graphical login screen.

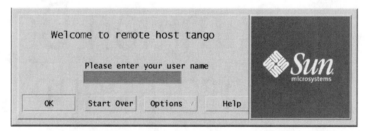

You must enter your username and click OK. A new screen will then appear, asking for the correct password for the login that you entered on the previous screen. If the username and password are authenticated, by using the password database (/etc/passwd), the CDE workspace will be launched, as shown in the following illustration. Typically, the Front Panel will appear, which consists of a toolbar that contains a set of hierarchical menus, from which various CDE applications may be launched.

One of the nice features of the CDE login screen, which is provided by the dtscreen application and managed by the dtlogin application, is that you can elect to use either the CDE workspace or the old Open Windows desktop, if you prefer. This selection can be made by selecting CDE or Open Windows from the Session menu. Prior to the adoption of CDE by Sun, Open Windows was the standard desktop for all Solaris systems, and some users may prefer Open Windows to CDE.

In addition, it is possible to configure a language to be used from the CDE login screen by selecting a language from one of the menus. Users may choose from all of the languages that are currently supported by Solaris or use the standard IEEE POSIX (Portable Operating System Interface) environment. There are two more menus that are available on the login screen: the remote login menu, where it is possible to log in directly to another host on the local area network using CDE, or the command line. In a local area network, it is very useful to be able to launch a CDE session on any host using the same terminal, rather than having to physically sit at another console. Alternatively, when performing system maintenance, it is often preferable to log in to a single-user session from the CDE login screen and boot into single-user mode. The dtlogin screen should disappear, and you should see the following message:

```
************************************************************
* Suspending Desktop Login
* If currently logged out, press [ENTER] for a console prompt.
* Desktop Login will resume shortly after you exit console session
************************************************************
```

If you press ENTER, you should see a login:

```
cassowary console login:
```

You may then proceed by performing system maintenance or rebooting the system.

CDE Workspace

The CDE workspace looks very similar to GNOME (for Linux users) and the Windows desktop (for Microsoft users). The main difference for Windows users is that CDE supports a middle mouse button, whereas only left-hand buttons are generally supported under Windows.

When an application is launched either from a menu on the Front Panel or from the Workspace menu (accessed by right-clicking anywhere in the workspace), it appears in its own separate window. For example, the terminal application (dtterm) may be launched by right-clicking the workspace, selecting the Programs menu, and selecting the Terminal option. A new CDE terminal window will then appear in the workspace, and it will be active (that is, it will have the focus). The terminal window activated is shown in the following illustration. The user's default login shell will be spawned, and commands can then be entered interactively on the command line.

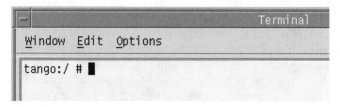

The CDE terminal window has three menus:

▼ The Window menu has two options: New window, which spawns another CDE terminal window, and Close, which closes the current CDE terminal window. The Close window option also has a keyboard shortcut equivalent (ALT+F4).

■ The Edit menu allows the user to copy and paste data to and from any CDE application, including other terminal windows, text editors, and so on.

▲ The Options menu is used to set the many different options supported by the CDE terminal window, including whether or not to display the menu and scroll bar, and the width of the terminal window (80 or 132 characters). In addition, a number of dialog boxes can be used to set global options, such as the cursor style, the cursor blink rate, and colors and sounds, as well as the font size and display.

The dtterm can be started with a number of command-line options, which can set some of these properties automatically. The benefit of this approach is that these parameters can be embedded in a script or startup file, so that your favorite settings will automatically be used every time dtterm is started. Table 4-1 shows the most commonly used dtterm command-line parameters.

CDE windows may be layered, one on top of the other, and activated by left-clicking any part of an inactive window. All CDE windows have a drop-down menu at their top left-hand corner. This menu has similar functions in both GNOME and Microsoft Windows.

Parameter	Purpose
-background	Sets the default background color of the terminal
-foreground	Sets the default text color of the terminal
-font	Sets the font size for the terminal
-geometry	Sets the width and height of the terminal window
-title	Sets the title of the window to the specified string

Table 4-1.   Commonly Used dtterm Options

It has items that allow the user to restore the window size, change the window size, lower the window, expand the window to occupy the entire workspace, toggle the display of the window menus, and close the window. In addition, windows may be minimized from the Window drop-down menu or maximized again by double-clicking the icon on the desktop. Figure 4-1 shows a series of minimized CDE windows in the workspace, including the Style Manager, Terminal, Process Viewer, Application Manager, and Mail.

In addition to a point-and-click interface, the CDE workspace supports a number of different keystroke options. This is particularly useful for users who have traditionally used the command line. Table 4-2 summarizes the main keystroke shortcuts used to shift the focus within a window, if that window is active, or within a dialog box that has popped up. These keystrokes can also be used to navigate the different menus on the Front Panel.

Keyboard navigation is slightly different within a workspace, since there are more possible actions than within a single window. Table 4-3 summarizes the main keystroke shortcuts used to shift the focus within a CDE workspace.

Within a menu, the arrow keys, rather than the TAB key, may be used to navigate between items.

Keystroke	Action
TAB	Moves to the next tab group
SHIFT+TAB	Moves to the previous tab group
DOWN ARROW	Moves to the next control in the tab group
UP ARROW	Moves to the previous control in a tab group

Table 4-2.   Keystrokes and Actions Within Windows, Dialog Boxes, and the Front Panel

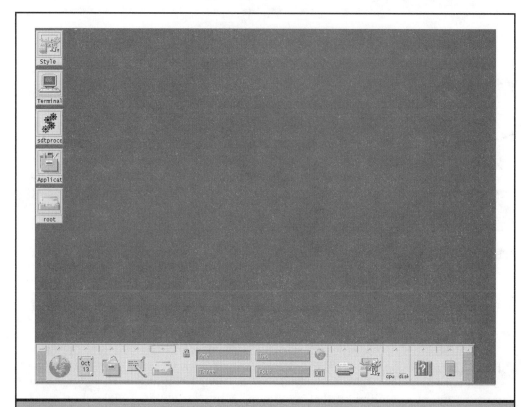

Figure 4-1.   Minimizing CDE windows

Keystroke	Action
ALT+TAB	Moves to the next window or icon
SHIFT+ALT+TAB	Moves to the previous window or icon
ALT+UP ARROW	Moves to the bottom window in a stack of windows (bringing it forward)
ALT+DOWN ARROW	Moves to the bottom of the window stack

Table 4-3.   Keystrokes and Actions Within the Workspace

Keystroke	Action
ALT+F6	Moves to the next window belonging to an application, or between the Front Panel and a subpanel
SHIFT+ALT+F6	Moves to the previous window belonging to an application, or between the Front Panel and a subpanel

Table 4-3. Keystrokes and Actions Within the Workspace *(continued)*

LAUNCHING APPLICATIONS

There are two ways to launch applications within CDE: either a command is issued through a shell, or from within a CDE terminal window, or it is selected from the Workspace menu or the Front Panel. For example, if we wanted to execute the clock application, we could run the following command from a shell:

```
bash-2.03% clock&
[1] 8836
bash-2.03%
```

By sending the clock process into the background, it is possible to continue to issue commands using the same shell. Alternatively, to run the clock from the Workspace menu, simply right-click anywhere in the workspace, select the Programs menu, and select the Clock item. Finally, you could select the Application Manager from the Applications menu, and open the OpenWindows (OW) collection of applications. After double-clicking the OW Clock icon, the clock will be executed.

The Workspace menu is the fastest way to get an application running and to perform CDE administrative tasks, such as adding new items to a menu. From the Workspace menu, it is possible to launch applications, manage workspace windows, customize the menu options displayed, lock the system display, and log out of the CDE desktop.

The Front Panel is more comprehensive than the Workspace menu, as there are nine menus instead of one. In addition, the CDE desktop allows for four different workspaces to be maintained: by simply clicking the One, Two, Three, or Four panels in the center of the Front Panel, users can maintain completely separate workspaces (one for development, one for system administration, one for playing games, and so on). Although Linux users will be familiar with multiple workspaces, Microsoft Windows users will find this a refreshing innovation. The nine menus included on the Front Panel are

- ▼ **Links** Including Clock, Web Browser, Personal Bookmarks, and Find Web Page
- ■ **Cards** Including Today's Card and Find Card
- ■ **Files** Including Home Folder, Open Floppy, Open CD-ROM, Properties, Encryption, Compress File, Archive, and Find File
- ■ **Applications** Including Text Note, Text Editor, Voice Note, and Application Manager
- ■ **Mail** Including Mailer and Suggestion Box
- ■ **Personal Printers** Including default printer and Print Manager
- ■ **Tools** Including Desktop Style, CDE Error Log, Customize Workspace Menu, Add Item to Menu, and Find Process
- ■ **Hosts** Including Performance Meter, This Host, System Info, Console, and Find Host
- ▲ **Help** Including Help Manager, SunSolve Online, Solaris Support, Information, Desktop Introduction, Front Panel Help, On Item Help, and AnswerBook 2

The Application Manager is the encyclopedic directory of most CDE applications on a Solaris system, as shown in Figure 4-2. The applications are divided into six categories:

- ▼ **Desktop Applications** Including Address Manager, Application Builder, Audio, Calculator, Calendar, Create Action, File Manager, and Help Viewer
- ■ **Desktop Controls** Including AccessX, Add Item To Menu, Customize Workspace Menu, Edit Dtwmrc, Reload Actions, Reload Applications, Reload Resources, and Restore The Front Panel
- ■ **Desktop Tools** Including Archive, Archive List Contents, Archive Unpack, Check Spelling, Clipboard Contents, Compare Files, Compress File, and Count Words
- ■ **Information** Including documentation for Solaris 8, AnswerBook, and sample bookmarks

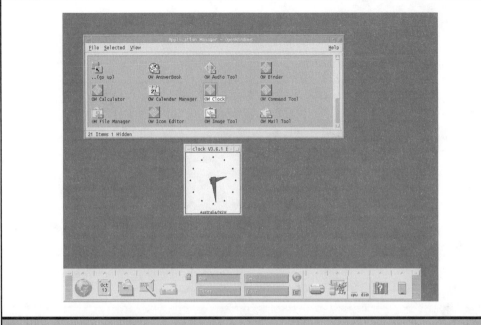

Figure 4-2.   CDE Application Manager

- ■ **Open Windows Applications**   Including old Open Windows AnswerBook, Audio Tool, OW Binder, OW Calculator, OW Calendar Manager, OW Clock, OW Command Tool, and OW File Manager

- ▲ **System Admin**   Including Admintool, AnswerBook Admin, Disk Usage, Eject CD-ROM, Eject Floppy, Format Floppy, Open CD-ROM, and Open Floppy

The main CDE applications that are available from the Workspace menu are discussed in the following sections.

File Manager

The main panel for the File Manager is shown in Figure 4-3, with a view of the devices directory (/dev). The File Manager shares many of the same features as those found in Microsoft Windows and Linux (for example, in K Desktop Environment (KDE) and GNOME). The contents of folders on different file systems may be viewed by double-clicking the appropriate icon. For example, if we clicked the pcmcia directory, we would see all of the PCMCIA card entries for the system. In addition, new files and folders may be created at any time by selecting the appropriate item from the File menu. Files can be located by using the Find facility, and individual file properties may be viewed by selecting the target file's icon and selecting the Properties item from the Selected menu.

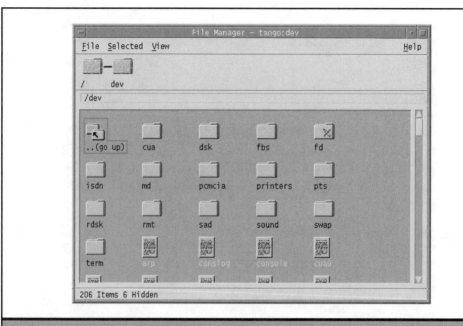

Figure 4-3.   The CDE File Manager

Text Editor

In order to write shell scripts, you must come to terms with using a Solaris editor, such as the vi visual editor program, which can be executed within a CDE terminal window. The visual editor is not as easy to use as some other editors available for Solaris, such as the pico editor bundled with the pine mail reading program. vi requires users to master separate control, editing, and data entry modes; and it requires the user to remember key commands for navigation, data insertion, and text deletion. In contrast, pico allows users to use WordStar-style control commands for copying and pasting text, saving files, and highlighting text. However, pico does not allow users to perform the complex search-and-replace utilities available to vi users. In this section, we examine how to use the vi editor to create shell scripts and any other text files that need to be created or modified (for example, application configuration files).

An easier alternative to vi is the text editor program that operates directly under CDE (dtpad), shown in Figure 4-4. This looks much more like Notepad, Write, and other editing programs that will be more familiar to users of Microsoft Windows. The dtpad application has a number of features that distinguish it from GUI editors in other operating systems. For example, it is possible to drag and drop data from other CDE applications. In addition, dtpad offers standard file and formatting options, including saving data to an

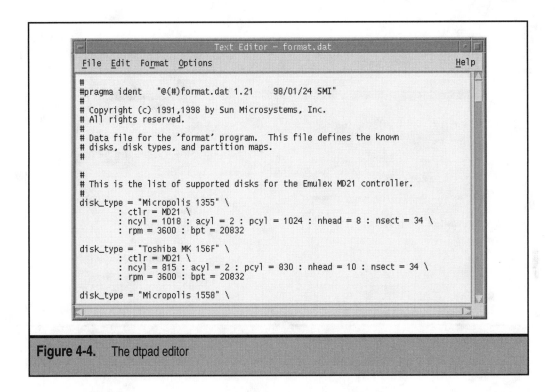

```
                        Text Editor — format.dat

   File  Edit  Format  Options                                      Help

   #
   #pragma ident    "@(#)format.dat 1.21     98/01/24 SMI"
   #
   # Copyright (c) 1991,1998 by Sun Microsystems, Inc.
   # All rights reserved.
   #
   # Data file for the 'format' program.  This file defines the known
   # disks, disk types, and partition maps.
   #

   #
   # This is the list of supported disks for the Emulex MD21 controller.
   #
   disk_type = "Micropolis 1355" \
           : ctlr = MD21 \
           : ncyl = 1018 : acyl = 2 : pcyl = 1024 : nhead = 8 : nsect = 34 \
           : rpm = 3600 : bpt = 20832

   disk_type = "Toshiba MK 156F" \
           : ctlr = MD21 \
           : ncyl = 815 : acyl = 2 : pcyl = 830 : nhead = 10 : nsect = 34 \
           : rpm = 3600 : bpt = 20832

   disk_type = "Micropolis 1558" \
```

Figure 4-4.   The dtpad editor

existing file; saving data to a new file; opening an existing file for editing; and a handy undo facility, which reverses the last change performed on the text. Users can perform global search-and-replace on specific text strings; and there is even a spell-checking facility, which is uncommon in a text-editing facility. Formatting options include the ability to insert text with overstriking, as well as line wrapping to 60 characters. A status bar, which is continuously updated, displays the total number of lines in the current document, as well as the line in which the cursor is currently located.

In the example shown in Figure 4-4, we have opened the /etc/format.dat system configuration file, which defines formatting data for all supported hard disks.

Mailer

Electronic mail (e-mail) has long been supported on Solaris for both local and remote users. CDE provides an easy-to-use e-mail client known as dtmail. The interface for the dtmail program is shown in Figure 4-5. The inbox for the root user is shown in the top panel. The user has 19 messages, the first of which is displayed in the bottom window (the message shows an error generated by the cron scheduling facility).

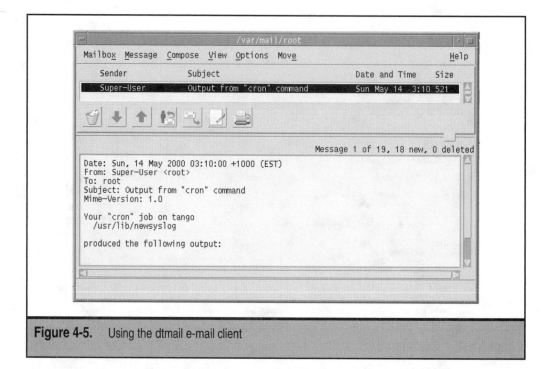

Figure 4-5. Using the dtmail e-mail client

The dtmail program can be controlled either through a menu system or by clicking one of the icons found on the middle panel—between the list of inbox messages and the text of the current message. The icons perform several different functions:

▼ Send the currently selected message to the trash

■ Read the next message down the list

■ Read the previous message in the list

■ Forward the current message to another user

■ Reply to the current message

■ Create a new message

▲ Print the current message

Using a mail client is only one side of the e-mail equation; it's also necessary to set up a mail server, which is covered in Chapter 11.

Calendar

The Calendar tool is a daily organizer that allows users to view past and current calendars month by month, and also to enter events to be remembered for particular days. The Calendar is shown in Figure 4-6, and is operated either by icons on a control panel at the top

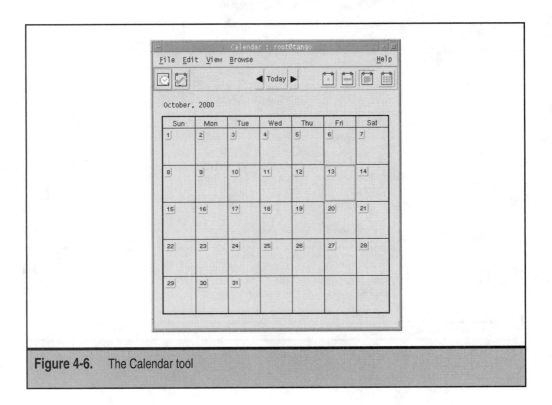

Figure 4-6.   The Calendar tool

of the screen or by using one of the menus, which contains options for file management, editing, viewing entries, and browsing entries.

Web Browser

Most Solaris systems will be connected to the Internet and will require a method of browsing the World Wide Web (WWW), using a Hypertext Transfer Protocol (HTTP)–compliant client. Solaris includes the HotJava client, which is a 100 percent Java implementation. While HotJava has few features compared to other Web browsers (such as Netscape Navigator), it is part of the Solaris environment and doesn't require any software or licenses from third parties to operate. It can be used in conjunction with the AnswerBook and any documentation set that is created using the Hypertext Markup Language (HTML). Figure 4-7 shows the HotJava client displaying the default page for the Apache Web server, which is now included in the Solaris operating environment.

HotJava is operated by using the icon bar located at the top of the screen. The icons displayed perform the following functions:

▼   Navigate backward to the last accessed document

■   Navigate forward to the next accessed document

■   Go to the home page

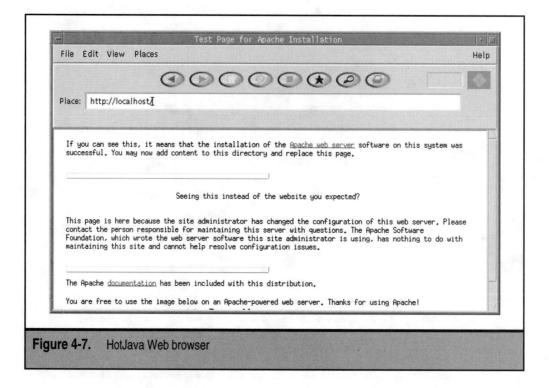

Figure 4-7.   HotJava Web browser

- Refresh the page contents
- Stop loading the current page
- Search for a page on the Internet
- ▲ Print the current page

Console

The console is similar to the dtterm; when executed, the user's default shell is spawned and commands can be executed interactively. The difference between dtterm and the console is that the latter displays informative messages about system status, which are normally sent to the screen of the physical console of a Solaris system. However, if the physical console is actually running CDE, then such messages would be lost. The console provides a facility to view these messages as they are generated. A sample CDE console is shown in the following illustration.

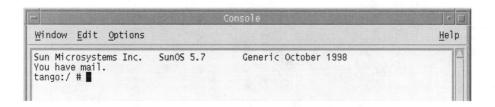

The kinds of messages displayed on the console are controlled by the syslog facility; thus, the file /etc/syslog.conf would need to be edited to either increase or decrease the number of messages piped to the console and to change the content of these messages. For example, a typical console message might warn the superuser that someone attempted to log in to an account, but typed the wrong password. You probably don't need to see the same message every time someone fumbles a login. However, another kind of message might warn that the file system is full and that applications can no longer write to the disk. This is a critical message, and further action should be taken immediately.

Calculator

The CDE calculator is a fully featured scientific calculator, that is capable of computing all trigonometric functions and the most commonly used exponential and factorial functions. Supported functions include the sine, cosine, and tangent, as well as computing e^x, where x is the desired exponent. There are memory facilities available for storing the results of computations, as well as creating expressions by enclosing individual operations within brackets. A number of different base-numbering systems are available, in addition to the decimal system, and results of trigonometric functions can be displayed in either degrees or radians. Figure 4-8 shows the interface for the CDE calculator.

Performance Meter

One of the most common questions a Solaris administrator is asked is, "Why is the system slow?" Usually, a Solaris system becomes slow for one of the following reasons:

▼   Too many processes are being spawned for the CPU to maintain concurrent execution of the applications being run by all users

■   Too many lightweight processes are being created

■   Disk I/O is being challenged by the needs of applications, such as databases, that are disk intensive

▲   The amount of disk space allocated to supporting virtual memory operations is insufficient to support all current applications

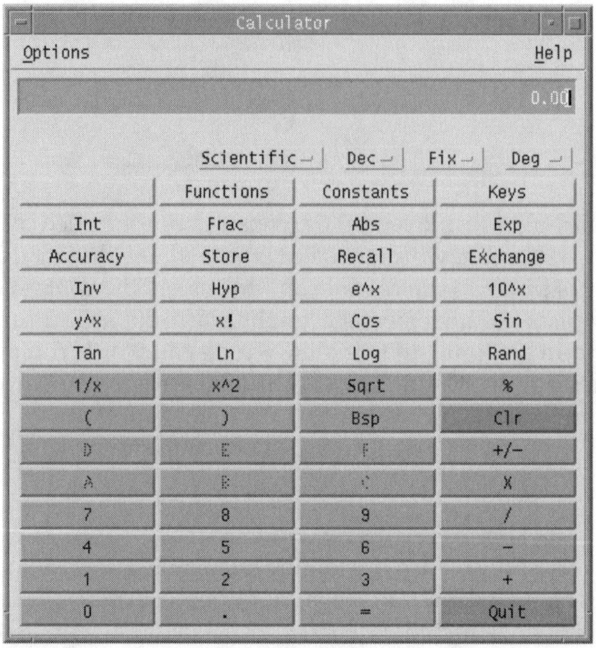

Figure 4-8. CDE calculator

If your system appears to be running more slowly than usual, the first place to look for trouble is the performance meter (perfmeter), which continuously prints the current system load, as shown in Figure 4-9. The performance meter often looks like a stock market chart—there are peaks and troughs, as more or fewer processes are executed. This activity is quite normal. However, if you begin to notice a sustained increase in the system load, well above the normal level of 1.0 for a system operating at capacity, then it may be time to begin examining which processes are hogging all of the system resources. The system load will be reduced if these processes have their nice value set to a lower priority.

Print Manager

Solaris supports a wide variety of printers, whether attached to a local parallel port, or accessed through a local area network by using Network File System (NFS) or Samba. One way to examine jobs that have been issued to various printers from a Solaris system is to use the Print Manager, which is similar to the print management facilities found in Linux and Microsoft Windows. Figure 4-10 shows the Find Print Jobs window from the Print Manager. To locate a print job in order to view its status or cancel it, the job name may be entered into the Job Name field, and searching initiated by clicking the Start Find button.

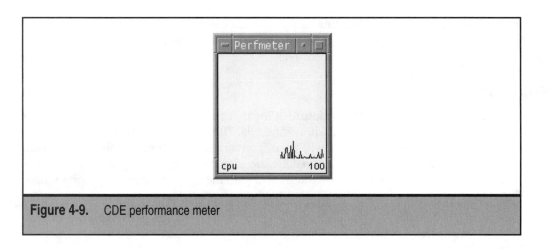

Figure 4-9.   CDE performance meter

Image Viewer

Solaris has multimedia support, including sound, movies, and images. Although many seasoned Linux users will be familiar with the xv program, which is available under both Solaris and Linux, CDE actually has its own image viewing and manipulation program. The image viewer has the ability to load and save images in a wide variety of popular formats, including GIF, JPEG, TIF, and output from the snapshot program reviewed in the

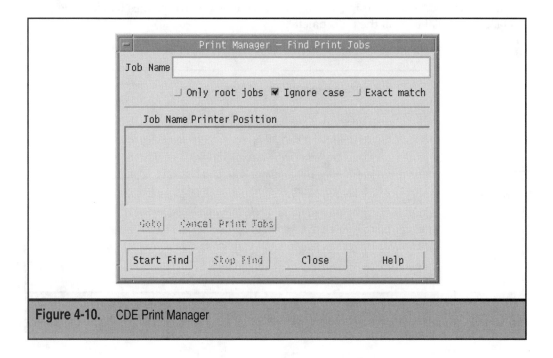

Figure 4-10.   CDE Print Manager

next section. It has cropping, cutting, copying, and pasting functions, as well as image rotation, image mirroring, and image reduction and enlargement. These functions are supported by the Palette shown in Figure 4-11.

Snapshot

The snapshot program is a screen-capture utility that can be used to capture the entire CDE workspace or the contents of individual windows. The screenshot utility has its own special file format (.rs files), which may be easily converted to PC-friendly file formats using the Image Convertor program. Fortunately, the snapshot interface actually has a button that allows the current snapshot to be launched with the Image Convertor program, making it easy to take a screenshot, edit its contents, and save it in your favorite file format. Many of the images contained in this book were captured using snapshot.

Icon Editor

As you will have realized after reading this chapter, the CDE uses icons extensively to represent files, applications, folders, and many other display objects within the workspace. However, you are not limited to using the icons supplied with Solaris to represent your own applications: CDE is supplied with an icon editor that allows you to create your own bitmapped images, as shown in Figure 4-12. These images may be used as icons that represent applications or actions within the CDE workspace. The images are 32×32 pixels (1,024 pixels), with a choice of eight different colors or shades of gray. In addition, it is possible to specify dynamic colors for the foreground and background. Standard image-editing tools are also included, with cropping, filling, and several geometric shapes (circles, lines, and rectangles) available from the tools palette.

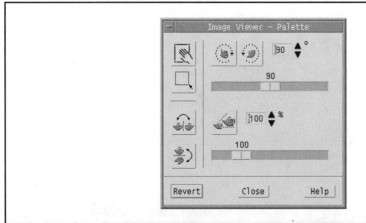

Figure 4-11.   CDE Image Viewer

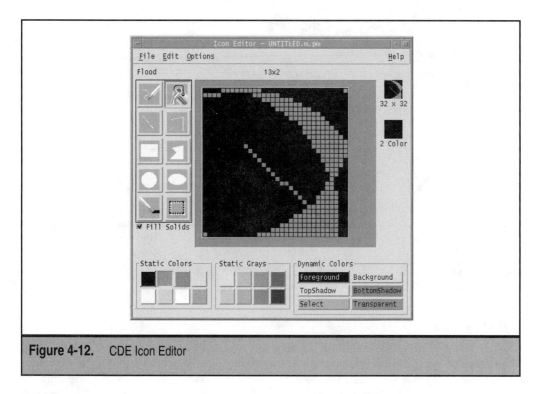

Figure 4-12.   CDE Icon Editor

Style Manager

The Style Manager is similar to the Desktop Themes or Display Settings options available under Microsoft Windows. The Style Manager is responsible for all aspects of presentation for the CDE workspace. It is possible to use different styles for the different workspaces available under the CDE desktop. The Style Manager has several different control panels that are available by clicking one of the icons displayed in the illustration.

These panels are used to set the following options:

▼   Available color schemes for the workspace

■   Default fonts for all text in CDE applications

■   Backdrop patterns for the workspace

■   Keyboard options, including key repeat rate

- Mouse configuration, including speed
- Beep settings for warnings
- Screen settings, including the screen saver
- Window options, including whether focus is set by clicking a mouse key or hovering over a window
▲ Startup configuration, including session saving and loading

Help

On most of the CDE screens we have seen, there has been a menu on the top right-hand corner that is the most important menu: the Help menu. The Help facility provides information and assistance on using and managing most of the applications that are supplied with the Solaris operating environment, including File Manager, Style Manager, and Print Manager. Users can browse available Help topics or search by keyword for topics relevant to the current application. For CDE applications that are developed in house, it is possible to provide customized help in the CDE Help format.

AnswerBook 2

Help is usually only applicable for the standard CDE applications. However, since the vast majority of the applications supplied with Solaris do not require CDE to operate, Solaris provides the AnswerBook facility. The AnswerBook has two components: the HotJava browser, which acts as the AnswerBook client, and the AnswerBook server, which is a Web server that only provides access to HTML versions of the main pages and the various reference manuals that accompany Solaris.

However, one of the best features of the AnswerBook is that it is available over the Internet, from http://docs.sun.com/. This means that any Solaris user, without local access to an AnswerBook, may freely download Portable Document Forrmat (PDF) versions of the reference manuals or search interactively across books in all AnswerBook collections.

SUMMARY

In this chapter, we have examined how to use the CDE workspace effectively to increase personal productivity. For users who prefer GUI-based tools to command-line interfaces, CDE provides easy access to the facilities provided by Solaris. In addition, CDE tools such as the HotJava browser can be used to access external services, such as the AnswerBook. We should point out that CDE is not the only desktop system available for use with X11 under Solaris; it is now possible to use GNOME and Enlightenment on Solaris, which may be useful if you come from a Linux background. However, CDE is now the standard UNIX desktop platform, and learning CDE will make your skills more transferable to other platforms.

PART II

Single Host Administration

CHAPTER 5

Shell Usage and Programming

A key Solaris concept is the functional separation between the user interface and the operating system. This distinction means that a user can access a Solaris system by using either a terminal-based Character User Interface (CUI) or a high-resolution Graphical User Interface (GUI), without modifying the underlying operating system. This approach is similar to the original concept of building Windows as a front-end extension to MS-DOS; the underlying operating system was not affected by the use of a fancy GUI interface. In addition, MS-DOS commands could still be executed within Windows, meaning that the two were functionally integrated but still separate programs. However, later versions of Windows (such as Windows NT and Windows 2000) have moved more and more to a complete integration of operating system and user interface; thus, while Windows NT users can access a command prompt and execute applications MS-DOS style, Windows NT is not dependent on MS-DOS and does not require MS-DOS to be running as the underlying operating system.

Linux has extended the concept of separation of operating system even further than traditional UNIX systems; the same Linux kernel can now be used in conjunction with a number of different displays and window and presentation managers, including GNOME (http://www.gnome.org), the K Desktop Environment (http://www.kde.org), and Enlightenment (http://www.enlightenment.org). The industry-wide move in enterprise has favored the development of a Common Desktop Environment (CDE), which is available on Solaris, Linux, HP/UX, and other leading systems. Since Windows no longer has a separation between the operating system and the user interface, it is not possible to run CDE on Windows.

NOTE: Sun Microsystems has now effectively dropped support for its Open Windows user interface in favor of the CDE. Most Solaris versions now support both Open Windows and CDE, although most system documentation and manuals are now focused on CDE.

If there has been so much attention paid to GUI environments, why are CUI environments still important to Solaris? Are they just a historical hangover that Windows has managed to overcome, or are they simply the tools of choice for long-haired network administrators who have never used a mouse? In fact, mastering the Solaris command line is one of the effective tools available under any UNIX environment, and the good news is, it's not that difficult to learn. Using the command line (or shell) has the following advantages over GUI environments:

▼   The shell is essential for programming repetitive tasks, which can only be performed laboriously through a GUI, for example, searching a file system for all document files that have changed each day, and making a copy of all these files (with the extension .doc) to a backup directory (with the extension .bak).

■   The shell can be used to search for, modify, edit, and replace Solaris configuration files, which are typically stored in text format. This is much like the approach taken with Windows .ini configuration files, which were text based. However, versions of Windows after Windows 95 used the Registry to store configuration information in a binary format, making the configuration information impossible to manually edit. All Solaris configuration files (including the startup scripts described in Chapters 2 and 3) are text based.

■ The shell has a number of built-in commands that typically mirror those provided in the C programming language. This means it is possible to write small programs as shell statements that are executed as sequential steps, without having to use a compiler (just like MS-DOS batch files are interpreted without requiring a compiler).

■ The shell can be used to launch applications that use a CUI, which is especially useful for logging in to a remote system and being able to use all the commands that the administrator can use on the console. In the era of global information systems, this is very useful. While Windows applications like Symantec's pcAnywhere can be used for remote access to the Windows desktop, they don't easily support multiuser access (or multiuser access where one user requires a CUI and another a GUI).

▲ The shell can be used to execute commands for which there is no equivalent GUI application. Although many operations could conceivably be performed using a GUI, it is usually easier to write a shell script than create a completely new GUI application.

Many applications in Solaris, Linux, and Windows are now available through a GUI interface. If you feel more comfortable using GUI interfaces, there is little reason to stop using them if you can find the tools to perform all of the tasks you need to undertake regularly, such as monitoring resource usage, and setting process alarms and diagnostics and/or remote access.

TIP: If you want to make the most of Solaris and competently administer the system, you will need to become familiar with the shell and command-line utilities.

In keeping with the philosophy that different administrators have different needs and styles, there are also several different shells available under Solaris that you can choose from:

▼ The Bourne shell (sh), the original UNIX shell that is used to write all system scripts by convention

■ The C shell (Csh), which has a command syntax similar to the C programming language

■ The Cornell shell (Tcsh), which has improved terminal handling compared to the original C shell

▲ The Bourne again shell (Bash), which is an open source, much improved version of the Bourne shell

In this chapter, we introduce the Bourne again shell (Bash), which is used as both a login shell and a shell that can be used to process scripts (the current version is 2.04). Bash has the advantage of being available in Linux and Windows NT, so it's possible that experienced administrators will have used it before. Using Bash, we will walk through some common scenarios for using the shell in interactive mode, such as executing commands, setting and accessing environment variables, and getting command help with the online manual system (man). Finally, we review the concepts of processes and signals, and examine how these are different from Linux and Windows NT/2000.

USING THE COMMAND-LINE INTERFACE

All shells, including Bash, have a command prompt. The prompt usually tells the user which shell is currently being used, who owns the shell, and/or the current working directory. For example the prompt

```
#
```

usually indicates that the current user has superuser privileges. Shell prompts are completely customizable. The default for Bash is just the name of the shell:

```
bash-2.04$
```

When you start a new terminal window from within the CDE, a shell is automatically spawned for you. This will be the same shell that is specified in your /etc/passwd entry:

```
apache:x:1003:10:apache user:/usr/local/apache:/usr/local/bin/bash
```

In this case, the Apache user has the Bash set as default. To be a valid login shell, /usr/local/bin/bash must also be included in the shell's database (stored in the file /etc/shells). The Bash spawned within a CDE window is shown in Figure 5-1.

If the default shell prompt is not to your liking, its format can easily be changed by setting two environment variables: PS1 and PS2. We cover environment variables in more detail in the following code listings; however, the Solaris environment is equivalent to that found in Linux and Windows NT. For example, to set the prompt to display the username and host, we would use the command

```
PS1='\u@\H> ' export PS1
```

The prompt displayed by the shell would then look like

```
oracle@db>
```

Many users like to display their current username, hostname, and current working directory, which can be set using the following command:

```
PS1='\u@\H:\w> '; export PS1
```

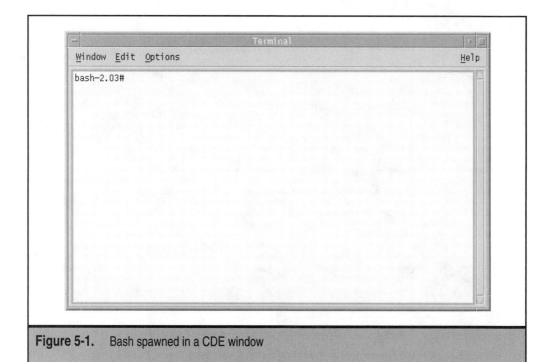

Figure 5-1.   Bash spawned in a CDE window

When executed, the shell prompt is changed to the following:

```
oracle@db:/usr/local>
```

where oracle is the current user, db is the hostname, and /usr/local is the current working directory. A list of different customization options for shell prompts is given in Table 5-1.

At the shell prompt, commands are entered in the order in which they are intended to be executed. For example, to execute the admintool from the command prompt, you would type the command

```
oracle@db:/usr/sbin> ./admintool
```

The ./ in this example indicates that the admintool application resides in the current directory. You could also execute the application using the command

```
oracle@db:/usr/sbin> /usr/sbin/admintool
```

The admintool window would then appear on the desktop, assuming that you're using a terminal window to execute a shell. Once the shell is executing a command in the foreground (like admintool), no other commands can be executed; however, by sending a command process into the background, it is possible to execute more than one command

Setting	Description	Output
\a	ASCII beep character	beep
\d	Date string	Wed Sep 6
\h	Short hostname	www
\H	Full hostname	www.paulwatters.com
\s	Shell name	bash
\t	Current time (12-hour format)	10:53:44
\T	Current time (24-hour format)	10:53:55
\@	Current time (A.M./P.M. format)	10:54am
\u	Username	root
\v	Shell version	2.03
\W	Shell version with revision	2.03.0
\!	Command history number	223
\$	Privilege indicator	#
\u\$	Username and privilege indicator	root#
\u:\!:\$	Username, command history number, and privilege indicator	root:173:#

Table 5-1.   Environment Variable Setting for Different Command Prompts Under Bash

in the shell. You can send a process into the background immediately by adding an ampersand (&) to the end of the command line:

```
oracle@db:/usr/sbin> ./admintool &
```

Alternatively, once a command has been executed, you can suspend it by pressing CTRL+Z, and then send it into the background by using the command **bg**:

```
oracle@db:/usr/sbin> ./admintool
^Z[1] + Stopped (SIGTSTP)          admintool
oracle@db:/usr/sbin> bg
[1] admintool&
oracle@db:/usr/sbin>
```

The application name is displayed along with the job number. You can bring an application back into the foreground by using the command

```
oracle@db:/usr/sbin> fg
admintool
```

This will bring job number 1 back into the foreground by default. However, if you had multiple jobs suspended, you would need to specify a job number with the **fg** command:

```
oracle@db:/usr/local/bin> ./netscape
^Z[2] + Stopped (SIGTSTP)          netscape
oracle@db:/usr/sbin> bg
[2] netscape&
oracle@db:/usr/sbin> fg
netscape
```

You can obtain a list of all running jobs in the current shell by typing the command

```
bash-2.04$ jobs
[2] +  Running                  ./netscape&
[1] -  Running                  admintool&
```

BASH COMMANDS

Every shell (including Bash) has a number of built-in commands, which are typically combined with standard Solaris utilities to perform everyday tasks. In this section, we look at some common examples of these commands.

Source (.)

The *source* command reads in and executes the lines of a shell script. The format of this command is

```
. file
```

where *file* is a valid filename that contains a Bash script. The first line should contain a directive that points to the absolute location of the shell:

```
#!/usr/local/bin/bash
```

Alternatively, Bash scripts can be executed by calling them with a new shell invocation, or calling them directly if the executable bit is set for the executing user. For example, the following three commands would each execute the script file myscript.sh:

```
bash-2.03$ . myscript.sh
bash-2.03$ sh myscript.sh
bash-2.03$ ./myscript.sh
```

However, only the source command (.) preserves any environment variable settings made in the script.

basename

The *basename* command strips a filename of its extension. The format of this command is

```
basename filename.ext
```

where filename.ext is a valid filename like mydata.dat. The basename command parses mydata.dat and extracts mydata. Since file extensions are not mandatory in Solaris, this command is very useful for processing files copied from Windows or MS-DOS.

cat

The *cat* command prints out the contents of the file, without any special screen control features like scrolling backward or forward in a file. The format of this command is

```
cat filename
```

To display the groups database, for example, we could run the command

```
bash-2.03$ cat /etc/group
root::0:root
other::1:
bin::2:root,bin,daemon
sys::3:root,bin,sys,adm
adm::4:root,adm,daemon
uucp::5:root,uucp
mail::6:root
tty::7:root,tty,adm
lp::8:root,lp,adm
nuucp::9:root,nuucp
staff::10:
```

cd

The *cd* command changes the current working directory to a new directory location, which can be specified in both absolute or relative terms. The format of this command is

```
cd directory
```

For example, if the current working directory is /usr/local, and we type the command

```
cd bin
```

then the new working directory would be /usr/local/bin. However, if we type the command

```
cd /bin
```

then the new working directory would be /bin. For interactive use, relative directory names are often used; however, scripts should always contain absolute directory references.

chgrp

The *chgrp* command modifies the default group membership of a file. The format of this command is

```
chgrp group file
```

where *group* is a valid group name defined in the groups database (/etc/groups), and *file* is a valid filename. Since permissions can be assigned to individual users, or groups of users, assigning a nondefault group membership can be useful for users who need to exchange data with members of different organizational units (for example, the Web master who swaps configuration files with the database administrator and also exchanges HTML files with Web developers). Only the file owner or the superuser can modify the group membership of a file.

chmod

The *chmod* command modifies the file access permissions for users, groups, and the file owner, and is similar to the ATTRIB command in Windows NT. File permissions allow users in different classes to have read, write, or execute access to a file.

NOTE: Only the file owner or the superuser can modify the permissions of a file.

The format of this command is

```
chmod permission file
```

where *permission* is a permission code (symbolic or octal format), and *file* is a valid filename.

date

The *date* command prints the current system date and time. The format of this command is

```
date
```

The default output for the command is of the form

```
Wednesday September  6 13:43:23 EST 2000
```

It is also possible to modify the output format, by using a number of parameters corresponding to days, months, hours, minutes, and so on. For example, the command

```
date '+Current Date: %d/%m/%y%nCurrent Time:%H:%M:%S'
```

produces the output

```
Current Date: 06/09/00
Current Time: 13:45:43
```

grep

The *grep* command searches a file for a string (specified by string) and prints the line wherever a match is found. The format of this command is

```
grep string file
```

The *grep* command is very useful for interpreting log files, where you only want to display a line that contains a particular code (for example, a Web server log file can be grepped for the string 404, which indicates a page not found).

head

The *head* command displays the first page of a file. The format of this command is

```
head filename
```

The *head* command is very useful for examining the first few lines of a very long file. For example, to display the first page of the name service switch configuration file (/etc/nsswitch.conf), we could use the command

```
bash-2.03$ head /etc/nsswitch.conf
root:189:# head /etc/nsswitch.conf
# /etc/nsswitch.nisplus:
# An example file that could be copied over to /etc/nsswitch.conf; it
# uses NIS+ (NIS Version 3) in conjunction with files.
# "hosts:" and "services:" in this file are used only if the
# /etc/netconfig file has a "-" for nametoaddr_libs of "inet" transports.
# the following two lines obviate the "+" entry in /etc/passwd and /etc/group.
```

less

The *less* command prints a file on the screen and allows searching backward and forward through the file. The format of this command is

```
less filename
```

To scroll through the contents of the system log configuration file (/etc/syslog.conf), you would use the command

```
less /etc/syslog.conf
#ident   "@(#)syslog.conf       1.4       96/10/11 SMI"   /* SunOS 5.0 */
# Copyright (c) 1991-1993, by Sun Microsystems, Inc.
# syslog configuration file.
# This file is processed by m4 so be careful to quote (`') names
# that match m4 reserved words. Also, within ifdef's, arguments
# containing commas must be quoted.
*.notice                                @loghost
*.err;kern.notice;auth.notice           /dev/console
*.err;kern.debug;daemon.notice;mail.crit;daemon.info
/var/adm/messages
*.alert;kern.err;daemon.err             operator
*.alert                                 root
```

The *less* command has a number of commands that can be issued interactively. For example, to move forward one window, just type **f**, or to move back one window, just type **b**. The *less* command also supports searching with the */pattern* command.

ls

The *ls* command prints the names of files contained in the directory dir (by default, the contents of the current working directory are displayed). The format of the command is

```
ls directory
```

where directory is the name of the directory whose contents you wish to list. For example, to list the contents of the /var/adm directory, which contains a number of system logs, you could use the command

```
bash-2.03$ ls /var/adm
aculog         log          messages.1    passwd       utmp         wtmp
ftpmessages    messages     messages.2    spellhist    utmpx        wtmpx
lastlog        messages.0   messages.3    sulog        vold.log
```

mkdir

The *mkdir* command makes new directory entries. The format of this command is

```
mkdir directory
```

For example, if the current working directory is /sbin, and we type the command

```
mkdir oracle
```

then the new directory would be /sbin/oracle. However, if we type the command

```
mkdir /oracle
```

then the new directory would be /oracle. For interactive use, relative directory names are often used; however, scripts should always contain absolute directory references.

more

The *more* command prints the contents of a file, like the *less* command, but only permits scrolling forward through a file. The format of this command is

```
more filename
```

To scroll through the contents of the disk device configuration file (/etc/format.dat), you would use the command

```
more /etc/format.dat
#pragma ident    "@(#)format.dat 1.21    98/01/24 SMI"
# Copyright (c) 1991,1998 by Sun Microsystems, Inc.
# All rights reserved.
# Data file for the 'format' program. This file defines the known
# disks, disk types, and partition maps.
# This is the list of supported disks for the Emulex MD21 controller.
disk_type = "Micropolis 1355" \
        : ctlr = MD21 \
        : ncyl = 1018 : acyl = 2 : pcyl = 1024 : nhead = 8 : nsect = 34 \
        : rpm = 3600 : bpt = 20832
```

The more command has a number of commands that can be issued interactively. For example, to move forward one window, just press the SPACEBAR; or to move forward one line, just press the ENTER key. More also supports searching with the /pattern command.

pwd

The *pwd* command prints the current working directory in absolute terms. The format of the command is

```
pwd
```

For example, if we change the directory to /etc and issue the *pwd* command, we would see the following result:

```
bash-2.03$ cd /etc
bash-2.03$ pwd
/etc
```

rmdir

The *rmdir* command deletes a directory; however, the directory concerned must be empty for the *rmdir* command to be successful. The format of this command is

```
rmdir directory
```

For example, if the current working directory is /usr/local, and we want to remove the directory "oldstuff," then we would use the command

```
rmdir oldstuff
```

However, we could use the command

```
rmdir /usr/local/oldstuff
```

to remove the directory as well. For interactive use, relative directory names are often used; however, scripts should always contain absolute directory references.

tail

The *tail* command displays the last page of a file. The format of this command is

```
tail filename
```

The *tail* command is very useful for examining the last few lines of a very long file. For example, to display the first page of a Web log file (/usr/local/apache/logs/access_log), we could use the command

```
bash-2.03$ tail /usr/local/apache/logs/access_log
192.168.205.238 - - [31/Aug/2000:09:35:59 +1000] "GET /images/picture10.gif
HTTP/1.1" 200 53
192.168.205.238 - - [31/Aug/2000:09:35:59 +1000] "GET /images/ picture1.gif
HTTP/1.1" 200 712
192.168.205.238 - - [31/Aug/2000:09:35:59 +1000] "GET /images/ picture5.gif
HTTP/1.1" 200 7090
192.168.205.238 - - [31/Aug/2000:09:35:59 +1000] "GET /images/ picture66.gif
HTTP/1.1" 200 997
192.168.205.238 - - [31/Aug/2000:09:35:59 +1000] "GET /images/ picture49.gif
HTTP/1.1" 200 2386
192.168.205.238 - - [31/Aug/2000:09:36:09 +1000] "GET /servlet/SimpleServlet
HTTP/1.1" 200 10497
```

The tail command also has an option that allows you to continuously monitor all new entries made to a file. This is very useful for monitoring a live service like Apache, where you need to observe any error made in real time. The format for this command is

```
tail -f filename
```

Help for each of these commands is usually available through the man facility or the GNU info command. To find out more about the Bash commands, you can use the command

```
bash-2.04$ man bash
Reformatting page. Wait... done
User Commands                                              BASH(1)
NAME
     bash - GNU Bourne-Again SHell
SYNOPSIS
     bash [options] [file]
COPYRIGHT
     Bash is Copyright (C) 1989-1999 by the Free Software Founda-
     tion, Inc.
DESCRIPTION
     Bash is an sh-compatible command language interpreter that
     executes commands read from the standard input or from a
     file. Bash also incorporates useful features from the Korn
     and C shells (ksh and csh).
```

INTRODUCTION TO PROCESSES AND SIGNALS

So far, we've looked at what common Solaris shell programs and commands do; however, we haven't really looked at how Solaris manages all of the applications that run on a system. Since Solaris is designed to handle many different concurrent users who all own their applications, which can be executed in the foreground or in the background, the operating system needs an intelligent method to keep track of these applications. Each program that runs on a Solaris system is associated with a unique process ID (PID), which distinguishes that program from all others. A PID is necessary because the same application can be started multiple times and, thus, cannot be referred to by a name alone. In addition, two different applications could be executed concurrently with the same name, or different users could both be executing the same application.

NOTE: Both Linux and Windows NT have a similar system for managing PIDs; however, there are some important differences.

Identifying Processes

While Windows NT only has the concept of a single PID for each process, the Solaris process model is more sophisticated, since each PID is associated with a parent process ID (PPID). This is very useful for grouping together groups of processes that were spawned by the same parent process. For example, the Samba daemon spawns several child processes to serve individual clients making requests for file access. The PID of each spawned process is different, but the PPID of each child process is the same:

```
hobart:/usr/local/abw > ps -eaf | grep smbd
   root   238     1  0   Aug 31 ?         0:00
/usr/local/samba/bin/smbd -D -l /var/adm/smblogs/log -s
/usr/local/samba/lib/sm
   root   172   238  0 08:09:54 ?         0:05
/usr/local/samba/bin/smbd -D -l /var/adm/smblogs/log -s
/usr/local/samba/lib/sm
   root   272   238  0 08:20:02 ?         0:07
/usr/local/samba/bin/smbd -D -l /var/adm/smblogs/log -s
/usr/local/samba/lib/sm
```

In this example, the original Samba PID is 238, which has the PPID of 1 (for example, it was started at system boot time). However, the Samba application spawned two child processes (172 and 272), which both have the PPID of 238. As we have already seen, the shell is the main entry point for applications on a Solaris system, so any applications started from a shell will have the PPID equivalent to the PID of that shell.

In the preceding Samba example, all of the Samba processes are owned by the root user; however, processes can be potentially owned by any user on the system. Owning a process confers some privileges to the owner: The process can be killed or restarted only by that user and the superuser. Other users cannot interfere with your work. The user is identified by a user ID (UID), and that user's default group is associated with a group ID (GID). The situation is also more complicated for some Solaris applications that can set the owner of a process to be a different user. These setuid programs are very powerful, because they allow unprivileged users to access some facilities that are normally reserved for the root user (for example, mounting a CD-ROM). However, they are also potentially dangerous if their capabilities are not closely audited. For example, a dangerous setuid application would allow unprivileged users to spawn an external shell and execute commands as root.

NOTE: There are also some situations in which applications can be executed setgid, where the group ID of the application can be set to a privileged group.

Parent and Child Processes

Technically speaking, when Solaris boots, the process that is responsible for spawning all child processes on the system is PID 1. However, when a shell is spawned by PID 1, it takes on its own PID. While the shell's PPID is 1, all of its child processes will have the PPID of the shell's PID. However, if the shell is killed while an application is running in the background, the PPID of the shell's child processes reverts to PID 1. All processes that have the PPID 1 are shut down only when the system is shut down by sending a kill command to PID 1.

As we saw in the preceding section, the *ps* command reveals some very useful information about the characteristics of processes on the system. In fact, the ps command has a large number of options that can be used to monitor all aspects of application performance on Solaris.

Process lists can be obtained for the processes owned by the current user or for all processes currently running on the system. Linux users will have encountered the *ps* command before; however, they will be more used to the BSD style of *ps* command options, which were found in early versions of Solaris, rather than the more modern System V commands.

Graphical Process Monitoring

Windows NT has a task manager that lists all processes in the GUI window. If you prefer this format to the text output of the ps command, you can use the process finder tool in the CDE, as shown in Figure 5-2. This is a highly configurable tool, and it displays information about processes, sorted by one of the following criteria:

- ▼ CPU time used by the process
- ■ Name of command
- ■ Physical RAM used by the process
- ■ PID
- ■ Process owner
- ■ Date/time that the process was initialized
- ■ PPID
- ▲ Virtual RAM used by the process

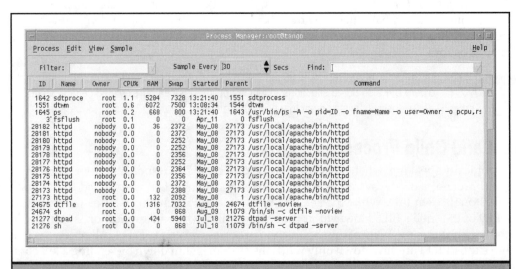

Figure 5-2.   CDE's graphical process finder

The ps Command

The *ps* command, by default, only displays the process spawned by the current user from the current shell:

```
bash-2.03# ps
    PID TTY        TIME CMD
   1653 pts/4     0:00 bash
   1584 pts/4     0:00 ksh
   1654 pts/4     0:00 ps
```

Four columns are displayed: the PID, the TTY on which the commands were executed, the CPU time used by the process, and the command name as executed on the command line. If this doesn't seem like a whole lot of information, the trick is to determine which combinations of options to the *ps* command will give you the information that you're looking for. For example, if you pass the option –l to the *ps* command, you will receive the long style of output from the command:

```
bash-2.03# ps -l
 F S   UID   PID  PPID  C PRI NI     ADDR     SZ    WCHAN TTY       TIME CMD
 8 R     0  1653  1584  0  51 20 e0b0a030    504          pts/4    0:00 bash
 8 S     0  1584  1582  0  51 20 e0f42058    375 e0f420c4 pts/4    0:00 ksh
 8 R     0  1656  1653  0  41 20 e1286768    196          pts/4    0:00 ps
```

In addition to the PID, the TTY on which the commands were executed, the CPU time used by the process, and the command name as executed on the command line, there are several other parameters displayed:

▼ Any flags (F) set by the process

■ The memory addresses (ADDR) used by the process

■ The memory addresses for processes that are sleeping (WCHAN)

■ The memory consumption (SZ)

■ The name of the command (CMD)

■ The nice value (NI), which indicates the priority of the process

■ The parent process ID (PPID)

■ The process priority (PRI)

▲ The run state (S) of the process, where S indicates a sleeping process and R indicates an active process

Any user can obtain information about all the other processes currently running on the system. This can be very useful if you suspect that another user is hogging all of the CPU time with their processes (the nice value, reported in the preceding list, can be set to a lower value by the root user on these kinds of processes). A typical *ps* command option combination is *-Af*, which prints a full list of all processes on the system, including details of

▼ The name of the user who started the process

■ The PID of the process

■ The PPID of the process

■ The scheduling class (C) of the process

■ The date/time when the process was started (STIME)

■ The terminal (TTY) on which the process was started

■ The CPU time consumed by the process since it was started

▲ The name of the command

A sample output from the *ps -Af* command is

```
bash-2.03# ps -Af
     UID   PID  PPID  C    STIME TTY       TIME CMD
    root     0     0  0   Apr 11 ?         0:00 sched
    root     1     0  0   Apr 11 ?         0:00 /etc/init -
    root     2     0  0   Apr 11 ?         0:03 pageout
    root     3     0  0   Apr 11 ?       119:21 fsflush
    root   190     1  0   Apr 11 ?         1:03 /usr/sbin/nscd -S passwd,yes -S
group,yes
    root   111     1  0   Apr 11 ?         0:01 /usr/sbin/rpcbind
    root   265     1  0   Apr 11 ?         0:00 /usr/lib/saf/sac -t 300
    root    63     1  0   Apr 11 ?         0:00 /usr/lib/devfsadm/devfseventd
    root    65     1  0   Apr 11 ?         0:00 /usr/lib/devfsadm/devfsadmd
    root   160     1  0   Apr 11 ?         0:23 /usr/lib/autofs/automountd
    root   115     1  0   Apr 11 ?         1:14 /usr/sbin/nis_cachemgr
    root 10994   256  0   Jul 13 vt01      1:33 /usr/openwin/bin/Xsun :0 -nobanner
-auth /var/dt/A:0-XiaaGa
    root   177     1  0   Apr 11 ?         0:01 /usr/sbin/cron
    root   155     1  0   Apr 11 ?         0:00 /usr/lib/nfs/lockd
    root   249     1  0   Apr 11 ?         0:00 /usr/lib/snmp/snmpdx -y -c
/etc/snmp/conf
    root   202     1  0   Apr 11 ?         0:00 /usr/lib/lpsched
  daemon   156     1  0   Apr 11 ?         0:00 /usr/lib/nfs/statd
    root   157     1  0   Apr 11 ?         0:00 /usr/sbin/inetd -s
    root   223     1  0   Apr 11 ?         0:00 /usr/sbin/vold
    root   214     1  0   Apr 11 ?         0:00 /usr/lib/power/powerd
    root  1653  1584  0 13:22:55 pts/4     0:00 bash
    root   225     1  0   Apr 11 ?         0:00 /usr/lib/utmpd
    root   257     1  0   Apr 11 ?         0:00 /usr/lib/dmi/dmispd
    root   266     1  0   Apr 11 console   0:00 /usr/lib/saf/ttymon -g -h -p tango
console login:  -T AT386 -d /dev/console -1
    root   247     1  0   Apr 11 ?         0:04 /usr/lib/sendmail -bd -q15m
    root 11091     1  0   Jul 13 ?         0:00 /bin/ksh /usr/dt/bin/sdtvolcheck -d
-z 5 cdrom
```

```
root 21276 11079  0   Jul 18 pts/2    0:00 /bin/sh -c dtpad -server
root   256     1  0   Apr 11 ?        0:00 /usr/dt/bin/dtlogin -daemon
root   272   249  0   Apr 11 ?        0:00 mibiisa -r -p 12416
```

The applications running on the system include the login daemon for the CDE (PID 256), the sendmail mail transport agent (PID 247), the Internet super daemon (PID 157), and the RPC server (PID 111). Table 5-2 summarizes the most commonly used options for the *ps* command.

Sending Signals

Processes can be controlled in the shell by using the *kill* command to send signals. These signals can result in one of two outcomes: a core dump, which is a file that contains a memory trace, or a process dying. However, there are some variations on these two possibilities. For example, sending a SIGHUP signal (kill –1) to a process results in the process restarting and typically rereading any configuration files. On the other hand, a SIGKILL signal (kill –9) will cause a process to die immediately. If you want to kill a process, and all of its child processes, you should send a SIGTERM signal (kill –15).

Option	Description
-a	Lists most frequently requested processes
-A, -e	Lists all processes
-c	Lists processes in scheduler format
-d	Lists all processes
-f	Prints comprehensive process information
-g	Prints process information on a group basis for a single group
-G	Prints process information on a group basis for a list of groups
-j	Includes SID and PGID in printout
-l	Prints complete process information
-L	Displays LWP details
-p	Lists process details for list of specified process
-P	Lists the CPU ID to which a process is bound
-s	Lists session leaders
-t	Lists all processes associated with a specific terminal
-u	Lists all processes for a specific user

Table 5-2.   Main Options for Listing Processes with ps

Let's take the Samba example earlier, where several processes were spawned by a single parent process. To restart one of the processes and force it to reread the smb.conf configuration file, we would use the command

```
bash-2.03# kill -1 203
```

If we wanted to kill the process altogether, we would use the command

```
bash-2.03# kill -9 203
```

This would leave all of the child processes running. However, if we wanted to kill all Samba processes, we would use the command

```
bash-2.03# kill -15 203
```

Table 5-3 shows the most commonly used signals in Solaris.

Code	Signal	Action	Description
1	SIGHUP	Exit	Hangup
2	SIGINT	Exit	Interrupt
3	SIGQUIT	Core	Quit
4	SIGILL	Core	Illegal Instruction
5	SIGTRAP	Core	Trace or Breakpoint Trap
6	SIGABRT	Core	Abort
7	SIGEMT	Core	Emulation Trap
8	SIGFPE	Core	Arithmetic Exception
9	SIGKILL	Exit	Killed
10	SIGBUS	Core	Bus Error
11	SIGSEGV	Core	Segmentation Fault
12	SIGSYS	Core	Bad System Call
13	SIGPIPE	Exit	Broken Pipe
14	SIGALRM	Exit	Alarm Clock
15	SIGTERM	Exit	Terminated

Table 5-3.   Signals Used for Process Communication

ENVIRONMENT VARIABLES

Environment variables are used to store information in a form that is accessible to commands within the shell and other applications that are spawned from the shell. You can obtain a list of all environment variables that have been set in a shell by using the command

```
bash-2.03$ set
BASH=/usr/local/bin/bash
BASH_VERSINFO=([0]="2" [1]="03" [2]="0" [3]="1" [4]="release" [5]="i386-pc-
solaris2.7")
BASH_VERSION='2.03.0(1)-release'
COLUMNS=80
DIRSTACK=()
DISPLAY=cassowary:0.0
EDITOR=/usr/bin/vi
ENV=/.kshrc
EUID=0
GROUPS=()
HELPPATH=/usr/openwin/lib/locale:/usr/openwin/lib/help
HISTFILE=/.sh_history
HISTFILESIZE=500
HISTSIZE=500
HOME=/
HOSTNAME=cassowary
HOSTTYPE=i386
IFS=' '
LANG=en_AU
LC_COLLATE=en_AU
LC_CTYPE=en_AU
LC_MESSAGES=C
LC_MONETARY=en_AU
LC_NUMERIC=en_AU
LC_TIME=en_AU
LD_LIBRARY_PATH=/usr/local/lib:/usr/openwin/lib:/usr/dt/lib
LINES=24
LOGNAME=root
MACHTYPE=i386-pc-solaris2.8
MAIL=/var/mail/root
MAILCHECK=60
MANPATH=/usr/dt/man:/usr/man:/usr/openwin/share/man
OPENWINHOME=/usr/openwin
OPTERR=1
OPTIND=1
OSTYPE=solaris2.7
PATH=/usr/sbin:/usr/bin:/bin:/usr/ucb:/usr/local/bin:/usr/openwin/bin:/usr/ccs/bin
PIPESTATUS=([0]="1")
PPID=1584
PS1='\s-\v\$ '
PS2='> '
PS4='+ '
```

```
PWD=/etc
SESSION_SVR=tango
SHELL=/bin/ksh
SHLVL=1
TERM=dtterm
TERMINAL_EMULATOR=dtterm
TZ=Australia/NSW
UID=0
USER=root
WINDOWID=58720265
```

Although this seems to be a lot of shell variables, the most significant ones include

- ▼ **BASH**   The path to the shell on the file system
- ■ **COLUMNS**   The column width for the terminal
- ■ **DISPLAY**   The display variable that is used for X11 graphics
- ■ **HOME**   The default home directory for the user
- ■ **HOSTNAME**   The hostname of the current system
- ■ **LD_LIBRARY_PATH**   The path to system and user libraries
- ■ **LOGNAME**   The username of the shell owner
- ■ **MANPATH**   The path to the system manuals
- ■ **NNTP SERVER**   The hostname of the NNTP server
- ■ **PATH**   The path that is searched to find applications when no absolute path is specified on the command line
- ■ **PPID**   The parent process ID
- ■ **TERM**   The terminal type (usually VT100)
- ■ **UID**   The user ID
- ▲ **WINDOWMANAGER**   The name of the X11 window manager

The values of all shell variables can be set on the command line by using the *export* command. For example, if we wanted to set the terminal type to VT220, we would use the command

```
bash-2.03$ TERM=vt220; export TERM
```

SUMMARY

In this chapter, we have examined the basics of using the shell to issue commands, manage jobs, monitor processes, and send signals. Although Windows NT administrators may find the shell daunting at first, it is a useful tool for performing repetitive actions and for monitoring resource usage on a system. Solaris provides users with a choice of shells, and users have the ability to select their own shell.

CHAPTER 6

Shell Programming

In Chapter 5, we examined how to use the Bourne again shell (Bash) command-line interface interactively to issue commands and execute utilities. This interface is similar to the command prompt found in Microsoft Windows systems and is identical to the Bash used under Linux. One of the major features of the Solaris shell is the ability to write complex scripts that perform repetitive actions and can process various kinds of decision logic. There are many more commands available for Bash than for MS-DOS batch files, which makes them very powerful. However, script files are more dependent on understanding file permissions than just using the shell to enter commands, which makes them more complex. In this chapter, we review basic Solaris file permissions, and we examine how to create executable scripts that can be used with Bash. In addition, we examine how to schedule shell scripts to run at regular intervals using the cron facility.

FILE OWNERSHIP

One of the most confusing issues for novice users of Solaris is understanding the Solaris file access permissions system. The basic approach to setting and interpreting relative file permissions is using a set of symbolic codes to represent users and permission types. Even advanced users may find it difficult to understand the octal permissions codes that are used to set absolute permissions. When combined with a default permission mask set in the user's shell (umask), octal permission codes are more powerful than symbolic permission codes. In this section, we review only relative file permissions using symbolic codes.

Symbolic Permission Codes

The Solaris UNIX File System (UFS) permits three basic kinds of file access: the ability to read (r), to write (w), and to execute (x) a file or directory. These permissions can be granted exclusively or nonexclusively on individual files, or on a group of files specified by a wildcard (*). These permissions can be set using the chmod command in combination with a "+" operator. Permissions can be easily removed with the chmod command by using the "−" operator.

For example, to set read permissions (for the current user) on the file /usr/local/lib/libproxy.a, we would use the command

```
bash-2.03$ chmod +r /usr/local/lib/libproxy.a
```

Alternatively, to set read permissions for all users on the file /usr/local/lib/libproxy.a, we would use the command

```
bash-2.03$ chmod a+r /usr/local/lib/libproxy.a
```

To remove read permissions on the file /usr/local/lib/libproxy.a for all users who are not members of the current user's default group, we would use the command

```
bash-2.03$ chmod o-r /usr/local/lib/libproxy.a
```

This does not remove the group and user read permissions that were set previously. Similarly, execute and write permissions can be set. For example, to set execute permissions on the /usr/local/bin/gcc files, for each class of user (current user, group, and world), we would use the commands

```
bash-2.03$ chmod u+x /usr/local/bin/gcc; chmod g+x /usr/local/bin/gcc; chmod o+x
/usr/local/bin/gcc
```

To explicitly remove write permissions on the /usr/local/bin/gcc files for each class of user (current user, group, and world), we would use the commands

```
bash-2.03$ chmod u-w /usr/local/bin/gcc; chmod g-w /usr/local/bin/gcc; chmod o-w
/usr/local/bin/gcc
```

The rationale behind using read and write permissions should be clear: permitting read access on a file allows an identified user to access the text of a file by reading it byte by byte, while write access permits the user to modify or delete any file on which the write permission is granted, regardless of who originally created the file; thus, individual users can create files that are readable and writeable by any other user on the system.

The permission to execute a file must be granted on scripts (such as shell scripts or Perl scripts) in order for them to be executed, while compiled and linked applications must also have the execute bit set on a specific application.

NOTE: The executable permission must also be granted on the special files that represent directories on the file system, if the directory's contents are to be accessed by a specific class of user.

The different options available for granting file access permissions can sometimes lead to interesting but confusing scenarios; for example, permissions can be set to allow a group to delete a file, but not to execute it. More usefully, a group might be given execute permission on an application, but be unable to write over it. In addition, setting file permissions using relative permission strings (rather than absolute octal permission codes) means that permissions set by a previous chmod are not revoked by any subsequent chmods.

However, the permissions themselves are only half the story. Unlike single-user file systems, permissions on Solaris are associated with different file owners (all files and processes on a Solaris system are "owned" by a specific user). In addition, groups of users can be granted read, write, and execute permissions on a file or set of files stored in a directory. Alternatively, file permissions can be granted on a systemwide basis, effectively granting file access without respect to file ownership. Since file systems can be exported using Network File System (NFS) and/or Samba, it's bad practice to grant systemwide read, write, and execute permissions on any file, unless every user needs access to that file. For example, all users need to read the password database (/etc/passwd), but only the root user should have read access to the shadow password database (/etc/shadow).

TIP: Blindly exporting all files with world read, write, or execute permissions on an NFS-shared volume is inviting trouble!

The three file system categories of ownership are defined by three permission setting categories: the user (u), who owns the file; the group members (g), who have access to the file; and all other users (o) on the system. The group specified by "g" can be the user's primary group (as defined in /etc/passwd) or secondary group to which the file has been assigned (defined in /etc/group). It is important to remember that there are ultimately few secrets on a Solaris file system: the root user has full access at all times (read, write, and execute) on all files in the file system. Even if a user removes all permissions on a file, the rule of root is absolute. If the contents of a file really need to be hidden, it is best to encrypt a file's contents using PGP, crypt, or a similar program. A root user can also change the ownership of a file; thus, a user's files do not absolutely belong to a specific user. The chown command can only be used by the superuser for this purpose.

Policies regarding default file permissions need to be set selectively in different environments. For example, in a production Web server system that processes credit card data, access should be denied, by default, to all users except those who are required to conduct online transactions (for example, the Apache user for the Apache Web server). On a system that supports team-based development, permissions will need to be set to allow the exchange of data between team partners, but to prevent the access to development files by others.

NOTE: There are very few Solaris systems that allow a default world-writeable policy on any file system, except for the temporary swap (/tmp) file system.

It is possible to enforce systemwide permissions by using a default umask, which sets the read, write, and execute permissions on all new files created by a specific user. If a user wishes to use a umask other than the default systemwide setting, this can be achieved by setting the umask on the command line when required or in the user's shell startup file (for example, .kshrc for Korn shell).

We start our examination of Solaris file permissions by examining how to create files, set permissions, change ownerships, group memberships, and use the ls command to examine existing file permissions. All of these commands can be used by nonprivileged users, except for the chown command.

The ls command is the main directory and file permission listing program used in Solaris. When displaying a long listing, it prints file access permissions, user and group ownerships, file size and creation date, and filename. For example, for the password file /etc/passwd, the output from the ls command would look like

```
bash-2.03# ls -l /etc/passwd
-r--r--r--   1 root     other          256 Sep  18 00:40 passwd
```

This directory entry can be read from left to right in the following way:

▼   The password file is not a directory, indicated by the first -

■   The password file has read-only permissions for the owner r -- (but not execute or write permissions)

■   The password file has read-only permissions for group members r --

- The password file has read-only permissions for other staff r --
- The password file is owned by the root user
- The password file has other group permissions
- The password file size is 256 kilobytes
- The password file was created on September 18, at 00:40 A.M.
▲ The name of the password file is passwd

The permissions string shown changes depending on the permissions that have been set by the owner. For example, if the password file had execute and write permissions for the root user, then the permissions string would read -rwxr--r--, rather than just -r-r-r-.

TIP: Each of the permissions can be set using symbolic or octal permissions codes by using the chmod command.

We've seen how a normal file looks under the ls command, but let's compare this with a directory entry, which is a special kind of file that is usually created by the mkdir command:

```
bash-2.03# mkdir samples
```

We can check the permissions of the directory entry by using the ls command:

```
bash-2.03# ls -l
total 8
drwxrwxr-x   2 root      other           512 Sep  5 13:41 samples
```

The directory entry for the directory samples can be read from left to right in the following way:

▼ The directory entry is a special file denoted by a leading "d"
- The directory entry has read, write, and execute permissions for the owner "rwx"
- The directory entry has read, write, and execute permissions for group members "rwx"
- The directory entry has read and execute permissions for other staff "r-x"
- The directory entry is owned by the root user
- The directory entry has other group permissions
- The directory entry size is 512 kilobytes
- The directory entry was created on September 5, at 1:41 P.M.
▲ The name of the directory is samples

For a directory to be accessible to a particular class of user, the executable bit must be set using chmod.

STANDARD UNIX UTILITIES

Solaris has many user commands available to perform tasks ranging from text processing, to file manipulation and terminal management. In this section, we will look at some standard UNIX utilities that are the core of using a shell in Solaris; however, readers are urged to obtain an up-to-date list of the utilities supplied with Solaris by typing the command

```
bash-2.03$ man intro
```

The cat command displays the contents of a file to standard output, without any kind of pagination or screen control. It is most useful for viewing small files or for passing the contents of a text file through another filter or utility (for example, the grep command, which searches for strings). To examine the contents of the groups database, for example, we would use this command:

```
bash-2.03# cat /etc/group
root::0:root
other::1:
bin::2:root,bin,daemon
sys::3:root,bin,sys,adm
adm::4:root,adm,daemon
uucp::5:root,uucp
mail::6:root
tty::7:root,tty,adm
lp::8:root,lp,adm
nuucp::9:root,nuucp
staff::10:
postgres::100:
daemon::12:root,daemon
sysadmin::14:
nobody::60001:
noaccess::60002:
nogroup::65534:
```

The cat command is not very useful for examining specific sections of a file. For example, if you need to examine the first few lines of a Web server's log files, then using cat would display them, but they would quickly scroll off the screen out of sight; however, you can use the head command to display only the first few lines of a file. In this example, we extract the lines from the log file of the Inprise Application Server:

```
bart:/usr/local/inprise/ias41/logs/bart/webpageservice > head access_log
203.16.206.43 - - [31/Aug/2000:14:32:52 +1000] ""GET /index.jsp HTTP/1.0"" 200
24077
203.16.206.43 - - [31/Aug/2000:14:32:52 +1000] ""GET /index.jsp HTTP/1.0"" 200
```

```
24077
203.16.206.43 - - [31/Aug/2000:14:32:52 +1000] ""GET /index.jsp HTTP/1.0"" 200
24077
203.16.206.43 - - [31/Aug/2000:14:32:52 +1000] ""GET /index.jsp HTTP/1.0"" 200
24077
203.16.206.43 - - [31/Aug/2000:14:32:52 +1000] ""GET /index.jsp HTTP/1.0"" 200
24077
203.16.206.43 - - [31/Aug/2000:14:32:52 +1000] ""GET /index.jsp HTTP/1.0"" 200
24077
203.16.206.43 - - [31/Aug/2000:14:32:52 +1000] ""GET /index.jsp HTTP/1.0"" 200
24077
203.16.206.43 - - [31/Aug/2000:14:32:53 +1000] ""GET /index.jsp HTTP/1.0"" 200
24077
203.16.206.43 - - [31/Aug/2000:14:32:53 +1000] ""GET /index.jsp HTTP/1.0"" 200
24077
203.16.206.43 - - [31/Aug/2000:14:32:53 +1000] ""GET /index.jsp HTTP/1.0"" 200
24077
```

Alternatively, if you just want to examine the last few lines of a file, you could use the cat command to display the entire file ending with the last few lines, or you could use the tail command to specifically display these lines. If the file is large (for example, an Inprise Application Server log file of 2MB), it would be a large waste of system resources to display the whole file using the cat command, whereas the tail command is very efficient. Here's an example of using the tail command to display the last few lines of a file:

```
bart:/usr/local/inprise/ias41/logs/bart/webpageservice > head access_log
203.16.206.43 - - [31/Aug/2000:14:32:52 +1000] ""GET /index.jsp HTTP/1.0"" 200
24077
203.16.206.43 - - [31/Aug/2000:14:32:52 +1000] ""GET /index.jsp HTTP/1.0"" 200
24077
203.16.206.43 - - [31/Aug/2000:14:32:52 +1000] ""GET /index.jsp HTTP/1.0"" 200
24077
203.16.206.43 - - [31/Aug/2000:14:32:52 +1000] ""GET /index.jsp HTTP/1.0"" 200
24077
203.16.206.43 - - [31/Aug/2000:14:32:52 +1000] ""GET /index.jsp HTTP/1.0"" 200
24077
203.16.206.43 - - [31/Aug/2000:14:32:52 +1000] ""GET /index.jsp HTTP/1.0"" 200
24077
203.16.206.43 - - [31/Aug/2000:14:32:52 +1000] ""GET /index.jsp HTTP/1.0"" 200
24077
203.16.206.43 - - [31/Aug/2000:14:32:53 +1000] ""GET /index.jsp HTTP/1.0"" 200
24077
203.16.206.43 - - [31/Aug/2000:14:32:53 +1000] ""GET /index.jsp HTTP/1.0"" 200
24077
203.16.206.43 - - [31/Aug/2000:14:32:53 +1000] ""GET /index.jsp HTTP/1.0"" 200
24077
```

Now, imagine that you are searching for a particular string within the access_log file, such as a 404 error code, which indicates that a page has been requested that does not exist. Web masters regularly check log files for this error code to create a list of links that need to be checked. To view this list, we can use the grep command to search the file for a specific string (in this case, "404"), and the more command can be used to display the results page by page:

```
bart:/usr/local/inprise/ias41/logs/bart/webpageservice > grep 404 access_log |
more
203.16.206.56 - - [31/Aug/2000:15:42:54 +1000] ""GET
/servlet/LibraryCatalog?command=mainmenu HTTP/1.1"" 200 21404
203.16.206.56 - - [01/Sep/2000:08:32:12 +1000] ""GET
/servlet/LibraryCatalog?command=searchbyname HTTP/1.1"" 200 14041
203.16.206.237 - - [01/Sep/2000:09:20:35 +1000] ""GET /images/L
INE.gif HTTP/1.1"" 404 1204
203.16.206.236 - - [01/Sep/2000:10:10:35 +1000] ""GET /images/L
INE.gif HTTP/1.1"" 404 1204
203.16.206.236 - - [01/Sep/2000:10:10:40 +1000] ""GET /images/L
INE.gif HTTP/1.1"" 404 1204
203.16.206.236 - - [01/Sep/2000:10:10:47 +1000] ""GET /images/L
INE.gif HTTP/1.1"" 404 1204
203.16.206.236 - - [01/Sep/2000:10:11:09 +1000] ""GET /images/L
INE.gif HTTP/1.1"" 404 1204
203.16.206.236 - - [01/Sep/2000:10:11:40 +1000] ""GET /images/L
INE.gif HTTP/1.1"" 404 1204
203.16.206.236 - - [01/Sep/2000:10:11:44 +1000] ""GET /images/L
INE.gif HTTP/1.1"" 404 1204
203.16.206.236 - - [01/Sep/2000:10:12:03 +1000] ""GET /images/L
INE.gif HTTP/1.1"" 404 1204
203.16.206.41 - - [01/Sep/2000:12:04:22 +1000] ""GET /data/books/576586955.pdf H
TTP/1.0"" 404 1204
--More--
```

These log files contain a line for each access to the Web server, with entries relating to the source IP address, date and time of access, the Hypertext Transfer Protocol (HTTP) request string sent, the protocol used, and the success/error code. When you see the --More-- prompt, the SPACEBAR can be pressed to advance to the next screen, or the ENTER key can be pressed to advance by a single line in the results.

NOTE: The pipeline operator | was used to pass the results of the grep command through to the more command.

In addition to the pipeline, there are four other operators that can be used on the command line to direct or append input streams to standard output, or output streams to standard input. Although that sounds convoluted, it can be very useful when working with files to direct the output of a command into a new file (or append it to an existing file). Alternatively, the input to a command can be generated from the output of another command. These operations are performed by

▼   >   Redirect standard output to a file

■   >>   Append standard output to a file

■   <   Redirect file contents to standard input

▲   <<   Append file contents to standard input

Bash also has logical operators, including the "less than" (lt) operator, which uses the test facility to make numerical comparisons between two operands. Other commonly used operators include

▼   a–eq b   a equals b

■   a–ne b   a not equal to b

■   a–gt b   a greater than b

■   a–ge b   a greater than or equal to b

▲   a–le b   a less than or equal to b

Let's look at an example with the echo command, which echoes the contents of a string or an environment variable that has been previously specified, and the cat command, which displays the contents of files. Starting with the echo command, imagine if we wanted to maintain a database of endangered species in a text file called animals.txt. If we wanted to add the first animal, "zebra," to an empty file, we could use the command

```
bash-2.03# echo ""zebra"" > animals.txt
```

We could then check the contents of the file animals.txt with the command

```
bash-2.03# cat animals.txt
zebra
```

This shows that the insertion was successful. Now, imagine that we want to add a second entry, "emu," to the animals.txt file. We could try using the command

```
bash-2.03# echo ""emu"" > animals.txt
```

However, the result may not be what we expected:

```
bash-2.03# cat animals.txt
emu
```

This is because the > operator always overwrites the contents of an existing file, while the >> operator always appends to the contents of an existing file. Let's run that command again with the correct operators:

```
bash-2.03# echo ""zebra"" > animals.txt
bash-2.03# echo ""emu"" >> animals.txt
```

Luckily, the output is just what we expected:

```
bash-2.03# cat animals.txt
zebra
emu
```

Once we have a file containing a list of all the animals, we would probably want to sort it alphabetically, making searching for specific entries easy. To do this, we can use the sort command:

```
bash-2.03# sort animals.txt
emu
zebra
```

The sorted entries are then displayed on the screen in alphabetical order. It is also possible to redirect the sorted list into another file (called sorted_animals.txt) by using the command

```
bash-2.03# sort animals.txt > animals_sorted.txt
```

If you wanted to check that the sorting process actually worked, you could compare the contents of the animals.txt file line by line with the sorted_animals.txt file, by using the diff command:

```
bash-2.03# diff animals.txt sorted_animals.txt
1d0
< zebra
2a2
> zebra
```

This result indicates that the first and second lines of the animals.txt and sorted_animals.txt files are different, as expected.

NOTE: If the sorting process had failed, the two files would have been identical and no differences would have been reported by the diff command.

A related facility is the basename facility, which is designed to remove file extensions from a filename specified as an argument. This is commonly used to convert files with one extension to another extension. For example, let's imagine that we had a graphic file conversion program that took as its first argument the name of a source JPEG file and then took the name of a target bitmap file. Somehow, we'd need to convert a filename of the form filename.jpg to a file of the form filename.bmp. We can do this with the basename command. In order to strip a file extension from an argument, we need to pass the filename and the extension as separate arguments to basename. For example, the command

```
bash-2.03# basename maya.gif .gif
```

will produce the output

```
"" 'maya
```

If we want the .gif extension to be replaced by a .bmp extension, we could use the command

```
bash-2.03# echo `basename maya.gif`.bmp
```

will produce the output

```
maya.bmp
```

Of course, we are not limited to extensions like .gif and .bmp. Also, keep in mind that the basename technique is entirely general; and since Solaris does not have mandatory filename extensions, the basename technique can be used for other purposes, such as generating a set of strings based on filenames.

WRITING SHELL SCRIPTS

Shell scripts are combinations of shell and user commands that are executed in non-interactive mode for a wide variety of purposes. Whether you require a script that converts a set of filename extensions, or you need to alert the system administrator by e-mail that disk space is running low, shell scripts can be used. The commands that you place inside a shell script should normally execute in the interactive shell mode as well, making it easy to take apart large scripts and debug them line by line in your normal login shell. In this section, we will only examine shell scripts that run under Bash.

TIP: Although many of the scripts will work without modification using other shells, it is always best to check the syntax chart of your own shell before attempting to run the scripts on a non-Bash shell.

Processing Shell Arguments

A common goal of writing shell scripts is to make them as general as possible, so that they can be used with many different kinds of input. For example, in the cat command examples presented earlier in the chapter, we wouldn't want to have to create an entirely new script for every file that we wanted to insert data into. Fortunately, shell scripts are able to make use of command-line parameters, which are numerically ordered arguments that are accessible from within a shell script. For example, a shell script to move files from one computer to another computer might require parameters for the source host, the destination host, and the name of the file to be moved. Obviously, we want to be able to pass these arguments to the script, rather than "hard wiring" them into the code. This is one advantage of shell scripts (and Perl scripts) over compiled languages like C— scripts are easy to modify, and their operation is completely transparent to the user.

Arguments to shell scripts can be identified by a simple scheme: the command executed is referred to with the argument $0, with the first parameter identified as $1, the second parameter identified as $2, and so on, up to a maximum of nine parameters.

Thus, a script executed with the parameters

```
bash-2.03% display_hardware.sh cdrom scsi ide
```

would refer internally to "cdrom" as $1, "scsi" as $2, and "ide" as $3. Let's see how arguments can be used effectively within a script to process input parameters. The first script we will create simply counts the number of lines in a file (using the wc command), specified by a single command-line argument ($1). To begin with, we create an empty script file:

```
bash-2.03% touch count_lines.sh
```

Next, we set the permissions on the file to be executable:

```
bash-2.03% chmod +x count_lines.sh
```

Next, we edit the file

```
bash-2.03% vi count_lines.sh
```

and add the appropriate code:

```
#!/bin/bash
echo ""Number of lines in file "" $1
wc -l $1
```

The script will take the first command-line argument, print the number of lines, and exit. We run the script with the command

```
bash-2.03# ./count_lines.sh /etc/group
```

which gives the output:

```
Number of lines in file /etc/group
43
```

Although the individual activity of scripts is quite variable, the procedure for creating the script file, setting its permissions, editing its contents, and executing it on the command line remains the same across scripts. Of course, you may wish to make the script only available to certain users or groups for execution: this can be enabled by using the chmod command and explicitly adding or removing permissions when necessary.

Testing File Properties

One of the assumptions that we made in the previous script was that the file specified by $1 actually existed; if it didn't exist, then we obviously would not be able to count the number of lines it contained. If the script is running from the command line, we can safely debug it and interpret any error conditions that arise (such as a file not existing, or having incorrect permissions). However, if a script is intended to run as a scheduled job (using the *cron* or *at* facility), then it is impossible to debug in real time. Thus, it is often useful to write scripts that can handle error conditions gracefully and intelligently, rather than leaving administrators wondering why a job didn't produce any output when it was scheduled to run.

NOTE: The number one cause of run-time execution errors is the incorrect setting of file permissions.

Although most users remember to set the executable bit on the script file itself, they often neglect to include error checking for the existence of data files that are used by the script. For example, if we want to write a script that checked the syntax of a configuration file (like the Apache configuration file, httpd.conf), then we need to check that the file actually exists before performing the check; otherwise, the script may not return an error message, and we may erroneously assume that the script file is correctly configured.

Fortunately, Bash makes it easy to test for the existence of files by using the (conveniently named) test facility. In addition to testing for file existence, files that exist can also be tested for read, write, and execute permissions prior to any read, write, or execute file access being attempted by the script. Let's revise our previous script that counted the number of lines in a file. First, we will verify that the target file (specified by $1) exists, and then print the result; otherwise, an error message will be displayed:

```
#!/bin/bash
if test -a $1 then
echo ""Number of lines in file "" $1
wc -l $1
else
        echo ""The file"" $1 ""does not exist""
fi
```

When we run this command, if a file exists, it should count the number of lines in the target file as before; otherwise, an error message will be printed. If the /etc/group file did not exist, for example, we'd really want to know about it:

```
bash-2.03# ./count_lines.sh /etc/group
The file /etc/group does not exist
```

There may be some situations in which we want to test another file property. For example, the /etc/shadow password database must only be readable by the superuser; thus, if we execute a script to check whether or not the /etc/shadow file is readable by a nonprivileged user, it should not return a positive result. We can check file readability by using the -r option rather than the -a option. Here's the revised script:

```
#!/bin/bash
if test -r $1 then
echo ""I can read the file "" $1
else
        echo ""I can''t read the file"" $1
fi
```

The following file permissions can also be tested using the test facility:

- ▼ -b   File is a special block file.
- ■ -c   File is a special character file.
- ■ -d   File is a directory.
- ■ -f   File is a normal file.
- ■ -h   File is a symbolic link.
- ■ -p   File is a named piped.
- ■ -s   File has nonzero size.
- ■ -w   File is writeable by the current user.
- ▲ -x   File is executable by the current user.

Looping

All programming languages have the ability to repeat blocks of code for a specified number of iterations. This makes performing repetitive actions very easy for a well-written program. Bash is no exception: it features a for loop, which repeats the actions of a code block for a specified number of iterations, as defined by a set of consecutive arguments to the for command. In addition, an iterator is available within the code block to indicate which of the sequence of iterations that will be performed is currently being performed. If that sounds a little complicated, let's have a look at a concrete example, which uses a for loop to generate a set of filenames. These filenames are then tested using the test facility to determine whether or not they exist:

```
#!/bin/bash
for i in apple orange lemon kiwi guava
do
        DATAFILE=$i"".dat""
        echo ""Checking"" $DATAFILE
```

```
        if test -s $FILENAME
        then
                echo ""$DATAFILE ""has zero-length""
        else
                echo $FILENAME ""is OK""
        fi
done
```

The for loop is repeated nine times, with the variable $i taking on the values apple, orange, lemon, kiwi, and guava; thus, when on the first iteration, when $i=apple, the shell interprets the for loop in the following way:

```
FILENAME=""apple.dat""
echo ""Checking apple.dat""
if test -s apple.dat
then
echo ""apple.dat has zero-length""
else
echo ""apple.dat is OK""
fi
```

If we run this script in a directory with files of zero length, then we would expect to see the following output:

```
bash-2.03# ./zero_length_check.sh
Checking apple.dat
apple.dat is zero-length
Checking orange.dat
orange.dat is zero-length
Checking lemon.dat
lemon.dat is zero-length
Checking kiwi.dat
kiwi.dat is zero-length
Checking guava.dat
guava.dat is zero-length
```

However, if we entered data into each of the files, then we should see them receive the "OK" message:

```
bash-2.03# ./zero_length_check.sh
Checking apple.dat
apple.dat is OK
Checking orange.dat
orange.dat is OK
Checking lemon.dat
```

```
lemon.dat is OK
Checking kiwi.dat
kiwi.dat is OK
Checking guava.dat
guava.dat is OK
```

Using Shell Variables

In the previous example, we assigned different values to a shell variable, which was used to generate filenames for checking. It is common to modify variables within scripts by using export and to attach error codes to instances when variables are not defined within a script. This is particularly useful if a variable that is available within a user's interactive shell is not available in the user's noninteractive shell. For example, we can create a script called show_errors.sh that returns an error message if the PATH variable is not set:

```
#!/bin/bash
echo ${PATH:?PATH_NOT_SET}
```

Of course, since the PATH variable is usually set, we should see output similar to the following:

```
bash-2.03# ./path_set.sh
/sbin:/bin:/usr/games/bin:/usr/sbin:/root/bin:/usr/local/bin:/usr/local
/sbin/:/usr/bin:
/usr/X11R6/bin: /usr/games:/opt/gnome/bin:/opt/kde/bin
```

However, if the PATH was not set, we would see the following error message:

```
./show_errors.sh: PATH_NOT_SET
```

It is also possible to use system-supplied error messages as well by not specifying the optional error string:

```
bash-2.03# ./path_set.sh
#!/bin/bash
echo ${PATH:?}
```

Thus, if the PATH variable is not set, we would see the following error message:

```
bash-2.03# ./path_set.sh
./showargs: PATH: parameter null or not set
```

We can also use the numbered shell variables ($1, $2, $3, and so on) to capture the space-delimited output of certain commands and to perform actions based on the value of these variables by using the set command. For example, the command

```
bash-2.03# set `ls`
```

will sequentially assign each of the fields within the returned directory listing to a numbered shell variable. For example, if our directory listing contained the entries

```
apple.dat    guava.dat    kiwi.dat    lemon.dat    orange.dat
```

we could retrieve the values of these filenames by using the echo command:

```
bash-2.03# echo $1
apple.dat
bash-2.03# echo $2
guava.dat
bash-2.03# echo $3
kiwi.dat
bash-2.03# echo $4
lemon.dat
bash-2.03# echo $5
orange.dat
```

This approach is very useful if your script needs to perform some action based on only one component of the date. For example, if you wanted to create a unique filename to assign to a compressed file, then you could combine the values of each variable, with a "Z" extension to produce a set of strings like "orange.dat.Z."

Cron Jobs

Running scripts interactively is very useful for development, but often administrators want to repeat a particular command at various times during the day. For example, as a security measure, an administrator might wish to be e-mailed a list of all users who are currently logged in to the system every hour. Such a script might look like

```
#!/bin/bash
finger | mailx -s ""User Report"" root
```

Solaris provides the cron facility to schedule the execution of shell scripts and other applications (such as backup programs, usually executed in the wee hours past midnight, when system usage is low). If we saved the preceding script in a file called /usr/local/bin/finger_check.sh, then we could enter it into the root user's crontab file, by using the command

```
bash-2.03$ crontab -e
```

If no crontab currently existed for the user, we would see the message

```
no crontab for root - using an empty one
crontab: installing new crontab
```

At this point, root's default editor would be invoked, and we could enter the following line into the crontab:

```
0 * * * * /usr/local/bin/finger_check.sh
```

This line means that the script will run at zero minutes (0) at every hour, on every day of the month (*), in every month (*), and on each day of the week(*). You can always verify the contents of a user's crontab file by examining the user's entry in /var/spool/cron/crontabs/:

```
bash-2.03# cat /var/spool/cron/crontabs/root
0 * * * * /usr/local/bin/finger_check.sh
```

In order for the job to run, the cron daemon needs to be running. All users may submit cron jobs. Combining shell scripts with the cron facility makes it easy to automate all kinds of processes in a system, reducing the need for manual intervention to enable repetitive tasks.

SUMMARY

In this chapter, we have examined how to use the shell as an effective tool for achieving all kinds of tasks involving running applications, managing file permissions, processes, and writing scripts. You have probably realized by now that the shell is much more complicated than the MS-DOS command prompt. However, the added complexity involved in dealing with file permissions and programming-like constructs pays dividends when repetitive, time-consuming tasks must be regularly performed.

CHAPTER 7

Managing Users and Groups

The concept of the user is central to Solaris—all processes and files on a Solaris system are owned by a particular user and are assigned to a specific user group. No data or activities on the system may exist without a valid user or group. Managing users and groups as a Solaris administrator can be a challenging activity—you will be responsible for assigning all of the privileges granted or denied to a user or group of users, and many of these permissions carry great risk. For example, a user with an inappropriate privilege level may execute commands as the superuser, causing damage to your system. In this chapter, the administrator will learn how to add users to the system, select an appropriate shell, and add and modify groups. In addition, the contents and structure of key user databases, including the password, shadow password, and group files, are examined in detail. Finally, we introduce the Solaris System Administration Menu Interface (admintool), which is a GUI-based user administration tool designed to make user management easier under Solaris.

ADDING AND MODIFYING USERS

All users on a Solaris system have a number of unique identifiers and characteristics that can be used to distinguish individual users from each other, and also to logically group related users. Most physical users of a Solaris system will have a unique login assigned to them, which is identified by a username with a maximum of eight characters. Once a user account is created, it can be used for the following purposes:

▼ Spawning a shell (like the Bourne again shell [bash] examined in Chapter 5)

■ Executing applications interactively

■ Scheduling applications to run at specific times and dates

▲ Access database applications and other system services

In addition to user accounts, Solaris also uses a number of system accounts (such as root, daemon, bin, sys, lp, adm, and uucp) to perform various kinds of routine maintenance, including

▼ Allocation of system resources to perform specific tasks

■ Running a mail server

■ Running a Web server

▲ Process management

Users may access a Solaris system by accessing the console, or through a remote terminal in either graphical or text mode. In each case, a set of authentication credentials is presented to the system, including the username and password. When entered, a user's password is compared to an encrypted string stored in the password database (/etc/passwd) or the shadow password database (/etc/shadow). Once the string entered by the user has been encrypted, it is matched against the already encrypted entry in the password database. If a match is made, authentication occurs, and the user may spawn a shell. A Solaris username may have a maximum of eight characters, as may a Solaris password.

TIP: Since the security of a Solaris system relies heavily on the difficulty of guessing passwords, user policies should be developed to either recommend or enforce the use of passwords containing random or semirandom character strings.

There are a number of other user characteristics that are associated with each user, in addition to a username and password. These features include

▼ The user ID (UID), which is a unique integer that begins with the root user (UID=1), with other UIDs typically (but not necessarily) being allocated sequentially. Some systems will reserve all UIDs below 1023 for system accounts (for example, the Apache user for managing the Apache Web server), while those UIDs above 1024 are designated for ordinary users. The UID of 0 designates the superuser account that is typically called root. This is equivalent to the Administrator account in Windows NT.

■ A flexible mechanism for distinguishing different classes of users, known as *groups*. Groups are not just sets of related users: the Solaris file system allows for group-designated read, write, and execute file access for groups, in addition to permissions granted to the individual user and to all users. Every UID is associated with a primary group ID (GID); however, UIDs may also be associated with more than one secondary group.

■ A home directory, which is the default file storage location for all files created by a particular user. If the automounter is used, then home directories may be exported using the Network File System (NFS) on /home. When a user spawns a login shell, the current working directory will always be the home directory.

■ A login shell, which can be used to issue commands interactively or to write simple programs, as reviewed in Chapters 5 and 6. A number of different shells are available under Solaris, including the Bourne shell (sh), C shell (csh), the Bourne again shell (bash), and the Cornell shell (tcsh). The choice of shell depends largely on personal preference, user experience with C-like programming constructs, and terminal handling.

▲ A comment, which is typically the user's full name, such as Paul Watters. However, system accounts may use names that describe their purpose (for example, the comment "Web server" might be associated with the Apache user).

Adding a user to a Solaris system is easy; however, this operation may only be performed by the root user. There are two options:. The first option is to edit the /etc/passwd file directly, incrementing the UID, adding the appropriate GID, adding a home directory (and remembering to physically create it on the file system), inserting a comment, and choosing a login name.

NOTE: A passwd for the user must be set using the passwd command.

Does this sound difficult? If so, then you should consider using the automated useradd command, which will do all of the hard work for you, as long as you supply the correct information. The useradd command has the following format:

```
bash# useradd -u uid -g gid -d home_directory -s path_to_shell -c comment
login_name
```

Let's add a user to our system and examine the results:

```
bash-2.03# useradd -u 1004 -g 10 -d /opt/www -s /bin/sh -c "Web User" www
```

Here, we are adding a Web User called "www" with the UID 1004, the GID 10, the home directory /opt/www, and the Bourne shell (sh) as the login shell. At the end of the useradd script, an appropriate line should appear in the /etc/passwd file:

```
bash-2.03# grep www /etc/passwd
www:x:1004:10:Web User:/opt/www:/bin/sh
```

However, the useradd command may fail under the following conditions:

▼ The UID that you specified has already been taken by another user. Unlike Windows NT, UIDs may be recycled as long as precautions are taken to ensure that a previous owner of the UID no longer owns files on the file system.

■ The GID that you specified does not exist. Verify its entry in the groups database (/etc/group).

■ The comment contains special characters such as double quotes (""), exclamation marks (!), or slashes (/).

▲ The shell that you specified does not exist. Check that the shell actually exists in the path specified and that the shell has an entry in the shells database (/etc/shells).

Once you have created a user account, it is possible to change any of its characteristics by directly editing the password database (/etc/passwd) or by using the usermod command. For example, if we wanted to modify the UID of the www account from 1004 to 1005, we would use the command

```
bash-2.03# usermod -u 1005 www
```

Again, we can verify that the change has been made correctly by examining the entry for www in the password database:

```
bash-2.03# grep www /etc/passwd
www:x:1005:10:Web User:/opt/www:/bin/sh
```

Remember: if you change a UID or GID, you must manually update existing directory and file ownerships by using the chmod, chgrp, and chown commands when appropriate.

Once a user account has been created, the next step is to set a password, which can be performed by the passwd command

```
bash-2.03# passwd user
```

where user is the login name for the account whose password you wish to change. In all cases, you will be required to enter the new password twice. If you happen to make a typing error, the password will not be changed and you will be warned that the two password strings entered did not match. Here's an example for the user www:

```
bash-2.03 # passwd www
New password:
Re-enter new password:
passwd(SYSTEM): They don't match; try again.
New password:
Re-enter new password:
passwd (SYSTEM): passwd successfully changed for www
```

After a password has been entered for a user, such as the www user, it should appear as an encrypted string in the shadow password database (/etc/shadow):

```
bash-2.03# grep www /etc/shadow
www:C4dMH8As4bGTM:::::::
```

Once a user has been granted an initial password, he or she may then enter a new password by using the passwd command with no options.

Now imagine that one of your prized employees has unexpectedly taken another job. Although you will eventually be able to change the ownership on all of her files, you cannot immediately restart some production applications. In this case, it is possible to temporarily disable logins to a specific account by using a command such as

```
bash-2.03# passwd -l karleen
```

This command would lock Karleen's account until the root user once again used the passwd command on this account to set a new password. A locked account can be identified in the password database by the characters LK:

```
bash-2.03# grep karleen /etc/shadow
karleen:*LK*:::::::
```

Once all of the user's files have been backed up, and any active processes have been killed by the superuser, the user account may be permanently deleted by using the userdel command. For example, to delete the user account karleen, and remove that user's home directory and all of the files underneath that directory, you would use the command

```
bash-2.03# userdel -r karleen
```

Alternatively, you could edit both the password and shadow password databases, and remove the appropriate lines containing the entries for the user karleen.

NOTE: You would also need to manually remove the user's home directory and all of her files underneath that directory.

There are also several system accounts that should remain locked at all times to prevent interactive logins, including adm, bin, listen, nobody, lp, sys, and uucp.

CHOOSING SHELLS

In Chapters 5 and 6, we examined how to use an interactive shell (the Bourne shell [sh]) and how to create shell scripts using the Bourne shell (sh). However, users have a wide variety of shells to choose from under Solaris, which is unlike Windows NT, where there is a single command prompt application with a single batch mode–processing language. In this section, we will review the major features of each of the major shells used in Solaris.

Solaris has a shells database, located in /etc/shells, which lists all of the registered shells on a system:

```
bash-2.03# cat /etc/shells
/bin/sh
/bin/csh
/bin/ksh
/bin/tcsh
/bin/bash
```

These shells are the Bourne shell (sh), the C shell (csh), the Korn shell (ksh), the Cornell shell (tcsh), and the Bourne again shell (bash).

Bourne Shell (sh)

The Bourne shell (sh) is the shell that, by convention, is always used by the superuser for scripting and issuing interactive commands. This special status exists because the Bourne shell (sh) is always guaranteed to be installed on every Solaris system, while most of the other shells are optionally installed from the Solaris distribution (for example, C shell [csh]) or by downloading them from the Internet (for example, bash).

The Bourne shell (sh) is always located in /bin/sh; thus, if you want to create a Bourne shell (sh) script, you would add the following to the top of your script:

```
#!/bin/sh
```

The Bourne shell (sh) provides facilities for job control and interpreting commands, using the decision logic commands described in Chapters 5 and 6. However, its terminal-handling facilities are very basic, which is why many users prefer to use bash.

TIP: If you need to write system startup scripts, such as those found in /etc/init.d, you will need to master the Bourne shell (sh).

Let's examine one of these scripts, which starts up the Samba fileserving daemon:

```
#!/bin/sh
# Samba service startup/shutdown script
case "$1" in
'start')
        /usr/local/samba/bin/smbd -D -l /var/adm/smblogs/log -s /usr/local/samba
/lib/smb.conf
        /usr/local/samba/bin/nmbd -D
        ;;
'stop')
        /usr/bin/pkill -x -u 0 smbd
        /usr/bin/pkill -x -u 0 nmbd
        ;;
*)
        echo "Usage: $0 { start | stop }"
        exit 1
        ;;
esac
exit 0
```

When past the parameter "start," this script starts up the Samba server and the associated naming service; but when it is past the parameter "stop," it performs a process kill on all of the Samba processes. The Bourne shell (sh) may seem esoteric and cryptic at first, but by examining script examples such as those found in /etc/init.d, you should quickly be able to master the major constructs.

Bourne Again Shell (bash)

Bash was covered in detail in Chapters 5 and 6. It is compliant with the Posix 1003.2 standard for shells and is a superset of the Bourne shell (sh). It is generally used by those who wish to maintain compatibility with the Bourne shell (sh), but who want improved terminal handling, including filename completion and a command history easily accessible from the terminal. In programming terms, bash also provides arrays, for loops and shell arithmetic, which are not fully supported in the Bourne shell (sh).

The bash FAQ is available from ftp://ftp.cwru.edu/pub/bash/FAQ, while the latest release of bash can always be downloaded from http://cnswww.cns.cwru.edu/~chet/bash/bashtop.html.

C Shell

The C shell (csh) is the main competitor to the Bourne shell (sh) and its variants, like bash. It features a C-like scripting language, in addition to advanced command history and terminal-handling features. Other variants, such as the Cornell shell (tcsh), are supersets of the original C shell: csh does not support command-line editing, for example, while Cornell shell (tcsh) does. The csh features command aliasing and history substitution, making it easy to retrieve and modify past commands for future execution.

A common alias set in the C shell is for the ls command, which forces a more meaningful display of directory items by using the -F parameter. The standard output for ls is

```
csh% ls /usr/local/jdk-1.2.2/bin
appletviewer  java-rmi.cgi  javap          policytool    sparc
extcheck      javac         jdb            rmic          tnameserv
jar           javadoc       keytool        rmid
jarsigner     javah         native2ascii   rmiregistry
java          javald        oldjava        serialver
```

Whereas the ls -F command produces the following output:

```
csh% ls -F
appletviewer@  java-rmi.cgi*  javap@          policytool@    sparc/
extcheck@      javac@         jdb@            rmic@          tnameserv@
jar@           javadoc@       keytool@        rmid@
jarsigner@     javah@         native2ascii@   rmiregistry@
java@          javald@        oldjava@        serialver@
```

Here, the @ symbol indicates that the file is a symbolic link, the / symbol indicates a directory entry, while the * symbol indicates an executable file. To create an alias for the ls command to execute the ls -F command, we would use the command

```
csh% alias ls 'ls -F'
```

Afterward, whenever we type ls, we should see the enhanced directory listing:

```
csh% ls
appletviewer@  java-rmi.cgi*  javap@          policytool@    sparc/
extcheck@      javac@         jdb@            rmic@          tnameserv@
jar@           javadoc@       keytool@        rmid@
jarsigner@     javah@         native2ascii@   rmiregistry@
java@          javald@        oldjava@        serialver@
```

As a Solaris administrator, you will find that many of your colleagues may have a favorite shell. Even if you mainly use a Bourne-like shell or a C-like shell in your daily work, it is often useful to be familiar with both kinds.

TIP: Learn the command syntax of all of the main shells.

ADDING AND MODIFYING GROUPS

Solaris provides a facility for identifying sets of related users into groups. Each user is associated with a primary GID, which is associated with a name. The group name and GID can be used interchangeably. In addition, users can also be associated with one or more secondary groups. This flexibility means that while users might have a primary group membership based on their employment or organizational status (for example, staff or managers), they can actively share data and system privileges with other groups based on their work group needs (for example, sales or engineers).

All information about groups in Solaris is stored in the groups database (/etc/group). Let's examine a typical sets of groups:

```
bash-2.03 # cat /etc/group
root::0:root
other::1:
bin::2:root,bin,daemon
sys::3:root,bin,sys,adm
adm::4:root,adm,daemon
uucp::5:root,uucp
mail::6:root
tty::7:root,tty,adm
lp::8:root,lp,adm
nuucp::9:root,nuucp
staff::10:paul,maya,brad,karleen
postgres:a.mBzQnr1ei2D.:100:postgres, paul
daemon::12:root,daemon
sysadmin::14:
nobody::60001:
noaccess::60002:
nogroup::65534:
```

We can see that the lower group numbers are associated with all of the system functions and accounts, such as the bin group, which has the members root, bin, and daemon, and the sys group, which has the members root, bin, sys, and adm. Higher numbered groups, such as staff, contain several different users, such as paul, maya, brad, and karleen. Notice also that paul has a secondary group membership in the postgres group, giving him database access privileges. A group password can also be set for each group, although most groups don't use this facility. In this group database, we can see that the postgres group is the only group that has an encrypted password (a.mBzQnr1ei2D.).

You can obtain a list of all groups that a user belongs to by using the groups command. For example, to view all of the groups that the root users belongs to, we use the command

```
bash-2.03# groups root
other root bin sys adm uucp mail tty lp nuucp daemon
```

To add a new group to the system, you may either manually edit the /etc/group file or use the groupadd command, which has the following syntax:

```
/usr/sbin/groupadd -g gid  group_name
```

Thus, to add a group called managers to the system, with a GID of 500, we would use the command

```
bash-2.03# groupadd -g 500 managers
```

We would then be able to verify the new group's existence by searching the groups database:

```
bash-2.03# grep management /etc/group
managers::500:
```

The groupadd command will fail if the GID that you specify has already been allocated to an existing group or if the group_name is greater than eight characters.

If you want to change your group from primary to secondary during an interactive session, to ensure that all of the files that you create are associated with the correct GID, you need to use the newgrp command. For example, the root user has the following primary group membership:

```
bash-2.03# id
uid=0(root) gid=0(root)
```

However, if the root user wishes to act as a member of another group, such as sys, the following command would have to be used:

```
bash-2.03# newgrp sys
```

The effective GID would then change to sys:

```
bash-2.03# id
uid=0(root) gid=3(sys)
```

Any operations that the root user performs after using the newgrp command, such as creating files, will be associated with the GID of 3 (sys) rather than 0 (root). For example, if we created a new file with the primary group, the group associated with the new file would be GID 0:

```
bash-2.03# touch root.txt
bash-2.03# ls -l root.txt
-rw-r--r--   1 root    root.0 Oct 12 11:17 root.txt
```

However, if the root user then changes groups to sys and creates a new file, then the group associated with the file will be sys, rather than root:

```
bash-2.03# newgrp sys
bash-2.03# touch sys.txt
bash-2.03# ls -l sys.txt
-rw-r--r--   1 root    sys    0 Oct 12 11:18 sys.txt
```

USING PASSWORD DATABASES

All Solaris users have a username and password associated with their account, except where a user account has been explicitly locked (designated *LK*) or where a system account has been specified not to have a password at all (NP).

NOTE: Many early exploits of Solaris systems were associated with default passwords used on some system accounts, and the most common method of gaining unauthorized access to a Solaris system remains password cracking and/or guessing.

In this section, we examine the password database (/etc/passwd) and its more secure counterpart, the shadow database (/etc/shadow); and we will examine strategies for making passwords safer.

The standard password database is stored in the file /etc/passwd and looks like this:

```
bash-2.03 # cat /etc/passwd
root:x:0:1:Super-User:/:/sbin/sh
daemon:x:1:1::/:
bin:x:2:2::/usr/bin:
sys:x:3:3::/:
adm:x:4:4:Admin:/var/adm:
lp:x:71:8:Line Printer Admin:/usr/spool/lp:
uucp:x:5:5:uucp Admin:/usr/lib/uucp:
nuucp:x:9:9:uucp Admin:/var/spool/uucppublic:/usr/lib/uucp/uucico
```

```
listen:x:37:4:Network Admin:/usr/net/nls:
nobody:x:60001:60001:Nobody:/:
noaccess:x:60002:60002:No Access User:/:
nobody4:x:65534:65534:SunOS 4.x Nobody:/:
postgres:x:1001:100:Postgres User:/usr/local/postgres:/bin/sh
htdig:x:1002:10:htdig:/opt/www:/usr/local/bin/bash
apache:x:1003:10:apache user:/usr/local/apache:/bin/sh
```

We have already seen some of the fields shown here when adding users to the system in a previous chapter:

▼ The username field, which has a maximum of eight characters

■ The encrypted password field, which in a system using shadow passwords is crossed with a x

■ The UID field, which contains the numeric and unique UID

■ The primary GID field, which contains the numeric GID

■ The user comment, which contains a description of the user

■ The path to the user's home directory

▲ The user's default shell

In older versions of Solaris, the encrypted password field would have contained an encrypted password string such as X14oLaiYg7bO2. However, this presented a security problem, as the login program required all users to have read access to the password file:

```
bash-2.03# ls -l /etc/passwd
-rw-r--r--   1 root      sys            605 Jul 24 11:04 /etc/passwd
```

Thus, any user with the lowest form privilege would be able to access the encrypted password field for the root user and attempt to gain root access by guessing the password. A number of programs were specifically developed for this purpose, such as crack, which takes a standard Solaris password file and uses a dictionary and some clever lexical rules to guess passwords. Once a root password has been obtained, a rogue user may perform any operation on a Solaris system, including formatting hard disks, installing Trojan horses, and launching attacks on other systems.

The cryptographic algorithm used by Solaris is not easy to crack: indeed, a brute force guess of a password composed of a completely random set of characters would take many CPUs years to compute. The task would be made even more difficult (if not impossible) if the root password was changed weekly, again with a random set of characters. However, the reality is that most users enter passwords that are easily guessed from a dictionary or with some knowledge about the user. Raise your hand if you've entered a spouse, parent, child, or pet name as a password! Or a password like root, sun, window, linux, and others. Since we are constantly required to use personal identification numbers (PINs) and passwords, people choose passwords that are easy to remember. However, easily remembered passwords are also the easiest to crack.

Solaris has reduced the chances of a rogue user obtaining the password file in the first place by implementing a shadow password facility. This creates a file called /etc/shadow, which is similar to the password file (/etc/passwd), but is only readable by root and contains the encrypted password fields for each UID. Thus, if a rogue user cannot obtain the encrypted password entries, it is impossible to use them as the basis for a crack attack. A shadow password file corresponding to the password file shown previously looks like

```
bash-2.03# cat /etc/shadow
root:X14oLaiYg7bO2:11033:::::::
daemon:NP:6445::::::
bin:NP:6445::::::
sys:NP:6445::::::
adm:NP:6445::::::
lp:NP:6445::::::
uucp:NP:6445::::::
nuucp:NP:6445::::::
listen:*LK*:::::::
nobody:NP:6445::::::
noaccess:NP:6445::::::
nobody4:NP:6445::::::
postgres:C4dMH8As4bGTM:::::::
htdig:kAa0lRg9IIDXo:::::::
apache::::::::
www:*LK*:::::::
```

However, it is still possible to write a shell script that continually attempts to log in to the root account by using easily guessable passwords, which could be generated from a crack program. While much less efficient than the method outlined earlier, this kind of attack is still possible. The best way to prevent this kind of attack is to select a secure root password. One way of doing this is to use Van Vleck's gpw password-generation program, which is available for binary download from ftp://nce.sun.ca/pub/freeware/intel/7/gpw-6.94-sol7-intel-local.gz. More information about the program can be obtained from http://www.multicians.org/thvv/tvvtools.html.

The gpw program generates a password that contains pronounceable syllables that are nonwords. This makes it impossible for a dictionary-based attack to succeed, while making it easy for users to remember their passwords. If we run gpw, by default we receive a list of ten safe candidate passwords:

```
bash-2.03# gpw
strudion
nathumen
atinfice
ofluceld
eldwarxe
```

```
illiersh
vatonyla
ladnerst
nieverwi
tgervell
```

It's often difficult to enforce the use of safe passwords on a system; however, it is possible to use options, such as password expiry with the passwd command, that force users to change their passwords regularly. If a safe password is changed regularly, then the chances of a rogue user guessing a password are virtually nil. In addition, one of the greatest risks to account security comes not from password guessing, but from packet-sniffing telnet sessions, where a user's username and password can be obtained by examining the contents of all packets being transmitted on a local area network or through any host that is on the network path between client and server. For example, if I were to telnet from a computer in Sydney to a host in the United States (such as www.paulwatters.com), my username and password could be intercepted by up to 16 hosts:

```
traceroute to paulwatters.com (209.67.50.203), 30 hops max, 40 byte packets
 1   FastEthernet6-0.civ-service1.Canberra.telstra.net (203.50.1.65)  0.542 ms
0.435 ms  0.536 ms
 2   Fddi0-0-0.civ-core2.Canberra.telstra.net (139.130.235.230)  1.342 ms  0.937 ms
1.397 ms
 3   GigabitEthernet4-0-0.dkn-core1.Canberra.telstra.net (203.50.6.126)  13.634 ms
1.557 ms  2.052 ms
 4   Pos0-1.ken-core1.Sydney.telstra.net (203.50.6.121)  4.742 ms  4.699 ms
4.956 ms
 5   Pos2-3.wel-core3.Perth.telstra.net (203.50.6.142)  53.078 ms  53.359 ms
54.186 ms
 6   GigabitEthernet4-0.wel-gw1.Perth.telstra.net (203.50.113.18)  54.171 ms
53.23 ms  52.961 ms
 7   Pos1-0.paix1.PaloAlto.telstra.net (203.50.126.30)  280.496 ms  281.26 ms
280.256 ms
 8   paix-f2-5.exodus.net (209.1.169.97)  281.142 ms  280.304 ms  281.401 ms
 9   209.185.249.25 (209.185.249.25)  283.595 ms  282.399 ms  281.884 ms
10   bbr02-p5-0.hrnd01.exodus.net (216.32.173.14)  361.305 ms  361.953 ms
363.847 ms
11   bbr01-g4-0.hrnd01.exodus.net (216.33.203.125)  361.747 ms  361.392 ms
361.36 ms
12   bbr01-p5-0.jrcy01.exodus.net (209.185.249.213)  358.342 ms  356.959 ms
358.572 ms
13   dcr03-g3-0.jrcy01.exodus.net (209.67.45.97)  358.972 ms  357.085 ms  357.259 ms
14   csr02-ve241.jrcy02.exodus.net (216.32.223.51)  355.898 ms  355.822 ms
356.114 ms
15   216.32.193.110 (216.32.193.110)  355.357 ms  355.681 ms  356.113 ms
16   futuresite.register.com (209.67.50.203)  357.54 ms  356.132 ms  357.223 ms
```

The risk of password interception can be removed by using a secure remote access tool, such as Secure Shell (SSH).

USING ADMINTOOL

So far, we have only examined user and group administration by using command-line tools, such as useradd and groupadd. This will suit administrators who have experience with Linux, because many of the commands have the same name as Solaris. However, Microsoft Windows administrators may find it difficult to remember command and option names after using the Windows NT User Manager, shown in Figure 7-1, which is a GUI-based administration tool. This application allows for the easy management of users and groups by pointing and clicking.

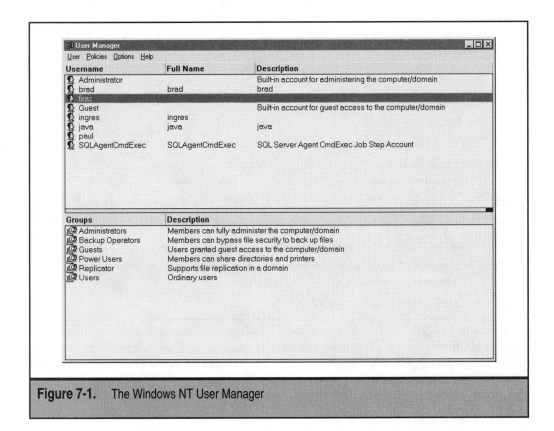

Figure 7-1. The Windows NT User Manager

Fortunately, Solaris also provides an easy-to-use administrative interface for adding users and groups to the system, the admintool. The admintool interface is shown in Figure 7-2. The interface shown is for user management, displaying the username, UID, and user comment. In addition to managing users and groups, admintool is also useful for managing hosts, printers, serial ports, and software. Each management option has its own interface, which is accessible from the Browse menu.

NOTE: When an interface is selected, such as the printers interface, administrators may then add, modify, or delete the entries that exist in the current database (in this case, administrators may add, delete, or modify the entries for printers).

Let's examine how to modify existing user information using the admintool, as shown in Figure 7-3. First, select the user whose data you wish to modify (for example, the adm user, one of the preconfigured system accounts that is created during Solaris installation). Next, select the Modify option from the admintool Edit menu. The user entry modification window is shown in Figure 7-3 for the adm user. Here, it is possible to modify the following options:

▼ The username

■ The primary group

■ All secondary groups

■ The user comment

■ The login shell, which can be selected from a drop-down list containing all valid shells defined in the shells database (/etc/shells)

■ The minimum and maximum days required before a password change

■ The maximum number of inactive days for an account

■ An expiry date for the user's account

■ The number of days' warning to give a user before their password must be changed

▲ The path to the user's home directory

Of course, all of this information can be set on the command line by using the passwd command; however, the admintool interface is easier to use and provides some additional functionality. For example, it is impossible to enter an invalid expiration date, because the day, month, and year are selected from drop-down lists. In addition, if there are any problems encountered during modification, no changes will be recorded.

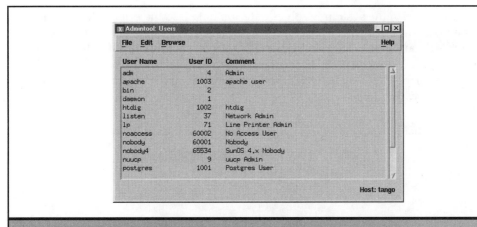

Figure 7-2. The Solaris admintool

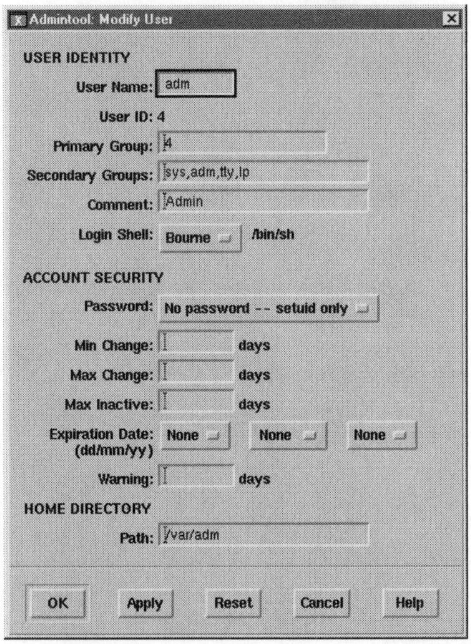

Figure 7-3. Modifying user details with admintool

Adding a user to the system involves entering data into the same interface used for modifying user details, as shown in Figure 7-4. The UID is sequentially generated, as is the default primary group, user shell, password option (not set until first login), and option to create a new directory for the user as his or her home directory. Again, admintool has advanced error-checking facilities that make it difficult to damage or overwrite system files with invalid data.

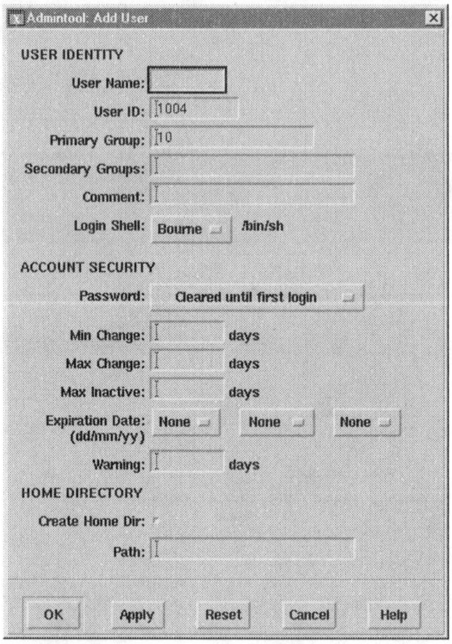

Figure 7-4.   Adding user details with admintool

Admintool can also be used as a group administration tool. Groups may be created, and users can be added or removed from specific groups. In addition, groups may also be deleted using admintool. To add a user to the group, simply select the adm group and click on the Add entry in the Edit menu. A comma-delimited list of users in the group will then be displayed. The bin user could be added to the adm group by inserting a comma after the last entry and adding the name bin to the list.

SUMMARY

In this chapter, we have examined a number of issues related to user and group management under Solaris, including selecting passwords, adding users on the command line, and managing groups using the admintool. Solaris provides both tools for command-line gurus from a Linux background, and GUI tools for administrators with more Microsoft Windows experience.

CHAPTER 8

Processes and System Resources

rocesses lie at the heart of all modern multiuser operating systems. By dividing system tasks into small, discrete elements, which are uniquely identified by a process ID (PID), Solaris is able to manage effectively all of the applications that may be concurrently executed by many different users. In addition, individual users may execute more than one application at any one time. Each Solaris process is associated with a user ID (UID) and a group ID (GID), just like a standard file. This means that only users may send signals to their own processes, except for the superuser, who may send signals to any process on the system. Signals are typically used to restart or terminate processes.

The multiuser, multitasking process model in Solaris ensures that system resources can be shared equally among all competing processes or allocated preferentially to the most important applications. For example, a firewall application would probably take precedence over all other system processes. Individual users and the superuser may allocate a priority level to active processes in real time.

In this chapter, we examine the concepts of understanding processes and managing file systems, Central Processing Unit (CPU), and memory resources. You will learn how to interpret process displays, trace system calls for processes that are resident in memory, and send signals to processes. In addition, we examine tools like top, which can be used for online monitoring of process activity. Finally, we review the /proc file system tools, which are used to extract real-time data about Lightweight Processes (LWPs) running on your system.

INTERPRETING PROCESS DISPLAYS

Most users obtain information about processes by using the ps command, which has a number of options, as shown in Table 8-1. By default, the ps command displays only the processes that are owned by the current user; however, it can also be configured to display details of all processes on a system. This is one reason why it is prudent to check your process list to determine whether or not sensitive information is available to other users. For example, if a user executed a database client and passed the username and password on the command line, it may be possible for another user to extract this information from the process list.

NOTE: Even less-privileged users may sometimes be able to extract useful information about processes being run by other users.

Parameter	Description
–a	Displays most frequently requested processes
–A, –e	Displays all processes
–c	Displays processes in scheduler format
–d	Displays all processes
–f	Displays comprehensive process information
–g	Displays process information on a group basis for a single group
–G	Displays process information on a group basis for a list of groups
–j	Displays SID and PGID in printout
–l	Displays complete process information
–L	Displays LWP details
–p	Displays process details for list of specified processes
–P	Displays the CPU ID to which a process is bound
–s	Displays session leaders
–t	Displays all processes associated with a specific terminal
–u	Displays all processes for a specific user

Table 8-1.   Commonly Used Options for the ps Command

One alternative to the ps command that has a Graphical User Interface (GUI) is the Common Desktop Environment (CDE) Process Manager, as seen in Figure 8-1. It presents a snapshot of all processes on a system and includes columns for PID, command name, user, CPU time consumed, physical RAM used, virtual RAM used, date the process was started, and full command string.

TIP: The display can be configured to refresh the display every 30 seconds or less, so that you can monitor process activities continuously.

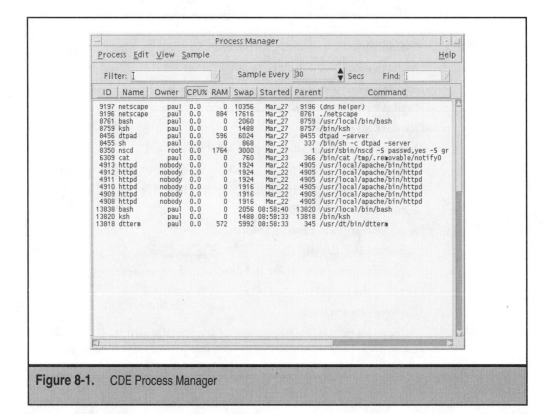

Figure 8-1.   CDE Process Manager

This manager is similar to the Windows NT Task Manager, as shown in Figure 8-2. Again, columns for the command name, PID, CPU usage, total CPU time, and total memory usage are shown.

In the following sections, we will examine the most commonly used process listings, and review their utility in light of process and user management issues.

Listing Frequently Requested Processes

The ps –a command lists most frequently requested processes, as shown in the following example:

```
bash-2.03# ps -a
   PID TTY        TIME CMD
  1511 pts/2      0:00 sh
  1531 pts/2      0:00 ttsessio
```

```
1532 pts/2    0:01 dtsessio
2878 pts/2    0:00 dtfile
3243 pts/3    0:00 netscape
3242 pts/3    0:22 netscape
2877 pts/2    0:00 sh
6809 pts/7    0:00 man
6824 pts/7    0:00 sh
6825 pts/7    0:00 more
6835 pts/5    0:00 dtterm
6640 pts/7    0:00 bash
6832 pts/5    0:00 ksh
6840 pts/8    0:00 ps
```

The results here are unsurprising: the most frequently requested process has a PID of 1511 and is the Bourne shell (sh) running on the terminal pts/2. We can also see several other processes spawned from the terminal pts/2, including CDE session and file management utilities. The TIME column displays the number of CPU minutes and seconds

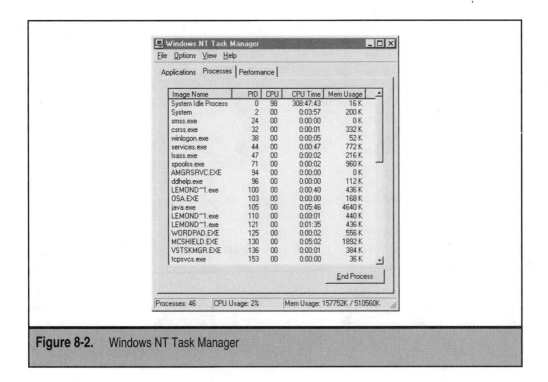

Figure 8-2.   Windows NT Task Manager

the process has consumed since being spawned. The netscape application (PID 3242) has consumed the most CPU time in this example.

Listing All Processes

To obtain a list of all processes currently running on a system, we use the ps –A command. In the example shown next, the first process spawned after booting is the scheduler, followed by the init process, which is ultimately the parent process for all user processes spawned on the system. Indeed, if you examine the parent process ID (PPID) for processes whose parents have been killed, you will find that the PPID reverts to PID 1. In the TTY column, a question mark is displayed wherever a process is not bound to a specific terminal. In this example, the process consuming the highest amount of CPU time is the file system flush process (fsflush), PID 3.

```
bash-2.03# ps -A
   PID TTY        TIME CMD
     0 ?         0:00 sched
     1 ?         0:00 init
     2 ?         0:00 pageout
     3 ?         5:09 fsflush
   410 ?         0:00 sac
   179 ?         0:00 ss_timed
   413 ?         0:00 ttymon
    66 ?         0:00 devfseve
    68 ?         0:00 devfsadm
   290 ?         0:00 automoun
   243 ?         0:00 keyserv
   121 ?         0:04 skipd
   178 ?         0:00 ss_logd
   298 ?         0:01 syslogd
   282 ?         0:00 lockd
   286 ?         0:00 statd
   361 ?         0:00 vold
```

Scheduler Format

The ps –c command lists processes in the scheduler format. It includes two extra columns: priority class (CLS) and process priority (PRI). In this case, the ps command and the Korn shell (ksh) are both members of the time-sharing class, meaning that a priority value may be assigned to each process. In the case of the ps process, this has a higher priority value than the Korn shell (ksh) process and, thus, has greater access to the system's resources.

```
bash-2.03# ps -c
   PID  CLS PRI TTY        TIME CMD
```

```
6842   TS   45 pts/8     0:00 ps
6837   TS   35 pts/8     0:00 ksh
```

If you actually wanted to give priority to the Korn shell (ksh) process, you could use the nice command to reduce the priority granted to the ps process by using the command

```
bash-2.03# nice -20 ps
```

However, a superuser may actually increase the priority of a process by using the command

```
bash-2.03# nice --10 ps
```

This command would result in the priority of the ps command being increased directly by 10.

Comprehensive Process Information

If you're an administrator, you'll typically want to keep an eye on all processes that are being run on your system. There are a number of good reasons to develop this kind of monitoring as a habit:

▼ **Performance**   It is critical to determine, during a general lag being experienced by interactive users on a system, which of the hundreds (or thousands) of processes are causing the bottleneck.

▲ **Security**   It is important to get an idea for the commands and applications that are typically executed by users on your system. Unusual and/or conspicuous activity may indicate a break-in attempt by a rogue user. You may decide, in an emergency, to suspend a process that appears suspicious and activate it again once its authenticity has been verified.

The most comprehensive process information can be obtained by running the ps –f command, as shown in the following example:

```
bash-2.03# ps -f
     UID    PID  PPID  C    STIME TTY      TIME CMD
    root   6846  6837  0 13:12:03 pts/8    0:00 ps -f
    root   6837  6835  0 13:10:42 pts/8    0:00 /bin/ksh
```

Here, we can see that there are several extra columns printed in addition to the standard process listing, including the PPID and the processor utilization column (C), which is only retained for historical purposes (this means that scripts that expect to see the C column will not crash just because the data is no longer available).

The ps –f command may be combined with the –e option to form the ps –ef command, which prints comprehensive details on all processes running on a system.

Group Process Information

Often, it's important to keep track of what a specific group of users is doing. For example, if you're running a student system at a college, you may wish to check only the processes run by members of the group "student," to check for password-cracking programs or other prohibited applications. Fortunately, the ps –G command prints group process data for a specified GID. In the following, we display process information on a group basis for members of the group GID 1, which includes the root user:

```
bash-2.03# ps -G 1
   PID TTY       TIME CMD
  1511 pts/2    0:00 sh
  1531 pts/2    0:00 ttsessio
  1475 ?        0:00 fbconsol
  1532 pts/2    0:01 dtsessio
  1544 ?        0:00 sdtvolch
  1539 ?        0:04 dtwm
  1541 ?        0:00 sdtperfm
  1515 ?        0:00 dsdm
  3207 ?        0:00 miniserv
```

Full Process Listing

If you haven't been satisfied by any of the process displays that we've already reviewed, then the next command, the ps –l command, should satisfy you, because it will print every piece of information that is collected about each individual process on the system. In the following example, each of these characteristics is reported:

▼ Command name (CMD)

■ CPU time consumed

■ Memory address (ADDR)

■ Memory address for sleeping processes (WCHAN)

■ Memory size (SZ)

■ Nice value (NI)

■ PPID

■ Process flags (F)

■ PID

■ PRI

■ Process state (S), including running processes (R) and sleeping processes (S)

▲ Processor utilization (C)

In the following example, the sleeping process PID 6837 has a PPID of 6835; a priority of 63; a nice value of 24; a memory address of e0f85050, with a total size of 373K; a WCHAN of e0f850bc; and negligible CPU time consumed:

```
bash-2.03# ps -l
 F S   UID   PID  PPID  C PRI NI     ADDR     SZ   WCHAN TTY      TIME CMD
 8 O     0  6861  6848  0  53 24 e1053780    196         pts/8    0:00 ps
 8 R     0  6848  6837  0  63 24 e128e098    501         pts/8    0:00 bash
 8 S     0  6837  6835  0  63 24 e0f85050    373 e0f850bc pts/8    0:00 ksh
```

Combining Process Options

One of the most useful features of the ps command is the ability to combine different process options into a single command. For example, if we wanted to print the list of all LWPs associated with every process on the system, we could use the ps –eL command. This produces a long list showing all LWPs, with the LWP number shown in the column LWP:

```
bash-2.03# ps -eL
   PID   LWP TTY       LTIME CMD
     0     1 ?          0:00 sched
     1     1 ?          0:00 init
     2     1 ?          0:00 pageout
     3     1 ?          5:09 fsflush
   410     1 ?          0:00 sac
   179     1 ?          0:00 ss_timed
   413     1 ?          0:00 ttymon
    66     1 ?          0:00 devfseve
   144     1 ?          0:00 httpd
   144     2 ?          0:00 httpd
   144     6 ?          0:00 httpd
   144     7 ?          0:00 httpd
   144     8 ?          0:00 httpd
   144     9 ?          0:00 httpd
   144    11 ?          0:00 httpd
   144    12 ?          0:00 httpd
   144    13 ?          0:00 httpd
```

Obviously, the Apache Web server daemon (httpd) has many LWPs associated with it. Another way to extract this information is to use the pgrep command, which displays a list of all processes with the same name and displays their PIDs.

```
bash-2.03# pgrep httpd
144
3610
3611
2901
3612
```

```
3603
3604
3605
3607
3608
3609
3606
```

MONITORING SYSTEM RESOURCES

Earlier in this chapter, we examined how to use the ps command to obtain interactive data about the number and type of processes being run on a Solaris system. In order to obtain real-time process information, however, many administrators prefer to use the top program, which is not supplied with Solaris 8 but can be downloaded from http://www.sunfreeware.com.

TIP: If you prefer to build from source, the current top version is available for download from ftp://ftp.groupsys.com/pub/top.

The following is a typical display from the top version:

```
last pid:  6911;  load averages:  0.05,  0.02,  0.02              13:16:05
74 processes:  73 sleeping, 1 on cpu
CPU states:      % idle,      % user,      % kernel,      % iowait,      % swap
Memory: 128M real, 9396K free, 106M swap in use, 137M swap free

   PID USERNAME THR PRI NICE  SIZE    RES STATE    TIME   CPU COMMAND
  6911 root       1  26    4 1264K   884K cpu      0:00  0.44% top
  6614 root       1  46    4 5924K  3780K sleep    0:00  0.13% dtterm
  6640 root       1  36    4 2008K  1456K sleep    0:00  0.02% bash

  6835 root       1  46    4 5940K  3840K sleep    0:00  0.01% dtterm
     1 root       1  58    0  628K   108K sleep    0:00  0.01% init
  6848 root       1  36    4 2004K  1412K sleep    0:00  0.01% bash
   669 root       1  59    0   15M    13M sleep    0:43  0.00% Xsun
  3242 root       1  57    4   15M    12M sleep    0:21  0.00% netscape
   317 root       7  51    0 2900K  2108K sleep    0:04  0.00% nscd
   245 root       3  58    0 1776K  1144K sleep    0:04  0.00% nis_cachemgr
   121 root       1  58    0 4616K   968K sleep    0:03  0.00% skipd
  1539 root       8  59    0 7576K  5064K sleep    0:03  0.00% dtwm
   376 root       1   1   19 2396K   408K sleep    0:01  0.00% sendmail
   298 root       9  58    0   13M  2588K sleep    0:01  0.00% syslogd
  1583 root       1  12    0  760K   540K sleep    0:00  0.00% cat
```

The top display is updated every few seconds so that all values reflect the current state of the system. We can see that at 1:16.05 P.M., the last PID used was 6911, and the 1-, 5-, and 15-minute load averages on the system were 0.05, 0.02, and 0.02, respectively. These values represent 5 percent, 2 percent, and 2 percent system load, respectively, meaning that the system is presently underutilized. A total of 74 processes were active, with all but one process (the top process) sleeping. The system in question has 128MB of physical RAM, of which almost 10MB is free. The system also has a total of 243MB of virtual RAM, of which approximately 106MB is being used. The process display is similar to the columns and values displayed in the preceding ps command examples: many of the processes have a number of LWPs associated with a single process (for example, the name service cache daemon [nscd] has 7 LWPs, while the top program only has one!).

TRACING SYSTEM CALLS

When developing applications, it is often useful to be able to examine what is going on behind the scenes in terms of processes being spawned and system calls being executed. Solaris provides the truss utility that tracks all of these details, which can be displayed interactively or dumped to a file. In addition, truss is often used by system administrators to determine why an application is failing to run. For example, if an application is attempting to read data from a configuration file that does not exist, or if it is trying to locate a library whose location does not exist in the path of the run-time user, then truss can reveal the calls that are failing.

In the following example, we trace the system calls involved in using the ls command. The first system call made is to the execve() function, which is called with the full name of the application that needs to be executed, a pointer to the list of arguments passed to the application (0xEFFFF740), and an environment pointer (0xEFFFF74C). Next, memory mapping operations are performed, followed by four attempts to open the library libc.so.1, which is checked against paths listed in the LD_LIBRARY_PATH environment variable. In this case, the library is not found in the /usr/local/lib/, /usr/openwin/lib/, or /usr/dt/lib/ directory, but is finally located in the /usr/lib directory. At the end of the truss, we can see the names of some of the files in the current directory being printed, including filesync, man, script, and zipinfo:

```
bash-2.03# truss ls
execve("/usr/bin/ls", 0x08047BB0, 0x08047BB8)  argc = 1
open("/dev/zero", O_RDONLY)                     = 3
mmap(0x00000000, 4096, PROT_READ|PROT_WRITE|PROT_EXEC, MAP_PRIVATE, 3, 0) =
0xDFBE1000
xstat(2, "/usr/bin/ls", 0x0804792C)            = 0
sysconfig(_CONFIG_PAGESIZE)                     = 4096
open("/usr/local/lib/libc.so.1", O_RDONLY)     Err#2 ENOENT
open("/usr/openwin/lib/libc.so.1", O_RDONLY)   Err#2 ENOENT
open("/usr/dt/lib/libc.so.1", O_RDONLY)        Err#2 ENOENT
open("/usr/lib/libc.so.1", O_RDONLY)           = 4
fxstat(2, 4, 0x0804776C)                        = 0
mmap(0x00000000, 4096, PROT_READ|PROT_EXEC, MAP_PRIVATE, 4, 0) = 0xDFBDF000
```

```
mmap(0x00000000, 598016, PROT_READ|PROT_EXEC, MAP_PRIVATE, 4, 0) = 0xDFB4C000
mmap(0xDFBD6000, 24392, PROT_READ|PROT_WRITE|PROT_EXEC, MAP_PRIVATE|MAP_FIXED, 4,
561152) = 0xDFBD6000
mmap(0xDFBDC000, 6356, PROT_READ|PROT_WRITE|PROT_EXEC, MAP_PRIVATE|MAP_FIXED, 3,
0) = 0xDFBDC000
close(4)                                        = 0
open("/usr/local/lib/libdl.so.1", O_RDONLY)     Err#2 ENOENT
open("/usr/openwin/lib/libdl.so.1", O_RDONLY)   Err#2 ENOENT
open("/usr/dt/lib/libdl.so.1", O_RDONLY)        Err#2 ENOENT

open("/usr/lib/libdl.so.1", O_RDONLY)           = 4
fxstat(2, 4, 0x0804776C)                        = 0
...
write(1, " f i l e              ".., 59)         = 59
filesync           man              script              zipinfo
write(1, " f i l e s y n c      ".., 62)         = 62
llseek(0, 0, SEEK_CUR)                           = 100860
_exit(0)
```

MULTI-CPU PROCESS MANAGEMENT

In addition to the ps and top commands, Solaris provides several other utilities that can be used to profile system performance on multiple CPU systems, including the mpstat and psrinfo commands, which print real-time process statistics on a per-processor basis and the uptime of individual CPUs, respectively. The mpstat command prints statistics for major faults (mjf) and minor faults (minf) experienced, the number of calls passed between the two CPUs (xcal), the number of interrupts (intr), the percentage of CPU time consumed by user processes (wt), and the percentage of CPU time taken up by system processes (sys).

```
bash-2.03$ mpstat
CPU minf mjf xcal  intr ithr  csw icsw migr smtx  srw syscl  usr sys  wt idl
  0   46   1  205   330  260  114   92   35   97    0    62   30  13   8  48
  1   45   1   35    50  138   89   89   35   94    0   256   35  13   8  45
```

In the following process information (psrinfo) output, we can see that both CPUs came online together and have not ceased operating since that time:

```
bash-2.03$ psrinfo
0       on-line   since 05/16/00 18:35:23
1       on-line   since 05/16/00 18:35:26
```

THE /PROC FILE SYSTEM

One of the key differences between Solaris and other network operating systems is the /proc file system: by representing all of the LWPs running on a system within a file system-like hierarchy, standard system calls may be used to retrieve information about these processes. Each LWP is associated with a PID, which is represented by a directory entry underneath the /proc directory. Each directory then contains a number of different files, in which run-time process data is stored.

The information that can be retrieved from /proc about LWPs is based on files that contain the following information:

- ▼ Address space (as)
- ■ Address space references (pagedata)
- ■ Control file (ctl)
- ■ Credential data (cred)
- ■ Current working directory (cwd)
- ■ File descriptor (fd)
- ■ Local descriptor table (ldt)
- ■ Process information (psinfo)
- ■ Reserved memory map (rmap)
- ■ Root directory (root)
- ■ Signals data (sigact)
- ■ Status file (status)
- ▲ Virtual memory map (map)

Solaris provides a number of different proc tools that may be used to extract process state information from the /proc filesystem in a form that is easily accessible to developers and administrators. In the following sections, we examine each of these tools and how they can be used to identify important run-time information about active LWPs.

pflags

The *pflags* command is used to display tracing flags, the data model, and any pending signals for a specified process. In the following example, the data model is revealed at _ILP32, the tracing flag is PR_PCINVAL, and there are two pending signals:

```
bash-2.03$ pflags 11635
11635:  bash
        data model = _ILP32
  /1:   flags = PR_PCINVAL
  sigmask = 0x00020002,0x00000000
```

pcred

The *pcred* command displays process credentials, which are evaluated by applications with respect to access and file permissions. The credentials that can be determined by the *pcred* command are the effective, real, and saved UIDs, and the effective, real, and saved GIDs of the target process. In the following example, the effective, real, and saved UID of the process is 501, while the effective, real, and saved GID of the process is 100. If the process being executed was setuid or setgid (that is, where the UID or GID was set to be something different than the executing user), then the effective, real, and saved UIDs and GIDs would be distinct:

```
bash-2.03$ pcred 11635
11635:  e/r/suid=501  e/r/sgid=100
        groups: 100 101
```

pmap

The *pmap* command is used to display a map of the address space associated with each process. It can be quite revealing to examine exactly what memory chunks are being consumed by an application and its associated files. In the following example, the Bourne again shell (bash) occupies memory directly; but system libraries, such as the nsl and socket libraries, are called by the shell and, therefore, require memory of their own:

```
bash-2.03$ pmap 11635
11635:  bash
00010000    488K read/exec          /usr/local/bin/bash
00098000     32K read/write/exec    /usr/local/bin/bash
000A0000    144K read/write/exec     [ heap ]
FF100000    656K read/exec          /usr/lib/libc.so.1
FF1B2000     32K read/write/exec    /usr/lib/libc.so.1
FF1BA000      8K read/write/exec     [ anon ]
FF200000    512K read/exec          /usr/lib/libnsl.so.1
FF28E000     40K read/write/exec    /usr/lib/libnsl.so.1
FF298000     32K read/write/exec     [ anon ]
FF2B0000      8K read/write/exec     [ anon ]
FF2C0000     16K read/exec          /usr/lib/locale/en_AU/en_AU.so.2
FF2D2000     16K read/write/exec    /usr/lib/locale/en_AU/en_AU.so.2
FF2E0000     16K read/exec          /usr/platform/sun4u/lib/libc_psr.so.1
FF2F0000     16K read/exec          /usr/lib/libmp.so.2
FF302000      8K read/write/exec    /usr/lib/libmp.so.2
FF320000     32K read/exec          /usr/lib/libsocket.so.1
FF336000     16K read/write/exec    /usr/lib/libsocket.so.1
FF340000    168K read/exec          /usr/lib/libcurses.so.1
FF378000     40K read/write/exec    /usr/lib/libcurses.so.1
FF382000      8K read/write/exec     [ anon ]
FF390000      8K read/exec          /usr/lib/libdl.so.1
FF3A0000      8K read/write/exec     [ anon ]
FF3B0000    120K read/exec          /usr/lib/ld.so.1
FF3DC000      8K read/write/exec    /usr/lib/ld.so.1
FFBEC000     16K read/write/exec     [ stack ]
 total     2448K
```

pldd

The *pldd* command displays a list of the libraries that are being currently used by a process. In combination with the *pmap* command, the *pldd* command provides a complete picture of the libraries that are being used at any one time by a process, and may help to determine which system libraries are retained and backed up, or which file size is monitored to detect Trojan horses in critical libraries.

```
bash-2.03$ pldd 11635
11635:  bash
/usr/lib/libcurses.so.1
/usr/lib/libsocket.so.1
/usr/lib/libnsl.so.1
/usr/lib/libdl.so.1
/usr/lib/libc.so.1
/usr/lib/libmp.so.2
/usr/platform/sun4u/lib/libc_psr.so.1
/usr/lib/locale/en_AU/en_AU.so.2
```

psig

The *psig* command displays all of the signals that are associated with the current process. Entries for the first nine process signals are displayed (for more information about these signals, see Table 8-2 later in the chapter), including SIGHUP, SIGINT, SIGILL, SIGTRAP, SIGABRT, SIGEMT, SIGFPE, and SIGKILL.

```
bash-2.03$ psig 11635
11635:  bash
HUP      caught  0         HUP,INT,ILL,TRAP,ABRT,EMT,FPE,BUS,SEGV,SYS,PIPE,ALRM,TER
M,USR1,USR2,VTALRM,PROF,XCPU,XFSZ,LOST
INT      blocked,caught  0
QUIT     ignored
ILL      caught  0         HUP,INT,ILL,TRAP,ABRT,EMT,FPE,BUS,SEGV,SYS,PIPE,ALRM,TER
M,USR1,USR2,VTALRM,PROF,XCPU,XFSZ,LOST
TRAP     caught  0         HUP,INT,ILL,TRAP,ABRT,EMT,FPE,BUS,SEGV,SYS,PIPE,ALRM,TER
M,USR1,USR2,VTALRM,PROF,XCPU,XFSZ,LOST
ABRT     caught  0         HUP,INT,ILL,TRAP,ABRT,EMT,FPE,BUS,SEGV,SYS,PIPE,ALRM,TER
M,USR1,USR2,VTALRM,PROF,XCPU,XFSZ,LOST
EMT      caught  0         HUP,INT,ILL,TRAP,ABRT,EMT,FPE,BUS,SEGV,SYS,PIPE,ALRM,TER
M,USR1,USR2,VTALRM,PROF,XCPU,XFSZ,LOST
FPE      caught  0         HUP,INT,ILL,TRAP,ABRT,EMT,FPE,BUS,SEGV,SYS,PIPE,ALRM,TER
M,USR1,USR2,VTALRM,PROF,XCPU,XFSZ,LOST
KILL     default
```

pstack

The *pstack* command is used to print a symbolic stack trace for the LWPs associated with the named process. In the following example, the symbols identified include waitid, _waitpid, and waitchld:

```
bash-2.03$ pstack 11635
11635:  bash
 ff198038 waitid    (7, 0, ffbef4c8, 7)
 ff157084 _waitpid (ffffffff, ffbef5ac, 4, 7, ff1b3968, 3d30c) + 54
 0003d30c waitchld (0, 0, ff00, 9a000, 1, 3661) + 78
 0003c4cc wait_for (3661, 0, ffffffff, 0, 0, bafd0) + 150
 00031020 execute_command_internal (0, 9a000, 5, ffffffff, 0, ff198140) + 768
 00031e54 execute_pipeline (bae90, 0, 5, ffffffff, c2b50, 0) + 254
 00032094 execute_connection (bb1d0, 0, ffffffff, ffffffff, c2b50, ab831) + 20c
 0003127c execute_command_internal (0, 0, ffffffff, ffffffff, 0, 0) + 9c4
 0003069c execute_command (bb1d0, 73, 99c00, a6414, bb1d0, a) + 48
 00027144 reader_loop (99c00, 1, 1, 1, ffbefb48, 1) + 1c4
 0002568c main      (0, ffbefa24, ffbefa2c, a0598, 0, 0) + 82c
 00024d7c _start    (0, 0, 0, 0, 0, 0) + 5c
8.5.8. pfiles
```

The *pfiles* command reports details about all of the files that have been opened by a specified process. In the following example, there are several files that have been opened with a number of different file permissions, including 0444, 0620, and 0644.

```
bash-2.03$ pfiles 11635
11635:  bash
  Current rlimit: 64 file descriptors
   0: S_IFCHR mode:0620 dev:136,0 ino:208102 uid:501 gid:7 rdev:24,3
      O_RDWR
   1: S_IFCHR mode:0620 dev:136,0 ino:208102 uid:501 gid:7 rdev:24,3
      O_RDWR
   2: S_IFCHR mode:0620 dev:136,0 ino:208102 uid:501 gid:7 rdev:24,3
      O_RDWR
   3: S_IFDOOR mode:0444 dev:176,0 ino:367 uid:0 gid:0 size:0
      O_RDONLY|O_LARGEFILE FD_CLOEXEC  door to nscd[184]
   4: S_IFDOOR mode:0644 dev:176,0 ino:373 uid:0 gid:0 size:0
      O_RDONLY  door to keyserv[106]
  63: S_IFCHR mode:0620 dev:136,0 ino:208102 uid:501 gid:7 rdev:24,3
      O_RDWR FD_CLOEXEC
```

pwdx

The *pwdx* command is similar to the *pwd* command: it prints the current working directory of the LWP, except that the data is derived from the /proc file system.

```
bash-2.03$ pwdx 11635
11635:  /etc/rc2.d
```

ptree

The *ptree* command displays a hierarchical diagram of all parent processes, with their child processes displayed beneath them. This pictorial representation makes it easy to obtain a quick snapshot of how all processes on the system are related to each other. In the following example, we can see that a telnet session (13961) spawned a Korn shell (ksh) (13963), which then spawned a bash shell (13978), which was then used to execute the *ptree* command (14012). Of course, some processes like rpcbind (104) have no child processes, but are still displayed because they are potential parent processes.

```
bash-2.03$ ptree
47    /usr/lib/devfsadm/devfseventd
49    /usr/lib/devfsadm/devfsadmd
104   /usr/sbin/rpcbind
106   /usr/sbin/keyserv
108   /usr/sbin/nis_cachemgr
150   /usr/sbin/inetd -s
  596   rpc.ttdbserverd
  10966 in.rlogind
    10968 -ksh
  13961 in.telnetd
    13963 -ksh
      13978 bash
        14012 ptree
149   /usr/lib/nfs/lockd
152   /usr/lib/nfs/statd
154   /usr/lib/autofs/automountd
166   /usr/sbin/syslogd
169   /usr/sbin/cron
184   /usr/sbin/nscd -S passwd,yes -S group,yes
190   /usr/lib/lpsched
204   /usr/lib/power/powerd
```

```
213   /usr/sbin/vold
215   /usr/lib/utmpd
219   /usr/local/sbin/sshd
223   /usr/lib/sendmail -bd -q15m
235   /usr/local/samba/bin/smbd -D -l /var/adm/smblogs/log -s /usr/local/samba/
  10483 /usr/local/samba/bin/smbd -D -l /var/adm/smblogs/log -s /usr/local/samb
  10678 /usr/local/samba/bin/smbd -D -l /var/adm/smblogs/log -s /usr/local/samb
```

ptime

The *ptime* command is similar to the time command: it displays the real, user, and system time required to execute a process. The difference between the *ptime* command and *time* command is that the former uses the /proc file system to obtain its data. In the following example, the *ls* command consumed 0.039 real seconds to execute, including 0.003 user seconds and 0.006 system seconds:

```
bash-2.03$ ptime /bin/ls /etc/rc3.d
README          S15nfs.server  S76snmpdx       S77dmi
real            0.039
user            0.003
sys             0.006
```

SENDING SIGNALS

Earlier, we saw that the *psig* command was used to display signals associated with LWPs. In this context, a signal is a message sent between processes by using the interprocess communication facilities of Solaris. Signals allow a process like the shell to communicate with child processes, telling them, among other things, to start, stop, or suspend their activities.

NOTE: These kinds of signals can also be sent directly from C programs, using the signal() system call.

Solaris supports all of the standard System V signal types, as shown in Table 8-2.

Signals are typically used in the shell to manage jobs that have been executed from the shell. In Microsoft Windows, a list of running processes may be obtained from the task manager, and a kill-like signal may be sent by clicking the End Process button. Sending signals within the shell to kill a process performs a similar function; however, there are many different signals that are for different purposes.

In order to launch a number of applications from a single shell, it is necessary to execute each application in the background by including an ampersand on the command line, leaving the shell interface free to issue new commands. This kind of multiprocessing is made possible because all processes that are sent into the background are associated with a specific job number, in addition to their process number. Once a job is in the background, it may be brought into the foreground by using the fg command within the shell

Signal	Code	Action	Description
SIGHUP	1	Exit	Hangup (see termio(7I))
SIGINT	2	Exit	Interrupt (see termio(7I))
SIGQUIT	3	Core	Quit (see termio(7I))
SIGILL	4	Core	Illegal Instruction
SIGTRAP	5	Core	Trace or Breakpoint Trap
SIGABRT	6	Core	Abort
SIGEMT	7	Core	Emulation Trap
SIGFPE	8	Core	Arithmetic Exception
SIGKILL	9	Exit	Killed
SIGBUS	10	Core	Bus Error
SIGSEGV	11	Core	Segmentation Fault
SIGSYS	12	Core	Bad System Call
SIGPIPE	13	Exit	Broken Pipe
SIGALRM	14	Exit	Alarm Clock
SIGTERM	15	Exit	Terminated

Table 8-2. Solaris Process Signals

and by specifying the job number that needs to be foregrounded. An alternative method for sending a process into the background is to launch it normally in the foreground, to suspend the process by sending a signal, and then to use the bg command to send the process into the background.

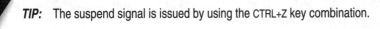

TIP: The suspend signal is issued by using the CTRL+Z key combination.

There are no limits to the number of applications that may be run in the background, but only one application may be run in the foreground at any one time. In the following example, we begin by executing an application in the foreground (bash), and then suspending it and sending it into the background. The process may be brought back into the foreground by using the fg command with the job number, after some other process (ls) has been run in the foreground and has exited:

```
csh% bash
bash-2.03$
^z
csh% bg
[1] 1024
csh% ls
data1.txt      data2.txt      data3.txt
csh% fg
bash-2.03$
```

To send a signal to a process, other than to suspend, background, or foreground, you need to use the kill command. Does the command name sound fatal? Well, signals sent by kill are usually sent to restart a process, terminate a process gracefully, or terminate a process ungracefully. The signal that you decide to send to a process will obviously depend on the urgency of the situation and the integrity of data being operated on by the process in question. For example, a database server process may be restarted by sending a kill –1 command, which should cause it to restart after shutting down gracefully, rereading its configuration file, and restarting. This process could take a long time. Alternatively, if you urgently need to shut down a process and don't care about the consequences, then you could send a kill –9 signal. Finally, if you need to kill a parent and all of its child processes, a kill –15 is often the most appropriate.

As an example, if you wanted to kill the Samba server with a PID 666, then typing

```
server# kill -1 666
```

would restart the Samba server, with its configuration updated from disk. However, if we issued the kill signal to the process with the command

```
server# kill -9 666
```

then the process would be stopped immediately and not restarted automatically.

SUMMARY

In this chapter, we have examined the basics of Solaris process management: how information about processes may be obtained in real time, and how processes may be controlled by using signals. In addition, some key Solaris process innovations, such as the /proc file system, were covered in depth, along with the set of /proc tools that can be used to examine the contents of the /proc file system.

CHAPTER 9

Package Management and Software Installation

All Solaris software that is installed as part of the operating environment comes in an archive known as a *package*. Solaris packages provide an easy way to bring together application binaries, configuration files, and documentation for distribution to other systems. In addition to the Solaris packaging system, Solaris also supports standard UNIX archiving and compression tools, such as tar (tape archive) and compress. In this chapter, we examine how to manage packages by using the standard Solaris packaging tools. Operations reviewed include installing packages, displaying information about packages, removing packages, and creating new packages.

Not all Solaris software is supplied in precompiled binary format, which is why we also examine how to build software distributions from source distributions, such as those provided by the GNU project. Although building large projects from source may initially seem daunting, the use of GNU configure scripts and the Makefile utility make it as easy as typing a few commands. Although building software from sources is time consuming, local optimizations may be performed by manipulating Makefiles, and sources can be checked for Trojan horses if the source of the software is unknown.

PACKAGE TOOLS

Packages are text files that contain an archive of binary applications, configuration files, documentation, or even source code. All files in the Solaris operating environment are now supplied as part of a package, meaning that it is easy to group files associated with different applications. If files are installed without packaging, then it becomes difficult over the years for administrators to remember which files were installed with particular applications. Packaging makes it easy to recognize application dependencies, since all files required by a specific application can be included within the archive. For example, we can use the *pkgchk* command to examine the package properties of a file that has already been installed:

```
bash-2.03# pkgchk -l -p /usr/bin/mkdir
Pathname: /usr/bin/mkdir
Type: regular file
Expected mode: 0555
Expected owner: bin
Expected group: bin
Expected file size (bytes): 9876
Expected sum(1) of contents: 38188
Expected last modification: Oct 06 05:47:55 PM 1998
Referenced by the following packages:
        SUNWcsu
Current status: installed
```

Another advantage of using packages is the standard installation interface provided to install Solaris packages. This means that all of Solaris is installed using the same application (pkgadd or admintool), rather than each application having its own installation program. This reduces coding time and makes it easier for administrators to install software, because only a single interface, with standard options such as overwriting existing files, needs to be learned.

Table 9-1 summarizes the various commands that are used to create, install, and remove packages.

In this section, we will examine how to install new packages, display information about downloaded packages, remove packages that have previously been installed on the system, and create new packages from compiled source code on the local system.

Examining Packages

At any time, we can examine which packages have been installed on a system by using the *pkginfo* command:

```
bash-2.03# pkginfo
application GNUlstdc        libstdc++
application GNUmake         make
system      NCRos86r        NCR Platform Support, OS Functionality (Root)
system      SFWaalib        ASCII Art Library
system      SFWaconf        GNU autoconf
system      SFWamake        GNU automake
system      SFWbison        GNU bison
system      SFWemacs        GNU Emacs
system      SFWflex         GNU flex
system      SFWfvwm         fvwm virtual window manager
system      SFWgcc          GNU compilers
system      SFWgdb          GNU source-level debugger
system      SFWgimp         GNU Image Manipulation Program
system      SFWglib         GLIB - Library of useful routines for C programming
system      SFWgm4          GNU m4
system      SFWgmake        GNU make
system      SFWgs           GNU Ghostscript
system      SFWgsfot        GNU Ghostscript Other Fonts
system      SFWgsfst        GNU Ghostscript Standard Fonts
system      SFWgtk          GTK - The GIMP Toolkit
system      SFWjpg          The Independent JPEG Groups JPEG software
system      SFWlxrun        lxrun
system      SFWmpage        mpage - print multiple pages per sheet
system      SFWmpeg         The MPEG Library
system      SFWncur         ncurses library
system      SFWolvwm        OPEN LOOK Virtual Window Manager
system      SFWpng          PNG reference library
```

This system has quite a few packages installed in both the system and application categories, including lxrun, the application that allows Linux binaries to be executed on Solaris Intel, and Gimp, a graphics-manipulation program.

Command	Description
Pkgproto	Creates a prototype file that specifies the files contained in a package
Pkgmk	Creates a package directory
Pkgadd	Installs a package from a package file
Pkgtrans	Converts a package directory into a file
Pkgrm	Uninstalls a package
Pkgchk	Verifies that a package is valid
Pkginfo	Prints the contents of a package

Table 9-1.   Solaris Packaging Commands

NOTE: There are very few restrictions on the kinds of files and applications that can be installed using packages.

Adding Packages

The best way to learn about adding packages is to use an example: in this section, we downloaded a package from www.sunfreeware.com called gpw-6.94-sol8-intel-local.gz, which is Van Vleck's random password-creation application. Let's look more closely at the package name to determine what software this package contains:

▼ The .gz extension means that the package file has been compressed using gzip after it was created. Other possible extensions include .Z, which indicates compression with the compress program, while a .z extension indicates compression by the pack program.

■ The local string indicates that the package contents will be installed under the directory /usr/local. Other typical installation targets include the /opt directory, where optional packages from the Solaris distribution are also installed.

■ The intel string states that the package is intended for use on Solaris Intel and not Solaris Sparc.

■ The 6.94 string indicates the current software revision level.

▲ The gpw string states the application's name.

To actually use the package file, we first need to decompress it by using the gzip command:

```
bash-2.03# gzip -d gpw-6.94-sol8-intel-local
```

Next, we can examine the contents of the file by using the head command:

```
bash-2.03# head gpw-6.94-sol8-intel-local
# PaCkAgE DaTaStReAm
TVVgpw 1 150
# end of header
NAME=gpw
ARCH=intel
VERSION=6.94
CATEGORY=application
VENDOR=Tom Van Vleck
EMAIL=steve@smc.vnet.net
```

This kind of header exists for all Solaris packages, and it makes it easy to understand what platform a package is designed for, who the vendor is, and who to contact for more information. Now that we have a package, we can begin the installation process by using the pkgadd command. In order to install the gpw-6.94-sol8-intel-local package, we use the following command:

```
bash-2.03# pkgadd -d gpw-6.94-sol8-intel-local
```

We would then see the following output:

```
The following packages are available:

  1  TVVgpw      gpw
                 (sparc) 6.94


Select package(s) you wish to process (or 'all' to process
all packages). (default: all) [?,??,q]: all
```

Pressing ENTER at this point will allow you to proceed with the installation:

```
Processing package instance <TVVgpw> from
</tmp/gpw-6.94-sol8-intel-local>


gpw
```

```
(sparc) 6.94
Tom Van Vleck
Using </usr/local> as the package base directory.
## Processing package information.
## Processing system information.
   2 package pathnames are already properly installed.
## Verifying disk space requirements.
## Checking for conflicts with packages already installed.
## Checking for setuid/setgid programs.

Installing gwp as <TVVgpw>

## Installing part 1 of 1.
/usr/local/bin/gpw
/usr/local/doc/gpw/README.gpw
[ verifying class <none> ]

Installation of <TVVgpw> was successful.
```

After processing package and system information, and checking that the required amount of disk space is available, the pkgadd command copies only two files from the archive to the local filesystem: /usr/local/bin/gpw and /usr/local/doc/gpw/README.gpw.

The package format is very flexible and is independent of the interface used to install specific packages. This means that while administrators from a Linux background may prefer to use the pkgadd command, administrators from a Windows background might find the package administration features of the admintool easier to use. As shown in Figure 9-1, the admintool provides an easy-to-use interface for installing packages, where the following options may be selected from drop-down lists:

▼ Check for existing files

■ Check for existing packages

■ Check for existing partial installations

■ Allow setuid/setgid files to be installed

■ Allow setuid/setgid scripts to be run

■ Check that installation dependencies have been met

■ Check that removal dependencies have been met

■ Check for correct run level

■ Check for sufficient space

■ Display copyrights

▲ Run the installation interactively

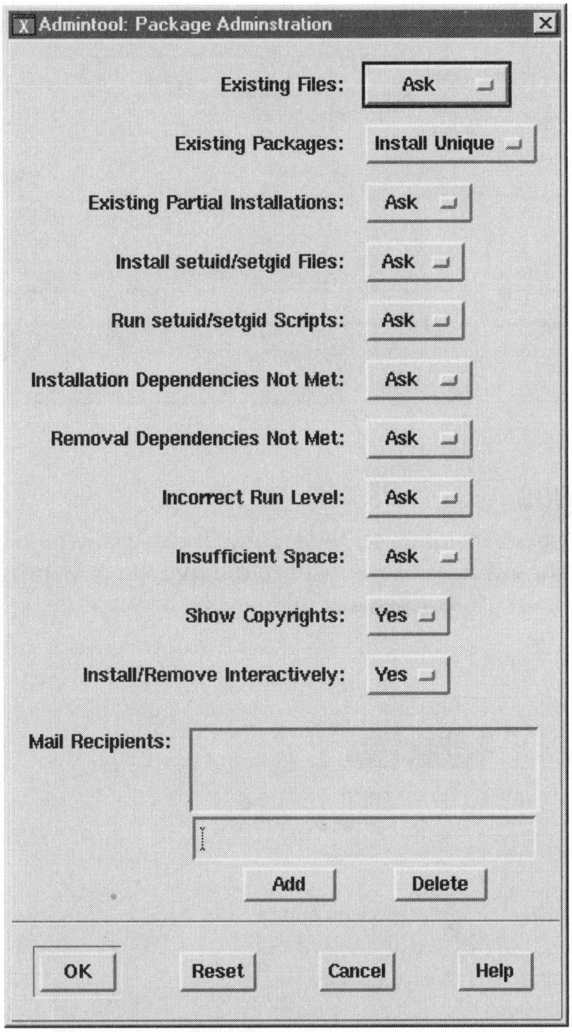

Figure 9-1.   The admintool interface for adding packages

The admintool also allows the administrator to specify an installation source so that packages may be installed directly from a CD-ROM or from a special spooling directory (/var/spool), as shown in Figure 9-2.

Figure 9-2. The admintool interface for selecting the package installation source

Removing Packages

Once a package has been installed on the system, it can easily be removed by using the pkgrm command. For example, if we want to remove the gpw program after it has installed in the /usr/local directory, we would use the command

```
bash-2.03# pkgrm TVVgpw

The following package is currently installed:
   TVVgpw          gpw
                   (sparc) 6.94

Do you want to remove this package? y

## Removing installed package instance <TVVgpw>
## Verifying package dependencies.
## Processing package information.
## Removing pathnames in class <none>
/usr/local/doc/gpw/README.gpw
/usr/local/doc/gpw
/usr/local/doc <shared pathname not removed>
/usr/local/bin/gpw
/usr/local/bin <shared pathname not removed>
## Updating system information.

Removal of <TVVgpw> was successful.
```

This book aims to make learning Solaris easy for experienced administrators of Microsoft Windows and Solaris. In the following pages, we present blueprints for commonly used Solaris networks and systems.

Solaris Administration Blueprints

Table of Contents

Solaris-Based Network

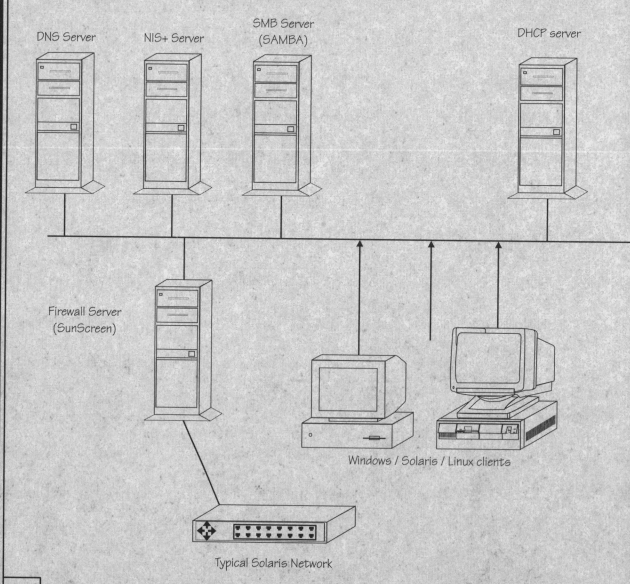

DNS Server

NIS+ Server

SMB Server
(SAMBA)

DHCP server

Firewall Server
(SunScreen)

Windows / Solaris / Linux clients

Typical Solaris Network

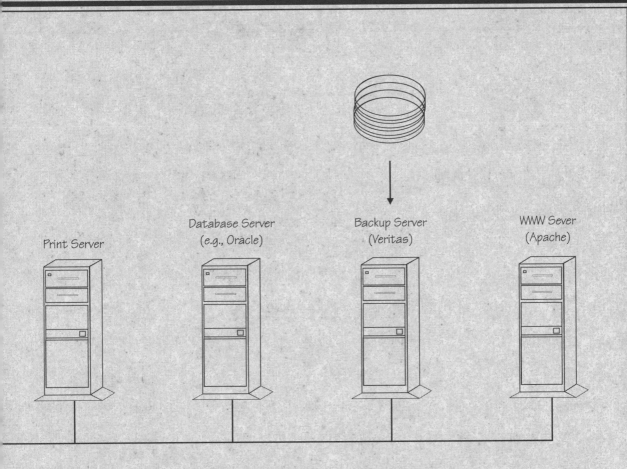

Print Server

Database Server
(e.g., Oracle)

Backup Server
(Veritas)

WWW Sever
(Apache)

A Solaris network supports Solaris, Linux, Windows and Macintosh clients, by providing services which support SMB file sharing, SMB printing, HTTP-compliant webserving, enterprise database services, backup systems with PC clients, and DNS and DHCP support

3

Linux vs. Windows NT/2000-Based Network

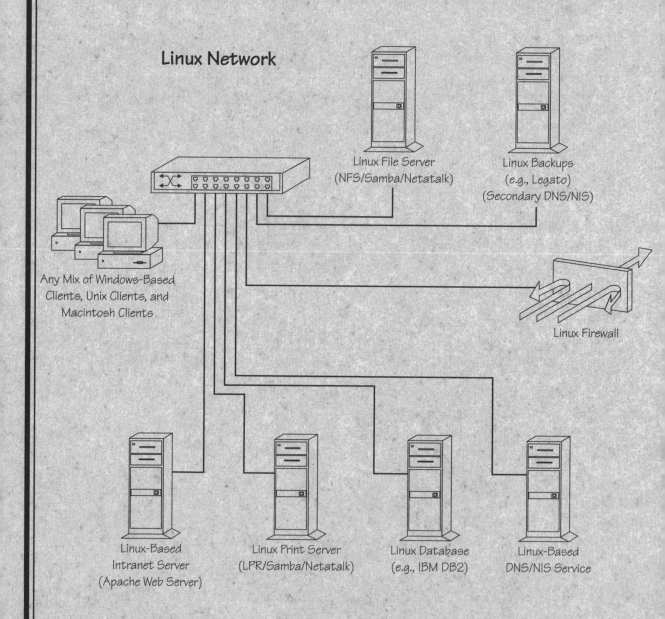

Linux Network

Linux File Server
(NFS/Samba/Netatalk)

Linux Backups
(e.g., Legato)
(Secondary DNS/NIS)

Any Mix of Windows-Based
Clients, Unix Clients, and
Macintosh Clients

Linux Firewall

Linux-Based
Intranet Server
(Apache Web Server)

Linux Print Server
(LPR/Samba/Netatalk)

Linux Database
(e.g., IBM DB2)

Linux-Based
DNS/NIS Service

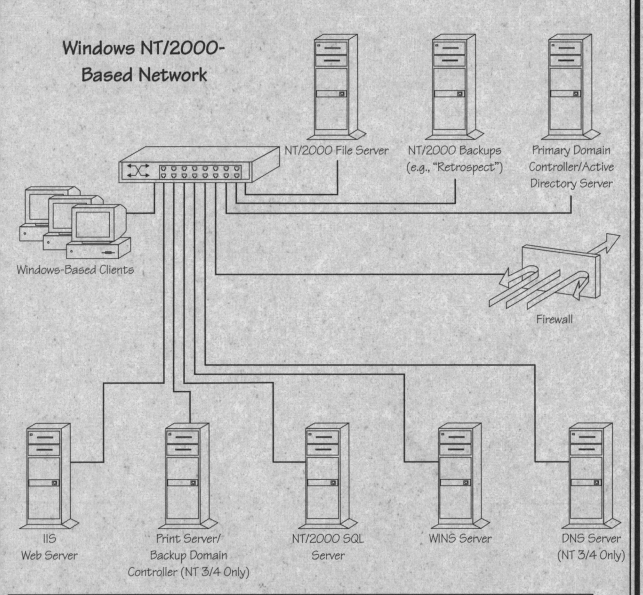

Windows NT/2000-Based Network

NT/2000 File Server

NT/2000 Backups (e.g., "Retrospect")

Primary Domain Controller/Active Directory Server

Windows-Based Clients

Firewall

IIS Web Server

Print Server/ Backup Domain Controller (NT 3/4 Only)

NT/2000 SQL Server

WINS Server

DNS Server (NT 3/4 Only)

Both networks are functionally equivalent: whatever NT/2000 can do, Linux can do as well. However, Linux can typically do this with fewer servers and can support Windows and Macintosh clients as well. This is accomplished with the Samba package for working with Windows clients, and Netatalk for working with Macintosh clients.

5

Linux vs. Windows NT/2000 Boot Process

The Linux Boot Process

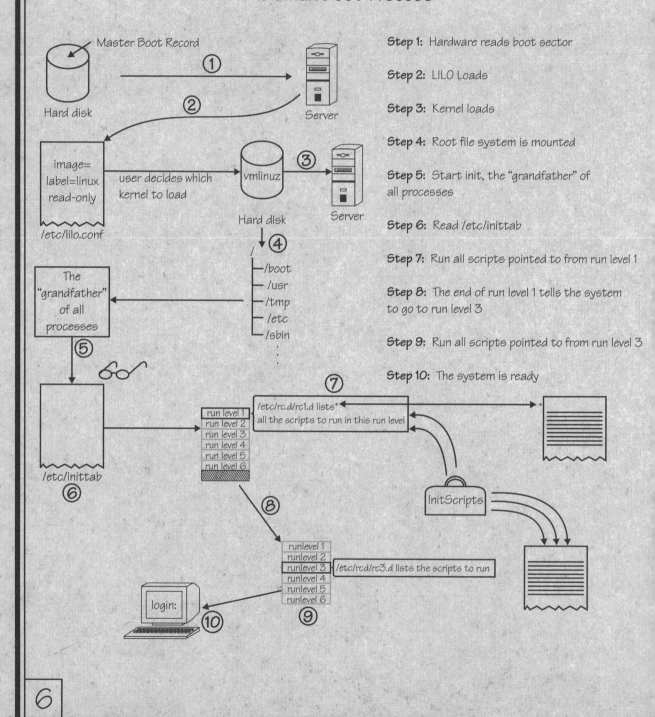

Step 1: Hardware reads boot sector

Step 2: LILO Loads

Step 3: Kernel loads

Step 4: Root file system is mounted

Step 5: Start init, the "grandfather" of all processes

Step 6: Read /etc/inittab

Step 7: Run all scripts pointed to from run level 1

Step 8: The end of run level 1 tells the system to go to run level 3

Step 9: Run all scripts pointed to from run level 3

Step 10: The system is ready

The NT/2000 Boot Process

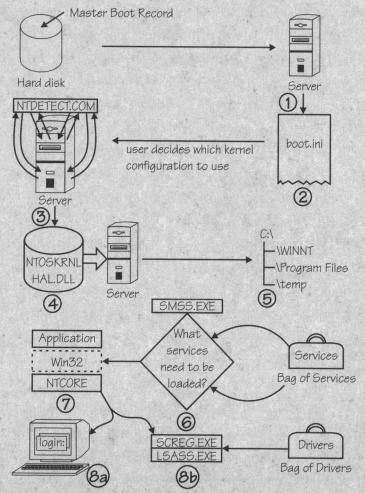

Master Boot Record

Hard disk

Server

NTDETECT.COM

user decides which kernel
configuration to use

boot.ini

Server

NTOSKRNL
HAL.DLL

Server

C:\
└ \WINNT
└ \Program Files
└ \temp

SMSS.EXE

Application

Win32

NTCORE

What
services
need to be
loaded?

Services

Bag of Services

login:

SCREG.EXE
LSASS.EXE

Drivers

Bag of Drivers

Step 1: Hardware reads boot sector

Step 2: NTLDR loads and reads BOOT.INI
(similar to LILO and /etc/lilo.conf)

Step 3: NTDETECT runs to probe the
hardware

Step 4: NTLDR loads NTOSKRNL.EXE, the
NT/2000 kernel and HAL.DLL, the Hardware
Abstraction Layer

Step 5: NT/2000 makes the C: drive available

Step 6: SMSS.EXE, the services manager
gets loaded. This reads the registry and
determines which services should be loaded

Step 7: The WIN32 system is loaded

Step 8a: Winlogon, which provides login
service, is started

Step 8b: SCREG, the Scan Registry Tool,
and LSASS, the Local Security Authority, are
started along with Winlogon. SCREG starts
auto loading drivers. The system is ready

The NT/2000 and Linux boot processes do strike parallels between each other.
If you understand the reasoning behind one, you can understand the reasoning
behind the other. They both start by reading the MBR, and they both end by
providing login: prompts for the user. Noteworthy points of similarity are the
NTLDR and LILO. They look different and act different, but in the end they do
exactly the same thing. NTDETECT, NTOSKRNL, and HAL are three components
that are all done in the Linux kernel. Although SMSS and init take very different
paths, their goal is one and the same: getting the necessary services started.

7

Solaris Boot Process

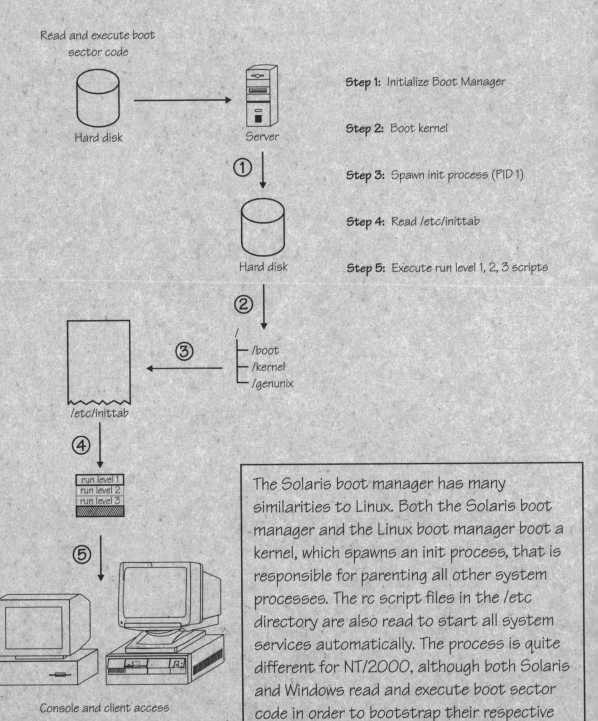

Read and execute boot sector code

Hard disk

Server

Hard disk

/
├── /boot
├── /kernel
└── /genunix

/etc/inittab

run level 1
run level 2
run level 3

Console and client access

Step 1: Initialize Boot Manager

Step 2: Boot kernel

Step 3: Spawn init process (PID 1)

Step 4: Read /etc/inittab

Step 5: Execute run level 1, 2, 3 scripts

The Solaris boot manager has many similarities to Linux. Both the Solaris boot manager and the Linux boot manager boot a kernel, which spawns an init process, that is responsible for parenting all other system processes. The rc script files in the /etc directory are also read to start all system services automatically. The process is quite different for NT/2000, although both Solaris and Windows read and execute boot sector code in order to bootstrap their respective systems.

8

The pkgrm command also operates in an interactive mode, where multiple packages may be removed using the same interface:

```
bash-2.03# pkgrm

The following packages are available:
  1  GNUlstdc      libstdc++
                   (i86pc) 2.8.1.1
  2  GNUmake       make
                   (i86pc) 3.77
  3  NCRos86r      NCR Platform Support, OS Functionality (Root)
                   (i386) 1.1.0,REV=1998.08.07.12.41
  4  SFWaalib      ASCII Art Library
                   (i386) 1.2,REV=1999.11.25.13.32
  5  SFWaconf      GNU autoconf
                   (i386) 2.13,REV=1999.11.25.13.32
  6  SFWamake      GNU automake
                   (i386) 1.4,REV=1999.11.25.13.32
  7  SFWbison      GNU bison
                   (i386) 1.28,REV=1999.11.25.13.32
  8  SFWemacs      GNU Emacs
                   (i386) 20.4,REV=1999.11.25.13.32
  9  SFWflex       GNU flex
                   (i386) 2.5.4,REV=1999.11.25.13.32
 10  SFWfvwm       fvwm virtual window manager
                   (i386) 2.2.2,REV=1999.11.25.13.32

... 288 more menu choices to follow;
<RETURN> for more choices, <CTRL-D> to stop display:
```

At this point, the number of the package that you wish to remove may be entered.

Creating Packages

Creating a package is easy if you follow a few simple steps. In this example, we compile and build the Apache Web server from source, and then customize for our local environment.

TIP: Instead of rebuilding Apache on every Web server from source, if we compile it once and then distribute it as a package to all of the local systems, we can save valuable time and CPU cycles.

The first step is to download the Apache source and build it according to the instructions supplied with the source package. After compiling the application into the source directory (for example, /usr/local/apache), local customizations should be made as appropriate. Next, we need to create the two files that are used to create the package: the prototype file, which contains a list of all the files to be stored in the archive and their file permissions; and the pkginfo file, which contains all of the descriptive information regarding the package, including the creator, architecture, and base directory.

To create the pkginfo file, we use the find command to create a list of all of the files below the base directory of the package installation. In the case of Apache, the base directory will be /usr/local/apache, if that is where the source was compiled:

```
bash-2.03# cd /usr/local/apache
bash-2.03# find . -print | pkgproto > prototype
```

This command will produce the prototype file in /usr/local/apache. It contains entries such as these:

```
d none bin 0755 nobody nobody
f none bin/httpd 0755 nobody nobody
f none bin/ab 0755 nobody nobody
f none bin/htpasswd 0755 nobody nobody
f none bin/htdigest 0755 nobody nobody
f none bin/apachectl 0755 nobody nobody
f none bin/dbmmanage 0755 nobody nobody
f none bin/logresolve 0755 nobody nobody
f none bin/rotatelogs 0755 nobody nobody
f none bin/apxs 0755 nobody nobody
d none libexec 0755 nobody nobody
d none man 0755 nobody nobody
d none man/man1 0755 nobody nobody
f none man/man1/htpasswd.1 0644 nobody nobody
f none man/man1/htdigest.1 0644 nobody nobody
f none man/man1/dbmmanage.1 0644 nobody nobody
d none man/man8 0755 nobody nobody
f none man/man8/httpd.8 0644 nobody nobody
f none man/man8/ab.8 0644 nobody nobody
f none man/man8/apachectl.8 0644 nobody nobody
```

Each entry is either an f (file) or a d (directory), with the octal permissions code and user and group ownership also displayed. After verifying that all of the files that you wish to package are listed in the pkginfo file, you then need to manually add an entry for the pkginfo file itself into the pkginfo file:

```
i pkginfo=./pkginfo
```

The pkginfo contains a description of your archive. Adding this entry will ensure that the pkginfo file is added to the archive. Next, you need to actually create the pkginfo file in the base directory of the package (for example, /usr/local/apache). The file needs to contain several customized entries, such as the following:

```
PKG="EDapache"
NAME="Apache"
ARCH="sparc"
VERSION="1.3.12"
CATEGORY="application"
VENDOR="Ethos Development Pty Ltd"
EMAIL="paul@ethos-development.com"
PSTAMP="Paul Watters"
BASEDIR="/usr/local/apache"
CLASSES="none"
```

Although these tags are self-explanatory, Table 9-2 contains a description of each of the options available for the pkginfo file.

Command	Description
PKG	The name of the package
NAME	The name of the application contained in the package
ARCH	The target system architecture (sparc or intel)
VERSION	The package version number
CATEGORY	Either an application or a system application
VENDOR	The supplier of the software
EMAIL	The e-mail address of the vendor
PSTAMP	The package builder's name
BASEDIR	The base directory where package files will be installed

Table 9-2.   Command Options for pkginfo Files

Once the pkginfo file has been created, we're ready to begin building the package. After changing into the package base directory, the following command should be executed:

```
bash-2.03# pkgmk -o -r /usr/local/apache
## Building pkgmap from package prototype file.
## Processing pkginfo file.
## Attempting to volumize 362 entries in pkgmap.
part  1 -- 6631 blocks, 363 entries
## Packaging one part.
/var/spool/pkg/EDapache/pkgmap
/var/spool/pkg/EDapache/pkginfo
/var/spool/pkg/EDapache/reloc/.bash_history
/var/spool/pkg/EDapache/reloc/.profile
/var/spool/pkg/EDapache/reloc/bin/ab
/var/spool/pkg/EDapache/reloc/bin/apachectl
/var/spool/pkg/EDapache/reloc/bin/apxs
/var/spool/pkg/EDapache/reloc/bin/dbmmanage
/var/spool/pkg/EDapache/reloc/bin/htdigest
/var/spool/pkg/EDapache/reloc/bin/htpasswd
```

A directory called "Edapache" will have been created in /var/spool/pkg, containing a copy of the source files, which are now ready to be packaged in the archive by using the pkgtrans command:

```
bash-2.03# cd /var/spool/pkg
bash-2.03# pkgtrans -s /var/spool/pkg /tmp/EDapache-1.3.12.tar

The following packages are available:
  1  EDapache      Apache
                   (sparc) 1.3.12

Select package(s) you wish to process (or 'all' to process
all packages). (default: all) [?,??,q]:
You need to select the EDapache package to be built by pressing the
Enter key:
Transferring <EDapache> package instance
```

The package (EDapache-1.3.12) has now been successfully created in the /tmp directory:

```
-rw-r--r--   1 root      other    3163648 Oct 18 10:09 EDapache-1.3.12
```

In order to reduce the size of the package file, the gzip command may be used to compress its contents:

```
bash-2.03# gzip EDapache-1.3.12
bash-2.03# ls -l EDapache-1.3.12.gz
-rw-r--r--   1 root      other       816536 Oct 18 10:09
EDapache-1.3.12.gz
```

The compressed package file may now be distributed to other users and installed using the pkgadd command.

ARCHIVING TOOLS

Using packages gives administrators the greatest level of control over how an archive is distributed and installed; however, creating the pkginfo and prototype files can be a time-consuming process for creating packages that are simply designed for a tape backup or for temporary use. In this case, it may be appropriate to create a tape archive, also called a "tar file," rather than a package.

TIP: Another advantage to using a tar file is that it can be distributed to colleagues using operating systems other than Solaris (such as Microsoft Windows and Linux) and unpacked with ease.

Creating a tar file is easy: for example, to create a tape archive containing the Apache distribution that we packaged in the previous section, we would use the command

```
bash-2.03# tar cvf /tmp/apache.tar *
a bin/ 0K
a bin/httpd 494K
a bin/ab 28K
a bin/htpasswd 39K
a bin/htdigest 16K
a bin/apachectl 7K
a bin/dbmmanage 7K
a bin/logresolve 10K
a bin/rotatelogs 7K
a bin/apxs 20K
a cgi-bin/ 0K
a cgi-bin/hello.c 1K
a cgi-bin/printenv 1K
```

```
a cgi-bin/test-cgi 1K
a cgi-bin/hello 7K
a cgi-bin/hello.cgi 7K
a cgi-bin/hello.sh 1K
a cgi-bin/prt 1K
a conf/ 0K
```

The cvf part of the tar command is an abbreviation of "create file using verbose mode and copy to a file." Originally, the tar command was designed to copy archive to a tape device; thus, an extra modifier is required to specify that the archive should be copied to a file instead. Table 9-3 summarizes the main modifiers used with the tar command.

The tar command takes either function letters or function modifiers. The main function letters used to specify operations with tar are given in the following sections.

Modifier	Name	Description
b	Blocking Factor	Specifies the number of tape blocks to be used during each read and write operation
e	Error	Specifies that tar should exit if an error is detected
f	File	Writes output to a file, rather than a tape drive
h	Symbolic Links	Archive files accessed through symbolic links
i	Ignore	Checksum errors are ignored during archive creation
k	Kilobytes	Specifies the size of the archive in kilobytes. If an archive is larger than this size, it will be split across multiple archives
o	Ownership	Modifies the user and group ownership of all archive files to the current owner
v	Verbose	Displays information about all files extracted or added to the archive

Table 9-3.   Tape Archive Function Modifiers

Replace Files

The function letter **r** is used to replace files in an existing archive. The named files are written at the end of the tar file, as shown in this example:

```
bash-2.03# tar rvf /tmp/apache.tar *
a bin/ 0K
a bin/httpd 494K
a bin/ab 28K
a bin/htpasswd 39K
a bin/htdigest 16K
a bin/apachectl 7K
a bin/dbmmanage 7K
a bin/logresolve 10K
a bin/rotatelogs 7K
a bin/apxs 20K
a cgi-bin/ 0K
a cgi-bin/hello.c 1K
a cgi-bin/printenv 1K
a cgi-bin/test-cgi 1K
a cgi-bin/hello 7K
a cgi-bin/hello.cgi 7K
a cgi-bin/hello.sh 1K
a cgi-bin/prt 1K
```

Table of Contents

The function letter **t** is used to extract the table of contents of an archive, which lists all of the files that have been archived within a specific file, as shown in this example:

```
bash-2.03# tar tvf /tmp/apache.tar *
drwxr-xr-x 1003/10          0 Mar 30 13:45 2000 bin/
-rwxr-xr-x 1003/10     505536 Mar 30 13:45 2000 bin/httpd
-rwxr-xr-x 1003/10      27896 Mar 30 13:45 2000 bin/ab
-rwxr-xr-x 1003/10      38916 Mar 30 13:45 2000 bin/htpasswd
-rwxr-xr-x 1003/10      16332 Mar 30 13:45 2000 bin/htdigest
-rwxr-xr-x 1003/10       7065 Mar 30 13:45 2000 bin/apachectl
-rwxr-xr-x 1003/10       6456 Mar 30 13:45 2000 bin/dbmmanage
```

```
-rwxr-xr-x 1003/10      9448 Mar 30 13:45 2000 bin/logresolve
-rwxr-xr-x 1003/10      6696 Mar 30 13:45 2000 bin/rotatelogs
-rwxr-xr-x 1003/10     20449 Mar 30 13:45 2000 bin/apxs
drwxr-xr-x 1003/10         0 Oct  5 14:36 2000 cgi-bin/
-rwxr-xr-x 1003/10       279 Oct  5 15:04 2000 cgi-bin/hello.c
-rwxr-xr-x 1003/10       274 Mar 30 13:45 2000 cgi-bin/printenv
-rwxr-xr-x 1003/10       757 Mar 30 13:45 2000 cgi-bin/test-cgi
-rwxr-xr-x 1003/10      7032 Oct  5 15:04 2000 cgi-bin/hello
-rwxr-xr-x 1003/10      6888 Oct  5 14:31 2000 cgi-bin/hello.cgi
-rwxr-xr-x 1003/10       179 Oct  5 15:09 2000 cgi-bin/hello.sh
-rwxr-xr-x 1003/10       274 Oct  5 14:34 2000 cgi-bin/prt
```

Extract Files

The function letter **x** is used to extract files from an archive, as shown in this example:

```
bash-2.03# tar xvf apache.tar
x bin, 0 bytes, 0 tape blocks
x bin/httpd, 505536 bytes, 988 tape blocks
x bin/ab, 27896 bytes, 55 tape blocks
x bin/htpasswd, 38916 bytes, 77 tape blocks
x bin/htdigest, 16332 bytes, 32 tape blocks
x bin/apachectl, 7065 bytes, 14 tape blocks
x bin/dbmmanage, 6456 bytes, 13 tape blocks
x bin/logresolve, 9448 bytes, 19 tape blocks
x bin/rotatelogs, 6696 bytes, 14 tape blocks
x bin/apxs, 20449 bytes, 40 tape blocks
x cgi-bin, 0 bytes, 0 tape blocks
x cgi-bin/hello.c, 279 bytes, 1 tape blocks
x cgi-bin/printenv, 274 bytes, 1 tape blocks
x cgi-bin/test-cgi, 757 bytes, 2 tape blocks
x cgi-bin/hello, 7032 bytes, 14 tape blocks
x cgi-bin/hello.cgi, 6888 bytes, 14 tape blocks
x cgi-bin/hello.sh, 179 bytes, 1 tape blocks
x cgi-bin/prt, 274 bytes, 1 tape blocks
```

COMPILING SOURCE DISTRIBUTIONS

In the previous sections, we examined how to create a Solaris package from compiled source and how to create a tape archive from source. However, many administrators who are new to Solaris may be unable to compile from source without some guidance. In this section, we walk through the compilation and building of a GNU package (the Text Utilities) and explain the procedure for downloading, configuring, compiling, and installing software supplied as source.

One of the most confusing aspects of building applications under Solaris is the lack of a C compiler, which is considered standard across all UNIX systems. Solaris used to have a C compiler; however, it is now sold separately by Sun Microsystems. Fortunately, the GNU C compiler (gcc) is completely free and can be installed for Solaris. A chicken-and-egg problem now presents itself, however: if you need a C compiler to build applications, how is it possible to build a compiler without already having a compiler?

Fortunately, you can download and install a precompiled package containing the gcc from www.sunfreeware.com for both Intel and Sparc platforms. You will need to download the following files:

ftp://ftp.sunfreeware.com/pub/freeware/sparc/8/gcc-2.95.2-sol8-sparc-local.gz

ftp://ftp.sunfreeware.com/pub/freeware/sparc9/glib-1.2.8-sol8-sparc-local.gz

Check that you have obtained the latest version of the gcc software before installing it. Once you have a compiler installed, you can check that it works by typing the following command:

```
bash-2.03# gcc -v
Reading specs from
/usr/local/lib/gcc-lib/i386-pc-solaris2.8/2.95.2/specs
gcc version 2.95.2 19991024 (release)
```

Alternatively, try writing a simple Hello World program to see whether the source code can be compiled and linked appropriately:

```
bash-2.03# cat hello.c
#include <stdio.h>
main()
{
        printf("Hello World!\n");
}
gcc hello.c -o hello
bash-2.03# ./hello
Hello World!
```

If you received any errors at this point, check that gcc can be found in your PATH environment variable and that the LD_LIBRARY_PATH contains the path to the gcc libraries directory.

Next, you will need to download the source code that you wish to compile. In this case, we downloaded the text utilities source file from www.gnu.org (textutils-2.0.tar.gz). The first step is to uncompress the source file:

```
gzip -d textutils-2.0.tar.gz
```

The tar file should then be extracted using the command

```
tar xvf textutils-2.0.tar
```

After changing to the source directory

```
cd textutils-2.0
```

the following files should be visible:

```
bash-2.03# ls
ABOUT-NLS       config.sub      INSTALL         Makefile.maint  src
acconfig.h      configure       install-sh      man             stamp-h.in
aclocal.m4      configure.in    intl            missing         tests
AUTHORS         COPYING         lib             mkinstalldirs   THANKS
ChangeLog       djgpp           m4              NEWS            TODO
config.guess    doc             Makefile.am     po
config.h.in     GNUmakefile     Makefile.in     README
```

Most source distributions are accompanied by a README file that contains all of the information that you need to know about a program, including what it's designed to do, what platforms it can be executed upon, and what its system requirements are. The first step in installing a source distribution is to read the README file:

```
bash-2.03# more README
These are the GNU text file (actually, file contents) processing
utilities. Most of these programs have significant advantages over
their Unix counterparts, such as greater speed, additional options,
and fewer arbitrary limits.

The programs that can be built with this package are: cat, cksum, comm,
csplit, cut, expand, fmt, fold, head, join, md5sum, nl, od, paste, pr,
ptx, sort, split, sum, tac, tail, tr, tsort, unexpand, uniq, and wc.

See the file NEWS for a list of major changes in the current release.

See the file INSTALL for compilation and installation instructions.
```

As the README file suggests, reading the INSTALL file will instruct you (often step by step) how to configure, make, and install the source package:

```
bash-2.03# more INSTALL
Basic Installation
==================

These are generic installation instructions.

The 'configure' shell script attempts to guess correct values for
various system-dependent variables used during compilation. It uses
those values to create a 'Makefile' in each directory of the package.
It may also create one or more '.h' files containing system-dependent
definitions. Finally, it creates a shell script 'config.status' that
you can run in the future to recreate the current configuration, a file
```

'config.cache' that saves the results of its tests to speed up
reconfiguring, and a file 'config.log' containing compiler output
(useful mainly for debugging 'configure').

To create an appropriate Makefile that matches the local system architecture, you must
run the configure script, which has been generated by the GNU Configure utility:

```
bash-2.03# ./configure
creating cache ./config.cache
checking host system type... i386-pc-solaris2.8
checking for a BSD compatible install... ./install-sh -c
checking whether build environment is sane... yes
checking whether make sets ${MAKE}... yes
checking for working aclocal... missing
checking for working autoconf... missing
checking for working automake... missing
checking for working autoheader... missing
checking for working makeinfo... missing
checking for gnutar... no
checking for gtar... no
```

After several pages of checking that various packages exist on your system, a series of
Makefiles will then be created:

```
creating ./config.status
creating Makefile
creating doc/Makefile
creating intl/Makefile
creating lib/Makefile
creating man/Makefile
creating m4/Makefile
creating po/Makefile.in
creating src/Makefile
creating djgpp/Makefile
```

If no problems are encountered, the source can then be built by using the make command:

```
bash-2.03# make
make  all-recursive
make[1]: Entering directory '/tmp/textutils-2.0'
Making all in lib
make[2]: Entering directory '/tmp/textutils-2.0/lib'
gcc -DHAVE_CONFIG_H -I. -I. -I.. -I.. -I. -I../intl     -g -O2 -c argmatch.c
gcc -DHAVE_CONFIG_H -I. -I. -I.. -I.. -I. -I../intl     -g -O2 -c closeout.c
gcc -DHAVE_CONFIG_H -I. -I. -I.. -I.. -I. -I../intl     -g -O2 -c diacrit.c
gcc -DHAVE_CONFIG_H -I. -I. -I.. -I.. -I. -I../intl     -g -O2 -c full-write.c
gcc -DHAVE_CONFIG_H -I. -I. -I.. -I.. -I. -I../intl     -g -O2 -c getopt.c
gcc -DHAVE_CONFIG_H -I. -I. -I.. -I.. -I. -I../intl     -g -O2 -c getopt1.c
gcc -DHAVE_CONFIG_H -I. -I. -I.. -I.. -I. -I../intl     -g -O2 -c hard-locale.c
gcc -DHAVE_CONFIG_H -I. -I. -I.. -I.. -I. -I../intl     -g -O2 -c human.c
```

```
gcc -DHAVE_CONFIG_H -I. -I. -I.. -I.. -I. -I../intl    -g -O2 -c linebuffer.c
gcc -DHAVE_CONFIG_H -I. -I. -I.. -I.. -I. -I../intl    -g -O2 -c long-options.c
gcc -DHAVE_CONFIG_H -I. -I. -I.. -I.. -I. -I../intl    -g -O2 -c md5.c
gcc -DHAVE_CONFIG_H -I. -I. -I.. -I.. -I. -I../intl    -g -O2 -c memcasecmp.c
gcc -DHAVE_CONFIG_H -I. -I. -I.. -I.. -I. -I../intl    -g -O2 -c memcoll.c
gcc -DHAVE_CONFIG_H -I. -I. -I.. -I.. -I. -I../intl    -g -O2 -c obstack.c
gcc -DHAVE_CONFIG_H -I. -I. -I.. -I.. -I. -I../intl    -g -O2 -c quotearg.c
gcc -DHAVE_CONFIG_H -I. -I. -I.. -I.. -I. -I../intl    -g -O2 -c readtokens.c
gcc -DHAVE_CONFIG_H -I. -I. -I.. -I.. -I. -I../intl    -g -O2 -c safe-read.c
gcc -DHAVE_CONFIG_H -I. -I. -I.. -I.. -I. -I../intl    -g -O2 -c version-etc.c
gcc -DHAVE_CONFIG_H -I. -I. -I.. -I.. -I. -I../intl    -g -O2 -c xmalloc.c
gcc -DHAVE_CONFIG_H -I. -I. -I.. -I.. -I. -I../intl    -g -O2 -c xstrdup.c
gcc -DHAVE_CONFIG_H -I. -I. -I.. -I.. -I. -I../intl    -g -O2 -c xstrtod.c
gcc -DHAVE_CONFIG_H -I. -I. -I.. -I.. -I. -I../intl    -g -O2 -c xstrtol.c
gcc -DHAVE_CONFIG_H -I. -I. -I.. -I.. -I. -I../intl    -g -O2 -c xstrtoul.c
gcc -DHAVE_CONFIG_H -I. -I. -I.. -I.. -I. -I../intl    -g -O2 -c xstrtoumax.c
gcc -DHAVE_CONFIG_H -I. -I. -I.. -I.. -I. -I../intl    -g -O2 -c mktime.c
gcc -DHAVE_CONFIG_H -I. -I. -I.. -I.. -I. -I../intl    -g -O2 -c strtoumax.c
gcc -DHAVE_CONFIG_H -I. -I. -I.. -I.. -I. -I../intl    -g -O2 -c regex.c
gcc -DHAVE_CONFIG_H -I. -I. -I.. -I.. -I. -I../intl    -g -O2 -c getline.c
gcc -DHAVE_CONFIG_H -I. -I. -I.. -I.. -I. -I../intl    -g -O2 -c stpcpy.c
gcc -DHAVE_CONFIG_H -I. -I. -I.. -I.. -I. -I../intl    -g -O2 -c error.c
```

After several pages of building, the source should be compiled, and you may then install the binaries:

```
bash-2.03# make install
Making install in lib
make[1]: Entering directory '/tmp/textutils-2.0/lib'
make[2]: Entering directory '/tmp/textutils-2.0/lib'
make[2]: Nothing to be done for 'install-exec-am'.
make[2]: Nothing to be done for 'install-data-am'.
make[2]: Leaving directory '/tmp/textutils-2.0/lib'
make[1]: Leaving directory '/tmp/textutils-2.0/lib'
Making install in intl
make[1]: Entering directory '/tmp/textutils-2.0/intl'
if test "textutils" = "gettext" \
  && test '' = 'intl-compat.o'; then \
  if test -r ./mkinstalldirs; then \
    ./mkinstalldirs /usr/local/lib /usr/local/include; \
  else \
    ../mkinstalldirs /usr/local/lib /usr/local/include; \
  fi; \
```

SUMMARY

In this chapter, we examined how to build software from source and distribute it to other users and systems, by using the Solaris package format and the platform-independent tape archive. All of the software supplied with Solaris (including system patches available from www.sunsolve.com) is now packaged using the package format; and many sites will build software from source, create a package from these binaries, and install a package, rather than copy files to the system directories manually. This makes it easier to manage dependencies and to understand how files are related to one another. Alternatively, the tar command is a quick and easy way to archive files, which can be distributed to colleagues using Microsoft Windows and Linux.

PART III

Managing Internet
Services

CHAPTER 10

Electronic Mail

Electronic mail (e-mail) is one of the foundation services offered by Solaris and other network operating systems such as Linux and Microsoft Windows. Solaris e-mail services allow the delivery of local messages for single stand-alone systems, as well as company intranets and the global Internet. Solaris provides both Mail Transport Agents (MTAs), such as the popular sendmail program, and Mail User Agents (MUAs), using a network protocol to retrieve mail from a Solaris server for display on a client system. For example, a Windows-based client network might use Qualcomm's Eudora program to read and send e-mail through the Internet by connecting to a Solaris sendmail server, using the Post Office Protocol (POP). Alternatively, in a mixed platform environment, client systems may all use the Program for Internet News and E-mail (pine) ("pine is not elm"), making use of the more advanced Internet Message Access Protocol (IMAP). A further option for Solaris users is to access their e-mail using one of the standard command-line clients, such as mailx or elm, both of which can be executed from any of the standard shells.

TIP: These clients do not require support for a third-party mail exchange protocol between client and server, as mail folders are accessed directly from the local filesystem.

In this chapter, we will examine how to configure and install Graphical User Interface (GUI) and command-line e-mail clients, as well as review the major configuration options for the sendmail MTA. We will also examine how to retrieve and install the latest version of sendmail, which may well fix bugs that have been identified in the vendor-supplied version provided by Sun. For example, the current revision of sendmail (sendmail 8.11.0) fixes an error with rmail that allowed overflowing of the recipient list, and it includes explicit support for Solaris 8 for the first time. Finally, we will explore some of the options for sending multimedia objects through e-mail messages by using metamail.

UNDERSTANDING E-MAIL SERVICES

Until relatively recently, many vendor-specific electronic messaging products used nonstandard, proprietary protocols for exchanging data. For example, UNIX systems often transferred e-mail using the UNIX-to-UNIX Copy Program (UUCP), while some systems designed for Microsoft Windows made use of the X.400 protocol. This made the exchange of e-mail between systems problematic because systems implementing these protocols could not communicate with each other.

RFC 821 suggested that a standard protocol should be implemented on all e-mail servers, and that the protocol should use a human-friendly command set, so that troubleshooting could be simplified.

NOTE: The Simple Mail Transfer Protocol (SMTP) is now the world standard for exchanging e-mail between hosts, although a more enhanced version of SMTP (known as ESMTP, or Extended Simple Mail Transfer Protocol) is supported by many different MTAs. SMTP delivery problems can be easily diagnosed by using standard tools like telnet.

The exchange of e-mail messages using SMTP operates using a client-server model: The sender of a message passes the text of the message, along with a recipient address to the local MTA. That MTA then establishes a client session with a remote mail server (possibly via an intermediate mail relay). After verifying that mail for the recipient can be accepted by the remote server, the server then requests that the message be passed, and it is delivered locally by a mail handler (like procmail). Delivery is then acknowledged by the server to the client. The exchange of data between the local e-mail client and the local MTA usually occurs by using POP or IMAP. The exchange of data between the local MTA and the remote MTA uses SMTP. Finally, the exchange of data between the remote MTA and the local e-mail client occurs by again using POP or IMAP. This configuration is shown in Figure 10-1.

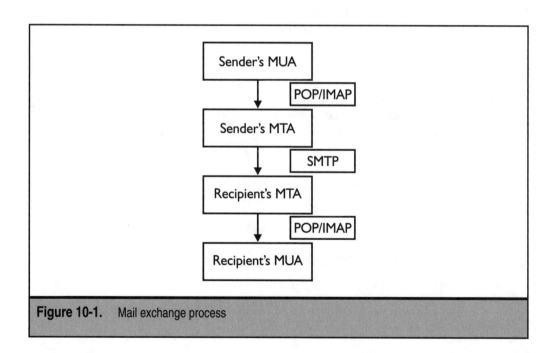

Figure 10-1. Mail exchange process

Sending and Receiving Mail

Let's look at a concrete example of how mail exchange works in real life. Imagine that the local user pwatters@cassowary.paulwatters.com wanted to send a message to the remote user sukhdev@ethos-development.com. We can examine the process as it occurs by using the test facility of the sendmail program.

TIP: Although we wouldn't normally use sendmail in this way as a normal mail client, we can more easily examine the steps taken when mail is being transferred.

```
cassowary:pwatters> /usr/lib/sendmail -v sukhdev@ethos-development.com
< message.txt
```

This command takes the contents of the file message.txt, and sends it using sendmail to the remote user sukhdev@ethos-development.com.

```
sukhdev@ethos-development.com... Connecting to
mail-incoming.hostsave.com (TCP)...
```

The following line documents the attempt to make a TCP connection on port 25 from cassowary.paulwatters.com to the mail host for ethos-development.com.

```
220 lmg.ahnet.net ZMailer Server 2.99.38 #1 ESMTP ready at Mon, 23 Oct
2000 19:16:43 -0700
```

The following line is the acknowledgement returned from the mail server for the domain ethos-development.com (lmg.ahnet.net). It also announces that the remote server speaks ESMTP as well as SMTP, and that the current local time is 7:16 P.M.

```
>>> HELO cassowary.paulwatters.com
```

The HELO command allows the local sender's host to be identified to the recipient's mail host.

```
250 lmg.ahnet.net Hello cassowary.paulwatters.com
```

The remote host acknowledges the local host.

```
>>> MAIL From:<pwatters@cassowary.paulwatters.com>
```

The local server announces a message from the local user pwatters@cassowary.paulwatters.com by using the MAIL command.

```
250 (verified non-local) Ok
```

The remote server acknowledges receipt of the request, and notes that the sending user is remote relative to its domain.

```
>>> RCPT To:<sukhdev@ethos-development.com>
```

The local server sends the RCPT command, which indicates the remote user to whom the mail is addressed.

```
250 (verified local) Ok
```

The remote server acknowledges receipt of the request, and notes that that the recipient is a user local to the domain.

```
>>> DATA
```

The DATA command is sent by the client to indicate that the message data will be now be uploaded.

```
354 Start mail input; end with <CRLF>.<CRLF>
```

The message upload request is acknowledged, and the message body may now be sent.

```
testing
>>> .
```

The message body is transferred and terminated by a single period at the end of the message.

```
250 2.6.0 Roger
```

Receipt of the message is acknowledged.

```
>>> QUIT
```

The local server requests a disconnection.

```
221 2.0.0 lmg.ahnet.net Out
sukhdev@ethos-development.com... Sent
```

The remote server accepts the disconnection and confirms delivery of the message.

Using a Relay

Of course, not every Solaris system is going to have a mail system running locally. In large organizations, a typical Internet gateway system may perform packet filtering, Web serving, and mail serving for an entire site. This means that mail originating from Solaris systems, in this situation, must be relayed through the gateway system. The domains that are accepted for relaying are defined in the /etc/mail/relay-domains file; thus, relaying mail for a local domain would require the local domain name to be entered.

TIP: If remote sites within an organization wish to use the mail relay, their domain names may also be entered.

Mail relaying used to be the norm with respect to handling e-mail. However, the growth of unsolicited commercial e-mail (or SPAM), which abuses the e-mail relay system, has seen relaying decrease in popularity over the years. The following example uses a mail relay, but mirrors the direct mail approach shown earlier:

```
cassowary % /usr/lib/sendmail -v sukhdev@ethos-development.com <
message.txt
sukhdev@ethos-development.com... Connecting to relay.paulwatters.com.
via relay...
220 relay.paulwatters.com ESMTP Sendmail 8.11.0/8.11.0; Tue, 17 Oct
2000 13:14:19 +1100 (EST)
>>> EHLO cassowary.paulwatters.com
250- relay.paulwatters.com Hello pwatters@cassowary.paulwatters.com
[10.64.128.16], pleased to meet you
250-EXPN
250-VERB
250-8BITMIME
250-SIZE 10000000
250-DSN
250-ONEX
250-ETRN
250-XUSR
250 HELP
>>> MAIL From:<pwatters@cassowary.paulwatters.com> SIZE=6819
250 <pwatters@cassowary.paulwatters.com >... Sender ok
>>> RCPT To:<sukhdev@ethos-development.com>
250 <sukhdev@ethos-development.com>... Recipient ok
>>> DATA
354 Enter mail, end with "." on a line by itself
message
>>> .
250 NAA13535 Message accepted for delivery
sukhdev@ethos-development.com... Sent (NAA13535 Message accepted for
delivery)
Closing connection to relay.paulwatters.com.
>>> QUIT
221 relay.paulwatters.com closing connection
```

Manual Testing

If you're not on a system that has sendmail (such as a Windows NT server), but you want to test whether a mail connection can be made with a remote host, the telnet utility may be used to make a connection directly on the SMTP port (port 25). Using this technique, SMTP commands and message data may be entered manually and transmitted to the remote server. The remote server doesn't really care that you aren't a sendmail server; it simply responds to the commands it receives. In the following example, a message is manually entered by a user from the system sender to a user on the system receiver. After exchanging the usual acknowledgements, the sender and recipients are identified and the message data is forwarded. The message is delivered and acknowledged:

```
sender:10:01:pwatters> telnet receiver 25
Trying 204.68.12.36 ...
Connected to receiver.ethos-development.com.
Escape character is '^]'.
220 receiver.ethos-development.com ESMTP Sendmail 8.8.8+Sun/8.8.8; Wed,
25 Oct 2000 09:53:55 +1000 (EST)
EHLO sender
250-receiver.ethos-development.com Hello sender.ethos-development.com
[203.64.12.36], pleased to meet you
MAIL FROM: <pwatters@sender.ethos-development.com>
250 <pwatters@sender.ethos-development.com>... Sender ok
RCPT TO: <pwatters@receiver.ethos-development.com>
250 <pwatters@receiver.ethos-development.com>... Recipient ok
DATA
354 Enter mail, end with "." on a line by itself
Testing...
1
2
3
.
250 MAA18353 Message accepted for delivery
QUIT
221 receiver.ethos-development.com closing connection
Connection closed by foreign host.
```

SMTP and ESMTP

Using the manual testing technique, it is possible to enter all SMTP and ESMTP commands interactively. In order to determine which SMTP commands are available from a particular server, you can simply type the HELP command once connected:

```
HELP
214-This is Sendmail version 8.8.8+Sun
```

```
214-Topics:
214-    HELO    EHLO    MAIL    RCPT    DATA
214-    RSET    NOOP    QUIT    HELP    VRFY
214-    EXPN    VERB    ETRN    DSN
214-For more info use "HELP <topic>".
214-To report bugs in the implementation contact Sun Microsystems
214-Technical Support.
214-For local information send email to Postmaster at your site.
214 End of HELP info
```

These SMTP commands perform the following functions:

▼ **DATA**   Indicates that the data being sent is message data

■ **EHLO**   Indicates that the host speaks ESMTP

■ **EXPN**   Lists local members of a mailing list

■ **HELO**   Indicates that the host speaks SMTP

■ **MAIL**   Contains the address of the sender

■ **QUIT**   Ends a session

■ **RCPT**   Contains the address of the recipient

▲ **VRFY**   Verifies that a recipient address exists as a user account on the system.

Alternatively, if you want to obtain a list of ESMTP commands that are available from an ESMTP server, you must use the EHLO command:

```
sender:12:08:pwatters> telnet receiver 25
Trying 204.68.12.36 ...
Connected to receiver.paulwatters.com.
Escape character is '^]'.
220 receiver.paulwatters.com ESMTP Sendmail 8.8.8+Sun/8.8.8; Tue, 24
Oct 2000 12:00:29 +1000 (EST)
EHLO sender
250-receiver.paulwatters.com Hello sender.paulwatters.com
[203.64.12.36], pleased to meet you
250-EXPN
250-VERB
250-8BITMIME
250-SIZE
250-DSN
250-ONEX
250-ETRN
250-XUSR
250 HELP
```

These commands perform the following functions:

▼ **8BITMIME**   Uses 8-bit data

■ **DSN**   Delivery status notification

■ **ETRN**   Initializes remote message queue

■ **ONEX**   Single message transmission

■ **SIZE**   Declares size of message

■ **VERB**   Starts verbose mode

▲ **XUSR**   Submits data for user

Understanding E-mail Headers

Every time an MTA generates a mail message and transmits it to a recipient at another system, a set of identifying lines are added to the top of the message. These identifiers are known as *headers,* and they can be used to trace the origin of a message, the date it was sent, and more. Historically, headers could be trusted to give authoritative information; however, since many MTAs do not prevent fake or incorrect information from being inserted into e-mail headers, companies that generate large volumes of SPAM mail are able to exploit the open nature of sendmail and other standard MTAs.

There are a number of mandatory and optional e-mail headers that must be generated in order to ensure that a message is delivered correctly. These include

▼ **Content-Length**   Contains the number of lines in the message

■ **Content-Type**   States the Multipurpose Internet Mail Extensions (MIME) type that the body of the message contains. This may be text, or any one of the multimedia types supported by MIME.

■ **Date**   Contains the time and date that the message was received

■ **From**   States the name and e-mail address of the sender

■ **Message-Id**   Contains a random string that uniquely identifies the message

■ **Received**   States how the message was received, including the name of the mail server

■ **Subject**   Contains the topic of the message, as inserted by the sender

▲ **To**   States the name and e-mail address of the recipient

These headers are used by mail clients to extract data for display about every message in each user's mailbox, as follows:

```
From Jane_Brownlow@mcgraw-hill.com Tue Oct 24 12:34 EST 2000
Received: from birds.paulwatters.com (root@birds.paulwatters.com
[137.111.216.
12])
```

```
        by emu.birds.paulwatters.com (8.9.1a/8.9.1) with ESMTP id
MAA07956
        for <pwatters@emu.birds.paulwatters.com>; Tue, 24 Oct 2000
12:34:23 +1100
(EST)
Received: from animals.paulwatters.com (animals.paulwatters.com
[137.111.1.11])
        by birds.paulwatters.com (8.8.8/8.8.8) with ESMTP id MAA12227
        for <pwatters@cassowary.paulwatters.com>; Tue, 24 Oct 2000
12:34:20 +1100 (EST)
Received: from corp148mr.mcgraw-hill.com (corp148mr.mcgraw-hill.com
[198.45.18.1
31])
        by animals.paulwatters.com (8.10.2/8.10.2) with ESMTP id
e9O1YAP07532
        for <pwatters@paulwatters.com>; Tue, 24 Oct 2000 12:34:11 +1100
(EST)
Message-Id: <200010240134.e9O1YAP07532@animals.paulwatters.com>
From: "Brownlow, Jane" <Jane_Brownlow@mcgraw-hill.com>
To: WATTERS Paul Andrew <pwatters@cassowary.paulwatters.com>
Subject: Solaris Book
Date: Sat, 21 Oct 2000 21:29:15 -0400
MIME-Version: 1.0
X-Mailer: Internet Mail Service (5.5.2650.21)
Content-Type: text/plain;
        charset="iso-8859-1"
Content-Length: 956
[Charset iso-8859-1 unsupported, filtering to ASCII...]
[You can also use 'v' to view or save this part.]
```

These headers indicate that the user Jane_Brownlow from the domain mcgraw-hill.com sent a message on 21 October at 9:29 P.M to pwatters in the domain paulwatters.com. The message passed through several relay hosts, including animals.paulwatters.com, to arrive at the destination. The message had 956 lines, had the subject "Solaris Book," and had the message ID 200010240134.e9O1YAP07532. The MIME version was 1.0, using the ISO-8859-1 character set and the content-type text/plain.

MIME

The MIME type found in the previous example is typical of mail messages that contain plain text. MIME were first outlined in RFC 2045, with the intention of providing a text-based encoding system by which multimedia documents (word processing documents, images, and movies) could be transmitted by e-mail. MIME are required because e-mail is an inherently text-based system for passing messages—but there are few restrictions on the content of these messages. This freedom can often be seen at work in the viruses that are passed through e-mail to infect host systems, where the mail reader has superuser privileges (a good reason never to execute an attachment as root!).

> **NOTE:** Since many MTAs have limitations on the size of messages that are accepted, MIME have the ability to encode multimedia content across different messages of a fixed size so that they may be reassembled at the destination.

As we saw above, there is a MIME type associated with every e-mail message, which is stated in the header with a line such as

```
Content-Type: text/plain; charset=us-ascii
```

The preceding line of code specifies that the message was composed in and sent in plain text and that there are no multimedia attachments.

Now, let's have a look at a message that does contain an encoded multimedia attachment:

```
This is a multi-part message in MIME format.

------=_NextPart_000_0008_01C033D3.0A46C4E0
Content-Type: text/plain;
        charset="iso-8859-1"
Content-Transfer-Encoding: 7bit

Gentlemen, Please find attached our current business plan.

-Paul W.

------=_NextPart_000_0008_01C033D3.0A46C4E0
Content-Type: application/msword;
        name="business.doc"
Content-Disposition: attachment;
        filename="business.doc"
Content-Transfer-Encoding: base64
```

```
0M8R4KGxGuEAAAAAAAAAAAAAAAAAAAAAPgADAP7/CQAGAAAAAAAAAAAAAABAAAAQgAAAAAAAAA
EAAARAAAAAEAAAD+////AAAAAEEAAAD//////////////////////////////////////////
//////////////////////////////////////////////////////////////////////////
//////////////////////////////////////////////////////////////////////////
//////////////////////////////////////////////////////////////////////////
//////////////////////////////////////////////////////////////////////////
```

As we can see from the MIME encoding definitions, this message contains an attachment of the application/msword format (Microsoft Word), which is called business.doc.

In order to extract the Microsoft Word file from the message, we need to either use a mail
program that handles MIME, or save the file as text and run it through metamail:

```
bash-2.03$ metamail business.meta
This message contains data in an unrecognized format,
application/msword,
which can either be viewed as text or written to a file.

What do you want to do with the application/msword data?
1 -- See it as text
2 -- Write it to a file
3 -- Just skip it

2
Please enter the name of a file to which the data should be written
(Default: business.doc) >
Wrote file business.doc
```

SENDMAIL

Sendmail is the MTA supplied with Solaris. It has been developed over many years on all
UNIX platforms and is, therefore, easily configurable across platforms. However, sendmail
configuration by hand is one of the most difficult operations performed by a Solaris system
administrator (it's no surprise that the O'Reilly Sendmail book is many hundreds of pages
long). We won't attempt to cover the complete configuration of sendmail, such as the rewriting rules, in this section. Instead, we will focus on some of key functions of sendmail,
especially supporting aliases and local mailing groups. In addition, we examine how to obtain the latest sendmail distribution, which you can build locally.

TIP: You may wish to do this if a major security flaw is exposed and a vendor-supplied patch
is not available.

Sendmail Distribution

The latest version of sendmail is always available at ftp.sendmail.org. In addition to the
source files, the ftp.sendmail.org login banner always contains the latest information
about the current sendmail release:

```
ftp ftp.sendmail.org
Connected to ftp.sendmail.org.
220 vorlon.sendmail.com FTP server (Version 6.00) ready.
Name (ftp.sendmail.org:paul): ftp
331 Guest login ok, send your email address as password.
```

Password:
230- This directory contains sendmail 8.x source distributions. Those
230- interested in mirroring the sendmail distribution tree should read
230- the MIRROR file in this directory.
230-
230- The latest version is available in sendmail.8.11.1.tar.{Z,gz,sig} --
230- the .Z file is compressed, the .gz file is the same bits gzipped, and
230- the .sig file is a PGP signature for the uncompressed bits in either
230- of the first two files. Please take ONLY ONE of the .Z or .gz files.
230-
230- A commercial version of sendmail 8.11 including precompiled ``push
230- button'' install and a GUI configuration and administration interface
230- is available from Sendmail, Inc. (see http://www.sendmail.com/
230- for details).
230-
230- Older versions are in sendmail.${VER}.tar.{Z,gz,sig}. Except for the
230- latest, these are unsupported by the Sendmail.ORG crew. The status of
230- various interesting ${VER}s is:
230-
230- 8.11.1 Many mostly minor fixes -- see RELEASE_NOTES for details.
230- 8.11.0 Add support for STARTTLS and SASL encryption. Some minor fixes.
230- 8.10.2 Detect and avoid a serious Linux capabilities security bug.
230- 8.10.1 Bug fix release: avoids dangerous AIX 4.X linker behavior
230- 8.10.0 Major new release: multiple queues, SMTP authentication, LDAP
230-   integration, IPv6, enhanced SMTP status codes, and more.
230- 8.9.3 header denial of service fixed. Minor fixes.
230- 8.9.2 accept() denial of service attack on Linux systems fixed.
230-   Berkeley DB 2.X integration fixed. Many minor fixes.
230- 8.9.1 Many mostly minor fixes -- see RELEASE_NOTES for details. Clarify
230-   LICENSE terms.
230- 8.9.0 New major release with focus on spam control with many other
230-   new features -- see RELEASE_NOTES for details.
230- 8.8.8 Many mostly minor fixes -- see RELEASE_NOTES for details.
230- 8.8.7 Fixes a few problems where 8.8.6 was too paranoid.
230- 8.8.6 Many mostly minor fixes -- see RELEASE_NOTES for details.
230- 8.8.5 Fixes a critical security bug as well as several small problems.
230- 8.8.4 Fixes several small bugs, including a potential security problem
230-   on some systems allowing local users to get the group permissions
230-   of other users, as well as a rare denial-of-service attack. It
230-   also fixes the "HUP to smtpd" root shell vulnerability in 8.8.2
230-   described in CERT Advisory CA-96.24.
230-
230- The following versions are unsupported:
230- 8.7.6 A security patch for CERT Advisory CA-96.20.
230-   *** SEE ALSO sendmail.8.7.6.patch.1 ***
230-   This version DOES NOT FIX the "HUP to smtpd" root shell problem.
230-
230- There is NO 8.6.* patch for CA-96.20. 8.6 is not supported, not secure,
230- and should not be run on any network-connected machine.

```
230-
230- Since sendmail 8.11 and later includes hooks to cryptography, the
230- following information from OpenSSL applies to sendmail as well.
230-
230- PLEASE REMEMBER THAT EXPORT/IMPORT AND/OR USE OF STRONG CRYPTOGRAPHY
230- SOFTWARE, PROVIDING CRYPTOGRAPHY HOOKS OR EVEN JUST COMMUNICATING
230- TECHNICAL DETAILS ABOUT CRYPTOGRAPHY SOFTWARE IS ILLEGAL IN SOME
230- PARTS OF THE WORLD.  SO, WHEN YOU IMPORT THIS PACKAGE TO YOUR
230- COUNTRY, RE-DISTRIBUTE IT FROM THERE OR EVEN JUST EMAIL TECHNICAL
230- SUGGESTIONS OR EVEN SOURCE PATCHES TO THE AUTHOR OR OTHER PEOPLE
230- YOU ARE STRONGLY ADVISED TO PAY CLOSE ATTENTION TO ANY EXPORT/IMPORT
230- AND/OR USE LAWS WHICH APPLY TO YOU. THE AUTHORS ARE NOT LIABLE FOR
230- ANY VIOLATIONS YOU MAKE HERE. SO BE CAREFUL, IT IS YOUR RESPONSIBILITY.
230-
230- $Revision: 8.5.4.6 $, Last updated $Date: 2000/09/28 18:04:28 $
230 Guest login ok, access restrictions apply.
```

The main issue to consider when upgrading sendmail is the compatibility of your existing sendmail.cf configuration file with the requirements of the new installation. Fortunately, most of the tags have remained constant throughout the various incarnations of sendmail, especially since the first V8 release.

sendmail.cf

The sendmail.cf file is divided into a number of sections:

▼ **Local Info**   Contains configuration information for the local host, including its official domain name, masquerading name, administrator's e-mail address, and mail hub

■ **Options**   Records sendmail-specific parameters, including 7- and 8-bit mail support, maximum message sizes, alias database options, and error modes

■ **Message Precedences**   Defines the delivery priorities of different message types

■ **Trusted Users**   Defines the list of users who may administer the mail system

■ **Format of Headers**   Defines exactly how the headers discussed in a previous section are to be printed on each e-mail

▲ **Rewriting Rules**   Determine how to find the host on which a particular user account exists, so that a message may be successfully delivered

Each line in the sendmail.cf file contains a comment, a rule, a macro, an option, or a mail header. The most common commands used in a sendmail.cf file are

▼ **C**   Prefixes a macro with more than one option

■ **D**   Prefixes a simple macro

■ **E**   Defines an environment variable

- **H** Prefixes a mail header used to construct a mail message
- **M** Contains the name and path of the local mail delivery agent (for example, the standard /bin/mail or the third-party procmail)
- **O** Prefixes an option
- **P** Specifies the message precedence options
- **R** Specifies an address rewriting rule
- ▲ **S** Prefixes the definition of a rule set

Aliases

One of the useful features of Solaris mail handling is the ability to define aliases that correspond to single users or mailing lists composed of multiple users. For example, the user pwatters might also be the local Web master, so it makes sense to redirect all mail sent to webmaster@some.host.com to pwatters@some.host.com using the aliases database. Similarly, if the users paul, maya, miki, and moppet were members of the coffee drinking club, club announcements could be sent to coffee@some.host.com if there was an alias set up in the database containing the users paul, maya, miki, and moppet.

In order to set up an alias for the Web master account just discussed, we would enter the following line into the /etc/aliases database:

```
webmaster: pwatters
```

Similarly, for the coffee group, we would enter the following line into the /etc/aliases database:

```
coffee: paul, maya, miki and moppet
```

NOTE: When a new alias like this is inserted into the aliases database, the newaliases command must be executed in order to update the files /etc/aliases.dir and /etc/aliases/pag.

A sample /etc/aliases file looks like this:

```
 Postmaster: root
MAILER-DAEMON: postmaster
nobody: /dev/null
staff:paul, brad, sukhdev, graham
solaris-users: paul, tim
help:          tim
helpdesk:      tim
support:          moppet
manager:          miki
```

NOTE: When new aliases are added, the newaliases command should be run to ensure that the aliases database is updated.

MAIL CLIENTS

There are several different mail clients available for Solaris. Some mail clients, such as mailx, elm, and pine, access mail directly from the local filesystem. Other clients, such as Netscape Mail, may POP or IMAP to retrieve their messages from a remote server. One advantage of using a mail client on the local mail server is that users can take advantage of programs like vacation, which sends a courtesy message to all users who e-mail you when you are away from your office.

NOTE: GUI clients are often the easiest to use for novice users or for those who wish to read their mail from a remote system.

Like other System V operating systems, Solaris has the standard mailx client, which may be executed by typing **mailx** on the command line. The mailx program has only basic message-handling facilities, and many users prefer to use a full-featured system such as pine or elm. One advantage of using a command-line client is that mail can be easily accessed by making a telnet (or secure shell) connection to the mail server, and spawning the client from the shell. This means that a simple terminal is all that is required to read e-mail, rather than bandwidth hungry graphics.

The elm interface is shown in Figure 10-2. Many of the single keystroke commands used in elm are listed on the bottom half of the screen. The elm program can be executed from the command line by using the command

```
bash-2.04$ elm
```

From the main menu, a number of different commands may be used to send mail, retrieve messages, and use mail folders, as listed here:

▼ **a**   Inserts an alias for the user associated with the current message into the address book

■ **b**   Returns the messages to the sender appearing as if delivery was unsuccessful

■ **c**   Opens a folder

■ **d**   Removes the current message from the mailbox

■ **f**   Sends the current message to another user

■ **m**   Makes a new mail message

■ **o**   Changes options that are saved in ~/.elm/elmrc

- **p**   Sends the current message to a printer
- **q**   Quits elm
- **s**   Copies the current message to a folder
▲ **x**   Exits elm

Most users include a signature that includes contact information at the end of their e-mail messages. My signature is

```
--
Paul A. Watters
Project Manager, Ethos Development
Sydney NSW Australia
paul@ethos-development.com
```

This signature should be contained in the file ~/.signature.

An alternative to using elm is a GUI-based client, such as Netscape Mail (Figure 10-3). This interface is particularly useful for administrators and users from a Microsoft Windows background, as they will already be familiar with the interface and commands used by the Netscape Mail client.

```
    Mailbox is '/var/mail/pwatters' with 21 messages [ELM 2.4ME+ PL71 (25)]

 O  21  Oct 23 owner-auug-announc (38)    [AUUG-ANNOUNCE]: AUUG Security Symposi




       |=pipe, !=shell, ?=help, <n>=set current to n, /=search pattern
 a)lias, C)opy, c)hange folder, d)elete, e)dit, f)orward, g)roup reply, m)ail,
  n)ext, o)ptions, p)rint, q)uit, r)eply, s)ave, t)ag, u)ndelete, or e(x)it

Command: █
```

Figure 10-2.   The elm mail user agent

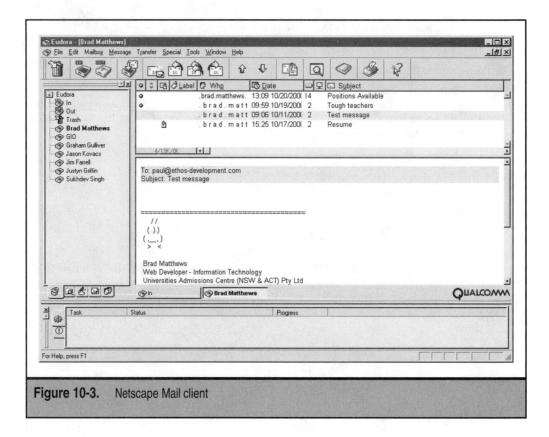

Figure 10-3. Netscape Mail client

SUMMARY

In this chapter, we have examined how e-mail is sent and received by the sendmail MTA. In addition, we have explored how sendmail is configured and how e-mail is accessed by using client applications. For more information on sendmail, readers should consult the sendmail FAQ, which is available at http://www.sendmail.org.

CHAPTER 11

Domain Name Service (DNS)

E very computer that is connected to the Internet must have an IP address, which identifies it uniquely within the network. For example, 192.18.97.241 is the IP address of the Web server at Sun. IP addresses are hard for humans to remember, and the addresses don't adequately describe the network on which a host resides. Thus, by examining the Fully Qualified Domain Name (FQDN) of 192.18.97.241—www.sun.com—it's immediately obvious that the host www lies within the sun.com domain. The mapping between human-friendly domain names and machine-friendly IP addresses is performed by a distributed naming service, known as the Domain Name Service (DNS).

Although Solaris has its own domain management system, known as the Network Information Service (NIS), described in Chapter 17, support is also provided for DNS. In this chapter, we examine how DNS servers manage records of network addresses and how this information can be accessed by Solaris applications. In addition, we examine how to build and configure the latest version of the Berkeley Internet Daemon (BIND) from source, if security issues leave your existing BIND service vulnerable to attack.

OVERVIEW OF DNS

The DNS is a distributed database that maps human-friendly hostnames, such as paulwatters.com, to a numeric IP address, such as 209.67.50.203. In the early days of the Internet, a single file was distributed to various hosts (called the HOSTS.TXT file), which contained an address-to-hostname mapping for known hosts. Administrators would periodically upload a list of any new hosts added to their networks, after which they would download the latest version of the file; however, as the Internet grew, maintaining this text database became impossible. A new system for mapping addresses to names was proposed in RFC 882 and 883, and was based on information about local networks being sourced from designated servers for each network. It should be noted that Solaris retains a variant of the HOSTS.TXT file in the form of the /etc/hosts file, which is typically used to map IP addresses to domain names for the localhost, as well as key network servers, such as the local domain name server. This is very useful in situations in which the DNS server is not responding while the system is being booted.

TIP: The /etc/hosts file is consulted by some applications, such as the syslog daemon (syslogd), to determine which host (the loghost) should be used for system logging.

The following is an example of a typical /etc/hosts file:

```
127.0.0.1          localhost
204.168.14.23  leura              leura.paulwatters.com          loghost
204.168.14.24  katoomba           katoomba.paulwatters.com
```

Of course, only key servers and the localhost should be defined in the /etc/hosts file; otherwise, any change in IP address for that server will not be reflected in the value resolved from /etc/hosts.

DNS works on a simple client/server principle: if you know the name of a DNS server for a particular network, you will be able to retrieve the IP address of any host within that network. For example, if I know that the name server for the domain paulwatters.com is dns20.register.com, I can contact dns20.register.com to retrieve the address for any host within the paulwatters.com domain (including www.paulwatters.com or 209.67.50.203). Of course, this leads us to a classic chicken-and-egg problem: how would we know, in the first instance, that the DNS server dns20.register.com was authoritative for paulwatters. com? The answer is that, in the same way that the addresses of all hosts under paulwatters.com are managed by the DNS server, the address of the DNS server is managed by the next server along the chain—in this case, the DNS server for the .com domain.

There are many such top-level domains now in existence, including the traditional .edu (educational organizations), .com (commercial organizations), and .net (network) top-level domains. Most countries now have their own top-level domains, including .au (Australia), .ck (Cook Islands), and .ph (Philippines). Underneath each top-level domain is a number of second-level domains; for example, Australia has .com.au (Australian commercial organizations), .edu.au (Australian educational organizations), and .asn.au (Australian nonprofit associations). The organizations that manage each top-level and second-level domain can also be quite different; while Network Solutions, Inc. (http://www.nsi.com/) is responsible for the wholesale allocation of domain names for the .com top-level domain, the .com.au second-level domain is managed by Melbourne IT (http://www.melbourneit.com.au/).

As an example, let's look at how the hostname www.finance.bigbank.com is resolved: the client resolver needs to determine which DNS server is authoritative for .com domains; followed by the DNS server that is authoritative for bigbank.com domains; potentially followed by the DNS server that is authoritative for the finance.bigbank.com domain, if all mappings for bigbank.com are not stored on a single server. The .com resolution is taken care of by the list of root servers provided by the WHOIS database (ftp://ftp.rs.internic.net/domain/named.root):

```
>>> Last update of whois database: Mon, 9 Oct 2000 09:43:11 EDT <<<

The Registry database contains ONLY .COM, .NET, .ORG, .EDU domains and
Registrars.

ftp://ftp.rs.internic.net/domain/named.root
;       This file holds the information on root name servers needed to
;       initialize cache of Internet domain name servers
;       (e.g. reference this file in the "cache  .  <file>"
;       configuration file of BIND domain name servers).
;
;       This file is made available by InterNIC registration services
;       under anonymous FTP as
;           file                    /domain/named.root
;           on server               FTP.RS.INTERNIC.NET
```

```
;              -OR- under Gopher at     RS.INTERNIC.NET
;                  under menu          InterNIC Registration Services (NSI)
;                     submenu          InterNIC Registration Archives
;                  file                named.root
;
;       last update:    Aug 22, 1997
;       related version of root zone:   1997082200
;
;
; formerly NS.INTERNIC.NET
;
.                          3600000  IN  NS    A.ROOT-SERVERS.NET.
A.ROOT-SERVERS.NET.        3600000      A     198.41.0.4
;
; formerly NS1.ISI.EDU
;
.                          3600000      NS    B.ROOT-SERVERS.NET.
B.ROOT-SERVERS.NET.        3600000      A     128.9.0.107
;
; formerly C.PSI.NET
;
.                          3600000      NS    C.ROOT-SERVERS.NET.
C.ROOT-SERVERS.NET.        3600000      A     192.33.4.12
;
; formerly TERP.UMD.EDU
;
.                          3600000      NS    D.ROOT-SERVERS.NET.
D.ROOT-SERVERS.NET.        3600000      A     128.8.10.90
;
; formerly NS.NASA.GOV
;
.                          3600000      NS    E.ROOT-SERVERS.NET.
E.ROOT-SERVERS.NET.        3600000      A     192.203.230.10
;
; formerly NS.ISC.ORG
;
.                          3600000      NS    F.ROOT-SERVERS.NET.
F.ROOT-SERVERS.NET.        3600000      A     192.5.5.241
;
; formerly NS.NIC.DDN.MIL
;
.                          3600000      NS    G.ROOT-SERVERS.NET.
G.ROOT-SERVERS.NET.        3600000      A     192.112.36.4
```

```
;
; formerly AOS.ARL.ARMY.MIL
;
.                          3600000      NS     H.ROOT-SERVERS.NET.
H.ROOT-SERVERS.NET.        3600000      A      128.63.2.53
;
; formerly NIC.NORDU.NET
;
.                          3600000      NS     I.ROOT-SERVERS.NET.
I.ROOT-SERVERS.NET.        3600000      A      192.36.148.17
;
; temporarily housed at NSI (InterNIC)
;
.                          3600000      NS     J.ROOT-SERVERS.NET.
J.ROOT-SERVERS.NET.        3600000      A      198.41.0.10
;
; housed in LINX, operated by RIPE NCC
;
.                          3600000      NS     K.ROOT-SERVERS.NET.
K.ROOT-SERVERS.NET.        3600000      A      193.0.14.129
;
; temporarily housed at ISI (IANA)
;
.                          3600000      NS     L.ROOT-SERVERS.NET.
L.ROOT-SERVERS.NET.        3600000      A      198.32.64.12
;
; housed in Japan, operated by WIDE
;
.                          3600000      NS     M.ROOT-SERVERS.NET.
M.ROOT-SERVERS.NET.        3600000      A      202.12.27.33
; End of File
```

The named.root file shown in the preceding code can be used by servers to resolve IP addresses for root DNS servers, if they do not run a local DNS server. After obtaining an IP address for a root server for the .com domain, a query is then made to bigbank.com for the address www.finance.bigbank.com. Two possible scenarios can occur at this point: either the DNS server that is authoritative for the entire bigbank.com domain can resolve the address; or, if the root server has delegated authority to another server, the query is passed to a DNS server for the finance.bigbank.com domain. In the latter situation, the bigbank.com DNS server does not know the IP address for any hosts within the finance.bigbank.com domain, except for the address of the DNS server.

NOTE: DNS is, therefore, a very flexible system for managing the mapping of domain names to IP addresses.

The software that carries out the client request for, and server resolution of, IP addresses is BIND.

NOTE: Although most vendors, including Sun, ship their own customized version of BIND, it is possible to download, compile, configure, and install your own version of BIND (available for download from http://www.isc.org).

DNS CLIENT TOOLS

Configuring a DNS client in Solaris is very easy and can be accomplished in a few easy steps. First, you must have installed the BIND package during system installation to use the DNS client tools. Alternatively, we examine later in this chapter how to build a new installation of BIND 9, that is more up to date than BIND 8, which is supplied with Solaris 8 by default. Second, you must configure the name service switch (/etc/nsswitch.conf) to consult DNS for domain name resolution, in addition to checking the /etc/hosts file and/or NIS/NIS+ maps or tables for hostnames. The following line must appear in /etc/nsswitch.conf for DNS to work correctly:

```
/etc/nsswitch.conf hosts:        dns [NOTFOUND=return] files
```

If you have NIS+ running, the line would appear this way:

```
/etc/nsswitch.conf hosts:        dns nisplus nis [NOTFOUND=return] files
```

Next, the name of the local domain should be entered into the file /etc/defaultdomain. For example, the /etc/defaultdomain file for the host www.paulwatters.com should have the following entry:

```
paulwatters.com
```

Finally, the /etc/resolv.conf file needs to contain the name of the local domain, as well as the IP addresses of the local primary DNS server and a secondary (off-site) DNS server. This means that even if your local DNS server goes down, you can rely on the secondary to provide up-to-date information about external hosts, relying on data within the /etc/hosts file to resolve local addresses. In the following example, we demonstrate how the /etc/resolv.conf file might look for the host www.finance.bigbank.com:

```
domain finance.bigbank.com
domain bigbank.com
nameserver 204.168.12.1
nameserver 204.168.12.16
nameserver 64.58.24.1
```

In the preceding code, there are two domains to which the host belongs: the subdomain finance.bigbank.com and the domain bigbank.com. Thus, there are two primary DNS servers listed within the local domain (204.168.12.1 and 204.168.12.16). In addition, an external secondary is also listed, corresponding to ns.bigisp.com, or 64.58.24.1.

Once the client resolver is configured in this way, we can use a number of tools to test whether DNS is working and to further examine how IP addresses are resolved. The most important tool for performing DNS resolutions is *nslookup*, which can be used in a simple command-line mode to look up fully qualified domain names from IP addresses, and vice versa.

TIP: nslookup also features an interactive mode that is very useful for retrieving name server characteristics for a particular domain and for determining which DNS servers are authoritative for a specific host or network.

Let's look at a simple example: if we wanted to determine the IP address of the host www.paulwatters.com, using a client on the host gamera.cassowary.net, we would use the following command:

```
godzilla:~:60 % nslookup www.paulwatters.com
The following response would be returned:
Server:   gamera.cassowary.net
Address:  206.68.216.16

Name:     paulwatters.com
Address:  209.67.50.203
Aliases:  www.paulwatters.com
```

This output indicates that the primary DNS server for the local (cassowary.net) domain is gamera.cassowary.net (206.68.216.16). This server then makes a connection through to the DNS server that is authoritative for the domain paulwatters.com (dns19.hostsave.com). This server then returns the canonical (actual) name for the host (paulwatters.com), as well as the alias name (www.paulwatters.com) and the desired IP address. If we reversed the process and instead supplied the IP address 209.67.50.203 on the command line, we would be able to perform a reverse lookup on that address, which would resolve to the domain name paulwatters.com.

If you want to verify that your DNS server is returning the correct IP address, or if you want to verify an address directly yourself, then running nslookup in interactive mode allows you to set the name of the DNS server to use for all lookups. For example, if we wanted to resolve the domain name for the Web server of the University of Sydney, we could use the following command:

```
godzilla:~:61 % nslookup www.usyd.edu.au
```

The following response would then be returned:

```
Server:   gamera.cassowary.net
Address:  206.68.216.16

Name: solo.ucc.usyd.edu.au
Address:  129.78.64.2
Aliases:  www.usyd.edu.au
```

We can verify that this IP address is indeed correct by setting our DNS server to be the DNS server that is authoritative for the ucc.usyd.edu.au domain:

```
> godzilla:~:62 % nslookup
Default Server:  gamera.cassowary.net
Address:  206.68.216.16.
```

Here, we enter the name of the DNS server that is authoritative for the target domain:

```
> server metro.ucc.su.oz.au
Default Server:  metro.ucc.su.oz.au
Address:  129.78.64.2
```

Next, we enter the name of the host to resolve:

```
> www.usyd.edu.au
Server:   metro.ucc.su.oz.au
Address:  129.78.64.2And the IP address is returned correctly:
Name:     solo.ucc.usyd.edu.au
ddress:  129.78.64.24
Aliases:  www.usyd.edu.au
```

If you wanted to determine some of the key characteristics of the DNS entry for www.usyd.edu.au, such as the DNS server that is authoritative for the host and the mail address of the administrator who is responsible for the host, it is possible to retrieve the Start of Authority (SOA) record through nslookup:

```
> godzilla:~:63 % nslookup
Default Server:  gamera.cassowary.net
Address:  206.68.216.16

> server metro.ucc.su.oz.au
Default Server:  metro.ucc.su.oz.au
Address:  129.78.64.2
> set q=soa
> www.usyd.edu.au
```

```
Server:  metro.ucc.su.oz.au
Address:  129.78.64.2

www.usyd.edu.au canonical name = solo.ucc.usyd.edu.au
ucc.usyd.edu.au
        origin = metro.ucc.usyd.edu.au
        mail addr = root.metro.ucc.usyd.edu.au
        serial = 316
        refresh = 3600 (1 hour)
        retry  = 1800 (30 mins)
        expire = 36000 (10 hours)
        minimum ttl = 43200 (12 hours)
```

This SOA record indicates the following:

▼ The canonical name of www.usyd.edu.au is solo.ucc.usyd.edu.au

■ The origin of the DNS record is metro.ucc.usyd.edu.au (and this server is authoritative for the host solo.ucc.usyd.edu.au)

■ The serial number for the current record is 316. Next time a change is made to the record, the serial number should be incremented

■ The refresh rate is 1 hour

■ The retry rate is 30 minutes

■ The expiry rate is 10 hours

▲ The TTL is 12 hours

We further examine the meaning of each field listed in the followng code when we discuss how to create DNS records for the server. The use of nslookup to determine which servers are authoritative for a particular query is not limited to individual hosts—in fact, the authoritative servers for entire networks can be determined by using nslookup. For example, if we wanted to determine which servers were authoritative for the Cook Islands top-level domain (.ck), we would use the following command:

```
godzilla:~:64 % nslookup
> set type=ns
> ck.
Server:  gamera.cassowary.net
Address:  206.68.216.16

Non-authoritative answer:
ck        nameserver = DOWNSTAGE.MCS.VUW.AC.NZ
ck        nameserver = NS1.WAIKATO.AC.NZ
ck        nameserver = PARAU.OYSTER.NET.ck
```

```
ck          nameserver = POIPARAU.OYSTER.NET.ck
ck          nameserver = CIRCA.MCS.VUW.AC.NZ

Authoritative answers can be found from:
DOWNSTAGE.MCS.VUW.AC.NZ internet address = 130.195.6.10
NS1.WAIKATO.AC.NZ        internet address = 140.200.128.13
PARAU.OYSTER.NET.ck      internet address = 202.65.32.128
POIPARAU.OYSTER.NET.ck   internet address = 202.65.32.127
CIRCA.MCS.VUW.AC.NZ      internet address = 130.195.5.12
```

Some servers that are authoritative for the top-level domains of the Cook Islands are located in New Zealand. This geographic separation may seem strange, but makes sense if you've ever lived through a tropical storm in Rarotonga: if the power to the OYSTER.NET.ck network was disrupted, hostnames could still be resolved through the backup servers at WAIKATO.AC.NZ.

It's also possible to obtain a list of all the networks and hosts within a particular top-level domain by using the ls command. Be warned, the output can be verbose:

```
godzilla:~:65 % nslookup
> set type=ns
> ls ck.
[DOWNSTAGE.MCS.VUW.AC.NZ]
 ck.                              server = parau.oyster.net.ck
 parau.oyster.net                 202.65.32.128
 ck.                              server = poiparau.oyster.net.ck
 poiparau.oyster.net              202.65.32.127
 ck.                              server = downstage.mcs.vuw.ac.nz
 ck.                              server = circa.mcs.vuw.ac.nz
 sda.org                          server = parau.oyster.net.ck
 parau.oyster.net                 202.65.32.128
 sda.org                          server = poiparau.oyster.net.ck
```

The final tool that is often useful for resolving hostnames is the whois command. The whois command uses InterNIC servers to perform all of the resolutions for you; and it includes useful information, such as the registrar of the domain name (useful when making complaints about SPAM or harassment on the net!). Here's the whois entry for paulwatters.com:

```
godzilla:~:66 % whois paulwatters

Whois Server Version 1.3
```

Domain names in the .com, .net, and .org domains can now be registered
with many different competing registrars. Go to http://www.internic.net
for detailed information.

```
Domain Name: PAULWATTERS.COM
Registrar: REGISTER.COM, INC.
Whois Server: whois.register.com
Referral URL: www.register.com
Name Server: DNS19.REGISTER.COM
Name Server: DNS20.REGISTER.COM
Updated Date: 30-may-2000
```

CONFIGURING A DNS SERVER

Now that we've examined DNS from a client viewpoint and explored concepts like
SOAs, IP-to-address mapping, and address-to-IP mapping, it should be clear what kind
of services a DNS server needs to provide to clients. In addition, DNS servers need to be
able to support both primary and secondary services, as described earlier in this chapter.

The BIND is the most commonly used DNS server for Solaris. It is supplied in a package that is generally installed during initial system configuration. Its main configuration
file is /etc/named.conf for BIND 8 supplied with Solaris 8. BIND 4 and earlier used a configuration file called /etc/named.boot; however, these versions are no longer supported
by the Internet Software Consortium (ISC), and administrators running BIND 4 should
upgrade to BIND 9 (as described in the next section).

The /etc/named.conf file is responsible for controlling the behavior of the DNS
servers, and it provides the following keywords that are used to define operational
statements:

▼ **acl**   Defines an access control list that determines which clients can use
   the server

■ **include**   Reads in an external file that contains statements in the same format
   as /etc/named.conf. This is very useful when your configuration file becomes
   very large, as different sections can be divided into logically related files.

■ **logging**   Determines which activities of the server are logged in the logfile
   specified by the statement

■ **options**   Defines local server operational characteristics

■ **server**   Defines operational characteristics of other servers

▲ **zone**   Creates local DNS zones

Let's examine a sample statement involving each of these keywords.

acl

If we want to define an access control list (acl) for all hosts on the local network (10.24.58.*), we would insert the statement

```
acl local_network {
10.24.58/24
};
```

Here, the 24 indicates the netmask 255.255.255.0 in prefix notation. Now, if our router was the host 10.24.58.32, and we wanted to prevent any access to the DNS server from that address, we would amend the preceding statement to the following:

```
acl local_network {
!10.24.58.32; 10.24.58/24
};
```

Note that the negation of a specific address from a subnet that is also permitted must precede the definition of that subnet in the statement.

include

A little later, we'll examine how to configure DNS zones. Since these definitions can be very long for large networks, administrators often place them in a separate file so that they can be managed separately from acl definitions and system options.; thus, to include all of the zone definitions from the file /var/named/zones.conf, we would insert the following statement into the /etc/named.conf file:

```
include "/var/named/zones.conf"
```

options

The options section sets key parameters that affect the run-time behavior of the BIND server. Typically, these are the directories in which the zone database are stored, and the file in which the process ID of the named process is stored. The following example gives the standard options for BIND 8:

```
options {
directory "/var/named";
pid-file "/var/named/pid";
}
```

server

The server statement defines characteristics of remote name servers. There are two main options that can be set with a server statement: whether or not a remote server is known to transmit incorrect information, and whether or not the remote server can answer multiple queries during a single request. The following is a sample server statement:

```
server 10.24.58.32
{
        bogus yes;
        transfer-format many-answers;
}
```

zone

A zone must be created for each network or subdomain that your DNS server manages. Zones can be created as either primary or secondary, depending on which server is authoritative for a particular domain. Entries for IP-to-name and name-to-IP mappings must also be included to correctly resolve both IP address and domain names. For the domain cassowary.net, the following zone entries would need to be created:

```
zone "cassowary.net"
{
      type master;
file "cassowary.net.db";
}
zone "58.24.10.in-addr.arpa"
{
      type master;
      file "cassowary.net.rev";
}
```

In this case, the two zone files /var/named/cassowary.net.db and /var/named/cassowary.net.rev need to be populated with host information. A sample /var/named/cassowary.net.db file would contain SOA entries like this:

```
@     IN     SOA     cassowary.net.     root.cassowary.net.     (
          2000011103      ;serial number
          10800       ;refresh every three hours
          1800;retry every 30 mins
          1209600      ;Two week expiry
          604800)      ;Minimum one week expiry
          IN     NS     ns.cassowary.net.
          IN     MX     10     firewall.cassowary.net.
          firewall     IN     A     10.24.58.1     ;firewall
```

```
emu           IN    A     10.24.58.2     ;webserver
quoll         IN    A     10.24.58.3     ;webserver
tazdevil      IN    A     10.24.58.4     ;kerberos
security      IN    CNAME    tazdevil
```

A sample /var/named/cassowary.net.rev file would contain SOA entries like this:

```
@    IN    SOA    58.24.10.in-addr.arpa.      root.cassowary.net. (
           2000011103    ;serial number
           10800      ;refresh every three hours
           1800;retry every 30 mins
           1209600     ;Two week expiry
           604800)     ;Minimum one week expiry
           IN    NS    ns.cassowary.net.
1          IN    PTR    firewall.cassowary.net.
2          IN    PTR    emu.cassowary.net.
3          IN    PTR    quoll.cassowary.net.
4          IN    PTR    tazdevil.cassowary.net.
```

Each host within the domain must have an IP-to-domain as well as a domain-to-IP mapping. Once a change is made to the zone file, the serial number should be incremented as appropriate. Note that in addition to address (A) and pointer (PTR) records for IP address and domain names, it is also possible to identify hosts as mail exchangers (MX) and by canonical names (CNAME). The former is required to define which host is responsible for handling mail within a domain, while the latter is used to create aliases for specific machines (thus, the tazdevil Kerberos server is also known as security.cassowary.net).

COMPILING A DNS SERVER

Most Solaris systems would currently be running BIND 8, so why should you upgrade to BIND 9? There are a number of new features in the new version that will be of particular interest to Solaris users:

▼ Improved DNS security with support for digitally signed zones, as well as DNS requests

■ Support for IPv6, the new standard for IP networking, which is supported more generally in Solaris 8 for the first time

■ Multiple views of a network's namespace, depending on whether the client is behind or in front of a firewall

▲ Support for symmetric multiprocessing. As many Solaris systems are multiprocessor, this greatly improves resolution performance

To compile BIND 9, you need to download the source, uncompress the source archive, and use tar to extract its contents. Next, you need to run the configure command that will produce output such as the following:

```
bash-2.03# ./configure
creating cache ./config.cache
checking host system type... i386-pc-solaris2.8
checking whether make sets ${MAKE}... yes
checking for ranlib... ranlib
checking for a BSD compatible install... ./install-sh -c
checking for ar... /usr/ccs/bin/ar
checking for etags... no
checking for emacs-etags... no
checking for perl5... no
checking for perl... /usr/local/bin/perl
checking whether byte ordering is bigendian... no
checking for compatible OpenSSL library... using private library
checking for gcc... gcc
checking whether the C compiler (gcc  ) works... yes
checking whether the C compiler (gcc  ) is a cross-compiler... no
checking whether we are using GNU C... yes
checking whether gcc accepts -g... yes
```

Next, you need to build the application binaries using the make command:

```
bash-2.03# make
making all in /tmp/bind-9.0.0/make
make[1]: Entering directory `/tmp/bind-9.0.0/make'
make[1]: Leaving directory `/tmp/bind-9.0.0/make'
making all in /tmp/bind-9.0.0/lib
make[1]: Entering directory `/tmp/bind-9.0.0/lib'
making all in /tmp/bind-9.0.0/lib/isc
make[2]: Entering directory `/tmp/bind-9.0.0/lib/isc'
making all in /tmp/bind-9.0.0/lib/isc/include
make[3]: Entering directory `/tmp/bind-9.0.0/lib/isc/include'
making all in /tmp/bind-9.0.0/lib/isc/include/isc
make[4]: Entering directory `/tmp/bind-9.0.0/lib/isc/include/isc'
make[4]: Leaving directory `/tmp/bind-9.0.0/lib/isc/include/isc'
make[3]: Leaving directory `/tmp/bind-9.0.0/lib/isc/include'
making all in /tmp/bind-9.0.0/lib/isc/unix
```

Finally, you need to test the binaries by building the test programs:

```
bash-2.03# make test
make[1]: Entering directory `/tmp/bind-9.0.0/bin/tests/db'
S:./t_db:Friday 03 November 12:23:27 2000
T:dns_db_load:1:A
A:A call to dns_db_load(db, filename) loads the contents of the database in file
name into db.
I:testing using file dns_db_load_1.data and name a.
R:PASS
T:dns_db_iscache:2:A
A:When the database db has cache semantics, a call to dns_db_iscache(db) returns
 ISC_TRUE.
I:testing using file dns_db_iscache_1.data
R:PASS
T:dns_db_iscache:3:A
A:When the database db has zone semantics, a call to dns_db_iscache(db) returns
ISC_FALSE.
I:testing using file dns_db_iscache_2.data
R:PASS
T:dns_db_iszone:4:A
A:When the database db has zone semantics, a call to dns_db_iszone(db) returns I
SC_TRUE.
I:testing using file dns_db_iszone_1.data
R:PASS
```

If all tests pass, then you may perform a make install to install the new binaries.

SUMMARY

In this chapter, we have examined how to install and configure DNS and the BIND DNS server. For more information, administrators should consult the BIND FAQ at http://www.nominum.com/resources/faqs/bind-faq.html.

CHAPTER 12

The Internet Daemon

1 ● netd is the super Internet daemon that is responsible for centrally managing many of the standard Internet services provided by Solaris through the application layer. For example, telnet, ftp, finger, talk, and uucp are all run from the inetd. Even third-party Web servers can often be run through inetd. Both User Datagram Protocol (UDP) and Transmission Control Protocol (TCP) transport layers are supported with inetd. The main benefit of managing all services centrally through inetd is reduced administrative overhead, since all services use a standard configuration format from a single file. Just like Microsoft Internet Information Server (IIS), the inetd is able to manage many network services with a single application.

However, there are several drawbacks to using inetd to run all of your services: There is now a single point of failure, meaning that if inetd crashes because one service fails, then all of the other inetd services may be affected; and the connection pooling for services like the Apache Web server is not supported under inetd. High-performance applications, where there are many concurrent client requests, should use a stand-alone daemon.

In this chapter, we will examine how to configure inetd and add new services, and we will review which services are currently provided by the Solaris inetd.

CONFIGURING THE INTERNET DAEMON

The Internet daemon relies on two files for configuration. The first is the /etc/inetd.conf file, the primary configuration file, consisting of a list of all services currently supported and their runtime parameters, such as the filesystem path to the daemon that is executed. The second is the /etc/services file that maintains a list of mappings between service names and port numbers, which is used to ensure that services are activated on the correct port.

Remember that every time you make a change to inetd.conf, you will need to send a HUP signal to the inetd process. You can identify the process ID (PID) of inetd by using the ps command and then sending a kill SIGHUP signal to that PID from the shell. In addition, commenting an entry in the /etc/services file will not necessarily prevent a service from running. Strictly speaking, only services that make the getprotobyname() call to retrieve their port number require the /etc/services file. So, for applications like sendmail, removing their entry in /etc/services has no effect.

TIP: To prevent sendmail from running, you would need to comment out its entry in /etc/inetd.conf and send a SIGHUP to the inetd process.

A service definition in /etc/inetd.conf has the following format:

```
service    socket    protocol    flags    user    server_name    arguments
```

where the service uses either datagrams or streams and uses UDP or TCP on the transport layer, with the server_name being executed by the user. An example entry is the UDP talk service:

```
talk    dgram    udp    wait    root    /usr/sbin/in.talkd    in.talkd
```

The talk service uses datagrams over UDP and is executed by the root user, with the talk daemon physically located in /usr/sbin/in.talkd. Once the talk daemon is running through inetd, it is used for interactive screen-based communication between two users (with at least one user talking on the local system). Figure 12-1 shows a talk request screen after the command

```
talk paul
```

has been executed. The login shell for paul would then display the following message:

```
Message from Talk_Daemon@cassowary at 10:50 ...
talk: connection requested by maya@cassowary.paulwatters.com.
talk: respond with:   talk maya@cassowary.paulwatters.com
```

To answer this call, you would then need to type

```
talk maya
```

In order to prevent users from using (or abusing) the talk facility, you would need to comment out the definition for the talk daemon in the /etc/inetd.conf file; thus, the line shown earlier would be changed to

```
#talk    dgram    udp    wait    root    /usr/sbin/in.talkd    in.talkd
```

In order for inetd to register the change, it needs to be restarted by using the kill command. To identify the PID for inetd, the following command may be used:

```
bash-2.03# ps -eaf | grep inetd
    root    206    1  0   May 16 ?        30:19 /usr/sbin/inetd -s
```

To restart the process, the following command would be used:

```
kill -1 206
```

The daemon would then restart after reading in the modified inetd.conf file.

Another useful feature of inetd is the capability to log all incoming TCP connections by starting the daemon with the –t option.

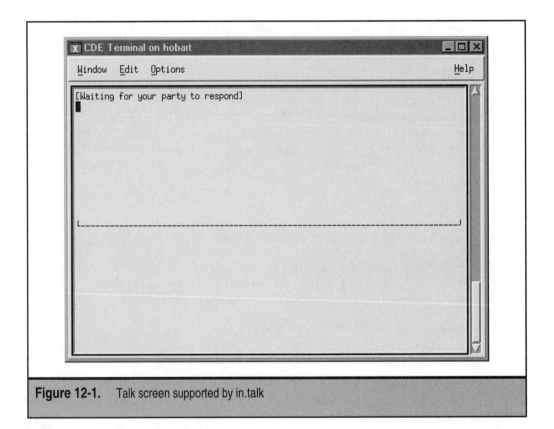

Figure 12-1. Talk screen supported by in.talk

TIP: More fine-grained logging is available from the TCP wrappers package, which can be downloaded from ftp://ftp.porcupine.org/pub/security/index.html#software.

/etc/inetd.conf

The sample inetd.conf file shown next contains entries for the most commonly used Internet services:

```
ftp      stream  tcp   nowait  root  /usr/sbin/in.ftpd     in.ftpd -l
telnet   stream  tcp   nowait  root  /usr/sbin/in.telnetd  in.telnetd
name     dgram   udp   wait    root  /usr/sbin/in.tnamed   in.tnamed
shell    stream  tcp   nowait  root  /usr/sbin/in.rshd     in.rshd
login    stream  tcp   nowait  root  /usr/sbin/in.rlogind  in.rlogind
exec     stream  tcp   nowait  root  /usr/sbin/in.rexecd   in.rexecd
comsat   dgram   udp   wait    root  /usr/sbin/in.comsat   in.comsat
talk     dgram   udp   wait    root  /usr/sbin/in.talkd    in.talkd
uucp     stream  tcp   nowait  root  /usr/sbin/in.uucpd    in.uucpd
```

```
tftp    dgram   udp     wait    root    /usr/sbin/in.tftpd      in.tftpd -s /tftpboot
finger  stream  tcp     nowait  nobody  /usr/sbin/in.fingerd    in.fingerd
systat  stream  tcp     nowait  root    /usr/bin/ps             ps -ef
netstat         stream  tcp     nowait  root    /usr/bin/netstat        netstat -f
inet
time    stream  tcp     nowait  root    internal
time    dgram   udp     wait    root    internal
echo    stream  tcp     nowait  root    internal
echo    dgram   udp     wait    root    internal
discard stream  tcp     nowait  root    internal
discard dgram   udp     wait    root    internal
daytime stream  tcp     nowait  root    internal
daytime dgram   udp     wait    root    internal
chargen stream  tcp     nowait  root    internal
chargen dgram   udp     wait    root    internal
100232/10       tli     rpc/udp wait root /usr/sbin/sadmind       sadmind
rquotad/1       tli     rpc/datagram_v  wait root /usr/lib/nfs/rquotad  rquotad
rusersd/2-3     tli     rpc/datagram_v,circuit_v        wait root
/usr/lib/netsvc/rusers/rpc.rusersd      rpc.rusersd
sprayd/1        tli     rpc/datagram_v  wait root /usr/lib/netsvc/spray/rpc.sprayd
rpc.sprayd
walld/1         tli     rpc/datagram_v  wait root /usr/lib/netsvc/rwall/rpc.rwalld
rpc.rwalld
rstatd/2-4      tli     rpc/datagram_v wait root /usr/lib/netsvc/rstat/rpc.rstatd
rpc.rstatd
rexd/1          tli     rpc/tcp wait root /usr/sbin/rpc.rexd      rpc.rexd
100083/1        tli     rpc/tcp wait root /usr/dt/bin/rpc.ttdbserverd
rpc.ttdbserverd
ufsd/1 tli      rpc/*   wait    root    /usr/lib/fs/ufs/ufsd    ufsd -p
100221/1        tli     rpc/tcp wait root /usr/openwin/bin/kcms_server  kcms_server
fs              stream  tcp     wait nobody /usr/openwin/lib/fs.auto     fs
100235/1 tli rpc/tcp wait root /usr/lib/fs/cachefs/cachefsd cachefsd
kerbd/4         tli     rpc/ticlts      wait    root    /usr/sbin/kerbd kerbd
printer         stream  tcp     nowait  root    /usr/lib/print/in.lpd   in.lpd
100234/1        tli     rpc/ticotsord   wait    root    /usr/lib/gss/gssd gssd
dtspc stream tcp nowait root /usr/dt/bin/dtspcd /usr/dt/bin/dtspcd
100068/2-5 dgram rpc/udp wait root /usr/dt/bin/rpc.cmsd rpc.cmsd
```

/etc/services

Many services must be mapped to a specific port number. An /etc/services file, sample shown next, defines port numbers for most of the commonly used services:

```
tcpmux          1/tcp
echo            7/tcp
echo            7/udp
discard         9/tcp           sink null
discard         9/udp           sink null
systat          11/tcp          users
```

```
daytime         13/tcp
daytime         13/udp
netstat         15/tcp
chargen         19/tcp          ttytst source
chargen         19/udp          ttytst source
ftp-data        20/tcp
ftp             21/tcp
telnet          23/tcp
smtp            25/tcp          mail
time            37/tcp          timserver
time            37/udp          timserver
name            42/udp          nameserver
whois           43/tcp          nicname
domain          53/udp
domain          53/tcp
bootps          67/udp
bootpc          68/udp
hostnames       101/tcp         hostname
pop2            109/tcp         pop-2
pop3            110/tcp
sunrpc          111/udp         rpcbind
sunrpc          111/tcp         rpcbind
imap            143/tcp         imap2
ldap            389/tcp
ldap            389/udp
ldaps           636/tcp
ldaps           636/udp
tftp            69/udp
rje             77/tcp
finger          79/tcp
link            87/tcp          ttylink
supdup          95/tcp
iso-tsap        102/tcp
x400            103/tcp
x400-snd        104/tcp
csnet-ns        105/tcp
pop-2           109/tcp
uucp-path       117/tcp
nntp            119/tcp         usenet
ntp             123/tcp
ntp             123/udp
NeWS            144/tcp         news
cvc_hostd       442/tcp
exec            512/tcp
login           513/tcp
shell           514/tcp         cmd
printer         515/tcp         spooler
```

```
courier          530/tcp       rpc
uucp             540/tcp       uucpd
biff             512/udp       comsat
who              513/udp       whod
syslog           514/udp
talk             517/udp
route            520/udp       router routed
klogin           543/tcp
new-rwho         550/udp       new-who
rmonitor         560/udp       rmonitord
monitor          561/udp
pcserver         600/tcp
kerberos-adm     749/tcp
kerberos-adm     749/udp
kerberos         750/udp       kdc
kerberos         750/tcp       kdc
krb5_prop        754/tcp
ufsd             1008/tcp      ufsd
ufsd             1008/udp      ufsd
cvc              1495/tcp
www-ldap-gw      1760/tcp
www-ldap-gw      1760/udp
listen           2766/tcp
nfsd             2049/udp      nfs
nfsd             2049/tcp      nfs
eklogin          2105/tcp
lockd            4045/udp
lockd            4045/tcp
dtspc            6112/tcp
fs               7100/tcp
```

FILE TRANSFER PROTOCOL (FTP)

Now that we have seen how inetd is configured, we will examine some of the services that are provided through inetd in detail. One of the most commonly used inetd services is the File Transfer Program (FTP). FTP allows users to retrieve files from accounts on different systems on the local area network or across the Internet. One popular variant of FTP is anonymous FTP, which is a convention by which remote access to a local filesystem is granted anonymously. This allows public users to download files from your system without having to provide any kind of authentication credentials.

NOTE: Many public software archives support anonymous FTP.

Let's examine a sample FTP session for the user pwatters on a system called emu. pwatters wants to transfer files to a system called cassowary using the remote account paul:

```
emu:/ $ ftp cassowary
Connected to cassowary.paulwatters.com.
220 cassowary FTP server (SunOS 5.8) ready.
Name (emu:pwatters): paul
331 Password required for paul.
Password:
230 User paul logged in.
ftp>
```

In this example, the user pwatters on emu connects to cassowary by using the standard ftp client program. However, pwatters could easily have used the FTP capacity of the Netscape Navigator program or the xftp application. The server cassowary responds to the client request by printing a welcome banner and asking for a valid username. Notice that the client's current username is displayed as part of the prompt: this means that if the account name on the FTP server is the same as the FTP client, the user may just press ENTER to accept the proposed username. However, in the example shown, the client username is pwatters, but the server username is paul, so "paul" must be entered directly.

Next, the password for the paul account is requested. If this is entered correctly, then the user will be logged into the server account, with the working directory root corresponding to the user's home directory. However, if the username and/or password are not correct, the following error message will be displayed:

```
530 Login incorrect.
Login failed.
ftp>
```

At the FTP prompt, it is possible to retry the authentication sequence without having to quit the FTP client and to restart by using the following commands:

```
ftp> user paul
331 Password required for paul.
Password:
230 User paul logged in.
ftp>
```

In the previous example, the correct password has been entered, and the remote user may then proceed to issue a number of commands through the FTP client. You can obtain a list of all supported commands on the FTP server by using the help command:

```
ftp> help
Commands may be abbreviated.  Commands are:

!               cr          macdef      proxy       send
$               delete      mdelete     sendport    status
```

```
account        debug          mdir           put            struct
append         dir            mget           pwd            sunique
ascii          disconnect     mkdir          quit           tenex
bell           form           mls            quote          trace
binary         get            mode           recv           type
bye            glob           mput           remotehelp     user
case           hash           nmap           rename         verbose
cd             help           ntrans         reset          ?
cdup           lcd            open           rmdir
close          ls             prompt         runique
```

Table 12-1 describes the most commonly used FTP commands. Most users will typically use only three or four commands during a session. The first command is usually to verify the current working directory, for which the PWD command is used:

```
ftp> pwd
257 "/home/paul" is current directory.
```

Next, the target directory should be selected. To determine which directories exist underneath the current directory, or to verify what files already exist in the current directory, the dir command may be used:

```
ftp> dir
200 PORT command successful.
150 ASCII data connection for /bin/ls (64.16.128.48,44879) (0 bytes).
total 34
drwxr-xr-x   2 paul     staff        512 May 10 13:53 .
drwxr-xr-x   6 paul     staff        512 May 15 09:10 ..
-rw-r--r--   1 paul     staff       1987 May 10 13:50 _GoodDayStub.java
-rw-r--r--   1 paul     staff        411 May 10 13:50 GoodDay.java
-rw-r--r--   1 paul     staff       4649 May 10 13:50 GoodDayHelper.java
-rw-r--r--   1 paul     staff        877 May 10 13:50 GoodDayHolder.java
-rw-r--r--   1 paul     staff        414 May 10 13:50 GoodDayOperations.java
-rw-r--r--   1 paul     staff       2522 May 10 13:50 GoodDayPOA.java
-rw-r--r--   1 paul     staff       1227 May 10 13:50 GoodDayPOATie.java
226 ASCII Transfer complete.
637 bytes received in 0.03 seconds (20.46 Kbytes/s)
```

In the previous example, we see that there are several Java source files in this directory. Now imagine that we wanted to download the GoodDay.java file to the local system. We would use the command

```
ftp> get GoodDay.java
200 PORT command successful.
150 Binary data connection for GoodDay.java (64.16.128.48,44879) (411 bytes).
226 Binary Transfer complete.
411 bytes received in 0.05 seconds (10.45 Kbytes/sec)
```

If we modified the file locally, added 4,000 bytes, and then wished to upload it back to the server, we could use the command

```
ftp> put GoodDay.java
200 PORT command successful.
150 Binary data connection for GoodDay.java (203.134.34.185,1036).
226 Transfer complete.
4411 bytes sent in 0.6 seconds (10.45 Kbytes/sec)
```

Once an FTP session has been completed, the quit command may be used to termi-nate the client session.

Command	Description
!	Spawns a shell
$	Runs a macro
?	Displays help
append	Appends data to a file
ascii	Transfer files as ASCII
bell	Sounds upon completion
bye	Quits FTP session
case	Enables case mapping
cd	Changes directory
cdup	Changes directory to parent
close	Quits FTP session
cr	Enables return key stripping
delete	Removes file
dir	Prints directory listing
disconnect	Quits FTP session
form	Specifies ASCII/binary format
glob	Enables filename expansion
hash	Enables hash printing
help	Displays help

Table 12-1. FTP Commands

Command	Description
lcd	Changes working directory on client
ls	Prints directory listing
macdef	Enters a macro
mdelete	Deletes files
mdir	Multiple directory listing
mkdir	Creates directory
mls	Multiple directory listing
mput	Uploads files
nmap	Enables templates
ntrans	Defines translation table
open	Opens connection
prompt	Toggles per-file prompting
proxy	Enables proxying
put	Uploads file
quit	Quits FTP session
quote	Executes command
remotehelp	Displays help
rename	Changes filename
reset	Resets connection
rmdir	Deletes directory
runique	Enables unique filenames
send	Uploads file
sendport	Enables port command
status	Displays status
struct	Defines file transfer structure
tenex	Toggles tenex file support
trace	Displays IP packet trace
user	User login
verbose	Displays verbose messages

Table 12-1.   FTP Commands *(continued)*

As we mentioned earlier, not every site uses login credentials retrieved from the password database to allow access to an FTP system. Many file archive sites allow anonymous FTP, that is, the capability to create an FTP session without providing a username and password. By convention, access to anonymous FTP is granted by the username "anonymous" or "ftp" and by any sequence of characters as a password, including the @ symbol.

TIP: In previous years, users would enter their e-mail addresses as a courtesy; however, some unscrupulous FTP operators have passed these addresses onto SPAM mailing lists for profit. It's unwise to enter your e-mail address unless you want SPAM.

Here is an example anonymous FTP session:

```
bash-2.03% ftp mirror.aarnet.edu.au
Connected to mirror.aarnet.edu.au.
220-
220- Welcome to Mirror.AARNet.EDU.AU in Australia
220-
220 AARNet FTP server ready.
Name (mirror.aarnet.edu.au:pwatters): ftp
331 Guest login ok, send your complete e-mail address as password.
Password:
230-
230- Welcome to Mirror.AARNet.EDU.AU in sunny Brisbane, located at ITS,
230- University of Queensland, Australia.
230-
230- Providing fast FTP/WWW access and bandwidth cost savings to AARNet
230- members using Sun hardware, Optus bandwidth and archive management
230- by the DSTC core mirror team of Jason Andrade, George Michaelson
230- and Paul Young.
230-
230- Questions/Suggestions/Feedback:    <mirror@mirror.aarnet.edu.au>
230-
230- *** DISCLAIMER: The AVCC/APL/DSTC/UQ are not liable for any    ***
230- *** use of, storage or transmission of files stored here.      ***
230- *** Unauthorized use of this server is strictly prohibited     ***
230-
230- *** For a list of hosted mirrors, please get: /pub/MIRRORS     ***
230- *** For a search engine look at http://mirror.aarnet.edu.au     ***
230-
230- 10 users of 200 (max).  Connection from: kookaburra.cassowary.net
230-
```

```
230- *** If you only see a few files when using ls, try using the  ***
230- *** http interface to mirror, or use "ls -l" instead          ***
230-
230 Guest login ok, access restrictions apply.
ftp>
```

Normal FTP commands may then be used to download files (get or mget), as per a normal FTP session.

telnet

Perhaps the second most commonly used service is the telnet service. Although many Windows NT administrators will have used FTP in the past, providing telnet services may be an unfamiliar concept, since it allows remote users to access an interactive shell as if they were physically logging in from the console. Both remote access for command-line commands and applications are available under Solaris, with Graphical User Interface (GUI) displays provided through Common Desktop Environment (CDE) and X11. Although products like pcAnywhere allow this kind of remote access for Windows, Solaris goes one step further to provide true multiuser access: many different users can run many different shells, applications, and CDE desktops concurrently, without interfering with each other's work.

telnet does not support the execution of applications requiring CDE and/or X11, unless the client provides support for X11. All Solaris systems provide this support, as do many other UNIX and Linux systems. It is even possible to use an X11 server for Windows to remotely execute CDE-based applications with their displays set to the Windows desktop.

TIP: Reflection X is an excellent product for Windows NT that is designed for this purpose.

Let's look at a sample telnet session between a system called "brolga" and a system called "currawong" and for the user pwatters:

```
brolga% telnet currawong
Trying 134.128.64.16...

Connected to currawong.cassowary.net.
Escape character is '^]'.


SunOS 5.7

login: pwatters
Password:
```

```
Last login: Tue Oct 24 10:03:02 from sparrow
Sun Microsystems Inc.    SunOS 5.8      Generic November1999

You have new mail.
currawong:11:41:pwatters>
```

The sequence of events is straightforward: the user enters a username on the remote system when prompted, presses ENTER, and then enters a password on the remote machine. If the username and password are accepted, the session proceeds and the user's default shell is spawned. The user may now issue commands interactively on the command-line as if he or she were sitting on the console.

The Solaris telnet client has an extensive help facility available, which can be viewed by keying the escape sequence (usually ^]), and typing the command "help." The main telnet commands are shown in Table 12-2.

Command	Description
close	Quits telnet session
logout	Closes connection
display	Prints connection characteristics
mode	Changes mode
open	Opens connection
quit	Quits telnet session
send	Sends special characters
set	Sets connection characteristics
unset	Unsets connection characteristics
status	Displays connection status
toggle	Changes connection characteristics
slc	Toggles special character mode
z	Suspends connection
!	Spawns shell
environ	Updates environment variables
?	Displays help
ENTER	Returns to session

Table 12-2.   Telnet Client Commands

The display command will print all of the current settings being used by your terminal:

```
telnet> display
will flush output when sending interrupt characters.
won't send interrupt characters in urgent mode.
won't skip reading of ~/.telnetrc file.
won't map carriage return on output.
will recognize certain control characters.
won't turn on socket level debugging.
won't print hexadecimal representation of network traffic.
won't print user readable output for "netdata".
won't show option processing.
won't print hexadecimal representation of terminal traffic.
echo            [^E]
escape          [^]]
rlogin          [off]
tracefile       "(standard output)"
flushoutput     [^O]
interrupt       [^C]
quit            [^\]
eof             [^D]
erase           [^?]
kill            [^U]
lnext           [^V]
susp            [^Z]
reprint         [^R]
worderase       [^W]
start           [^Q]
stop            [^S]
forw1           [off]
forw2           [off]
ayt             [^T]
```

The status command reveals the characteristics of the current telnet connection:

```
telnet> status
Connected to currawong.cassowary.net.
Operating in single character mode
Catching signals locally
Remote character echo
Escape character is '^]'.
```

To resume the telnet session, simply press the ENTER key at the telnet> prompt.

OTHER SERVICES

As we discussed earlier, there are many different services offered through inetd.

TIP: If you look at the manpage for each of the services, you will be able to learn more about how each command is used.

For example, the finger command displays all of the currently logged-in users and is supported by the in.fingerd daemon, which is spawned through inetd:

```
bash-2.03$ finger
Login      Name           TTY         Idle    When     Where
paul       Paul Watters   pts/1       10d Mon 13:08    emu
maya       Maya Watters   pts/2        6 Fri 10:48     cassowary
```

The man page for finger gives many different options for executing the command.

SUMMARY

In this chapter, we have examined how the Internet super daemon (inetd) is used to spawn instances of various system services and how services are mapped to ports using the services database. All of the services listed in /etc/inetd.conf have man pages associated with them, making it easy to determine which services should be enabled or disabled at any one time.

CHAPTER 13

Remote Access

Following from Chapter 12, in this chapter we will extend coverage of network services to include common remote access tools, such as more secure alternatives to telnet. We will begin by examining how to install and configure anonymous FTP. Next, we will review the remote access "r" commands such as rsh and rlogin. Then we will investigate why these applications are inherently insecure and discuss methods for replacing them with more secure alternatives.

ANONYMOUS FTP

As we saw in the previous chapter, FTP is a useful client/server protocol for transferring individual files or groups of files of binary or plain text data between hosts. So far, we've focused on the situation in which the user attempting to log in from a remote host has a valid username and password on the FTP server, that is, can be identified and authenticated using the standard Solaris username and password matching routines. However, one of the most widespread uses of FTP is providing remote access to unidentifiable clients—in other words, the users of the FTP service remain anonymous because their credentials are not validated on the server side.

Anonymous FTP services are not supported by default in Solaris, unlike most Linux distributions, and also unlike Windows, in which the Internet Information Server (IIS) provides anonymous FTP access. However, a simple procedure, which we will review in this section, can be followed to enable anonymous FTP on Solaris. First, we will examine the limitations and restrictions placed on anonymous FTP services by Solaris, and then we'll discuss various strategies that can be used to secure anonymous FTP.

Obviously, the greatest fear in opening up access to your system for anonymous users is that they will abuse the system or find a way to penetrate the protective layers that you put in place to protect the system. For example, if you must provide anonymous FTP uploads, then you run the risk of allowing users to upload very large files that could be used to literally fill the filesystem to capacity. Imagine further that the filesystem on which the anonymous FTP user's home directory resides was the same filesystem on which every other user's files were located. Authenticated users would not be able to create new files without deleting others first, making it very difficult to work effectively.

One solution to this problem is to create a single partition with a capacity equal to the total estimated space required for uploads; thus, if an anonymous user fills this partition with junk in order to deny service to other users, service will only be disrupted for other anonymous users. Most sites that provide anonymous FTP services only allow the anonymous downloading of files from an archive, rather than allowing unauthenticated write access to the remote filesystem.

TIP: If a remote user really does need to upload files, it's best to create a new account for him or her using admintool, and place a quota on his or her ability to create files on the filesystem.

Anonymous FTP is supported by all FTP clients, including the XFTP client, developed by the Lawrence Livermore National Laboratory (available for download from http://www.llnl.gov/ia/xftp.html). Figure 13-1 shows the XFTP client logging in anonymously to a remote host—the files can be downloaded and uploaded according to the file permissions set for the FTP user's home directory and below. When logging in anonymously, users must use the username "ftp" or "anonymous," which enables the user to bypass the normal authentication mechanisms.

Anonymous FTP works by setting the root directory of the anonymous FTP account to something other than the real root directory; this gives the remote user a view of the Solaris system that appears to have all of the normal system directories and mount points (such as /usr, /etc, and /lib). However, this virtual root directory is actually located well below the root directory for authenticated users.

For example, imagine that we created a 150MB slice, such as /dev/dsk/c1t1d1s7, which was only to be used for anonymous FTP. If we created a mount point called /anon and mounted the filesystem /dev/dsk/c1t1d1s7 there, then the root directory for the anonymous FTP user would actually be /anon. Thus, if an anonymous FTP user typed **cd /**, he or she would literally be changing the working directory to /anon.

The home directory of the anonymous FTP user would then be set to /anon, and he or she would not be allowed to own files on other file systems. Provided that no symbolic links were created between the /anon file system and the directories on other file systems,

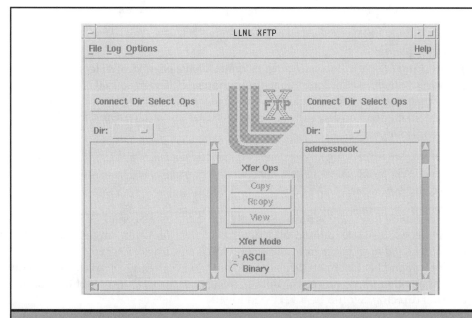

Figure 13-1.   Accessing anonymous FTP archives with XFTP

the /anon file system would be completely separate from every other user's files. Of course, it is necessary to provide copies of various system files and directories in the mini-root file system, such as a skeleton password file and the ls command. This allows files to be listed through the FTP client interface, and it allows the files to be owned by a valid user defined in the skeleton password file (including the user ID [UID] and group ID [GID] of accounts like root).

NOTE: No real passwords should be stored in this password file—all entries should be removed, except for root, and password shadowing should be enabled. We will cover these steps later in this section.

Traditionally when you connect to an anonymous FTP server, you identify yourself as the user "ftp" or the user "anonymous," after which you are asked to enter your e-mail address:

```
client% ftp ftp.sun.com
Connected to ftp.sun.com.
220-Welcome to Sun Microsystems Corporate FTP Server.
220-
220 ftp FTP server (ftpd Wed Oct 30 23:31:06 PST 1996) ready.
Name (ftp.sun.com:pwatters): anonymous
331 Guest login ok, send your complete e-mail address as password.
Password:
230 Guest login ok, access restrictions apply.
```

However, some unscrupulous site administrators have been known to sell lists of all e-mail addresses that are entered into their anonymous FTP server so that companies can send them targeted unsolicited commercial e-mail to the address entered. It is, therefore, wise to enter a fake e-mail address that contains at least one @ character, as this is typically used for validation.

TIP: Never enter a valid password from your own system, as this could be recorded and used to break into your local account in the future.

An anonymous FTP session is almost exactly the same as a normal FTP session: the same commands are used to upload and download files (get, put, mget, and mput), change directories (cd and lcd), print the current working directory (pwd), and get a directory listing (dir and ls). The main difference is that you will not be logged into the same system area as all other users, unless the home directory of the FTP user is set to / (for example, the root directory would be a very bad idea!).

NOTE: Most anonymous FTP servers have a README or INDEX file that explains what files are available to download, and what restrictions might be placed on anonymous users, such as download size and connect time limits.

If you experience any difficulties with setting up anonymous FAQ on Solaris, you should consult the Anonymous FTP FAQ file available at ftp://rtfm.mit.edu/pub/usenet/news.answers/computer-security/anonymous-ftp-faq. Security patches are released periodically for all Internet daemons, including in.ftpd, through SunSolve. In addition, CERT advisories, which contain important late-breaking news about vulnerabilities that have been discovered by vendors or that have been widely publicized on the Internet, are available at http://www.cert.org.

Solaris 8 provides the ftpconfig command to install anonymous FTP. However, when setting up such a sensitive service, it is useful to understand what manual steps are involved. To set up anonymous FTP, you must first create a group for the anonymous FTP user called "ftp," which only has the member ftp, by using the following command:

```
bash-2.03# groupadd -g 200 ftp
```

It is important to note that the GID of 200 must not be used for another group. Next, the user account ftp must be created by using the useradd command:

```
bash-2.03# useradd -u 1024 -g 200 -d /anon -s /bin/false -c "Anon FTP User" ftp
```

The useradd command creates the ftp user account with UID 1024, GID 100, a home directory of /anon, and the /bin/false program as the default shell. This prevents any remote user from accessing the system by using telnet, since the user must have a valid shell for the system to permit logins. Again, the UID of 1024 must not be used by any other user. These two steps could be undertaken using the admintool if you prefer to use a Graphical User Interface (GUI).

The next stage of the process is to set the file permissions on /anon to 555:

```
bash# chmod -R 555 /anon
```

Setting the file permissions on /anon to 555 prevents writing to the filesystem by all users, but permits reading and executing. The latter is necessary so that directories can be accessed by all users. In addition, it is often a good policy to change the ownership of all files in the /anon directory to be owned by root and not by FTP, since we want the ftp user to have as little control as possible over the files in /anon.

Next, a mini Solaris root system needs to be installed into the /anon filesystem. The following steps need to be followed:

▼ Create the directories /anon/bin, /anon/etc, /anon/lib, and /anon/pub as the root user, and set the permissions to 555 (read and execute, but no writing)

■ Copy the ls program from /bin to the directory /anon/bin directory, and set the permissions to be 555

■ Copy /etc/passwd to /anon/etc/passwd, and replace any encrypted passwords with the * character. This prevents anonymous users from obtaining a copy of the encrypted passwords stored on your computer, which they could use to break into your system.

■ Remove all entries from /anon/etc/passwd except for root and the ftp user. The example password file should look similar to this:

```
root:*:0:0:Super User::
ftp:*:1024:200:Anon FTP User::
```

■ Copy the /etc/group file into the /anon/etc directory, and delete all entries except for GID 0 and GID 200 (for example, root's default group and the ftp user's default group)

▲ Create an /anon/pub/README file that describes the purpose of your site and outlines any special access policies, such as download limits

After these steps have been taken, the /anon directory should have the following entries:

```
dr-xr-xr-x  7    root     root   512 Nov 5        16:36 ./
 dr-xr-xr-x 25    root     root   512 Nov 5        16:36 ../
 dr-xr-xr-x  2    root     root   512 Nov 5        16:36 bin/
 dr-xr-xr-x  2    root     root   512 Nov 5        16:36 etc/
dr-xr-xr-x  2    root      root  512  Nov 5        16:36 etc/
          dr-xr-xr-x 10    root     root  512 Nov 5        16:36 pub/
-r-xr-xr-x  1    root      root  256  Nov 5        16:36 README
```

If you encounter problems with anonymous FTP, it's often possible to determine what the problem is by examining the FTP status codes that are returned from all FTP commands sent to the server. The most likely cause of access problems is file permissions—you need to ensure that all anonymous FTP files are world readable and that directories are world executable. A full list of error codes in given in Table 13-1.

Code	Description
110	Restart marker reply
120	Service ready in *nnn* minutes
125	Data connection already open; transfer starting
150	File status okay; about to open data connection
200	Command okay
202	Command not implemented, superfluous at this site
211	System status or system help reply
212	Directory status
213	File status

Table 13-1.   FTP Status Codes

Code	Description
214	Help message
215	NAME system type
220	Service ready for new user
221	Service closing control connection
225	Data connection open; no transfer in progress
226	Closing data connection
227	Entering Passive Mode (h1, h2, h3, h4, p1, p2)
230	User logged in; proceed
250	Requested file action okay; completed
257	"PATHNAME" created
331	User name okay; need password
332	Need account for login
350	Requested file action pending further information
421	Service not available; closing control connection
425	Can't open data connection
426	Connection closed; transfer aborted
450	Requested file action not taken
451	Requested action aborted: local error in processing
452	Requested action not taken
500	Syntax error: command unrecognized
501	Syntax error in parameters or arguments
502	Command not implemented
503	Bad sequence of commands
504	Command not implemented for that parameter
530	Not logged in
532	Need account for storing files
550	Requested action not taken
551	Requested action aborted: page type unknown
552	Requested file action aborted
553	Requested action not taken

Table 13-1.   FTP Status Codes *(continued)*

For more information about how FTP operates, including anonymous FTP, see the following RFCs:

▼ RFC 2640: Internationalization of the File Transfer Protocol

■ RFC 2389: Feature negotiation mechanism for the File Transfer Protocol

■ RFC 1986: Experiments with a Simple File Transfer Protocol for Radio Links Using Enhanced Trivial File Transfer Protocol (ETFTP)

■ RFC 1440: SIFT/UFT: Sender-Initiated/Unsolicited File Transfer

■ RFC 1068: Background File Transfer Program (BFTP)

■ RFC 2585: Internet X.509 Public Key Infrastructure Operational Protocols: FTP and HTTP

■ RFC 2428: FTP Extensions for IPv6 and NATs

■ RFC 2228: FTP Security Extensions

▲ RFC 1639: FTP Operation Over Big Address Records (FOOBAR)

Although Solaris comes with a standard FTP server, you may decide to install one of the many third-party FTP servers that are available on the Internet. This is because some third-party FTP servers offer some extra features that are useful for supporting anonymous FTP, because they support upload/download quotas and sophisticated group access facilities. One of the most popular servers is the Washington University FTP (WU-FTP) server, which can be downloaded from ftp://ftp.wu.edu. One of the nicest features of WU-FTPD is the ability to examine the source code and customize it to meet your own requirements; thus, if you wanted to incorporate a new security feature into the FTP server, you could easily make the change. Unfortunately, giving the source code away to crackers on the Internet makes the system more vulnerable to attack because a weakness may be identified in the source. For example, many standard daemons (until recently) did not perform bounds checking on command parameter arrays, which meant that servers could easily be compromised by passing parameter strings greater than the declared size of the parameter array. However, these problems have been largely rectified in recent years, and having access to the source code can also help developers identify any potential weaknesses.

The Washington University FTP daemon (WU-FTPD) is very useful for managing anonymous FTP because file download limits can be set on a per-user, per-session basis, rather than just on the filesystem. This can be useful for preventing denial-of-service attacks, as well as allowing a more equitable distribution of download bandwidth from a public server during peak periods. Options for the WU-FTPD can be set for various functions, including the ability to delete, overwrite, rename, change permissions, and set umasks for the anonymous FTP client:

```
delete      yes    guest,anonymous
overwrite   yes    guest,anonymous
rename      no     guest,anonymous
chmod       yes    anonymous
umask       no     anonymous
```

Once the WU-FTPD has been installed and configured, it can be started by adding the following line to the /etc/inetd.conf file:

```
ftp  stream  tcp  nowait  root  /usr/local/wu-ftpd/ftpd  ftpd -laio
```

The line that contained the original FTP daemon configuration should be commented out, and the inetd process should then be restarted.

SERVICE TESTING

If you're having trouble getting anonymous FTP to work, or any of the Transmission Control Protocol /Internet Protocol (TCP/IP) services supported by Solaris, you can always test the protocol commands manually by using a telnet client to make a TCP connection to the target port on the server. In the case of FTP, you can issue commands interactively to port 21 and verify the response accordingly. The port number can be specified on the command line after the server hostname. To test an anonymous FTP server, you could use the following command:

```
client% telnet server 21
Trying 203.64.22.1...
Connected to server.
Escape character is '^]'.
220 server FTP server (UNIX(r) System V Release 4.0) ready.
```

This means that the FTP server is ready to serve queries. If your FTP server needs to be highly available, it's easy to write a script that uses telnet to test that a server is operational 24/7. To test the availability of other remote access services, you simply need to specify the port number on the command line. For example, to test the sendmail service, you could use the command

```
client% telnet server 25
Trying 203.64.22.1...
Connected to server.
Escape character is '^]'.
220 server ESMTP Sendmail 9.0.0a/9.0.0; Sat, 11 Nov 2000 08:34:01 +1100 (EST)
```

In addition to testing connectivity, it is also possible to issue commands and test their responses. For example, if you're running a Web server that should always serve the same index page, you could write a script that used telnet to determine whether or not the Web page was actually being served by the server. A get command can be issued using HTTP, and the contents of the returned page can be matched with the expected page (rather than a 404 error page, which would indicate that the page had not been found). To retrieve the default index.html page on the server, the following command could be used:

```
client% telnet server
Trying 203.64.22.1...
Connected to server.
```

```
Escape character is '^]'.
GET index.html
<!DOCTYPE HTML PUBLIC "-//IETF//DTD HTML 3.0//EN">
<HTML><HEAD>
<TITLE>Index Page</TITLE></HEAD>
<h1>Hopefully this is the page you wanted to see!</h1>
```

R COMMANDS

So far, we've focused on the telnet and FTP commands to perform remote access operations; however, there is another set of remote access commands known as the "r" commands. These can be used to spawn remote shells, using the rsh command, and execute commands remotely, using the rlogin command. The rsh application is used to execute commands remotely on a server that has the remote shell daemon running. The command that is to be executed can be specified on the command line. As an example, you can run the who command on a remote server, to see who is currently logged in:

```
client% rsh server who
```

The output from the command is piped to standard output, meaning that it can be redirected to a file on the client system. For example, if the preceding command was run once hourly as a security measure to log all active users every hour, the output could be redirected to a running logfile, an example of which follows:

```
client% rsh server who >> /var/log/server.who.log
```

The /var/log/server.who.log file would then contain all of the entries for the command, every time it is executed. A cron job could be created that schedules this command to run hourly, in which case, all logged entries will appear sequentially in the file. Once the application has been executed on the remote server, terminal control returns to the client.

The rlogin command is different to the rsh command because the client is remotely logged into a server after spawning a remote shell; thus, the rlogin command does not terminate once a connection has been established, and a shell has been spawned. To make a connection to a server running the rlogin daemon, you would need to use the following command:

```
client% rlogin server
```

You would then be prompted to enter your password:

```
password:
```

If the username and password can be authenticated, then a shell will be spawned, and you will be able to enter commands directly. Alternatively, if your remote username is different from your local username, you may pass it on the command line by using the

–l parameter. For example, the local user bill may have an account called "william" on the remote server, in which case the following command could be used:

```
bill@client% rlogin server -l william
```

The r commands are used as alternatives to telnet in a number of different situations. Using rlogin is typically faster than using telnet; and in some networks, the telnet service may be completely disabled. Authentication in this case may rely on Kerberos or another distributed authentication mechanism. This means that each user would have a single password in the domain, meaning if the user authenticated at one server, he or she can rlogin to another without authentication. This is a very useful feature for managing large networks of hosts that have similar configurations, and it can be set by defining hosts as equivalent in the /etc/hosts.equiv file.

Another nice trick for servers running X11 is that it is possible to telnet from one system to another and to remotely execute applications whose display is set to the current system's console. For example, if we logged into the host "chile" on the console, but we wished to run a statistical analysis package on the host "ecuador," then we would simply telnet to ecuador from chile and execute the application. The application would run on the remote system, but all input and output would be redirected to the current terminal. However, two steps are usually required to get this process working properly. First, you must set the DISPLAY environment variable on the server ecuador to be chile, with the following command:

```
ecuador$ DISPLAY=chile:0.0; export DISPLAY
```

In addition, if you get a message such as

```
Error: Can't open display: chile:0
```

You will need to explicitly allow connections from ecuador to chile's display by executing the following command:

```
chile$ xhost + ecuador
```

This procedure is very useful when a central server has many CPUs, lots of RAM, and all of the major applications installed, and your local client system is not powerful. An example is the Sun Ray thin client, which is the size of a small book and which executes all processes on a central workgroup server, such as an Enterprise 450, as shown in Figure 13-2.

SECURITY ISSUES

Remote access tools like telnet, ftp, rlogin, and rsh are very useful applications in their own right, which is why they continue to be supported under Solaris. When your staff is completely trusted, they are completely safe to be used in a local area network, which is protected by a packet filtering firewall. If you want to make a remote connection across

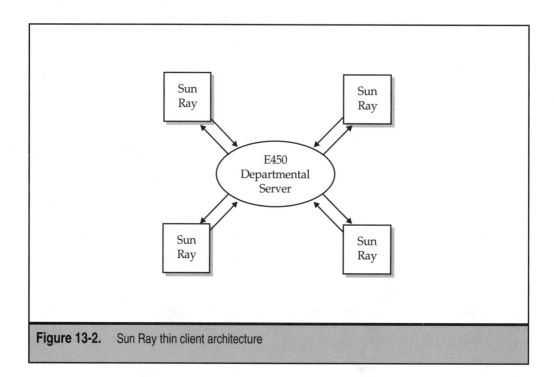

Figure 13-2. Sun Ray thin client architecture

the Internet, there is a possibility that someone is intercepting your telnet, rlogin, rsh, or ftp packets on an intermediate host. You can obtain an idea of how many potential sniffers could be capturing your data packets by examining a list of all intermediate hosts between the client and server, using the traceroute command:

```
client% traceroute www.sun.com
Tracing route to wwwwseast.usec.sun.com [192.9.49.30]
over a maximum of 30 hops:
  1    184 ms    142 ms    138 ms  202.10.4.131
  2    147 ms    144 ms    138 ms  202.10.4.129
  3    150 ms    142 ms    144 ms  202.10.1.73
  4    150 ms    144 ms    141 ms  atm11-0-0-11.ia4.optus.net.au [202.139.32.17]
  5    148 ms    143 ms    139 ms  202.139.1.197
  6    490 ms    489 ms    474 ms  hssi9-0-0.sf1.optus.net.au [192.65.89.246]
  7    526 ms    480 ms    485 ms  g-sfd-br-02-f12-0.gn.cwix.net [207.124.109.57]
  8    494 ms    482 ms    485 ms  core7-hssi6-0-0.SanFrancisco.cw.net [204.70.10.9]
  9    483 ms    489 ms    484 ms  corerouter2.SanFrancisco.cw.net [204.70.9.132]
 10    557 ms    552 ms    561 ms  xcore3.Boston.cw.net [204.70.150.81]
 11    566 ms    572 ms    554 ms  sun-micro-system.Boston.cw.net [204.70.179.102]
 12    577 ms    574 ms    558 ms  wwwwseast.usec.sun.com [192.9.49.30]
Trace complete.
```

If your username and password are sent in the clear (for example, not encrypted), as rlogin, rsh, telnet, and ftp all are, then these two authentication credentials could be intercepted by using the snoop command. You can see for yourself the power of the snoop command by running it on your local system to intercept all packets generated by telnet running on port 23:

```
bash-2.03# snoop tcp port 23
Using device /dev/hme0 (promiscuous mode)
moppet.paulwatters.com -> miki.paulwatters.com TELNET C port=62421
miki.paulwatters.com -> moppet.paulwatters.com TELNET R port=62421 Using device
/dev/hme0
moppet.paulwatters.com -> miki.paulwatters.com TELNET C port=62421
miki.paulwatters.com -> moppet.paulwatters.com TELNET R port=62421
moppet.paulwatters.com ->
moppet.paulwatters.com -> miki.paulwatters.com TELNET C port=62421
miki.paulwatters.com -> moppet.paulwatters.com TELNET R port=62421
miki.paulwatters.com ->
moppet.paulwatters.com -> miki.paulwatters.com TELNET C port=62421
miki.paulwatters.com -> moppet.paulwatters.com TELNET R port=62421
miki.paulwatters.com ->
moppet.paulwatters.com -> miki.paulwatters.com TELNET C port=62421
miki.paulwatters.com -> moppet.paulwatters.com TELNET R port=62421
moppet.paulwatters.com ->
moppet.paulwatters.com -> miki.paulwatters.com TELNET C port=62421
miki.paulwatters.com -> moppet.paulwatters.com TELNET R port=62421
miki.paulwatters.com ->
moppet.paulwatters.com -> miki.paulwatters.com TELNET C port=62421
miki.paulwatters.com -> moppet.paulwatters.com TELNET R port=62421
moppet.paulwatters.com ->
moppet.paulwatters.com -> miki.paulwatters.com TELNET C port=62421
```

In the preceding code listing, we can see that telnet data is being transferred between the hosts miki and moppet. To actually see what data is being transmitted, such as a username and password, you simply switch to verbose mode by specifying the –v option on the command line:

```
bash-2.03# snoop -v tcp port 23
Using device /dev/hme0 (promiscuous mode)
ETHER:  ----- Ether Header -----
ETHER:
ETHER:  Packet 1 arrived at 14:13:22.14
ETHER:  Packet size = 60 bytes
ETHER:  Destination = 1:58:4:16:8a:34,
ETHER:  Source      = 2:60:5:12:6b:35, Sun
ETHER:  Ethertype = 0800 (IP)
ETHER:
IP:    ----- IP Header -----
IP:
```

```
IP:    Version =
IP:    Header length = 20 bytes
IP:    Type of service = 0x00
IP:          xxx. .... = 0 (precedence)
IP:          ...0 .... = normal delay
IP:          .... 0... = normal throughput
IP:          .... .0.. = normal reliability
IP:    Total length = 40 bytes
IP:    Identification = 46864
IP:    Flags = 0x4
IP:          .1.. .... = do not fragment
IP:          ..0. .... = last fragment
IP:    Fragment offset = 0 bytes
IP:    Time to live = 255 seconds/hops
IP:    Protocol = 6 (TCP)
IP:    Header checksum = 11a9
IP:    Source address = 64.23.168.76, moppet.paulwatters.com
IP:    Destination address = 64.23.168.48, miki.paulwatters.com
IP:    No options
IP:
TCP:   ----- TCP Header -----
TCP:
TCP:   Source port = 62421
TCP:   Destination port = 23 (TELNET)
TCP:   Sequence number = 796159562
TCP:   Acknowledgement number = 105859685
TCP:   Data offset = 20 bytes
TCP:   Flags = 0x10
TCP:          ..0. .... = No urgent pointer
TCP:          ...1 .... = Acknowledgement
TCP:          .... 0... = No push
TCP:          .... .0.. = No reset
TCP:          .... ..0. = No Syn
TCP:          .... ...0 = No Fin
TCP:   Window = 8760
TCP:   Checksum = 0x8f8f
TCP:   Urgent pointer = 0
TCP:   No options
TCP:
TELNET:  ----- TELNET:    -----
TELNET:
TELNET:  ""
TELNET:
```

The details listed in the preceding are only for a single packet, which is a lot of information made available to all who are listening. One method for reducing the risk of exposing authentication credentials to public scrutiny is to use a remote access client, which encrypts the exchange of username and password data between the client and the server.

This means that, although the username and password strings can still be captured, their contents would need to be cracked by using a brute force method.

Such a method is extremely unlikely to succeed if a password is selected that is difficult to crack (for example, a password composed of eight random numbers and characters). Alternatively, the entire session may be encrypted making it ever more difficult for an eavesdropper to determine what data is being exchanged.

One of the most popular applications for securing remote access is the Secure Shell (SSH), which is available in both freeware and commercially supported editions. If you wish to use the SSH developed as part of the OpenBSD project, you can download the latest portable release from http://www.openssh.com/portable.html. Alternatively, if you must use commercial products, you can download and purchase a commercial SSH from http://www.ssh.com.

Both of these packages support the Secure Shell 1 (SSH1) (RSA-based) and Secure Shell 2 (SSH2) (DH/DSA-based) protocols, developed by the IETF (http://www.ietf.org/html.charters/secsh-charter.html), as well as support multiple encryption algorithms (for example, 3DES and Blowfish). In addition to using SSH as an alternative for shell-based interactive logins, the scp and sftp programs can be used as alternatives to rcp (remote copy) and FTP, respectively.

SUMMARY

In this chapter, we have further examined the remote access tools that are supplied with Solaris, and we have covered how to secure them. Most sites that are connected to the Internet would choose to disable telnet services and install SSH instead.

CHAPTER 14

Web Services

The World Wide Web (WWW) has become one of the most dominant Internet services provided by organizations and individuals worldwide. Everyone has a home page that they wish to share with the rest of the world, and many companies offer goods and services through the Internet. In this chapter, you will learn how to install and configure the popular Apache Web server, and write simple Common Gateway Interface (CGI) applications using Practical Extraction and Report Language (perl). In addition, we will examine how to use the Apache JServ Java servlet runner to deploy server-side Java applications to the WWW.

INSTALLING APACHE

Apache is the de facto industry standard for Web servers, with more than 50 percent of Internet sites using Apache as their primary Web servers. Many Internet Web servers combine the functionality of Apache with the stability of Solaris to ensure 24/7 reliability. With the release of Solaris 8, Sun has finally bowed to pressure and has included the Apache binaries with the operating environment distribution. This means that you won't need to build Apache from sources to get started with Apache. However, you may decide to recompile Apache from sources in the future, if you wish to take advantage of the different kinds of module support available for Apache.

Apache's main task is to serve files to clients using Hypertext Transfer Protocol (HTTP). Web browsers typically make a Transmission Control Protocol (TCP) connection to port 80 on the Web server, issue a get or post request, and then parse the Hypertext Markup Language (HTML) tags that are interpreted on the client side to produce the Web pages that we all know and love. Figure 14-1 shows a Netscape client on Solaris retrieving an HTML page from a Solaris server running Apache.

Running Apache for Web hosting is designed to be easy. In addition, you'll be pleased to know that Apache also performs a number of different tasks, including

▼ Providing a CGI for client access to server-side processes and applications. CGI applications can be written in C, C++, Perl, the Bourne shell, or the language of your choice

■ Supporting the hosting of multiple sites on a single server, where each site is associated with a unique, fully qualified domain name. Thus, a single Solaris system, in an ISP environment, can host multiple Web sites, such as www.java-support.com, www.paulwatters.com, and others, using a single instance of Apache

■ Securing the transmission of credit card details and other sensitive data by supporting the Secure Socket Layer (SSL). This allows for key-based encryption of the HTTP (called HTTPS) with key sizes of up to 128 bits

■ Providing a fully featured proxy/cache server, which provides an extra level of protection for clients behind a firewall and also keeps a copy of the most commonly retrieved documents from the WWW

▲ Offering customized access, agent, and error logs that can be used for marketing and reporting purposes

Figure 14-1.   A Netscape client running on Solaris retrieves an HTML page from a Solaris server running Apache

The main Apache configuration file is httpd.conf, which contains three sections:

▼ The global environment section, which sets key server information such as the root directory for the Apache installation, and several process management settings, such as the number of concurrent requests permitted per server process

■ The main server configuration section, which sets runtime parameters for the server, including the port on which the server listens, the server name, the root directory for the HTML documents and images that comprise the site, and the server authorization configuration if required

▲ The virtual hosts configuration section, which configures the Apache server to run servers for multiple domains. Many of the configuration options that are set for the main server can also be customized for each of the virtual servers.

We will now examine the configuration options in each of these sections in detail.

Global Environment Configuration

The following options are commonly set in the global environment configuration section:

```
ServerType standalone
ServerRoot "/opt/apache1.3"
PidFile /opt/apache1.3/logs/httpd.pid
ScoreBoardFile /opt/apache1.3/logs/apache_status
Timeout 300
KeepAlive On
MaxKeepAliveRequests 100
KeepAliveTimeout 15
MaxRequestsPerChild 0
ThreadsPerChild 50
LoadModule auth_module modules/mod_auth.so
```

The server configuration shown here does not run as a service of the Internet super daemon (inetd); rather, Apache runs as a stand-alone daemon. This gives Apache more flexibility in its configuration, as well as better performance than running through inetd. Since Apache is able to service more than one client through a single process (using the KeepAlive facility), no production system should ever use the inetd mode.

The ServerRoot for the Apache installation is set to /opt/apache1.3 in this installation. There is no need to install Apache in a specific location, as long as you define its root location in the inetd.conf.

NOTE: All of the key files required by Apache are located below this directory root, such as the lock file, the scoreboard file, and the file that records the process ID (PID) of the current Apache process.

Each of the clients that connect to the server has an expiry date in the form of a time-out. In this configuration, the timeout is set to 300 seconds (5 minutes). This is the period of inactivity after which a client is deemed to have timed out. Requests are kept alive, with up to 100 requests. There is no limit to the number of requests per child process; however, there is a limit of 50 threads per child.

Main Server Configuration

The following options are commonly set in the main server configuration:

```
Port 80
ServerAdmin paul@ethos-development.com
ServerName www.ethos-development.com
DocumentRoot "/opt/apache1.3/htdocs"
<Directory/>
    Options FollowSymLinks
    AllowOverride None
</Directory>
<Directory "/opt/apache1.3/htdocs">
    Options Indexes FollowSymLinks MultiViews
    AllowOverride None
    Order allow,deny
    Allow from all
</Directory>
UserDir "/opt/apache1.3/users/"
DirectoryIndex index.html
AccessFileName .htaccess
<Files .htaccess>
    Order allow,deny
    Deny from all
</Files>
UseCanonicalName On
TypesConfig /opt/apache1.3/conf/mime.types
DefaultType text/plain
HostnameLookups Off
ErrorLog /opt/apache1.3/logs/error.log
LogLevel warn
LogFormat "%h %l %u %t \"%r\" %>s %b \"%{Referer}i\" \"%{User-Agent}i\"" combined
LogFormat "%h %l %u %t \"%r\" %>s %b" common
LogFormat "%{Referer}i -> %U" referer
LogFormat "%{User-agent}i" agent
CustomLog /opt/apache1.3/logs/access.log common
CustomLog /opt/apache1.3/logs/access.log combined
ServerSignature On
Alias /icons/ "/opt/apache1.3/icons/"
ScriptAlias /cgi-bin/ "/opt/apache1.3/cgi-bin/"
```

```
<Directory "/opt/apache1.3/cgi-bin">
    AllowOverride None
    Options None
</Directory>
IndexOptions FancyIndexing
AddIconByEncoding (CMP,/icons/compressed.gif) x-compress x-gzip
AddIconByType (TXT,/icons/text.gif) text/*
AddIconByType (IMG,/icons/image2.gif) image/*
AddIconByType (SND,/icons/sound2.gif) audio/*
AddIconByType (VID,/icons/movie.gif) video/*
AddIcon /icons/binary.gif .bin .exe
AddIcon /icons/binhex.gif .hqx
AddIcon /icons/tar.gif .tar
AddIcon /icons/world2.gif .wrl .wrl.gz .vrml .vrm .iv
AddIcon /icons/compressed.gif .Z .z .tgz .gz .zip
AddIcon /icons/a.gif .ps .ai .eps
AddIcon /icons/layout.gif .html .shtml .htm .pdf
AddIcon /icons/text.gif .txt
AddIcon /icons/c.gif .c
AddIcon /icons/p.gif .pl .py
AddIcon /icons/f.gif .for
AddIcon /icons/dvi.gif .dvi
AddIcon /icons/uuencoded.gif .uu
AddIcon /icons/script.gif .conf .sh .shar .csh .ksh .tcl
AddIcon /icons/tex.gif .tex
AddIcon /icons/bomb.gif core
AddIcon /icons/back.gif
AddIcon /icons/hand.right.gif README
AddIcon /icons/folder.gif ^^DIRECTORY^^
AddIcon /icons/blank.gif ^^BLANKICON^^
DefaultIcon /icons/unknown.gif
ReadmeName README
HeaderName HEADER
IndexIgnore .??* *~ *# HEADER* README* RCS CVS *,v *,t
AddEncoding x-compress Z
AddEncoding x-gzip gz tgz
AddLanguage da .dk
AddLanguage nl .nl
AddLanguage en .en
AddLanguage et .ee
AddLanguage fr .fr
AddLanguage de .de
AddLanguage el .el
AddLanguage it .it
AddLanguage pt .pt
AddLanguage ltz .lu
```

```
AddLanguage ca .ca
AddLanguage es .es
AddLanguage sv .se
AddLanguage cz .cz
LanguagePriority en da nl et fr de el it pt ltz ca es sv
AddType application/x-tar .tgz
BrowserMatch "Mozilla/2" nokeepalive
BrowserMatch "MSIE 4\.0b2;" nokeepalive downgrade-1.0 force-response-1.0
BrowserMatch "RealPlayer 4\.0" force-response-1.0
BrowserMatch "Java/1\.0" force-response-1.0
BrowserMatch "JDK/1\.0" force-response-1.0
```

The parameters in this section determine the main runtime characteristics of the Apache server. The first parameter is the port on which the Apache server will run. If the server is being executed by an unprivileged user, then this port must be set at 1024 or higher. However, if a privileged user (like root) is executing the process, then any unreserved port may be used (you can check the services database, /etc/services, for ports allocated to specific services).

NOTE: The default port is 80.

Next, some details about the server are entered, including the hostname of the system, which is to be displayed in all URLs, and a contact e-mail address for the server. This address is usually displayed on all error and CGI misconfiguration pages. The root directory for all HTML and other content for the Web site must also be supplied. This allows for both absolute and relative Uniform Resource Locators (URLs) to be constructed and interpreted by the server.

In this case, the htdocs subdirectory underneath the main Apache directory is used. Thus, the file index.html in this directory will be the default page displayed when no specific page is specified in the URL.

There are several options that can be specified for the htdocs directory, including whether or not to ignore symbolic links to directories that do not reside underneath the htdocs subdirectory. This is useful when you have files available on CD-ROMs and other filesystems that do not need to copied onto a hard drive, but simply served through the WWW.

Apache has a simple user authentication system available, which is similar to the Solaris password database (/etc/passwd) in that it makes use of encrypted passwords, but it does not make use of the Solaris password database. This means that a separate list of users and passwords must be maintained. Thus, when a password-protected page is requested by a user, a username and matching password must be entered using a dialog box, as shown in Figure 14-2. Any directory that appears underneath the main htdocs directory can be password protected using this mechanism.

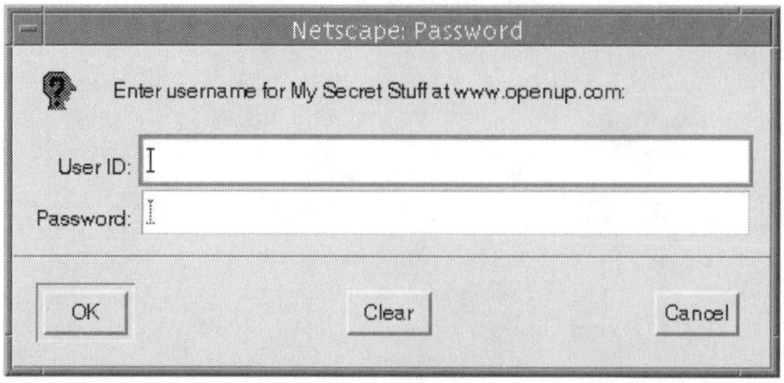

Figure 14-2.   User authentication using Netscape

Next, the various Multipurpose Internet Mail Extension (MIME) types that can be processed by the server are defined in a separate file called mime.types. Let's look at some examples of the MIME types defined for the server:

```
application/mac-binhex40          hqx
application/mac-compactpro        cpt
application/msword                doc
application/pdf                   pdf
application/postscript            ai eps ps
application/x-bcpio               bcpio
application/x-cdlink              vcd
application/x-chess-pgn           pgn
application/x-compress
application/x-cpio                cpio
application/x-csh                 csh
application/x-director            dcr dir dxr
application/x-dvi                 dvi
application/x-futuresplash        spl
application/x-gtar                gtar
application/x-gzip
application/x-hdf                 hdf
application/x-javascript          js
application/x-koan                skp skd skt skm
```

We can see the file types defined here for many popular applications, including compression utilities (Macintosh BinHex, application/mac-binhex40, with the extension .hqx), word-processing documents (Microsoft Word, application/msword, with the extension .doc), and C shell scripts (application/x-csh, with the extension .csh).

The next section deals with logfile formats. The first directive switches off hostname lookups on clients before logging their activities. Since performing a reverse DNS lookup on every client making a connection is a CPU- and bandwidth-intensive task, many sites prefer to switch it off.

However, if you need to gather marketing statistics on where your clients are connecting from (for example, by geographical region or by second-level domain type), then you may need to switch hostname lookups on. In addition, an error log is specified as a separate entity to the access log. A typical set of access log entries looks like this:

```
192.64.32.12 - - [06/Sep/2000:20:55:36 +1000] "GET /cgi-bin/printenv HTTP/1.1" 200
1024
192.64.32.12 - - [06/Sep/2000:20:56:07 +1000] "GET
/cgi-bin/Search.cgi?term=solaris&type=simple HTTP/1.1" 200 85527
192.64.32.12 - - [06/Sep/2000:20:58:44 +1000] "GET /index.html HTTP/1.1" 200 94151
192.64.32.12 - - [06/Sep/2000:20:59:58 +1000] "GET /pdf/secret.pdf HTTP/1.1" 403 29
```

The first example in the previous code listing shows that the client 192.64.32.12 accessed the CGI application printenv on 6 September 2000, at 8:55 P.M. The result code for the transaction was 200, which indicates a successful transfer. The printenv script comes standard with Apache, and it displays the current environment variables being passed from the client. The output is very useful for debugging, and looks like the following:

```
DOCUMENT_ROOT="/usr/local/apache-1.3.12/htdocs"
GATEWAY_INTERFACE="CGI/1.1"
HTTP_ACCEPT="image/gif, image/x-xbitmap, image/jpeg, image/pjpeg,
application/vnd.ms-excel, application/msword, application/vnd.ms-powerpoint, */*"
HTTP_ACCEPT_ENCODING="gzip, deflate"
HTTP_ACCEPT_LANGUAGE="en-au"
HTTP_CONNECTION="Keep-Alive"
HTTP_HOST="www"
HTTP_USER_AGENT="Mozilla/4.75 (X11; I; SunOS 5.8 i86pc; Nav)"
PATH="/usr/sbin:/usr/bin:/bin:/usr/ucb:/usr/local/bin:/usr/openwin/bin:/usr/dt/bin:/usr/ccs/bin"
QUERY_STRING=""
REMOTE_ADDR="209.67.50.55"
REMOTE_PORT="3399"
REQUEST_METHOD="GET"
REQUEST_URI="/cgi-bin/printenv"
SCRIPT_FILENAME="/usr/local/apache/cgi-bin/printenv"
SCRIPT_NAME="/cgi-bin/printenv"
SERVER_ADDR="209.67.50.203"
SERVER_ADMIN="paul@paulwatters.com"
SERVER_NAME="www.paulwatters.com"
SERVER_PORT="80"
SERVER_PROTOCOL="HTTP/1.1"
SERVER_SIGNATURE="Apache/1.3.12 Server at www.paulwatters.com Port 80\n"
SERVER_SOFTWARE="Apache/1.3.12 (Unix)" TZ="Australia/NSW"
```

The second line from the log shows that a client running from the same system successfully executed the CGI program Search.cgi, passing two get parameters: a search term of "solaris", and a search type of "simple". The size of the generated response page was 85,527 bytes. The third line shows a plain HTML page being successfully retrieved, with a response code of 200 and a file size of 94,151 bytes.

The fourth line demonstrates one of the many HTTP error codes being returned, instead of the 200 success code. In this case, a request to retrieve the file /pdf/secret.pdf is denied with a 403 code being returned to the browser. This code would be returned if the file permissions set on the /pdf/secret.pdf file did not grant read access to the user executing Apache (for example, nobody). A list of HTTP codes for transmission success, client failure, and server failure is shown in Table 14-1.

Code Type	Code	Description
Successful Transmission	200	OK
	201	Created
	202	Accepted
	203	Nonauthoritative Information
	204	No Content
	205	Reset Content
	206	Partial Content
Client Errors	400	Bad Request
	401	Unauthorized
	402	Payment Required
	403	Forbidden
	404	Not Found
	405	Method Not Allowed
	406	Not Acceptable
	407	Proxy Authentication Required
	408	Request Timeout
	409	Conflict
	410	Gone
	411	Length Required

Table 14-1. HTTP Response Codes

Code Type	Code	Description
	412	Precondition Failed
	413	Request Entity Too Large
	414	Request-URI Too Long
	415	Unsupported Media Type
	416	Expectation Failed
Server Errors	500	Internal Server Error
	501	Not Implemented
	502	Bad Gateway
	503	Service Unavailable
	504	Gateway Timeout
	505	HTTP Version Not Supported

Table 14-1.   HTTP Response Codes *(continued)*

Virtual Hosts Configuration

The following options are commonly set in the main server configuration:

```
<VirtualHost www.java-support.com>
    ServerAdmin webmaster@www.java-support
    DocumentRoot /opt/apache1.3/htdocs/www.java-support.com
    ServerName www.java-support.com
    ErrorLog /opt/apache1.3/logs/www.java-support.com-error_log
    CustomLog /opt/apache1.3/logs/www.java-support.com-access_log common
</VirtualHost>
```

In the preceding code, we define a single virtual host (www.java-support.com), in addition to the default host for the Apache Web server. Virtual host support allows administrators to keep separate logs for errors and access, as well as a completely separate document root to the default server. This makes it very easy to maintain multiple virtual servers on a single physical machine.

Running Apache

In recent versions, Apache has come bundled with a control script (apachectl) that can be used to start, stop, and report on the status of the server. To obtain help on the apachectl script, change to the bin subdirectory under the Apache installation directory, and use the following command:

```
bash-2.03$ ./apachectl help
usage: ./apachectl
(start|stop|restart|fullstatus|status|graceful|configtest|help)

start      - start httpd
stop       - stop httpd
restart    - restart httpd if running by sending a SIGHUP or start if
             not running
fullstatus - dump a full status screen; requires lynx and mod_status enabled
status     - dump a short status screen; requires lynx and mod_status enabled
graceful   - do a graceful restart by sending a SIGUSR1 or start if not running
configtest - do a configuration syntax test
help       - this screen
```

To start Apache, you simply need to issue the following command from the same directory:

```
bash-2.03$ ./apachectl start
```

In order to stop the service, the following command may be used from the same directory:

```
bash-2.03$ ./apachectl stop
```

If you change the Apache configuration file, and you need to restart the service so that the server is updated, you can simply use the following command from the same directory:

```
bash-2.03$ ./apachectl restart
```

Once Apache is running on port 80, clients will be able to begin requesting HTML pages and other content.

Recently, Apache has grown to be more than a simple Web server. It has a number of modules that can be used to extend its features, including the following:

▼ **mod_access**   Allows or denies access to the Web server based on the originating Internet Protocol (IP) address of the request

■ **mod_actions**   Associates MIME types of files requested by a specific CGI application

■ **mod_autoindex**   Creates indexes for directory listings automatically

■ **mod_info**   Prints information about the runtime configuration of the Apache server, including the number and type of modules loaded

▲ **mod_usertrack**   Supports the use of cookies to store client-side data

TIP: For more information on modules, check the entry on managing modules in the Apache manual (http://localhost/manual/mod).

Adding modules at run time is easy: to load the mod_usertrack, for example, you would need to include the following lines in the httpd.conf file:

```
LoadModule usertrack_module        modules/mod_usertrack.so
ddModule        mod_usertrack.c
```

Graphical User Interface (GUI) Administration Using Webmin

If you're a Windows administrator, you've probably cringed at the amount of configuration file editing required to configure the Apache Web server. Fortunately, there is an alternative to manual configuration, which comes in the form of a webmin module. Webmin is a browser-based UNIX system configuration system, which comes with its own simplified Web server (miniserv.pl).

The management interface consists of dynamically generated HTML on the client side, CGI applications on the server side, and Java applets. Although webmin is the ideal tool to manage Apache services, it can also be used for user administration, boot management, the domain name service, and almost every kind of system management required on Solaris. The webmin interface is shown in Figure 14-3.

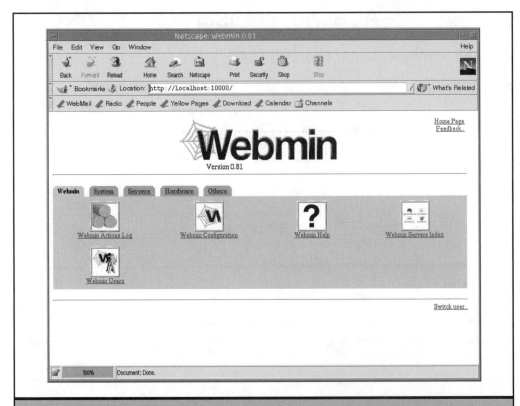

Figure 14-3.   The webmin administration interface

To install webmin, you need to download the source or binary archive from http://www.webmin.com/webmin/. Binary distributions are only available for Solaris Sparc, however, so you'll need to install Solaris Intel from source. The current source version is available at http://www.webmin.com/webmin/download/solaris-pkg/webmin-0.81.pkg.gz.

Many of the CGI scripts use perl, which is included as part of the Solaris 8 distribution. To administer Apache, you will also require the Apache module, which can be downloaded from http://www.webmin.com/webmin/download/modules/apache.wbm. Once installed, the Apache interface will become available, as shown in Figure 14-4.

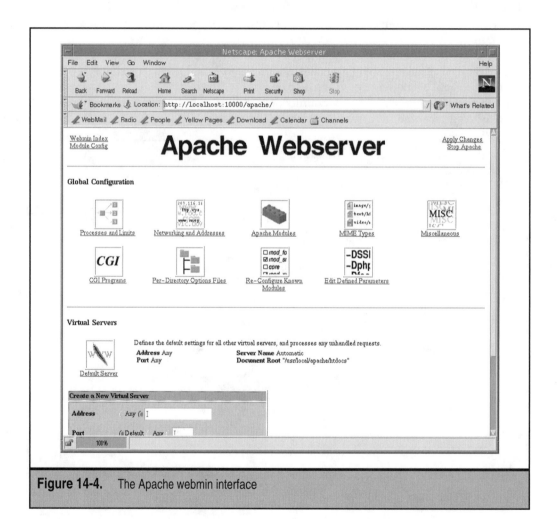

Figure 14-4. The Apache webmin interface

The Apache webmin interface allows you to configure all aspects of the Apache Web server without having to manually edit the configuration file. There are several different pages that are used to make configuration changes and to restart the server if necessary, including

▼ Managing processes and server limits

■ Setting network addresses

■ Adding Apache modules

■ Configuring MIME types

■ Installing CGI programs

▲ Modifying module configuration

Each of these pages has a distinct purpose. For example, the Processes and Limits page, shown in Figure 14-5, allows you to insert values for the following options:

▼ Maximum headers in request

■ Maximum request line size

■ Maximum requests per server process

■ Minimum spare server processes

■ Maximum request header size

■ Maximum concurrent requests

■ Maximum spare server processes

▲ Initial server processes

Once installed, the webmin Web server will be started, and you will be able to connect to your local server on port 10000. In addition to administering Apache by using webmin, you may also run webmin through Apache, by running it as root and setting the DocumentRoot to the installation directory.

TIP: If you find webmin to be useful, you can sign up on the webmin mailing list at http://www.webmin.com/webmin/mailing.html. There is also a very useful user's guide provided by Caldera at http://www.calderasystems.com/edesktop/usersguide/ch10.html.

Configuring CGI and Writing CGI Applications

Apache supports CGI applications natively, so there's no special configuration required to run CGI applications. A CGI application needs only two requirements: (1) read and execute permissions on the script or application that is to be run, and (2) the string "Content-type: text/html" must be printed, followed by two newline characters. One of the nice features of the CGI standard is that a CGI application can be written in the language of your choice: C, C++, Perl, Bourne shell scripts, or any language that your organization has expertise in. In addition, there are enhancements that speed up the sometimes slow execution of CGI applications. For example, there is a mod_perl Apache module that reduces overhead due to the invocation of the Perl interpreter by interpreting the Perl code within the Apache server itself.

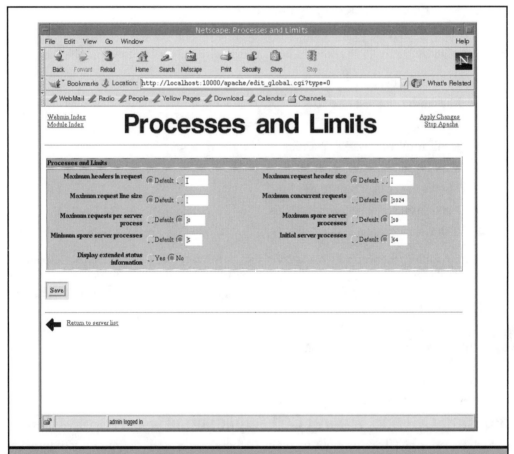

Figure 14-5.   Managing Processes and Limits in Apache

Let's examine how CGI works with a simple application that can be written in one of several different languages. The goal is to print out the following HTML:

```
<HTML>
<HEAD>
<TITLE>Hello World!</TITLE>
</HEAD>
<BODY>
Hello World!
</BODY>
</HTML>
```

The preceding HTML code prints a simple "Hello World!" message in the browser window, as well as "Hello World!" in the title bar. We can easily write a CGI program in C to print out this HTML, by using the following code:

```
#include <stdio.h>
main()
{
  printf("Content-type: text/html\n\n");
  printf("<HTML>\n");
  printf("<HEAD>\n");
  printf("<TITLE>Hello World!</TITLE>\n");
  printf("</HEAD>\n");
  printf("<BODY>\n");
  printf("Hello World!\n");
  printf("</BODY>\n");
  printf("</HTML>\n");
}
```

To compile this code, you need to use gcc:

```
bash-2.03$ gcc hello_world.c -o hello.cgi
```

Next, copy the hello.cgi program to the Apache cgi-bin directory:

```
bash-2.03$ cp hello.cgi /usr/local/apache1.3/cgi-bin/
```

Finally, you need to set the permissions correctly for the user who actually runs the Apache process:

```
bash-2.03$ chmod 755 hello.cgi
```

To execute the CGI program, you simply request the following URL:

```
http://localhost/cgi-bin/hello.cgi
```

SUMMARY

In this chapter, we have examined how to install and configure the Apache Web server. In addition, we have examined how to use the webmin GUI administration tool, which can be used to manage all aspects of Apache runtime operation. Finally, we examined how to write server-side CGI applications that can be executed by a client browser. Apache has many functions in addition to Web serving, including acting as a proxy/cache. Administrators can choose to use Apache just as a Web server, or they can take advantage of these advanced features to build efficient Web information systems.

CHAPTER 15

Security

Security is a central concern to system administrators of all network operating systems, because all services may potentially have inherent flaws or weaknesses revealed through undetected bugs that may compromise a networked system. Solaris is no exception, and new Solaris administrators will find themselves revisiting issues that they may have encountered with other operating systems.

For example, Linux, Microsoft Windows, and Solaris all run database systems that have daemons that listen for connections coming through the Internet. These servers may be shipped with default user accounts with well-known passwords, which are not inactivated by local administrators after configuration and administration. Consequently, exploits involving such services are broadcast on USENET newsgroups, cracking mailing lists and Web sites.

Alternatively, some security issues are specific to Solaris: username and password sniffing while a remote user is using telnet to spawn a local shell is unique to Solaris and other UNIX systems, since PC-based products that provide remote access (such as Symantec's pcAnywhere product) encrypt the exchange of authentication credentials by default.

In this chapter, we will focus on laying the groundwork for an understanding of the vulnerabilities of the Solaris operating system, as well as the techniques used by Solaris managers to reduce the risk of a successful attack by a rogue user. We also examine some of the many resources on the Internet that may be used to learn more about Solaris security, as well as implement specific Solaris security solutions.

SECURITY AUDITING

After installing a new Solaris system, or after inheriting an old Solaris system, one of the first tasks that should be conducted is a security audit. The audit should conform to the local site security policy (there is a security policy, right?). A typical security policy might specify the services that are allowed to run from your server and prohibit the running of any other services. Often, the security policy will be determined by the requirements of your Internet Service Provider (ISP), since the security of their network ultimately depends on the security of local hosts.

A security audit should first examine what services are being offered, and then determine an action plan based on services that should be disabled. In addition, monitoring and logging solutions should be installed for services that are sanctioned, so that it is possible at all times to determine what activity is occurring on any service.

For example, a denial-of-service attack may involve hitting a specific port (such as port 80, the Web server port) with a large number of packets, aimed at reducing overall performance of the Web server and the host system. If you don't have logs of all this activity, it will be difficult to determine why your system performance is slow and/or where any potential attacks have originated.

The final phase of a security audit involves comparing the current list of services running on the system to the security bulletins that are released by the Computer Emergency Response Team (CERT) (http://www.cert.org) and similar computer security groups.

TIP: After determining the versions of software running on your system, you should determine which packages require patching and/or upgrading in order to eliminate the risks from known vulnerabilities.

Introducing SAINT

As you can guess from this to-do list, running a security audit and implementing solutions based on the audit can be a time-consuming task. Fortunately, there are a number of tools available that can significantly reduce the amount of time required to conduct security audits and cross-check existing applications with known security holes.

One of these programs is called the Security Administrator's Integrated Network Tool (SAINT), which is freely available from World Wide Digital Security, Inc., at http://www.wwdsi.com/saint. SAINT, currently in version 3.0, is based in part on an earlier auditing tool known as SATAN. Both SATAN and SAINT have the ability to scan all of your system services and identify potential and/or known vulnerabilities. These are classified according to their risk: some items may be critical, requiring immediate attention, while other items may come in the form of suggestions rather than requirements.

For example, while many local services are vulnerable to a buffer overflow, where the fixed boundaries on an array are deliberately overwritten by a remote client to crash the system, other issues, such as the use of "r" remote access commands, may be risky but acceptable in suitably protected local area networks. Thus, SAINT is not prescriptive in all cases, and suggested actions are always to be performed at the discretion of the local administrator.

Some administrators are concerned that using programs like SAINT actually contributes to cracking and system break-ins, because they provide a ready-made toolkit that can be used to identify system weaknesses in preparation for a break-in. However, if sites devote the necessary resources to monitoring system usage and identifying potential security threats, the risk posed by SAINT is minimal (particularly if its "suggestions" are acted upon).

Indeed, World Wide Digital Security, Inc., actually uses a Web version of SAINT (called WebSAINT) as the basis for their security consulting. For a fee, they will conduct a comprehensive security audit of your network from the perspective of a remote (rather than a local) user. This can be very useful when attempting to identify potential weaknesses in your front-line systems, such as routers, gateways, and Web servers.

In this section, we will examine how to install and configure the SAINT program and run an audit on a newly installed Solaris 8 system (in this example, a Solaris Intel system). This will reveal many of the common issues that arise when Solaris is installed out of the box. Most of these issues are covered by CERT advisories. Sun often releases patches very soon after a CERT vulnerability is discovered on shipped Solaris products. For example, a patch that is available for a well-known vulnerability existing in the Berkeley Internet Daemon (BIND) package matches IP addresses with fully qualified domain names (http://www.cert.org/advisories/CA-99-14-bind.html).

However, some CERT advisories are of a more general nature, since no specific code fix will solve the problem. One example is the identification of a distributed denial-of-service system called "Stacheldraht," which combines the processing power and network resources of a group of systems (that are geographically distributed) and can prevent Web servers from serving pages to clients (http://www.cert.org/advisories/CA-2000-01.html).

NOTE: CERT releases advisories on a regular basis, so it's advisable to keep up to date with all current security issues by reading their news.

One of the great strengths of the SAINT system is that it has an extensive catalog of CERT advisories and in-depth explanations of what each CERT advisory means for the local system. Every SAINT vulnerability is associated with a Common Vulnerabilities and Exposures (CVE) number that matches descriptions of each security issue from the CVE database (http://cve.mitre.org). Each identified vulnerability will contain a hyperlink back to the CVE database, so that information displayed about every issue is updated directly from the source. New patches and bug fixes are also listed.

SAINT has the capability to identify security issues for the following services:

▼ **Domain Name Service (DNS)**   Responsible for mapping the fully qualified domain name of Internet hosts to a machine-friendly IP address. In particular, BIND, commonly used for DNS resolution, is susceptible to vulnerabilities.

■ **File Transfer Program (FTP)**   Allows remote users to retrieve files from the local filesystem; has historically been associated with serious daemon buffer overflow problems.

■ **Internet Message Access Protocol (IMAP)**   Supports advanced e-mail exchange facilities between mail clients and mail servers; also has buffer overflow issues that have previously allowed remote users to execute privileged commands arbitrarily on the mail server.

■ **Network File System (NFS) Service**   Shares disk partitions to remote client systems; is often misconfigured to provide world read access to all shared volumes when this access should only be granted to specific users.

■ **Network Information Service (NIS)**   A distributed network service that shares maps of users, groups, and passwords among hosts to minimize administrative overheads; can be compromised if a rogue user can detect the NIS service operating.

▲ **Sendmail Mail Transport Agent (MTA)**   Allows Solaris commands to be embedded within e-mails that were executed without authentication on the server side.

SAINT works by systematically scanning ports for services that have well-known exploits and then reporting these exploits back to the user. In addition, it runs a large number of password checks for default passwords on system accounts or accounts that often have no password. SAINT checks all of the services and exploits that it knows about, and the database of known exploits grows with each new release.

SAINT also tests the susceptibility of your system to denial-of-service attacks, where a large number of large-sized packets are directed to a specific port on your system. This tactic is typically used against Web servers. Some high-profile cases in recent years have highlighted the inherent weakness of networked systems that allow traffic on specific ports without some kind of regulation.

Many of the system daemons checked by SAINT will have a so-called buffer overflow problem, where a system may be crashed because memory is overwritten with arbitrary values outside the declared size of an array. Without appropriate bounds checking, passing a get request to a Web server of 1025 bytes when the array size is 1024 would clearly result in unpredictable behavior, as the C language does not prevent a program from doing this.

TIP: Since Solaris daemons are typically written in C, a number have been fixed in recent years to prevent this problem from occurring (but you may be surprised at just how often new weaknesses are exposed).

Installing SAINT

The latest release of SAINT may be downloaded from http://www.wwdsi.com/saint>. To run SAINT, you will need to install the GNU C compiler or the Sun C compiler. The Perl interpreter and Netscape Web browser supplied with Solaris 8 are also required. After downloading and unpacking the source, the preinstallation configuration can be performed with the following command:

```
cassowary# ./configure
```

The configuration program will check that you have all of the necessary software to run SAINT on your local system, including a C compiler, socket libraries, ANSI C header files, Perl, and Remote Procedure Call (RPC) commands:

```
bash-2.03# ./configure
loading cache ./config.cache
checking for gcc... (cached) gcc
checking whether the C compiler (gcc  ) works... yes
checking whether the C compiler (gcc  ) is a cross-compiler... no
checking whether we are using GNU C... (cached) yes
checking whether gcc accepts -g... (cached) yes
checking for a BSD compatible install... ./install-sh -c
checking whether make sets ${MAKE}... (cached) yes
```

```
checking for main in -lPW... (cached) no
checking for main in -lX11_s... (cached) no
checking for main in -lXm_s... (cached) no
checking for main in -lXt_s... (cached) no
checking for main in -lc_s... (cached) no
checking for main in -lnsl... (cached) yes
checking for main in -lresolv... (cached) yes
checking for main in -lrpc... (cached) no
checking for rpc socket compatibility... yes
checking for runtime linkage option... yes
checking for main in -lsocket... (cached) yes
checking for getpwnam in -lsun... (cached) no
checking for +DAportable... no
checking how to run the C preprocessor... (cached) gcc -E
checking for linux/limits.h... (cached) no
checking for /usr/src/linux... no
checking for ANSI C header files... (cached) yes
checking for uid_t in sys/types.h... (cached) yes
checking type of array argument to getgroups... (cached) gid_t
checking if sys_errlist is declared... no
checking if system netinet headers work... yes
checking for rpcgen... (cached) /usr/bin/rpcgen
creating ./config.status
creating Makefile
Reconfiguring...
Checking to make sure all the targets are here...
Trying to find Perl... /usr/local/bin/perl5.00503
Changing the source in PERL scripts...
Trying to find HTML/WWW browser...
Looking for UNIX commands...
Found /bin/remsh; using this instead of rsh
Can't find nmap
Can't find nmblookup
Can't find smbclient
Doing substitutions on the shell scripts...
Changing paths in config/paths.pl...
Changing paths in config/paths.sh...
```

Although some programs, such as the Samba daemons (smbd and nmbd) and nmap are not installed, this will not prevent SAINT from running. After configuration has been completed, the scripts config/paths.pl and config/paths.sh will be updated with the new settings. The binaries may then be built by using the following command:

```
cassowary# make
```

The sources will then be compiled by using the C compiler and the make utility:

```
bash-2.03# make
make[1]: Entering directory `/tmp/saint-3.0'
cd src/misc; make "LIBS=-L/usr/ucblib -R/usr/ucblib -lrpcsvc -lrpcsoc
-lnsl -lresolv -lsocket" "XFLAGS=-g -O2    -DSTDC_HEADERS=1
-DGETGROUPS_T=gid_t " "RPCGEN=/usr/bin/rpcgen"
make[2]: Entering directory `/tmp/saint-3.0/src/misc'
gcc -O -I. -g -O2    -DSTDC_HEADERS=1 -DGETGROUPS_T=gid_t     -c md5.c -o
md5.o
gcc -O -I. -g -O2    -DSTDC_HEADERS=1 -DGETGROUPS_T=gid_t     -c md5c.c -o
md5c.o
gcc -O -I. -g -O2    -DSTDC_HEADERS=1 -DGETGROUPS_T=gid_t   -o ../../bin/md5
md5.o md5c.o
gcc -O -I. -g -O2    -DSTDC_HEADERS=1 -DGETGROUPS_T=gid_t   -o
../../bin/sys_socket sys_socket.c
gcc -O -I. -g -O2    -DSTDC_HEADERS=1 -DGETGROUPS_T=gid_t   -o
../../bin/timeout timeout.c
gcc -O -I. -g -O2    -DSTDC_HEADERS=1 -DGETGROUPS_T=gid_t   -o ../../bin/rcmd
rcmd.c -L/usr/ucblib -R/usr/ucblib -lrpcsvc -lrpcsoc  -lnsl -lresolv
-lsocket
gcc -O -I. -g -O2    -DSTDC_HEADERS=1 -DGETGROUPS_T=gid_t   -o
../../bin/safe_finger safe_finger.c
/usr/bin/rpcgen rex.x 2>/dev/null
gcc -O -I. -g -O2    -DSTDC_HEADERS=1 -DGETGROUPS_T=gid_t     -c rex.c -o
rex.o
gcc -O -I. -g -O2    -DSTDC_HEADERS=1 -DGETGROUPS_T=gid_t     -c rex_xdr.c -o
rex_xdr.o
. . . .
```

All of the source files will be built during this phase. If the build is successful, you should see the following lines at the end of the display:

```
$MOSAIC="/opt/netscape/netscape";
$TCP_SCAN="bin/tcp_scan";
$FTP_SCAN="bin/ftp-scan";
$UDP_SCAN="bin/udp_scan";
```

```
$FPING="bin/fping";
$NFS_CHK="bin/nfs-chk";
$YP_CHK="bin/yp-chk";
$SAFE_FINGER="bin/safe_finger";
$MD5="bin/md5";
$SYS_SOCKET="bin/sys_socket";
```

When you're building cross-platform applications like SAINT, you may see some warnings generated by the compiler about data types and casts. These can usually be ignored.

On the other hand, if an error is encountered, then you'll need to check your environment and perhaps make a bug report to WWDSI. For example, if your LD_LIBRARY_PATH is not set to include the appropriate system library directories, then you'll need to update its value in your shell.

After making SAINT successfully, you may also install the man page:

```
bash-2.03# make install
mkdir -p /usr/local/man/man1
./install-sh -c -o root -g 0 -m 444 saint.1 /usr/local/man/man1/saint.1
```

At this point, you're ready to begin your SAINT security audit.

Running SAINT

SAINT can be started by typing the following command:

```
cassowary# ./saint
```

This starts up the Netscape Web browser, shown in Figure 15-1. The following message is printed in the shell window:

```
Security Administrator's Integrated Network Tool
Portions copyright (C) 2000 World Wide Digital Security, Inc.
Portions copyright (C) 1995 by Satan Developers.
SAINT is starting up...
```

SAINT has several pages, including Data Management, Target Selection, Data Analysis, and Configuration Management. These pages can be visited sequentially to conduct your audit. The Data Management page, shown in Figure 15-2, allows you to create a new SAINT database in which to store the results of your current audit. Alternatively, you may open an existing SAINT database if you have created one previously, and/or you can merge data from other SAINT scans.

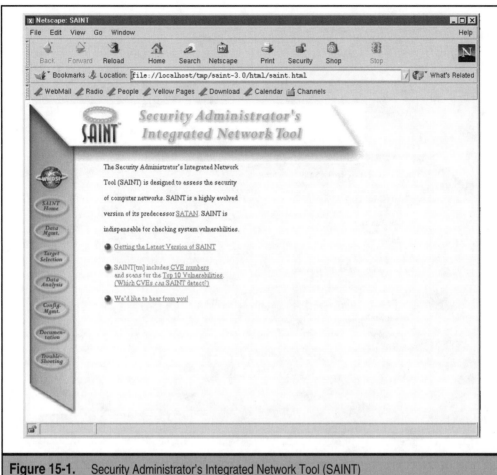

Figure 15-1. Security Administrator's Integrated Network Tool (SAINT)

Next, you will need to use the Target Selection page to identify the host system that you wish to scan using SAINT, as shown in Figure 15-3. Here, you need to enter the fully qualified domain name of the host that you wish to scan.

Alternatively, if you have a large number of hosts to scan, it may be more useful to create a file containing a list of hosts. This file could then be used by a system behind the firewall to identify locally visible weaknesses, and also be used by a system external to the firewall to re-

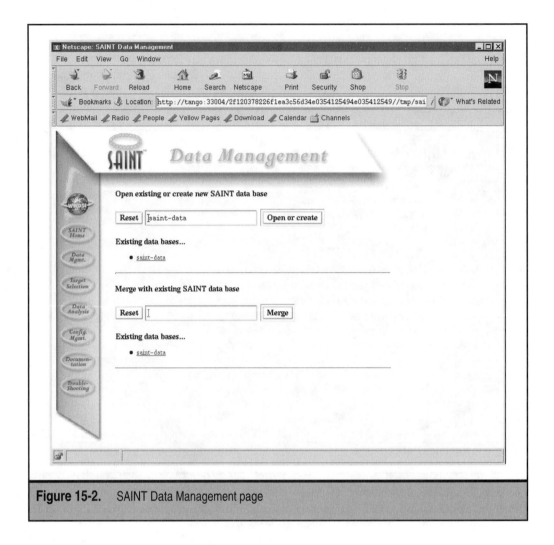

Figure 15-2. SAINT Data Management page

veal any threats visible to the outside world. You may also elect to scan all hosts in the local area network, which should only be performed out of normal working hours, as it places a heavy load on network bandwidth.

You need to select a scanning level option, which include the following:

▼ **Light scanning**   Difficult to detect

■ **Normal scanning**   Easy to detect

■ **Heavy scanning**   Won't crash Windows NT targets

▲ **Heavy+ scanning**   May crash Windows NT targets

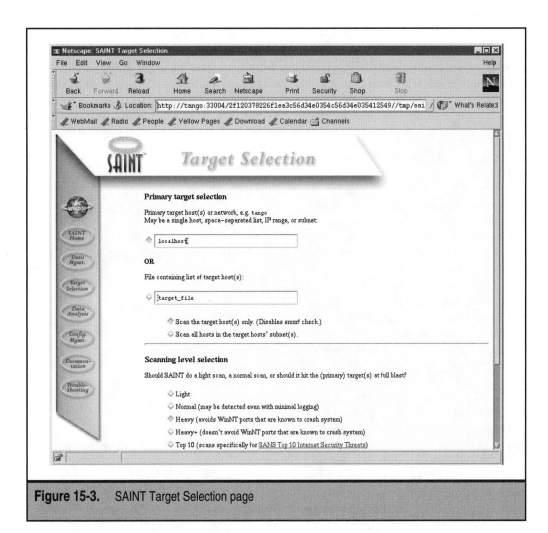

Figure 15-3. SAINT Target Selection page

There is a final option that just checks the top ten security flaws, as identified by the report at http://www.sans.org/topten.htm. These flaws include BIND weaknesses; vulnerable Common Gateway Interface (CGI) programs; RPC weaknesses; Sendmail buffer overflow; mountd; UNIX NFS exports; User IDs, especially root/administrator with no passwords; IMAP and Post Office Protocol (POP) buffer overflow vulnerabilities; and Simple Network Management Protocol (SNMP) community strings set to public and private.

TIP: Always remember that attempting to break into a computer system is a criminal offense in many jurisdictions: you should obtain written authorization from the owner of your system before embarking on a security-related exercise of this kind; otherwise, it may be misconstrued as a real attack.

Once the target selection is complete, the data collection process begins by executing a number of scripts on the server and reporting the results through the Web browser. Data is collected by testing many different Solaris services, including ping, finger, RPC, login, rsh, sendmail, tooltalk, snmp, and rstatd. A number of status messages will appear in the browser window, as shown here.

```
Data collection in progress...
10/25/00-13:43:16 bin/timeout 60 bin/fping cassowary.paulwatters.com
10/25/00-13:43:16 bin/timeout 20 bin/finger.saint
cassowary.paulwatters.com .PLUS
10/25/00-13:43:16 bin/timeout 20 bin/ostype.saint
cassowary.paulwatters.com .PLUS
10/25/00-13:43:16 bin/timeout 60 bin/udpscan.saint
19,53,69,111,137-139,161-162,177,8999,1-18,20-52,54-68,70-110,112-136,1
40-160,163-176,178-1760,1763-2050,32767-33500 cassowary.paulwatters.com
.PLUS
10/25/00-13:43:16 bin/timeout 20 bin/dns.saint
cassowary.paulwatters.com .PLUS
10/25/00-13:43:16 bin/timeout 20 bin/rpc.saint
cassowary.paulwatters.com .PLUS
10/25/00-13:43:16 bin/timeout 60 bin/tcpscan.saint
12754,15104,16660,20432,27665,1-9999 cassowary.paulwatters.com .PLUS
10/25/00-13:43:17 bin/timeout 20 bin/ddos.saint
cassowary.paulwatters.com .PLUS
10/25/00-13:44:16 bin/timeout 20 bin/rsh.saint
cassowary.paulwatters.com .PLUS
10/25/00-13:44:16 bin/timeout 20 bin/login.saint -o -u deanna -p deanna
telnet cassowary.paulwatters.com .PLUS
10/25/00-13:44:16 bin/timeout 20 bin/rsh.saint -u ua_inf0
cassowary.paulwatters.com .PLUS
10/25/00-13:44:17 bin/timeout 20 bin/login.saint -o -u ua_de0 telnet
cassowary.paulwatters.com .PLUS
10/25/00-13:44:17 bin/timeout 20 bin/sadmind.saint SunOS 5.7
cassowary.paulwatters.com .PLUS
10/25/00-13:44:17 bin/timeout 20 bin/login.saint -o -u ua_os8 telnet
cassowary.paulwatters.com .PLUS
10/25/00-13:44:17 bin/timeout 20 bin/rsh.saint -u root
cassowary.paulwatters.com .PLUS
10/25/00-13:44:18 bin/timeout 20 bin/login.saint -o -u ua_de4 telnet
cassowary.paulwatters.com .PLUS
10/25/00-13:44:19 bin/timeout 20 bin/login.saint -o -u uaprod -p uaprod
telnet cassowary.paulwatters.com .PLUS
10/25/00-13:44:22 bin/timeout 20 bin/login.saint -o -u ua_de8 telnet
cassowary.paulwatters.com .PLUS
```

```
10/25/00-13:44:22 bin/timeout 20 bin/login.saint -o -u ua_osa telnet
cassowary.paulwatters.com .PLUS
10/25/00-13:44:22 bin/timeout 20 bin/login.saint -o -u ua_de0 -p ua_de0
telnet cassowary.paulwatters.com .PLUS
10/25/00-13:44:25 bin/timeout 20 bin/rsh.saint -u ua_os6
cassowary.paulwatters.com .PLUS
10/25/00-13:44:25 bin/timeout 20 bin/rsh.saint -u ua_os7
cassowary.paulwatters.com .PLUS
10/25/00-13:44:25 bin/timeout 20 bin/rsh.saint -u ua_os8
cassowary.paulwatters.com .PLUS
10/25/00-13:44:25 bin/timeout 20 bin/login.saint -o -u auspost -p
auspost telnet cassowary.paulwatters.com .PLUS
10/25/00-13:44:26 bin/timeout 20 bin/login.saint -o -u ua_de1 -p ua_de1
telnet cassowary.paulwatters.com .PLUS
10/25/00-13:44:27 bin/timeout 20 bin/rsh.saint -u ua_os9
cassowary.paulwatters.com .PLUS
10/25/00-13:44:27 bin/timeout 20 bin/login.saint -o -u ce_ass2 -p
ce_ass2 telnet cassowary.paulwatters.com .PLUS
10/25/00-13:44:28 bin/timeout 20 bin/login.saint -o -u ua_de2 -p ua_de2
telnet cassowary.paulwatters.com .PLUS
10/25/00-13:44:29 bin/timeout 20 bin/login.saint -o -u ua_de3 -p ua_de3
telnet cassowary.paulwatters.com .PLUS
10/25/00-13:44:31 bin/timeout 20 bin/login.saint -o -u ua_inf0 -p
ua_inf0 telnet cassowary.paulwatters.com .PLUS
10/25/00-13:44:32 bin/timeout 20 bin/login.saint -o -u ua_de4 -p ua_de4
telnet cassowary.paulwatters.com .PLUS
10/25/00-13:44:33 bin/timeout 20 bin/login.saint -o -u ua_inf0 telnet
cassowary.paulwatters.com .PLUS
10/25/00-13:44:34 bin/timeout 20 bin/login.saint -o -u ua_de5 -p ua_de5
telnet cassowary.paulwatters.com .PLUS
10/25/00-13:44:34 bin/timeout 20 bin/login.saint -o -u schoolemails
telnet cassowary.paulwatters.com .PLUS
10/25/00-13:44:37 bin/timeout 20 bin/login.saint -o -u puborder telnet
cassowary.paulwatters.com .PLUS
10/25/00-13:44:38 bin/timeout 20 bin/login.saint -o -u ua_de6 -p ua_de6
telnet cassowary.paulwatters.com .PLUS
10/25/00-13:44:38 bin/timeout 20 bin/login.saint -o -u ua_de7 -p ua_de7
telnet cassowary.paulwatters.com .PLUS
10/25/00-13:44:39 bin/timeout 20 bin/login.saint -o -u ua_de8 -p ua_de8
telnet cassowary.paulwatters.com .PLUS
10/25/00-13:44:39 bin/timeout 20 bin/rsh.saint -u un_ass4
cassowary.paulwatters.com .PLUS
10/25/00-13:44:40 bin/timeout 20 bin/login.saint -o -u ua_sa telnet
cassowary.paulwatters.com .PLUS
```

```
10/25/00-13:44:43 bin/timeout 20 bin/login.saint -o -u adviser_help -p
adviser_help telnet cassowary.paulwatters.com .PLUS
10/25/00-13:44:44 bin/timeout 20 bin/rsh.saint -u cc_ass2
cassowary.paulwatters.com .PLUS
10/25/00-13:44:44 bin/timeout 20 bin/rsh.saint -u sys
cassowary.paulwatters.com .PLUS
10/25/00-13:44:44 bin/timeout 20 bin/login.saint -o -u ua_de9 -p ua_de9
telnet cassowary.paulwatters.com .PLUS
10/25/00-13:44:44 bin/timeout 20 bin/login.saint -o -u ua_osa -p ua_osa
telnet cassowary.paulwatters.com .PLUS
10/25/00-13:44:45 bin/timeout 20 bin/login.saint -o -u ua_os7 telnet
cassowary.paulwatters.com .PLUS
10/25/00-13:44:46 bin/timeout 20 bin/sendmail.saint smtp
cassowary.paulwatters.com .PLUS
10/25/00-13:44:49 bin/timeout 20 bin/login.saint -o -u ua_osb -p ua_osb
telnet cassowary.paulwatters.com .PLUS
10/25/00-13:44:50 bin/timeout 20 bin/rsh.saint -u schoolemails
cassowary.paulwatters.com .PLUS
10/25/00-13:44:50 bin/timeout 20 bin/rsh.saint -u puborder
cassowary.paulwatters.com .PLUS
10/25/00-13:44:51 bin/timeout 20 bin/login.saint -o -u ua_osc -p ua_osc
telnet cassowary.paulwatters.com .PLUS
10/25/00-13:44:51 bin/timeout 20 bin/login.saint -o -u ua_de3 telnet
cassowary.paulwatters.com .PLUS
10/25/00-13:44:51 bin/timeout 20 bin/login.saint -o -u sq_ass1 -p
sq_ass1 telnet cassowary.paulwatters.com .PLUS
10/25/00-13:44:55 bin/timeout 20 bin/rexec.saint
cassowary.paulwatters.com .PLUS
10/25/00-13:44:55 bin/timeout 20 bin/login.saint -o -u ua_de7 telnet
cassowary.paulwatters.com .PLUS
10/25/00-13:44:55 bin/timeout 20 bin/login.saint -o -u un_ass4 -p
un_ass4 telnet cassowary.paulwatters.com .PLUS
10/25/00-13:44:56 bin/timeout 20 bin/tooltalk.saint SunOS 5.7
cassowary.paulwatters.com .PLUS
10/25/00-13:44:56 bin/timeout 20 bin/xhost.saint -d
cassowary.paulwatters.com:0 cassowary.paulwatters.com .PLUS
10/25/00-13:44:57 bin/timeout 20 bin/login.saint -o -u cc_ass2 telnet
cassowary.paulwatters.com .PLUS
10/25/00-13:44:57 bin/timeout 120 bin/snmp.saint -w
cassowary.paulwatters.com .PLUS
10/25/00-13:44:57 bin/timeout 20 bin/login.saint -o -u ce_ass2 telnet
cassowary.paulwatters.com .PLUS
10/25/00-13:45:01 bin/timeout 20 bin/login.saint -r -u wank -p wank
telnet cassowary.paulwatters.com .PLUS
```

```
10/25/00-13:45:02 bin/timeout 20 bin/rsh.saint -u ua_osa
cassowary.paulwatters.com .PLUS
10/25/00-13:45:03 bin/timeout 20 bin/rsh.saint -u ua_osb
cassowary.paulwatters.com .PLUS
10/25/00-13:45:03 bin/timeout 20 bin/rsh.saint -u bin
cassowary.paulwatters.com .PLUS
10/25/00-13:45:03 bin/timeout 20 bin/rsh.saint -u ua_osc
cassowary.paulwatters.com .PLUS
10/25/00-13:45:04 bin/timeout 20 bin/login.saint -o -u ua_os6 telnet
cassowary.paulwatters.com .PLUS
10/25/00-13:45:04 bin/timeout 20 bin/rstatd.saint
cassowary.paulwatters.com .PLUS
10/25/00-13:45:06 bin/timeout 20 bin/statd.saint SunOS 5.7
cassowary.paulwatters.com .PLUS
10/25/00-13:45:06 bin/timeout 20 bin/login.saint -o -u ua_sa -p ua_sa
telnet cassowary.paulwatters.com .PLUS
10/25/00-13:45:07 bin/timeout 20 bin/login.saint -o -u ua_de2 telnet
cassowary.paulwatters.com .PLUS
10/25/00-13:45:10 bin/timeout 20 bin/login.saint -o -u ua_de6 telnet
cassowary.paulwatters.com .PLUS
10/25/00-13:45:11 bin/timeout 20 bin/cmsd.saint SunOS 5.7
cassowary.paulwatters.com .PLUS
10/25/00-13:45:11 bin/timeout 20 bin/login.saint -o -u ua_os6 -p ua_os6
telnet cassowary.paulwatters.com .PLUS
10/25/00-13:45:13 bin/timeout 20 bin/login.saint -o -u ua_os7 -p ua_os7
telnet cassowary.paulwatters.com .PLUS
10/25/00-13:45:16 bin/timeout 20 bin/login.saint -o -u cc_ass2 -p
cc_ass2 telnet cassowary.paulwatters.com .PLUS
10/25/00-13:45:17 bin/timeout 20 bin/login.saint -o -u ua_osc telnet
cassowary.paulwatters.com .PLUS
10/25/00-13:45:17 bin/timeout 20 bin/login.saint -o -u ua_dp2 telnet
cassowary.paulwatters.com .PLUS
10/25/00-13:45:20 bin/timeout 20 bin/login.saint -o -u ua_os8 -p ua_os8
telnet cassowary.paulwatters.com .PLUS
10/25/00-13:45:22 bin/timeout 20 bin/login.saint -o -u ua_os9 -p ua_os9
telnet cassowary.paulwatters.com .PLUS
10/25/00-13:45:22 bin/timeout 20 bin/login.saint -o -u un_ass4 telnet
cassowary.paulwatters.com .PLUS
10/25/00-13:45:23 bin/timeout 20 bin/rsh.saint -u daemon
cassowary.paulwatters.com .PLUS
10/25/00-13:45:24 bin/timeout 20 bin/rsh.saint -u adviser_help
cassowary.paulwatters.com .PLUS
10/25/00-13:45:24 bin/timeout 20 bin/login.saint -o -u hc_ass2 telnet
cassowary.paulwatters.com .PLUS
```

```
10/25/00-13:45:25 bin/timeout 20 bin/login.saint -o -u root telnet
cassowary.paulwatters.com .PLUS
10/25/00-13:45:26 bin/timeout 20 bin/login.saint -o -u deanna telnet
cassowary.paulwatters.com .PLUS
10/25/00-13:45:28 bin/timeout 20 bin/rsh.saint -u ua_dp2
cassowary.paulwatters.com .PLUS
10/25/00-13:45:29 bin/timeout 20 bin/rlogin.saint
cassowary.paulwatters.com .PLUS
10/25/00-13:45:29 bin/timeout 20 bin/login.saint -o -u uaprod telnet
cassowary.paulwatters.com .PLUS
10/25/00-13:45:30 bin/timeout 20 bin/rsh.saint -u ce_ass2
cassowary.paulwatters.com .PLUS
10/25/00-13:45:31 bin/timeout 20 bin/rsh.saint -u peterb
cassowary.paulwatters.com .PLUS
10/25/00-13:45:31 bin/timeout 20 bin/login.saint -o -u auspost telnet
cassowary.paulwatters.com .PLUS
10/25/00-13:45:32 bin/timeout 20 bin/login.saint -o -u ua_de1 telnet
cassowary.paulwatters.com .PLUS
10/25/00-13:45:32 bin/timeout 20 bin/rsh.saint -u hc_ass2
cassowary.paulwatters.com .PLUS
10/25/00-13:45:33 bin/timeout 20 bin/login.saint -o -u ua_os9 telnet
cassowary.paulwatters.com .PLUS
10/25/00-13:45:35 bin/timeout 20 bin/login.saint -o -u ua_de5 telnet
cassowary.paulwatters.com .PLUS
10/25/00-13:45:37 bin/timeout 20 bin/rsh.saint -u deanna
cassowary.paulwatters.com .PLUS
10/25/00-13:45:38 bin/timeout 20 bin/login.saint -o -u ua_dp2 -p ua_dp2
telnet cassowary.paulwatters.com .PLUS
10/25/00-13:45:38 bin/timeout 20 bin/login.saint -r -u rewt -p satori
telnet cassowary.paulwatters.com .PLUS
10/25/00-13:45:39 bin/timeout 20 bin/rsh.saint -u ua_sa
cassowary.paulwatters.com .PLUS
10/25/00-13:45:39 bin/timeout 20 bin/login.saint -o -u adviser_help
telnet cassowary.paulwatters.com .PLUS
10/25/00-13:45:41 bin/timeout 20 bin/login.saint -o -u ua_de9 telnet
cassowary.paulwatters.com .PLUS
10/25/00-13:45:43 bin/timeout 20 bin/rsh.saint -u uaprod
cassowary.paulwatters.com .PLUS
10/25/00-13:45:44 bin/timeout 20 bin/login.saint -o -u ua_osb telnet
cassowary.paulwatters.com .PLUS
10/25/00-13:45:44 bin/timeout 20 bin/relay.saint
cassowary.paulwatters.com .PLUS
10/25/00-13:45:45 bin/timeout 20 bin/rsh.saint -u ua_de0
cassowary.paulwatters.com .PLUS
10/25/00-13:45:45 bin/timeout 20 bin/rsh.saint -u auspost
```

```
cassowary.paulwatters.com .PLUS
10/25/00-13:45:45 bin/timeout 20 bin/rsh.saint -u ua_de1
cassowary.paulwatters.com .PLUS
10/25/00-13:45:46 bin/timeout 20 bin/login.saint -o -u sq_ass1 telnet
cassowary.paulwatters.com .PLUS
10/25/00-13:45:46 bin/timeout 20 bin/rsh.saint -u ua_de2
cassowary.paulwatters.com .PLUS
10/25/00-13:45:46 bin/timeout 20 bin/rsh.saint -u ua_de3
cassowary.paulwatters.com .PLUS
10/25/00-13:45:47 bin/timeout 20 bin/rsh.saint -u ua_de4
cassowary.paulwatters.com .PLUS
10/25/00-13:45:47 bin/timeout 20 bin/rsh.saint -u ua_de5
cassowary.paulwatters.com .PLUS
10/25/00-13:45:48 bin/timeout 20 bin/rsh.saint -u ua_de6
cassowary.paulwatters.com .PLUS
10/25/00-13:45:49 bin/timeout 20 bin/login.saint -o -u peterb -p peterb
telnet cassowary.paulwatters.com .PLUS
10/25/00-13:45:49 bin/timeout 20 bin/rsh.saint -u ua_de7
cassowary.paulwatters.com .PLUS
10/25/00-13:45:49 bin/timeout 20 bin/rusers.saint
cassowary.paulwatters.com .PLUS
10/25/00-13:45:50 bin/timeout 20 bin/login.saint -o -u peterb telnet
cassowary.paulwatters.com .PLUS
10/25/00-13:45:50 bin/timeout 20 bin/rsh.saint -u ua_de8
cassowary.paulwatters.com .PLUS
10/25/00-13:45:50 bin/timeout 20 bin/rsh.saint -u ua_de9
cassowary.paulwatters.com .PLUS
10/25/00-13:45:51 bin/timeout 20 bin/login.saint -o -u hc_ass2 -p
hc_ass2 telnet cassowary.paulwatters.com .PLUS
10/25/00-13:45:51 bin/timeout 20 bin/login.saint -o -u schoolemails -p
schoolemails telnet cassowary.paulwatters.com .PLUS
10/25/00-13:45:54 bin/timeout 20 bin/login.saint -o -u puborder -p
puborder telnet cassowary.paulwatters.com .PLUS
10/25/00-13:45:55 bin/timeout 20 bin/login.saint -o -u root -p root
telnet cassowary.paulwatters.com .PLUS
10/25/00-13:45:58 bin/timeout 20 bin/rsh.saint -u sq_ass1
cassowary.paulwatters.com .PLUS
10/25/00-13:45:58 bin/timeout 20 bin/ftp.saint
cassowary.paulwatters.com .PLUS
10/25/00-13:46:00 SAINT run completed
```

SAINT uses several different modules to probe vulnerabilities in the system, including tcpscan, which scans for Transmission Control Protocol (TCP) denial-of-service issues; udpscan, which scans for User Datagram Protocol (UDP) denial-of-service issues; and ddos. In addition, a number of well-known username and password combinations are also attempted in order to break into an account. You would imagine that root/root would never be used as a username and password combination, but it does happen.

Once all of the data has been collected, the results of the scan are then displayed on the Data Analysis page, shown in Figure 15-4. It is possible to list vulnerabilities by their danger level, by the type of vulnerability, or by the number of vulnerabilities in a specific category. Most administrators will want to deal with the most dangerous vulnerabilities, so the first option should be selected. In addition, it is possible to view information about the target system by class of service, type of system, domain name, subnet, and hostname.

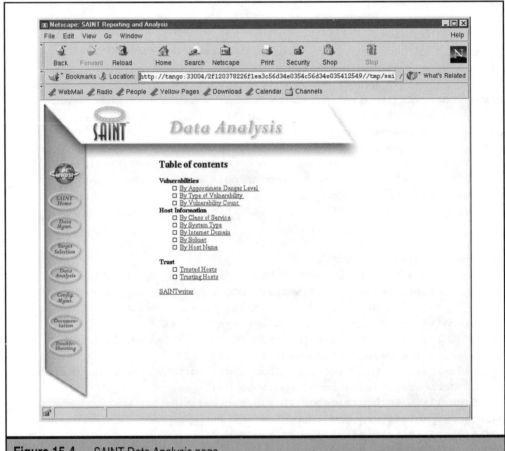

Figure 15-4. SAINT Data Analysis page

Vulnerabilities are listed in terms of danger level: there are Critical Problems, Areas of Concern, and Potential Problems, as shown in Figure 15-5. For the local host cassowary, which was a standard Solaris install out-of-the-box, two critical problems were identified, both associated with gaining root access via buffer overflow:

▼   **The Common Desktop Environment (CDE)–based Calendar Manager Service**   May be vulnerable to a buffer overflow attack, as identified in CVE 1999-0320 and 1999-0696. The Calendar Manager is used to manage appointments and other date/time-based functions.

▲   **The Remote Administration Daemon (sadmind)**   May be vulnerable to a buffer overflow attack, as described in CVE 1999-0977. The remote administration daemon is used to manage system administration activities across a number of different hosts.

There were also two areas of concern identified, with information gathering vulnerabilities exposed:

▼   **The Finger Daemon (fingerd)**   Returned personal information about users that could be used to stage an attack. For example, the home directory, full name, and project were displayed (CVE 1999-0612).

▲   **The Remote Users List Daemon (ruserd)**   Was active, providing a list of users on the system to any remote user (CVE 1999-0626). Like the fingerd, information gathered from the ruserd could be used to stage an attack.

Two possible vulnerabilities were identified:

▼   **The Chargen Program**   Vulnerable to UDP flooding used in denial-of-service attacks, such as Fraggle (CVE 1999-0103).

▲   **The Sendmail Server**   Allows mail relaying, which may be used by remote users to forward mail using the server. This makes it easy for companies promoting SPAM to make it appear as if their mail originated from your server. See Chapter 10 for more information.

Six recommendations were made to limit Internet access, including stopping all of the "r" services: these make it easy for a remote user to execute commands on the local system, such as spawning a shell or obtaining information about system load, and have been used in the past to break into systems. In addition, some sendmail commands (such as EXPN and VRFY) are allowed by the sendmail configuration: this allows remote users to obtain a list of all users on the current system, which is often the first step in obtaining their passwords.

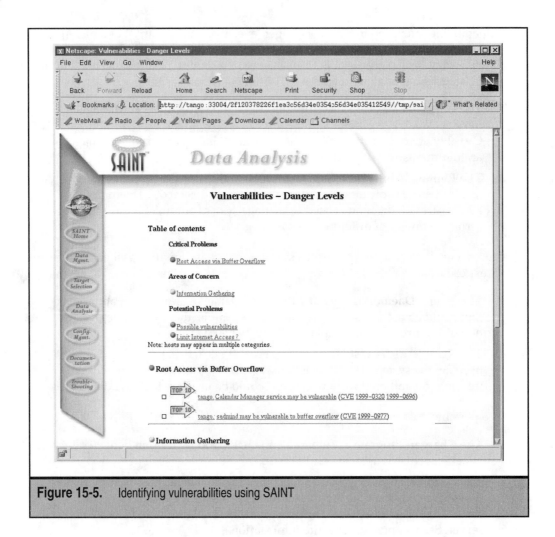

Figure 15-5. Identifying vulnerabilities using SAINT

If you are concerned that a rogue user may be using SAINT against your network, you may download and run one of the many SAINT-detecting programs, such as Courtney (http://ciac.llnl.gov/ciac/ToolsUnixNetMon.html#Courtney). Courtney monitors TCP traffic to determine whether or not a single remote machine is systematically scanning the ports within a specified time frame. This program is useful for detecting all kinds of port scanning and not just SAINT.

DISABLING IP PORTS

The first step in preventing unauthorized access of the kind SAINT reports as vulnerabilities is to disable access to specific IP ports by disabling entries in the services database. This prevents services from operating, even if the Internet super daemon (inetd) attempts to accept a connection for a service because it is still defined in /etc/inetd.conf. In this section, we will examine how to disable specific services from inetd, in conjunction with the services database.

The following services are typically enabled in /etc/services and configured in /etc/inetd.conf. Most sites will want to disable them and install more secure equivalents. For example, the ftp and telnet services may be replaced by the encrypted secure copy and Secure Shell (SSH) programs respectively.

To disable the ftp, telnet, shell, login, exec, comsat, talk, uucp, and finger services, we would *comment out* their entries in /etc/inetd.conf by inserting a hash character (#) at the first character position of the line that defines the service. The following configuration enables the ftp, telnet, shell, login, exec, comsat, talk, uucp, and finger services in /etc/inetd.conf:

```
ftp      stream  tcp   nowait  root    /usr/sbin/in.ftpd      in.ftpd -l
telnet   stream  tcp   nowait  root    /usr/sbin/in.telnetd   in.telnetd
shell    stream  tcp   nowait  root    /usr/sbin/in.rshd      in.rshd
login    stream  tcp   nowait  root    /usr/sbin/in.rlogind   in.rlogind
exec     stream  tcp   nowait  root    /usr/sbin/in.rexecd    in.rexecd
comsat   dgram   udp   wait    root    /usr/sbin/in.comsat    in.comsat
talk     dgram   udp   wait    root    /usr/sbin/in.talkd     in.talkd
uucp     stream  tcp   nowait  root    /usr/sbin/in.uucpd     in.uucpd
finger   stream  tcp   nowait  nobody  /usr/sbin/in.fingerd   in.fingerd
```

The following configuration disables the ftp, telnet, shell, login, exec, comsat, talk, uucp, and finger services in /etc/inetd.conf:

```
#ftp      stream  tcp   nowait  root    /usr/sbin/in.ftpd      in.ftpd -l
#telnet   stream  tcp   nowait  root    /usr/sbin/in.telnetd   in.telnetd
#shell    stream  tcp   nowait  root    /usr/sbin/in.rshd      in.rshd
#login    stream  tcp   nowait  root    /usr/sbin/in.rlogind   in.rlogind
#exec     stream  tcp   nowait  root    /usr/sbin/in.rexecd    in.rexecd
#comsat   dgram   udp   wait    root    /usr/sbin/in.comsat    in.comsat
#talk     dgram   udp   wait    root    /usr/sbin/in.talkd     in.talkd
#uucp     stream  tcp   nowait  root    /usr/sbin/in.uucpd     in.uucpd
#finger   stream  tcp   nowait  nobody  /usr/sbin/in.fingerd   in.fingerd
```

The following configuration enables the ftp, telnet, shell, login, exec, comsat, talk, uucp, and finger services in /etc/services:

```
ftp             21/tcp
telnet          23/tcp
shell           514/tcp         cmd
login           513/tcp
exec            512/tcp
biff            512/udp         comsat
talk            517/udp
uucp            540/tcp         uucpd
finger  stream  tcp       nowait  nobody  /usr/sbin/in.fingerd     in.fingerd
```

The following configuration disables the ftp, telnet, shell, login, exec, comsat, talk, uucp, and finger services in /etc/services:

```
#ftp            21/tcp
#telnet         23/tcp
#shell          514/tcp         cmd
#login          513/tcp
#exec           512/tcp
#biff           512/udp         comsat
#talk           517/udp
#uucp           540/tcp         uucpd
#finger  stream  tcp      nowait  nobody  /usr/sbin/in.fingerd     in.fingerd
```

PACKET FILTERING

The basic idea behind many firewall products is to filter the IP packets that arrive at a router, and selectively permit them to be processed by the kernel and passed through the router, or explicitly rejected. This is useful for allowing external users to send mail on port 25 or to retrieve Web pages on port 80, while preventing Secure Shell (SSH) access on port 22.

Conversely, IP packets that arrive from behind a firewall may also be blocked on specific ports. This allows local users to ping external hosts or establish an FTP connection to a remote archive while preventing them from using services that are not sanctioned. Firewall systems are also available for both Microsoft Windows and Linux systems; while the former tend to be Graphical User Interface (GUI)-oriented, such as Checkpoint's Firewall-1 (http://www.checkpoint.com), Linux firewalls are typically configured from the command line. An example is the IP Filter program, available from http://cheops.anu.edu.au/~avalon/ip-filter.html, which works with both Solaris and Linux.

The best system for users who are new to Solaris is Sun's own SunScreen firewall (http://www.sun.com/software/securenet/lite/download.html). It comes in both a free and commercial edition, with the latter more than adequate for protecting small networks. It is available for both Solaris Intel and Solaris Sparc. The current release version is 3.1, which supports gigabit ethernet, SNMP management, and direct editing of security policy tables; however, it does not currently support Internet Protocol version 6 (IPv6). The firewall may be administered locally or remotely by using a secure session.

There are several important limitations that are placed on the SunScreen Lite version:

▼ It is designed to work with a system that is already acting as a router (if it wasn't, why would you want SunScreen anyway?).

■ It does not operate in the special stealth mode employed by the commercial edition.

■ It does not support any of the High Availability features of the commercial version.

■ It does not support more than two network interfaces; however, as most routers only have two interfaces, this should not be an issue for small networks.

▲ It does not provide support for proxying.

SunScreen can be operated either in GUI mode, through a standard Web browser such as Netscape, or by directly editing the system's configuration files. It is easy to install using the Web Start Wizard that is provided with the installation package.

To install the software, you need to run the /opt/SUNWicg/SunScreen/bin/ss_install script. There are several options that need to be configured for SunScreen to operate as desired:

▼ Routing or stealth mode operation

■ Local or remote administration

■ Restrictive, secure, or permissive security level

▲ Support for DNS resolution

After choosing the appropriate option for your system, the following message will be displayed:

```
--Adding interfaces & interface addresses
--Initialize 'vars' databases
--Initialize 'authuser' & 'proxyuser' databases
--Initialize 'logmacro' database
--Applying edits
--Activating configuration
loading skip keystore.
Successfully initialized certificate database in /etc/skip/certdb
starting skip key manager daemon.
```

```
Configuration activated successfully on cassowary.
Reboot the machine now for changes to take effect.
```

After rebooting the system, the firewall software will be loaded into the kernel, and you will then need to add rules to the firewall by using your browser to set the appropriate administration options. Figure 15-6 shows the browser starting on port 3852 on the localhost.

When first installed, the SunScreen username and password will be "admin" and "admin," entered into the Admin User and Password fields. After clicking the Login button, the SunScreen Information page is displayed, as shown in Figure 15-7. There are several options available at this point: firewall logs may be viewed, as may connection statistics. However, most users will want to create a set of security policies immediately upon starting the firewall service.

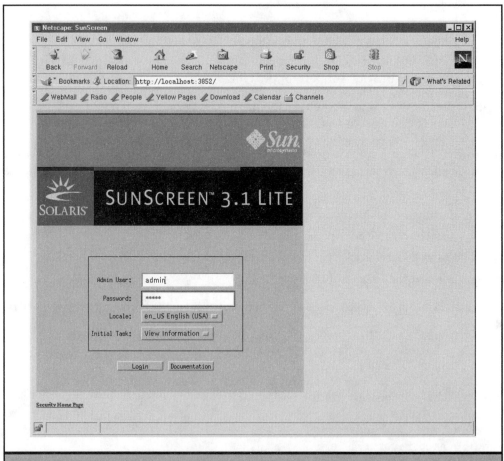

Figure 15-6.   Starting the SunScreen administrative interface

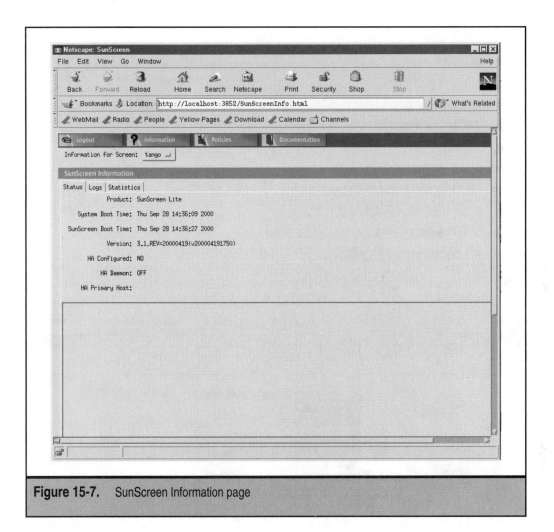

Figure 15-7.   SunScreen Information page

Security policies are based on rules that either allow or deny a packet to be transmitted from a source to a destination address. Alternatively, an address class may be specified by using wildcards. The main actions associated with allow rules are

▼ LOG_NONE

■ LOG_SUMMARY

■ LOG_DETAIL

■ SNMP_NONE

▲ SNMP

The main actions associated with deny rules are

▼ LOG_NONE

■ LOG_SUMMARY

■ LOG_DETAIL

■ SNMP_NONE

■ SNMP

■ ICMP_NONE

■ ICMP_NET_UNREACHABLE

■ ICMP_HOST_UNREACHABLE

■ ICMP_PORT_UNREACHABLE

■ ICMP_NET_FORBIDDEN

▲ ICMP_HOST_FORBIDDEN

Figure 15-8 shows how to define a rule with actions for the SMTP service, which is operated by sendmail. This allows mail to be transferred from local users to remote hosts. If we wanted to block all mail being sent to and from our network, we could create a deny

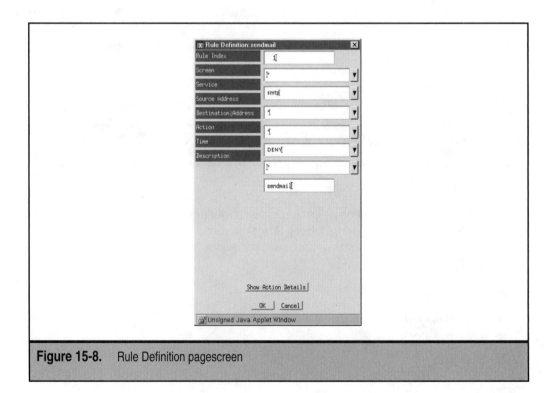

Figure 15-8.   Rule Definition pagescreen

action within the rule for the SMTP service. The rule could be applied selectively to specific local subnets or remote destinations.

Another useful feature is the ability to apply rules only for specific time periods. For example, if you worked in a bank, you could prevent all e-mails from being sent externally after 5 P.M. and before 9 A.M.

Once the new rule has been entered, it can be viewed on the Policy Rules panel, along with any other rules, as shown in Figure 15-9. The panel allows new rules to be added and existing rules to be edited, moved, or deleted. For each packet-filtering rule, the service, source address, destination address, action timeframe, and name are shown.

SunScreen performs more than just packet filtering: it can be used to setup a virtual private network (VPN) and can perform advanced network address translation (NAT) functions.

Figure 15-9. Policy Rules interface

RESOURCES

The most comprehensive security archive on the Internet is the COAST archive (ftp://coast.cs.purdue.edu/pub/tools/unix). Here, you will find the sources to cryptographic software, replacements for standard daemons, firewalls, intrusion-detection systems, security libraries, logging tools, network and password utilities, scanners, and various system utilities.

Another good source of tools is Wietse Venema's software repository (ftp://ftp.porcupine.org/pub/security/index.html#software). This includes tools such as the Coroner's Toolkit, used for computer forensics; a secure replacement for sendmail called postfix; TCP wrappers, which are used to log connections to selected network daemons; and a replacement for the standard RPC portmapper.

The following books are recommended reading for learning more about Solaris security:

▼ *Solaris Security* by Peter Gregory (Prentice-Hall, 2000).

■ *Applied Cryptography* by Bruce Schneier (Wiley, 1996).

■ *Building Internet Firewalls* by Brent Chapman and Elizabeth Zwicky (O'Reilly, 1996).

▲ *Practical UNIX and Internet Security* by Simon Garfinkel and Gene Spafford (O'Reilly, 1996).

SUMMARY

In this chapter, we have looked at security from a Solaris administrator's perspective. We have outlined the processes involved in conducting a security audit of a Solaris system to identify any potential weaknesses, and we have covered how to resolve the issues raised. In addition, we examined how to disable network services in Solaris and how to block traffic from using specific ports by using a packet filter.

PART IV

Managing Intranet Services

CHAPTER 16

Samba

Microsoft Windows systems make extensive use of the Session Message Block (SMB) protocol to make file systems and printers available for access by remote clients. For example, read/write access rights to shared directories and networked printers may be granted in a Windows NT domain. It is also possible to mount remotely exported file systems as virtual local drives, making it easy to integrate centralized data storage with local data management systems (such as databases).

Fortunately, Solaris supports SMB networking through the Samba suite of programs, which even includes a NetBIOS name service. In this chapter, we examine how Samba can be used to share Solaris file systems and printers to any client that supports SMB networking, including Windows, Linux, and MacOS clients. This means that Solaris can be used as a reliable, centralized fileserver, replacing unreliable servers running other operating systems. In this chapter, the reader will learn how to export file systems, share printers, and share file systems between Samba servers.

SAMBA SERVER

Samba is a package that makes it easy to bring the Windows and Solaris networking environments closer together. Although both Windows and Solaris support standard Transmission Control Protocol /Internet Protocol (TCP/IP) networking, both Microsoft and Sun have tended to develop their own versions of file system and printer sharing.

Microsoft's Explorer program, as shown in Figure 16-1, is used to create combined views of all local and remote file systems within a domain: in the example given, there are two local drives (C: and D:) and a local CD-ROM drive, as well as the computer Tiger, as shown in the Network Neighborhood. If the entry for Tiger was expanded, several shared disks could potentially be mounted, if access rights were granted to the local user for the remote volumes, through Security Access Manager. In addition, printers attached to Tiger could also be accessed, and print jobs could be managed using the printer control panel.

In contrast, Sun developed the Network File System (NFS) protocol, which also allows file systems and printers to be shared to other clients (NFS is described in detail in Chapter 18). There are even Windows-based NFS clients that allow Windows clients to access Solaris NFS shares. The choice between using NFS and Samba in a heterogeneous environment may be one of cost (PC-NFS costs money, Samba is free); but the choice is more likely a question of numbers: would you rather install NFS client software on hundreds of Windows systems that already have SMB support, or would you prefer to install a single SMB-compliant server (such as Samba)?

TIP: Using Samba as a centralized Windows reduces the need to buy extra server licenses for file and print servers, since these functions could be provided by a Solaris Intel or Solaris SPARC system running Samba. Samba also runs on Linux systems.

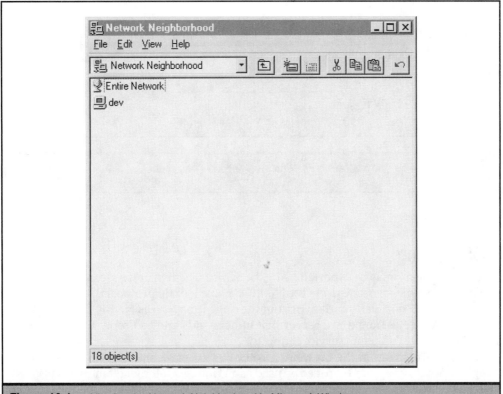

Figure 16-1.   Viewing the Network Neighborhood in Microsoft Windows

Figure 16-2 shows a concrete example of how Samba can be useful on the (Microsoft Windows) client side: a remote file system (\\elp\servlets) being exported using Samba running on Solaris allows a Microsoft Windows user to map a local drive letter (K:) to that file system. As far as the Windows client is concerned, the Samba volume is equivalent to a file system being shared from Windows NT server or equivalent.

Samba is not part of the Solaris operating environment, but may be downloaded from http://www.samba.org and compiled locally. Alternatively, the binaries may be downloaded from http://www.sunfreeware.com. There are two main services that must be run in order to use Samba: the nmbd NetBIOS name lookup service and the smbd Samba daemon. The NetBIOS service is necessary to find local Windows clients and all SMB servers within the local domain. The smbd daemon takes care of the actual file and print sharing operations. A new process is created for every client that connects to smbd, although only one nmbd is ever created.

Figure 16-2.   Mapping a Solaris file system to a Windows drive letter

NetBIOS Naming

Before file systems may be exported using the Samba Daemon, it is necessary to locate the client and server systems by using the NetBIOS name lookup protocol. The nmbd service runs on port 137 on Solaris and carries out the same functions as NetBIOS naming under Microsoft Windows. nmbd is a server that understands and can reply to NetBIOS over Internet Protocol (IP) name service requests.

It also participates in the browsing protocols that make up the Windows Network Neighborhood view. nmbd can also be used as a Windows Internet Name Server (WINS). We can best gain an insight into how this operates by looking at some of the Windows NT commands that can be used to browse SMB shares, and by comparing these with the equivalent Linux commands that perform the same tasks.

In order to view a list of client systems that are currently accessing a Windows NT server, we would use the command

```
C:\WINNT\SYSTEM32>nbtstat -s
```

The following output would then be displayed:

```
            NetBIOS Connection Table

Local Name  State        In/Out  Remote Host        Input    Output
-----------------------------------------------------------------------
RICHMOND <00>  Connected   Out    CHARLOTTE   <20>   101KB    15KB
RICHMOND <00>  Connected   Out    ATLANTA     <20>   1MB      100MB
RICHMOND <00>  Connected   Out    JAMESTOWN   <20>   203KB    205KB
```

This output states that the server RICHMOND is serving the remote systems CHARLOTTE, ATLANTA, and JAMESTOWN. It is possible to examine how much data has been uploaded and downloaded to and from the server by looking at the input/output column: in the case of CHARLOTTE, the input is greater than the output; while for ATLANTA, the output greatly exceeds the input, which would be expected of a fileserving system. In contrast, Jamestown has similar levels of input and output.

In order to view all of the hosts available for connections within a specific Windows NT domain, the net view command may be used:

```
C:\WINNT\SYSTEM32>net view
```

This produces output similar to the following:

```
Server Name            Remark

-------------------------------------------------------------------------
\\CHARLOTTE        Regional Server
\\RICHMOND            Capital Server
\\JAMESTOWN          Regional Server
\\RALEIGH            Capital Server
\\SMOKYMTS         Web Server
\\SHENANDOAH       Web Server
\\OAKTON           Kerberos Server
\\FALLSCHURCH        Anonymous FTP Server
The command completed successfully.
```

Here, we can see that a number of systems are available within the local EASTUSA domain: there are several fileservers for capital cities and regional cities, as well as two Web servers, as Kerberos servers, and an anonymous FTP server. These kinds of systems would typically be found in a modern network, and all would potentially require remote file access to other systems. For example, the two Web servers might require access to some files on the anonymous FTP server; this access could be provided by Samba.

Solaris systems don't have the net view command; however, Samba does provide a number of tools such as nmblookup, which can be used to list all of the systems within a specific domain. For example, to display all of the systems within the EASTUSA domain, we would use the following command:

```
bash-2.03$ nmblookup EASTUSA
Added interface ip=62.12.48.43 bcast=62.12.48.255 nmask=255.255.255.0
Sending queries to 62.12.48.255
Got a positive name query response from 62.12.48.39 (62.12.48.39)
Got a positive name query response from 62.12.48.41 (62.12.48.41)
Got a positive name query response from 62.12.48.42 (62.12.48.42)
```

```
Got a positive name query response from 62.12.48.43 (62.12.48.43)
Got a positive name query response from 62.12.48.50 (62.12.48.50)
Got a positive name query response from 62.12.48.57 (62.12.48.57)
Got a positive name query response from 62.12.48.58 (62.12.48.58)
```

It's important to remember that any of these hosts could be Samba servers running on Linux or Solaris, as well as Microsoft Windows servers and clients using native SMB networking.

The nmbd daemon may be started with the following command:

```
bash-2.03# /usr/local/samba/bin/nmbd -D
```

TIP: The –D option specifies that the NetBIOS name service daemon should run as a stand-alone daemon, rather than as a service through the Internet super daemon (inetd) (described in Chapter 12).

Configuring the Samba Daemon

The smbd server can be started with the following command:

```
bash-2.03# /usr/local/samba/bin/smbd -D
```

Again, the –D option specifies that the NetBIOS name service daemon should run as a stand-alone daemon, rather than as a service through inetd (described in Chapter 12).

The Samba daemon has a special configuration file, called smb.conf. It is usually stored in the /usr/local/samba/lib directory. The smb.conf can either be very short or very long, depending on the extent to which your local system requires customization and how many file systems need to be exported. The following is a sample smb.conf file:

```
[global]
workgroup = EASTUSA
netbios name = RICHMOND
server string = Solaris Samba Server V2.0.6
interfaces = 62.12.48.43
security = SHARE
log file = /usr/local/samba/log/log.%m
max log size = 500
socket options = TCP_NODELAY SO_RCVBUF=4096 SO_SNDBUF=4096
dns proxy = Yes
guest account = guest
hosts allow = localhost, 62.12.48.43/255.255.255.0

[printers]
comment = RICHMOND HP Printer
path = /var/spool/hp
print ok = Yes
```

```
browseable = Yes

 [homes]
comment = User Home Directories
read only = No
browseable = Yes

 [answerbook]
comment = Sun Answerbook Docs
path = /usr/answerbook/
guest ok = Yes
```

The global section defines several key parameters that affect the operation of smbd, including the name of the workgroup (EASTUSA), the name of the local server (RICHMOND), the server string that identifies the system (Solaris Samba Server V2.0.6), the primary network interface IP address (62.12.48.43), the security level (standard share level), the path to the Samba log file (/usr/local/samba/log), Transmission Control Protocol (TCP) parameters (such as send and receive buffer sizes in bytes), and the name of the guest account (guest).

Next, the local hp printer is specified as a share in the printers section. In addition, two different file systems are shared: the homes file system shares the local home directory for each user on the system, while the answerbook file system shares the local copy of Sun's answerbooks. Although NFS provides the automounter service through NFS that makes it easy for users to retrieve files from a single home directory on a server, the homes facility on Samba can be just as versatile.

NOTE: Most of the settings in smb.conf are easy to interpret, but, if needed, the complete Samba manual may be found online at the Samba site (http://www.samba.org).

One of the nice features of Samba is the configuration script checking program testparm. The testparm program will alert you to any configuration errors prior to starting a Samba service. In addition, testparm prints out all of the Samba parameters associated with the system in general and for each share, not just those that were explicitly declared in the smb.conf file:

```
bash-2.03$ testparm
Load smb config files from /usr/local/samba/lib/smb.conf
Processing section "[printers]"
Processing section "[homes]"
Processing section "[answerbook]"
Loaded services file OK.
WARNING: You have some share names that are longer than 8 chars
These may give errors while browsing or may not be accessible
to some older clients
```

```
Press enter to see a dump of your service definitions
# Global parameters
[global]
        workgroup = EASTUSA
        netbios name =
        netbios aliases =
        server string = Samba 2.0.6
        interfaces =
        bind interfaces only = No
        security = USER
        encrypt passwords = Yes
        update encrypted = No
        allow trusted domains = Yes
        hosts equiv =
        min passwd length = 5
        map to guest = Never
        null passwords = No
        password server =
        smb passwd file = /usr/local/samba/private/smbpasswd
        root directory = /
        passwd program = /bin/passwd
        passwd chat = *old*password* %o\n *new*password* %n\n
*new*password* %n\n *changed*
        passwd chat debug = No
        username map =
        password level = 0
        username level = 0
        unix password sync = No
        restrict anonymous = No
        use rhosts = No
        log level = 2
        syslog = 1
        syslog only = No
        log file = /usr/local/samba/log/log.%m
        max log size = 50
        timestamp logs = Yes
        protocol = NT1
        read bmpx = No
        read raw = Yes
        write raw = Yes
        nt smb support = Yes
        nt pipe support = Yes
        nt acl support = Yes
        announce version = 4.2
```

```
announce as = NT
max mux = 50
max xmit = 65535
name resolve order = lmhosts host bcast
max packet = 65535
max ttl = 259200
max wins ttl = 518400
min wins ttl = 21600
time server = No
change notify timeout = 60
deadtime = 0
getwd cache = Yes
keepalive = 300
lpq cache time = 10
max disk size = 0
max open files = 10000
read prediction = No
read size = 16384
shared mem size = 1048576
socket options =
stat cache size = 50
load printers = Yes
printcap name = lpstat
printer driver file = /usr/local/samba/lib/printers.def
strip dot = No
character set =
mangled stack = 50
coding system =
client code page = 850
stat cache = Yes
domain groups =
domain admin group =
domain guest group =
domain admin users =
domain guest users =
machine password timeout = 604800
add user script =
delete user script =
logon script =
logon path = \\%N\%U\profile
logon drive =
logon home = \\%N\%U
domain logons = No
os level = 0
```

```
lm announce = Auto
lm interval = 60
preferred master = No
local master = Yes
domain master = No
browse list = Yes
dns proxy = Yes
wins proxy = No
wins server =
wins support = No
kernel oplocks = Yes
ole locking compatibility = Yes
oplock break wait time = 10
smbrun = /usr/local/samba/bin/smbrun
config file =
preload =
lock dir = /usr/local/samba/var/locks
default service =
message command =
dfree command =
valid chars =
remote announce =
remote browse sync =
socket address = 0.0.0.0
homedir map =
time offset = 0
unix realname = No
NIS homedir = No
panic action =
comment =
path =
alternate permissions = No
revalidate = No
username =
guest account = nobody
invalid users =
valid users =
admin users =
read list =
write list =
force user =
force group =
read only = Yes
create mask = 0744
```

```
force create mode = 00
security mask = 037777777777
force security mode = 037777777777
directory mask = 0755
force directory mode = 00
directory security mask = 037777777777
force directory security mode = 037777777777
guest only = No
guest ok = No
only user = No
hosts allow =
hosts deny =
status = Yes
max connections = 0
min print space = 0
strict sync = No
sync always = No
print ok = No
postscript = No
printing = sysv
print command = lp -c -d%p %s; rm %s
lpq command = lpstat -o%p
lprm command = cancel %p-%j
lppause command = lp -i %p-%j -H hold
lpresume command = lp -i %p-%j -H resume
queuepause command = lpc stop %p
queueresume command = lpc start %p
printer name =
printer driver = NULL
printer driver location =
default case = lower
case sensitive = No
preserve case = Yes
short preserve case = Yes
mangle case = No
mangling char = ~
 hide dot files = Yes
delete veto files = No
veto files =
hide files =
veto oplock files =
map system = No
map hidden = No
map archive = Yes
```

```
            mangled names = Yes
            mangled map =
            browseable = Yes
            blocking locks = Yes
            fake oplocks = No
            locking = Yes
            mangle locks = Yes
            oplocks = Yes
            level2 oplocks = No
            oplock contention limit = 2
            strict locking = No
            share modes = Yes
            copy =
            include =
            exec =
            postexec =
            root preexec =
            root postexec =
            available = Yes
            volume =
            fstype = NTFS
            set directory = No
            wide links = Yes
            follow symlinks = Yes
            dont descend =
            magic script =
            magic output =
            delete readonly = No
            dos filetimes = No
            dos filetime resolution = No
            fake directory create times = No
[printers]
comment = RICHMOND HP Printer
path = /var/spool/hp
print ok = Yes
browseable = Yes

  [homes]
comment = User Home Directories
read only = No
browseable = Yes

  [answerbook]
comment = Sun Answerbook Docs
path = /usr/answerbook/
```

```
guest ok = Yes
 dont descend =
 magic script =
 magic output =
 delete readonly = No
 dos filetimes = No
 dos filetime resolution = No
 fake directory create times = No
```

Samba Daemon Status

After the Samba server has been started on port 139, it is easy to keep track of the server status by using the smbstatus command:

```
bash-2.03$ smbstatus
```

This will return a list of all current clients accessing data through the local Samba system:

```
Samba version 2.0.6
Service     uid       gid      pid      machine
-------------------------------------------------
answerbook  root      root     344      atlanta    Wed Nov 1 10:45:00 2000
homes       root      root     345      atlanta    Wed Nov 1 10:45:30 2000
homes       julian    staff    1023     charlotte  Thu Nov 2 00:15:34 2000
answerbook  steve     staff    2333     jamestown  Wed Nov 1 10:45:30 2000
```

In addition to the share name being accessed, the user ID (UID), group ID (GID), and process ID (PID) of the smbd process associated with the client are shown, along with the client system name and the date that the connection was established. For example, the root user from the system Atlanta opened the answerbook and the root home directory on Wednesday, November 1, 2000, at 10:45 A.M.

The smbstatus command also displays details of actual files being opened by the users who have established connections to the local Samba server. This can be very useful when trying to determine why a file on the local server file system can't be modified—a remote user may have placed a lock on it, which will not be released until the user has closed the file:

```
Locked files:
Pid    DenyMode   R/W      Oplock        Name
-------------------------------------------------
345    DENY_NONE  RDWR     NONE          /root/data.txt    Wed Nov 1 10:51:34
2000
345    DENY_NONE  RDONLY   NONE          /root/db.txt      Wed Nov 1 10:56:21
2000
1023   DENY_NONE  RDWR     NONE          /home/julian/address_book.txt   Thu
Nov 2 00:20:34 2000
```

The details of all currently locked files are displayed: along with the PID of the Samba daemon spawned for each client process, the read/write status and the full path to the locked file is displayed, along with the time and date that the file was first opened.

Finally, smbstatus displays some useful statistics regarding shared memory usage, which can be useful when trying to size the amount of RAM required by a departmental server or similar system that services a large number of Samba clients:

```
Share mode memory usage (bytes):
   2096928(99%) free + 112(0%) used + 112(0%) overhead = 2097152(100%) total
```

In this situation, almost all of the allocated memory is free, meaning that many more Samba clients may be serviced.

Samba Graphical User Interfaces (GUIs)

If manually configuring Samba by using the smb.conf file is a bit daunting, there are several third-party GUIs that may be used to automate the process of creating a smb.conf through a browser. One of the most popular tools is the Samba Web Administration Tool (SWAT), which runs as a service through the inetd on port 901.

SWAT can be administered locally, through a browser running on Solaris, or remotely, through a browser running on Microsoft Windows. The current Samba source distribution will build SWAT by default; however, a number of configuration changes need to be made in order to enable the SWAT service.

TIP: If you're unsure about how to edit the inetd.conf file or restart the inetd service, see Chapter 12.

The first step is to map the SWAT service name to the required TCP port (901), by adding the following line to the /etc/services files:

```
swat    901/tcp
```

The following line then needs to be added to the /etc/inetd.conf file:

```
swat    stream  tcp  nowait  root  /usr/local/samba-2.0.5/bin/swat  swat
```

For the changes to take effect, the inetd service must be restarted by using the following steps:

```
bash-2.03# ps -eaf | grep inetd
    root    200     1  0   Nov 1 ?         01:25 /usr/sbin/inetd -s
```

The PID of inetd is 200, so the command to restart the service with the modified inetd.conf file is

```
kill -1 200
```

After opening a browser, the SWAT interface may then be accessed by using the URL http://richmond:901, as shown in Figure 16-3.

Samba Clients

There are a number of ways to make a client connection to a Samba server: if you are using a Windows NT Workstation system or similar, the Samba server should simply appear as a normal Windows NT server, with individual file systems listed as shares (as determined by the smb.conf program). In addition, Solaris file systems may be mapped as local Windows NT drives. This makes Samba an ideal solution for servicing multiple Windows NT Workstation systems as a reliable fileserver.

For Linux users, the smbmount command can be used to mount shared Solaris file systems. In order to mount the answerbook share on the Samba server Richmond, for example, the following command would be issued from a Linux system:

```
linux# smbmount //richmond/answerbook /usr/local/answerbook
```

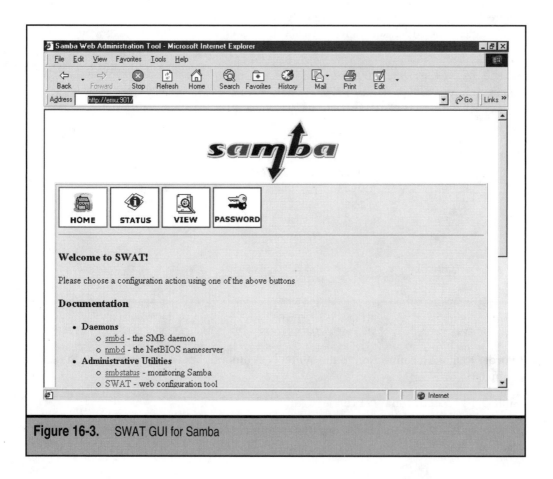

Figure 16-3.   SWAT GUI for Samba

This would mount the remote answerbook share onto the local file system on the mount point /usr/local/answerbook. Of course, the mount point would need to be created prior to mounting by using the following command:

```
linux# mkdir -p /usr/local/answerbook
```

To unmount the share once it is no longer required, the following command would be used:

```
linux# umount /usr/local/answerbook
```

Solaris users who wish to access remote Samba shares (from Solaris, Windows NT, or Linux servers) typically use the smbclient program, which runs from the command line and has a simple command set that is similar to that used by FTP. smbclient provides a very useful and compact way to upload, download, and delete files on a remote server. In order to make an initial connection, we would use a command of the form

```
bash-2.03# smbclient -L system
```

where "system" is the name of the remote Samba server.

To determine which shares were available on the server Richmond, we would use the command

```
bash-2.03# smbclient -L richmond
Added interface ip=62.12.48.43 bcast=62.12.48.43 nmask=255.255.255.0
Domain=[EASTUSA] OS=[Unix] Server=[Samba 2.0.6]

        Sharename      Type       Comment
        ---------      ----       -------
        answerbook     Disk       Sun Answerbooks
        homes          Disk       User Home Directories
        IPC$           IPC        IPC Service (Samba 2.0.6)

        Server                    Comment
        ---------                 -------
        RICHMOND                  Samba 2.0.6

        Workgroup                 Master
        ---------                 -------
        EASTUSA                   JAMESTOWN
```

In order to make a connection to the share //richmond/answerbook, we would use the command

```
bash-2.03# smbclient //richmond/answerbook
```

We would then be able to use one of the commands listed in Table 16-1 to list directory contents, change working directories, and upload and download files.

Command	Action
cd <dir>	Change working directory
dir <dir>	Display directory contents
get <file>	Retrieve a single file from the server
ls <dir>	Display directory contents
mget <files>	Retrieve multiple files from the server
mput <files>	Store multiple files on the server
put <file>	Store a single file on the server

Table 16-1.   Basic smbclient Commands

Accessing a remote printer using Samba is slightly different: the -P option must be supplied to the smbclient command in order to identify that target share as a printer. For example, to mount the printer called "hp" on the Samba server Richmond, we would use the following command:

```
bash-2.03$ smbclient -P //richmond/hp
```

A local file (such as address_book.txt) may then be printed by using a command like

```
smb:\> print address_book.txt
```

The standard printing tools may then be used to examine print queues to determine whether the print job was successfully completed.

SUMMARY

In this chapter, we have examined how to set up and configure the Samba service on Solaris and how to access Solaris shares by using clients on Microsoft Windows and Linux. Samba is a great cross-platform tool that can be used to set up a Solaris system as a departmental fileserver with the benefits of high availability that may be absent from other operating systems.

CHAPTER 17

Dynamic Host Configuration Protocol (DHCP)

In this chapter, we examine the (DHCP), which is an easy way to dynamically manage Internet Protocol (IP) addresses in Class A, Class B, and Class C networks using time-based leases for client addresses. Since at any one time, only a few IP addresses on a network may be in use, it makes sense to organize their allocation dynamically, rather than statically assigning them to individual hosts. This is particularly important for ever-expanding Class C networks, where less than three-hundred addresses are available.

In this chapter, readers will learn the background of DHCP and similar protocols, such as Reverse Address Resolution Protocol (RARP) and Bootstrap Protocol (BOOTP). In addition, we will walk through how to install a Solaris DHCP server and how to configure DHCP clients.

OVERVIEW OF DHCP

The Internet is a worldwide, networked environment through which information can be exchanged by using a number of well-defined network protocols, such as Transmission Control Protocol (TCP) and User Datagram Protocol (UDP). Each host on the Internet can be identified by a single machine-friendly number (for example, 128.43.22.1), which is mapped to a human-friendly, fully qualified domain name (for example, www.paulwatters.com). This mapping is provided by a globally distributed database, known as the Domain Name Service (DNS), allowing local networks to statically assign IP address ranges to all their local hosts. (DNS for Solaris is covered in Chapter 11.)

When DNS was first introduced, the exponential growth of networks and hosts connected to the Internet was not anticipated. IP address allocations initially reserved for Class A, B, and C networks were rather generous in hindsight—many address ranges were not used to their full capacity. Nowadays, there is a critical shortage of available IP address space using the current Internet Protocol version 4 (IPv4) standard.

Although the new Internet Protocol version 6 (IPv6) (supported by Solaris 8) will provide many more potential addresses, organizations worldwide are seeking solutions to use their existing resources more efficiently. While IPv6 is currently being adopted by many organizations, widespread deployment is not anticipated in the near future.

NOTE: While IPv6 is expected to solve the IP allocation dilemma in the short term, once the forecasted billions of Internet-enabled devices are connected to the mbone (http://www.mbone.com), the IP address allocation dilemma will come to the fore once again.

As an alternative to static IP address allocation, a practical alternative IP address management strategy is to use the DHCP. This protocol allows a server to dynamically allocate IP addresses from a central DHCP server to all configured DHCP clients on the local network. DHCP provides a mechanism by which computers using Transmission Control Protocol/Internet Protocol (TCP/IP) can obtain protocol configuration parameters automatically by using a lease mechanism, without having to rely on static addresses, which could be incorrect or outdated.

This means that only hosts that are up will be taking an IP address from the pool of existing addresses assigned to a particular network, by requesting and accepting an IP address lease from the DHCP server. For a Class C network, the pool of available addresses is (at most) 254, excluding the broadcast address, which is insufficient for many growing organizations.

TIP: If an organization changes its Internet Service Provider (ISP), they ordinarily need to change the network configuration parameters for each client system—a manual and inefficient process that consumes the valuable time of network administrators.

DHCP is not the only protocol to lease out IP addresses in this way. Previously, Solaris clients used the RARP to obtain an IP address dynamically from a RARP server. This protocol is particularly important for diskless clients who cannot store their IP addresses, locally. However, DHCP is better than RARP because it supports clients from Solaris, Linux, and Microsoft Windows, as well as serving more parameters than just an IP address. In addition, RARP servers can only provide addresses to a single network, while DHCP is capable of serving multiple networks from a single server, provided that routing is correctly set up.

On the other hand, Microsoft Windows administrators will be familiar with the BOOTP, which provides IP addresses dynamically in the same way that DHCP does. In fact, DHCP can be considered a superset of BOOTP, and DHCP servers are generally backward compatible with BOOTP. The relationship between DHCP and BOOTP is historical: the BOOTP protocol is the foundation on which DHCP was built. Many similarities remain: the packet formats for DHCP and BOOTP are the same, although BOOTP packets are fixed length and DHCP packets are variable length.

NOTE: The DHCP packet length is negotiated between the client and the server.

Another advantage of DHCP over proprietary protocols is that it is an open network standard, developed through the Internet Engineering Task Force (IETF). It is based on a client-server paradigm, in which the DHCP client (for example, a PC running Microsoft Windows) contacts a DHCP server (for example, a server running Solaris) for its network configuration parameters. The DHCP server is typically centrally located and is under the control of the network administrator.

Since the server is secure, DHCP clients can obtain reliable information for dynamic configuration, with parameters that reflect up-to-date changes in the current network architecture. For example, if a client is moved to a new network, it must be assigned a new IP address for that new network. DHCP can be used to manage these assignments automatically.

Readers interested in finding out more about how DHCP works can refer to RFC 2131. There is also a reference implementation of a DHCP server, client, and relay agent available from the Internet Software Consortium (ISC) (http://www.isc.org). While unsuitable for production purposes, the ISC implementation uses a modular API, which is designed to work with both Portable Operating System Interface for Computer Environments (POSIX)–compliant and non-POSIX-compliant operating systems. It also includes source code, making it useful for understanding how DHCP works behind the scenes.

In addition to dynamically allocating IP addresses, DHCP also serves other key network configuration parameters, such as the subnet mask, default router, and DNS server. Again, this goes beyond the capabilities of competing protocols like RARP. By deploying a DHCP server, network administrators can reduce repetitive client-based configuration of individual computers, which often requires the use of confusing operating system specific setup applications. Instead, clients can obtain all their required network configuration parameters automatically, without manual intervention, from a centrally managed DHCP server.

Both commercial and freeware versions of DHCP clients and servers are available for all platforms. For example, Checkpoint's DHCP server can be integrated with its firewall product, Firewall-1, to maximize the security potential of centralized network configuration management. Advanced network management protocols are supported by DHCP, like the Simple Network Management Protocol (SNMP). In addition, configuration change management issues, such as IP mobility and managing addresses for multiple subnets, can all be handled from a single DHCP server.

Implementation of DHCP should always be evaluated in the context of other network management protocols, such as SNMP, and other directory services, such as the Lightweight Directory Access Protocol (LDAP). Both LDAP and SNMP are crucial to the management of hosts and users in large and distributed networks. Since DHCP is responsible for the allocation of network configuration parameters, it is essential that SNMP agents obtain the correct information about hosts that they manage. In addition, LDAP servers need to be aware that host IP addresses will change over time.

This chapter will cover practical issues associated with installing DHCP servers and configuring DHCP clients on Windows, Linux, and Solaris systems. It is assumed that most readers will be familiar with the DNS and with TCP/IP stacks implemented on Solaris, Linux, or Windows systems. Starting with a description of the DHCP protocol and its historical roots in the BOOTP protocol, this chapter aims to provide a reference of the DHCP protocol, and practical installation and configuration procedures for heterogeneous environments.

RUNNING DHCP

The basic DHCP process is a straightforward two-phase process involving a single DHCP client and at least one DHCP server. When the DHCP client (dhcpagent) is started on a client, it broadcasts a DHCPDISCOVER request for an IP address on the local network, which is received by all available servers running a DHCP server (in.dhcpd). Next, all

DHCP servers that have spare IP addresses answer the client's request through a DHCPOFFER message, which contains an IP address, subnet mask, default router name, and DNS server IP address.

If there are multiple DHCP servers that have IP addresses available, it is possible that multiple servers will respond to the client request. The client simply accepts the first DHCPOFFER that it receives, upon which it broadcasts a DHCPREQUEST message, indicating that a lease has been obtained. Once the server has received this second request, it confirms the lease with a DHCPACK message. After a client has finished using the IP address, a DHCPRELEASE message is sent to the server.

In the situation in which a server has proposed a lease in the first phase that it is unable to fulfill in the second phase, it must respond with a DHCPNACK message. This means that the client will then broadcast a DHCPDISCOVER message, and the process will start again. A DHCPNACK message is usually sent if a time-out has occurred between the original DHCPDISCOVER request and the subsequent reception at the server side of a DHCPREQUEST message. This is often due to network outages or congestion. The list of all possible DHCP messages is shown in Table 17-1.

The DHCPOFFER message specifies the lease period, after which the lease will be deemed to have expired and will be made available to other clients. However, clients also have the option of renewing an existing lease, so that their existing IP address can be retained. The DHCP protocol defines fixed intervals prior to actual lease expiry, at which time a client should indicate whether or not it wishes to extend the lease.

TIP: If these renewals are not made in time, a DHCPRELEASE message will be broadcast and the lease will be invalid.

DHCP has three ways to allocate leases to a client. Automatic allocation grants an IP address permanently to a client. This is useful for granting IP addresses to servers that

Code	Description
DHCPDISCOVER	Broadcasts from client to all reachable servers
DHCPOFFER	Server responds to DHCPDISCOVER requests
DHCPREQUEST	Client accepts lease proposal from only one server
DHCPACK	Server acknowledges lease
DHCPNACK	Server refuses to accept DHCPREQUEST
DHCPRELEASE	Lease no longer required

Table 17-1.   DHCP Codes and Their Meanings

require a static IP address. A DNS server typically requires a static IP address that can be registered in host records lodged with InterNIC. The majority of clients will have addresses assigned dynamically by the server, which allows the greatest reuse of addresses. Alternatively, an administrator may manually assign an address to a specific client.

The process of allocating a DHCP lease is shown in Figure 17-1.

CONFIGURING A SOLARIS DHCP SERVER

The Solaris client (dhcpagent) and server (in.dhcpd) solution features backward compatibility with other methods already in use, particularly the RARP and static configurations. In addition, the address of any workstation's network interfaces can be changed after the system has been booted.

The dhcpagent client for Solaris features caching and automated lease renewal, and it is fully integrated with IP configuration (ifconfig). The in.dhcpd server for Solaris can provide both primary and secondary DHCP services, and it is fully integrated with Network Information Services (NIS+). The Solaris DHCP server has the ability to handle hundreds of concurrent requests, and also has the ability to boot diskless clients. Multiple DHCP support is provided through the Network File System (NFS).

TIP: Although we won't cover these advanced features in this chapter, it's worthwhile considering them when making a decision to use RARP or DHCP (or some other competing dynamic IP allocation method).

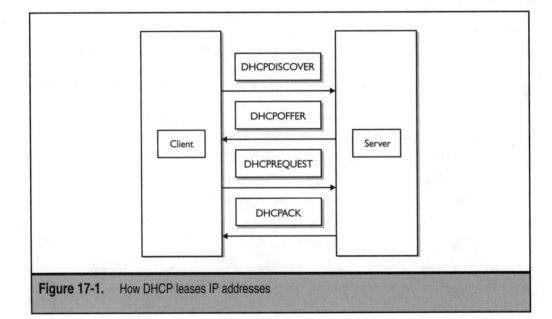

Figure 17-1.   How DHCP leases IP addresses

The main program used to configure DHCP under Solaris is /usr/sbin/dhcpconfig, which is a shell script that performs the entire configuration for you. Alternatively, you can use the dhtadm or pntadm applications to manage the DHCP configuration table (/var/dhcp/dhcptab). The dhcpconfig program is menu based, making it easy to use. The first menu displayed when you start the program looks like this:

```
***                     DHCP Configuration               ***
    Would you like to:
    1)          Configure DHCP Service
    2)          Configure BOOTP Relay Agent
    3)          Unconfigure DHCP or Relay Service
    4)          Exit
    Choice:
```

The first menu option allows the DHCP service to be configured for initial use. If your system has never used DHCP before, then you must start with the option. You will be asked to confirm DHCP startup options, such as the time-out periods made on lease offers (for example, between sending DHCPOFFER and receiving a DHCPREQUEST), and whether or not to support legacy BOOTP clients. You will also be asked about bootstrapping configuration, including the following settings. These settings can all be offered to the client as part of the DHCPOFFER message:

▼ Timezone

■ DNS server

■ NIS server

■ NIS+ server

■ Default router

■ Subnet mask

▲ Broadcast address

The second menu option allows the DHCP server to act simply as a relay agent. After entering a list of BOOTP or DHCP servers to which requests can be forwarded, the relay agent should be operational. Finally, you may choose to unconfigure either the full DHCP service or the relay service, which will revert all configuration files.

If you selected option 1, you will be asked if you want to stop any current DHCP services:

```
Would you like to stop the DHCP service? (recommended) ([Y]/N)
```

Obviously, if you are supporting live clients, then you should not shut down the service. This is why DHCP configuration needs to take place outside normal business hours so that normal service is not disrupted. If you have ensured that no clients are depending on the in.dhcpd service, you can answer yes to this question and proceed.

Next, you will be asked to identify the datastore for the DHCP database:

```
### DHCP Service Configuration ###
### Configure DHCP Database Type and Location ###
Enter datastore (files or nisplus) [nisplus]:
```

The default value is the NIS+, covered in Chapter 19. However, if you are not using NIS+ to manage network information, then you may choose the files option. If you choose the files option, you will need to identify the path to the DHCP datastore directory:

```
Enter absolute path to datastore directory [/var/dhcp]:
```

The default path is the /var/dhcp directory; however, if your /var partition is small or running low on space, and you have a large network to manage, you may wish to locate the datastore directory somewhere else. You will then be asked if you wish to enter any nondefault DHCP options:

```
Would you like to specify nondefault daemon options (Y/[N]:
```

Most users will choose the standard options. However, if you wish to enable additional facilities like BOOTP support, you will need to answer yes to this question.

You will then be asked whether you want to have transaction logging enabled:

```
Do you want to enable transaction logging? (Y/[N]:Y
```

Transaction logs are very useful for debugging, but they grow rapidly in size over time, especially on a busy network. The size of the file will depend on the syslog level that you wish to enable:

```
Which syslog local facility [0-7] do you wish to log to? [0]:
```

Next, you will be asked to enter expiry times for leases that have been offered to a client:

```
How long (in seconds) should the DHCP server keep outstanding OFFERs? [10]:
```

The default is ten seconds, which is satisfactory for a fast network; however, if you are operating on a slow network, or expect to be servicing slow clients (like 486 PCs and slower), then you may wish to increase the time-out. In addition, you can also specify that the dhcptab file be reread during a specified interval, which is useful only if you have made manual changes using dhtadm:

```
How often (in minutes) should the DHCP server rescan the dhcptab? [Never]:
```

If you wish to support BOOTP clients, you should indicate this at the next prompt:

```
Do you want to enable BOOTP compatibility mode? (Y/[N]):
```

After configuring these nondefault options, you will be asked to configure the standard DHCP options. The first option is the default lease time, which is specified in days:

```
Enter default DHCP lease policy (in days) [3]:
```

This value is largely subjective, although it can be estimated from the address congestion of your network. If you are only using an average 50 percent of the address on your network, then you can probably set this value to 7 days without concern. If you are at the 75 percent level, then you may wish to use the default value of 3 days. If you are approaching saturation, then you should select daily lease renewal. Finally, if the number of hosts exceeds the number of available IP addresses, you may need to enter a fractional value to ensure the most equitable distribution of addresses.

Most sites will allow clients to renegotiate their existing leases:

```
Do you want to allow clients to renegotiate their leases? ([Y]/N):
```

However, just like a normal landlord, you may sometimes be compelled to reject requests for lease renewal, especially if your network is saturated. You must now enable DHCP support for at least one network for DHCP to operate:

```
Enable DHCP/BOOTP support of networks you select? ([Y]/N):
```

You will be asked the following questions (using an example local network of 192.65.34.0):

```
Configure BOOTP/DHCP on local LAN network: 192.65.34.0? ([Y]/N):
```

You should (of course!) answer yes, if this is the network that you wish to configure DHCP for.

Next, you will need to determine whether you wish DHCP to insert hostnames into the hosts file for you, based on the DHCP data:

```
Do you want hostnames generated and inserted in the files hosts table? (Y/[N]):
```

Most sites will use DNS or similar for name resolution, rather than the hosts file, so answering "Y" is not recommended.

One situation in which you may wish to generate hostnames is a terminal server or Web server pool, where the hostnames are arbitrary and frequently change in number. In this case, you simply need to enter a sensible basename for the hostnames to be generated from:

```
What rootname do you want to use for generated names? [yourserver-]:
```

For a Web server bank, you could use a descriptive name like "www."

Next, you will be asked to define the IP address range that you want the DHCP server to manage, beginning with the starting address:

```
Enter starting IP address [192.65.34.0]:
```

Next, you must specify the number of clients. In our Class C network, this will be 254:

```
Enter the number of clients you want to add (x < 65535):
```

Once you have defined the network that you wish to support, you're ready to start using DHCP.

CONFIGURING A SOLARIS DHCP CLIENT

Once the DHCP server has been configured, it is then very easy to configure a Solaris client. When installing the client, you will be asked whether you wish to install DHCP support. At this point, you should answer yes. You will not be asked to enter a static IP address as per a normal installation, as this will be supplied by the DHCP server with a DHCPOFFER message.

If you wish to enable support for DHCP on a client that has already been installed, you will need to use the sys-unconfig command, which can be used on all systems to reconfigure network and system settings without having to manually edit configuration

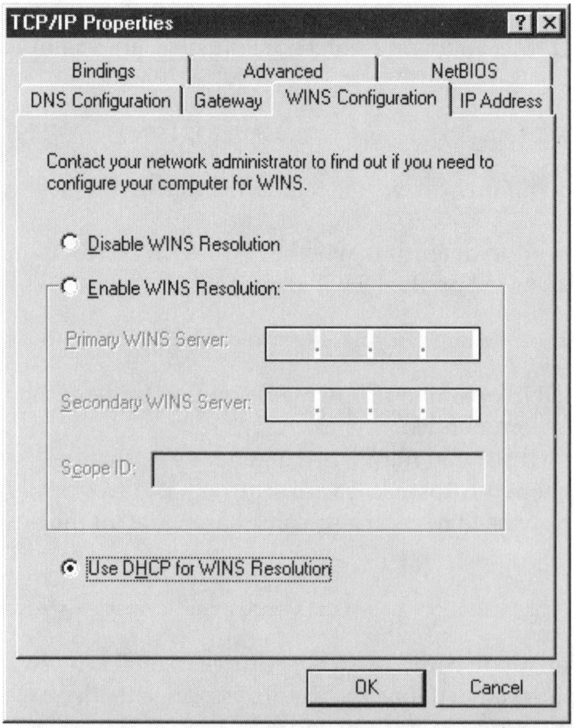

Figure 17-2.   DHCP Client for Microsoft Windows

files. The sys-unconfig command reboots the system in order to perform this task, so users should be given plenty of warning before reconfiguration commences. Again, you will be asked during configuration to install DHCP support, to which you should answer yes.

CONFIGURING A WINDOWS DHCP CLIENT

Setting up support for a Microsoft Windows client is easy: you simply select the DHCP support option in the TCP/IP section of the Network Control Panel, which can be found in most versions of Windows. A DHCP client for Windows 95 is shown in Figure 17-2 on the previous page. Once DHCP support is enabled, it is no longer necessary to enter any static IP address information.

SUMMARY

In this chapter, we have examined how to easily set up a Solaris DHCP server, which can be used to dynamically allocate IP addresses to clients from several different operating systems. Although DHCP server setup involves making some complex decisions about your network architecture, setting up DHCP clients is easy. It's generally considered easier to configure a single server per subnet than 254 clients who all require their settings to be entered manually! However, DHCP administrators should be aware of a number of important security issues, such as the possibility of IP spoofing occurring, and they should watch the CERT site (http://www.cert.org) for any advisories.

CHAPTER 18

Network File System (NFS)

In this chapter, we will examine Sun's Network File System (NFS), which is a distributed file system architecture based on the Remote Procedure Call (RPC). RPC is a standard method of allocating and managing shared resources among Solaris systems. Although NFS is similar to Samba in concept (transparent file system sharing among systems), as presented in Chapter 16, NFS features high data throughput because of dedicated support in the Solaris kernel, and support for both NFS 2 and 3 (Linux, for example, only supports NFS 2).

NFS was one of the first distributed network applications to ever be successfully deployed on local area networks. It allows users to mount volumes of other systems connected to the network. It also possesses the ability to change permissions, delete and create files, and apply security measures as any other locally mounted file system. One of the great advantages of NFS is its efficient use, with RPC, of network bandwidth.

In Solaris 8, the NFS concept has been extended to the Internet, with the new Web Network File System (WebNFS) providing file system access through a URL similar to that used for Web pages. In this chapter, we will examine the theory behind distributed file systems, and we will examine how they can best be established in practice.

Prior to Solaris 2.5, NFS 2 was deployed; it used the unreliable User Datagram Protocol (UDP) for data transfer, hence NFS 2's poor reputation for data integrity. The more modern NFS 3 protocol, based on Transmission Control Protocol (TCP), is now implemented in all new Solaris releases. NFS 3 allows an NFS server to cache NFS client requests in RAM, speeding up disk-writing operations and NFS transactions. In addition, Solaris 2.6 and onward provide support for a new type of NFS: Web Network File System (WebNFS).

The WebNFS protocol allows file systems to be shared across the Internet, as an alternative to traditional Internet file-sharing techniques like File Transfer Program (FTP). In addition, initial testing has shown that Sun's WebNFS server has greater bandwidth than a traditional Web server, meaning that it might one day replace Hypertext Transfer Protocol (HTTP) as the Web standard for transferring data.

In this chapter, the reader will learn how to set up and install an NFS server and an NFS client, and how to export file systems. In addition, we examine how to set up the automounter, so that a user's home directory across all machines on an intranet is automatically shared and available, irrespective of his or her login host.

NFS ARCHITECTURES

Any Solaris system can share any of its file systems with other systems, making these file systems available for remote mounting. NFS considers the system that shares the file system to be a server, and the system that remotely mounts the file system to be a client. When an NFS client mounts a remote file system, it is connected to a mount point on the local file system, which means it appears to local users as just another file system. For example, a system called "london" may make its mail directory /var/mail available for remote mounting by NFS clients.

This would allow users on machines like oxford, colchester, and luton to read their mail stored actually on london to be read locally from their own machines, without their having to explicitly log in to london. This means that a single mail server that acts as an NFS server can serve all NFS clients on a local area network with mail. Figure 18-1 shows this configuration.

However, one important aspect of NFS is the ability to export file systems and mount them on a remote mount point that is different from the original shared directory. For example, the NFS server london may also export its Sun Answerbook files (from the directory /opt/answerbook) to the clients oxford, colchester, and luton; however, luton mounts these files in the /usr/local/www/htdocs directory, as it publishes them via the World Wide Web (WWW), while oxford mounts them in /opt/doc/answerbook. The client colchester mounts them in /opt/answerbook, just like they are exported from london. The point is that the remote mount point can be completely different from the actual directory exported by an NFS server. This configuration is shown in Figure 18-2.

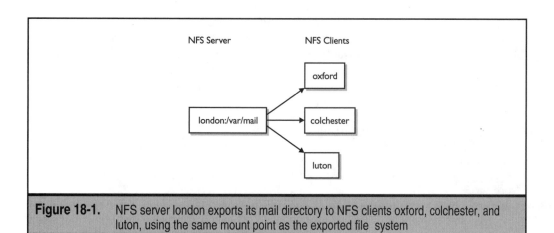

Figure 18-1.   NFS server london exports its mail directory to NFS clients oxford, colchester, and luton, using the same mount point as the exported file system

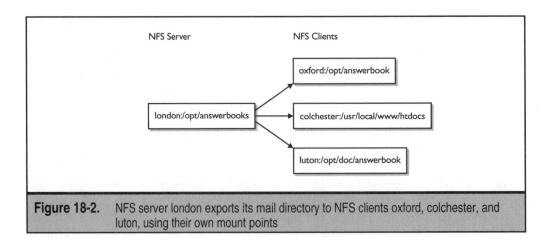

Figure 18-2.   NFS server london exports its mail directory to NFS clients oxford, colchester, and luton, using their own mount points

Configuring NFS

If you installed the NFS server during installation, a startup script called nfs.server will have been created in /etc/init.d. Thus, the NFS server can be started manually by typing the following command:

```
bash-2.03# /etc/init.d/nfs.server start
```

The previous command will start at least two daemons: the NFS server (/usr/lib/nfs/nfsd) and the mount daemon (/usr/lib/nfs/mountd). The nfsd daemon is responsible for answering access requests from clients for shared volumes on the server, while the mountd daemon is responsible for providing information about mounted file systems.

To check whether or not the NFS server has started correctly, it is possible to examine the process list for nfsd and mountd by using the following commands:

```
bash-2.03# ps -eaf | grep nfsd
    root 19961    1  0   Aug 31 ?        0:09 /usr/lib/nfs/nfsd -a 16
bash-2.03#  ps -eaf | grep mountd
    root   370    1  0   May 16 ?        2:49 /usr/lib/nfs/mountd
```

In this case, both nfsd and mountd are operating correctly.

In order to stop the NFS server, the following command may be used:

```
bash-2.03# /etc/init.d/nfs.server stop
```

There are some optional services started by the NFS server startup script, including daemons that support diskless booting (the Reverse Address Resolution Protocol (RARP) daemon, /usr/sbin/in.rarpd, and the boot parameter server, /usr/sbin/rpc.bootparamd). In addition, a separate daemon for x86 boot support (/usr/sbin/rpld), using the Network

Booting Remote Program Load (RPL), may also be started. You only need to configure these services if you wish to provide diskless booting for local clients; otherwise, they can be safely commented from the /etc/init.d/nfs.server script.

RPC

As mentioned earlier, NFS makes use of RPC technology, which makes it easy for systems to make requests for remote execution of procedures on server systems. RPC is currently supported across a number of different operating systems, including Solaris, Linux, and Microsoft Windows.

The purpose of RPC is to abstract the connection details and methods required to access procedures across networks: that is, the client and server programs do not need to implement separate networking code, as a simple Application Programming Interface (API) is provided for finding services through a service called the *portmapper* (or rpcbind). The portmapper must be running on both the client and the server for NFS to operate correctly. The portmapper is registered with both UDP and TCP 111, since requests may be generated for or received using NFS 2 or NFS 3, respectively.

rpcinfo

If you're having trouble starting the NFS daemon, it's often an rpc problem. In order to determine whether an rpc portmapper is running, you may use the rpcinfo command:

```
bash-2.03# rpcinfo -p
   program vers proto    port  service
    100000    4   tcp     111  rpcbind
    100000    3   tcp     111  rpcbind
    100000    2   tcp     111  rpcbind
    100000    4   udp     111  rpcbind
    100000    3   udp     111  rpcbind
    100000    2   udp     111  rpcbind
    100007    3   udp   32774  ypbind
    100007    2   udp   32774  ypbind
    100007    1   udp   32774  ypbind
    100007    3   tcp   32771  ypbind
    100007    2   tcp   32771  ypbind
    100007    1   tcp   32771  ypbind
    100011    1   udp   32785  rquotad
    100024    1   udp   32789  status
    100024    1   tcp   32775  status
    100021    1   udp    4045  nlockmgr
    100021    2   udp    4045  nlockmgr
    100021    3   udp    4045  nlockmgr
    100021    4   udp    4045  nlockmgr
    100068    2   udp   32809
    100068    3   udp   32809
```

```
100068   4   udp   32809
100068   5   udp   32809
100083   1   tcp   32795
100021   1   tcp    4045   nlockmgr
100021   2   tcp    4045   nlockmgr
100021   3   tcp    4045   nlockmgr
100021   4   tcp    4045   nlockmgr
100005   1   udp   32859   mountd
100005   2   udp   32859   mountd
100005   3   udp   32859   mountd
100005   1   tcp   32813   mountd
100005   2   tcp   32813   mountd
100005   3   tcp   32813   mountd
100026   1   udp   32866   bootparam
100026   1   tcp   32815   bootparam
```

In the previous example, both the mountd and nfsd are running, along with several other services, so the NFS daemon should have no problems executing. However, the RPL service is not active, so x86 clients would not be able to use the local server as a boot server.

SHARING FILE SYSTEMS

To actually share file systems and directories, you can use the share command with the options shown in Table 18-1. For example, if you want to share the /var/mail directory from london to clacton, you could use the following command:

```
london# share -F nfs -o rw=clacton /var/mail
```

In the previous example, "-F nfs" stands for "a file system of type NFS." Of course, we really want to share the volume with frinton and colchester as well, so we would use the following command:

```
london# share -F nfs -o rw=clacton,frinton,colchester /var/mail
```

In the previous example, /var/mail volume is shared to these clients because users on these systems need to read and write their e-mail. However, if we need to share a CD-ROM volume, we obviously need to share it read only:

```
london# share -F nfs -o ro /cdrom
```

Normally, the volumes to be shared are identified in the /etc/dfs/dfstab file. One of the really innovative features of NFS is that a system that shares volumes to other systems can actually remotely mount shared volumes from its own clients. For example, while london might share the volume /cdrom to clacton, colchester, and frinton, frinton might

Parameter	Description
anon	Maps requests between users anonymously
nosuid	Prevents applications from executing as set-uid
ro	Prevents writing to an exported file system
root	Equates remote access by root to local root access
rw	Permits reading and writing to an exported file system

Table 18-1.   NFS Server Options

share the /staff directory, which contains home directories, to london, clacton, and colchester, using the following command:

```
frinton# share -F nfs -o rw=clacton,london,colchester /staff
```

file systems can be unshared using the unshare command. For example, if we are going to change a CD-ROM on london that is shared to clients using NFS, it might be wise to unmount it first:

```
london# unshare -F nfs /cdrom
```

The command dfmounts shows that the local resources shared through the networked file system are currently mounted by specific clients:

```
london# dfmounts
RESOURCE   SERVER PATHNAME                 CLIENTS
           london /cdrom                   frinton,clacton
    -       london /var/mail               colchester,frinton,clacton
    -      london /opt/answerbook          colchester
```

However, dfmounts does not provide information about the permissions with which directories and file systems are shared, nor does it show those shared resources that have no clients currently using them. To display this information, we need to use the share command with no arguments. On frinton, this looks like

```
frinton# share
/staff rw=clacton,colchester,london   "staff"
```

while on london, the volumes are different:

```
london# share
    -               /cdrom   ro=clacton,colchester,london "cdrom"
                  /var/mail  rw=clacton,colchester,london "mail"
```

Alternatively, the showmounts command may be used:

```
bash-2.03$ showmount -e
```

And the output will be similar to the following:

```
export list for london:
/cdrom clacton.cassowary.net,colchester.cassowary.net,london.cassowary.net
```

INSTALLING AN NFS CLIENT

In order to access file systems being shared from an NFS server, a separate NFS client must be operating on the client system. There are two main daemon processes that must be running in order to use the mount command to access shared volumes: the NFS lock daemon (/usr/lib/nfs/lockd) and the NFS stat daemon (/usr/lib/nfs/statd). The lockd daemon manages file sharing and locking at the user level, while the statd daemon is used for file recovery after connection outage.

If NFS was installed during the initial system setup, then a file called nfs.client should have been created in /etc/init.d. In order to run the NFS client, the following command must be executed:

```
bash-2.03# /etc/init.d/nfs.client start
```

Just like the NFS server, you can verify that the NFS daemons have started correctly by using the following commands:

```
bash-2.03# ps -eaf | grep statd
   daemon   211    1  0   May 16 ?           0:04 /usr/lib/nfs/statd
bash-2.03# ps -eaf | grep lockd
     root   213    1  0   May 16 ?           0:03 /usr/lib/nfs/lockd
```

If these two daemons are not active, then the NFS client will not run. The next step is for the client to consult the /etc/vfstab file, which lists both the UFS and NFS file systems that need to be mounted, and it attempts to mount the latter if they are available by using the mountall command.

To stop the NFS client once it is operating, the following command may be used:

```
bash-2.03# /etc/init.d/nfs.client stop
```

The NFS server is usually started automatically during run level 3.

MOUNTING REMOTE FILE SYSTEMS

On the client side, if we want to mount a volume that has been shared from an NFS server, we use the mount command. For example, if we want to mount the exported CD-ROM from london on the NFS client frinton, we would use the command:

```
frinton# mount -F nfs -o ro london:/cdrom /cdrom
```

Like the /etc/dfs/dfstab file, which records a list of volumes to be exported, the /etc/ vfstab file can contain entries for NFS volumes to be mounted from remote servers. For example, on the machine colchester, if we wanted the /var/mail volume on london to be mounted locally as /var/mail, we would enter the following line in /etc/vfstab:

```
london:/var/mail          /var/mail    nfs         yes    rw
```

The prevsious line can be interpreted as a request to mount /var/mail from london read/write on the local mount point /var/mail as an NFS volume that should be mounted at boot time.

If you make changes to the /etc/vfstab file on frinton, and you want to mount the /var/mail partition, you can use the command

```
frinton# mount /var/mail
```

which will attempt to mount the remote /var/mail directory from the server london. Alternatively, you can use the command

```
frinton# mountall
```

which will mount all partitions that are listed in /etc/vfstab, but that have not yet been mounted. This should identify and mount all available partitions.

File systems can be unmounted by using the umount command. For example, if the /cdrom file system on london is mounted on frinton as /cdrom, then the command

```
frinton# umount /cdrom
```

will unmount the mounted NFS volume.

Alternatively, the unmountall command can be used, which unmounts all currently mounted NFS volumes. For example, the command

```
london# umountall -F nfs
```

unmounts all volumes that are currently mounted through NFS.

When a remote volume is mounted on a local client, it should be visible to the system just like a normal disk; so commands like df can be used to display disk slice information:

```
colchester# df -k
london:/cdrom 412456 341700   70756     83%     /cdrom
london:/var/mail    4194304 343234   3851070   8%      /var/mail
london:/opt/answerbook       2097152  1345634    750618  64%
/opt/answerbook
```

The main options available for mounting NFS file systems are shown in Table 18-2.

MEASURING NFS PERFORMANCE

NFS used to have a bad reputation as a slow, error-prone system for exchanging data. For example, many database vendors recommend against storing database files on NFS-mounted volumes, since data integrity could be severely affected if rollback logs, for example, were suddenly unavailable to the server. While this is still good advice for databases, NFS 3 is intended for high-performance fileserving applications.

In conjunction with the automounter and NIS+, NFS is often used to centralize home directories on a single server, that has Redundant Arrays of Inexpensive Disks (RAID) mirroring and striping enabled (using DiskSuite), to maximize redundancy of data storage, as well as increase the total amount of virtual addressable disk space.

If your entire user base relies on good NFS performance, it's critical to monitor the performance of the NFS server at all times, especially periods of peak load. The parameters that affect NFS performance are available network bandwidth, the amount of free virtual and physical RAM, and the system load. In this section, we will examine how to combine data from several different Solaris commands to continuously monitor the performance of NFS servers.

Option	Description
ro	Mounts a file system read-only permissions
rw	Mounts a file system read/write permissions
Hard	No timeouts permitted. The client will repeatedly attempt to make a connection.
Soft	Timeouts permitted. The client will attempt a connection and give an error message if connection fails.
Bg	Attempts to mount a remote file system in the background if connection fails

Table 18-2.   NFS Client Options

nfsstat

The nfsstat command can be used to examine the characteristics of all NFS shares, as well as their overall performance. For example, if two volumes were mounted by the client frinton from the server london (/staff and /cdrom) using NFS 3, then the default characteristics as reported by nfsstat –m would look like this:

```
bash-2.03# nfsstat -m
/staff from london:/staff
 Flags:
vers=3,proto=tcp,sec=sys,hard,intr,link,symlink,acl,rsize=32768,wsize=32768,retrans=5
/usr/answerbook from london:/usr/answerbook
 Flags:
vers=3,proto=tcp,sec=sys,hard,intr,link,symlink,acl,rsize=32768,wsize=32768,retrans=5
```

In the previous output, the two volumes have been mounted using the same NFS mount options, including the read and write packet sizes, as well as a packet retransmission count of 5. In order to obtain the performance characteristics of the shared volumes, we would use the nfsstat command with the –s option, which reports both connection-oriented and connectionless statistics:

```
london# nfsstat -s
Server rpc:
Connection oriented:
calls           badcalls        nullrecv        badlen          xdrcall
418029153       0               0               0               0
dupchecks       dupreqs
2291698         0
```

The previous output indicates that, for connection-oriented statistics, there have been 418029153 RPC calls registered by the server since it was last started, and 2291698 duplicated RPC caching checks carried out. The duplicated check-to-RPC calls ratio is approximately 0.5 percent, which is quite acceptable. There were no other RPC call types recorded, such as badcalls (where the RPC call was not accepted); no RPC calls with an impossible size (badlen); and no duplicate requests (dupreqs) or calls that were impossible to interpret (xdrcall).

```
Connectionless:
calls           badcalls        nullrecv        badlen          xdrcall
6385714         0               0               0               0
dupchecks       dupreqs
0               0
```

In the previous output, connectionless statistics are even more encouraging: although 6385714 RPC calls were recorded, there were no badcall, nullrecv, badlen xdrcall, dupchecks, or dupreqs recorded. These figures suggest that the network bandwidth is currently sufficient for the processing of RPC calls; however, should a large number of badcalls or xdrcalls be noted, a network analyzer may be required to determine where the bottleneck is occurring.

Specific to NFS, we can examine the functions of the various RPC calls that were recorded for both NFS 2 and NFS 3:

```
Server nfs:
calls           badcalls
424410642       0
Version 2: (6149413 calls)
null            getattr         setattr         root            lookup
49 0%           789279 12%      0 0%            0 0%            2283432 37%
readlink        read            wrcache         write           create
2050 0%         2333064 37%     0 0%            0 0%            2152 0%
remove          rename          link            symlink         mkdir
42 0%           13 0%           0 0%            0 0%            0 0%
rmdir           readdir         statfs
0 0%            737956 12%      1376 0%
Version 3: (416101332 calls)
null            getattr         setattr         lookup          access
347397 0%       295158834 70%   22595 0%        44046984 10%    67088057 16%
readlink        read            write           create          mkdir
638029 0%       5287349 1%      105316 0%       191586 0%       1480 0%
symlink         mknod           remove          rmdir           rename
178 0%          0 0%            4703 0%         991 0%          441 0%
link            readdir         readdirplus     fsstat          fsinfo
124 0%          1210283 0%      1962077 0%      3466 0%         4635 0%
pathconf        commit
25789 0%        1018 0%
```

For NFS 2, the highest number of calls are related to actual file reads (37%) and lookups (37%), with the remainder associated with retrieving client attributes through the cache (12%) and reading directories (12%). For NFS 3, the picture is a little more troubling, with some 70% of the calls being associated with retrieving client attributes through the cache and only 1% of calls being related to actual file reads. This suggests that the NFS server is performing poorly and the size of the Directory Name Lookup Cache (NDLC) should be expanded to improve performance.

vmstat

One of the greatest performance issues in NFS tuning is virtual memory capacity and performance. If your NFS server is using large amounts of swap, then using a slow disk will result in poor performance, since the cache will be hit hard. One application that reports on the current state of virtual memory is the vmstat command, which displays a large collection of statistics concerning virtual memory performance.

As you can see from the following display, the virtual memory report on the london server is not encouraging: 1346736431 total address translation faults were recorded, as well as 38736546 major faults, 1346736431 minor faults, and 332163181 copy-on-write faults. This suggests that more virtual memory is required to support NFS or, at least, that the disk on which the swap partition is placed should be upgraded to 10,000 RPM:

```
london# vmstat -s
        253 swap ins
    237 swap outs
    253 pages swapped in
  705684 pages swapped out
1346736431 total address trans. faults taken
 56389345 page ins
 23909231 page outs
152308597 pages paged in
 83982504 pages paged out
 26682276 total reclaims
 26199677 reclaims from free list
        0 micro (hat) faults
1346736431 minor (as) faults
 38736546 major faults
332163181 copy-on-write faults
316702360 zero fill page faults
 99616426 pages examined by the clock daemon
      782 revolutions of the clock hand
126834545 pages freed by the clock daemon
 14771875 forks
  3824010 vforks
 29303326 execs
160142153 cpu context switches
2072002374 device interrupts
3735561061 traps
2081699655 system calls
1167634213 total name lookups (cache hits 70%)
 46612294 toolong
964665958 user    cpu
399229996 system cpu
1343911025 idle    cpu
227505892 wait    cpu
```

mpstat

Another factor influencing NFS performance is the system load: a system that runs a large number of process and consistently has a load of greater than 1.0 cannot be relied upon to give adequate performance in times of need. The mpstat command can be used to examine a number of system parameters, including the system load, over a number of regular intervals.

Many administrators take several hundred samples using mpstat and compute an average system load for specific times of the day when a peak load is expected. This can greatly assist in capacity planning of CPUs to sustain NFS throughput. Fortunately, Sun hardware architectures support up to 64 CPUs, so it's not difficult to scale up to meet demand.

mpstat contains several columns that measure the following parameters:

▼ Context switches

■ Cross calls between CPUs

■ Idle percentage of CPU time

■ Interrupts

■ Minor and major faults

■ Sys percentage of CPU time

■ Thread migrations

▲ User percentage of CPU time

In the following output for the server london, the proportion of system time consumed is well below 100 percent—the peak value is 57 percent for only one of the CPUs in this dual-processor system. Sustained values of sys at or near the 100 percent level indicate that more CPUs should be added to the system:

```
london# mpstat 5
CPU minf mjf xcal  intr ithr  csw icsw migr smtx  srw syscl  usr sys  wt idl
  0   46   1  250    39  260  162   94   35  104    0    75   31  14   8  47
  1   45   1   84   100  139  140   92   35  102    0    14   35  13   7  45
CPU minf mjf xcal  intr ithr  csw icsw migr smtx  srw syscl  usr sys  wt idl
  0  141   3  397   591  448  539  233   38  111    0 26914   64  35   1   0
  1  119   0 1136   426  136  390  165   40  132    0 21371   67  33   0   0
CPU minf mjf xcal  intr ithr  csw icsw migr smtx  srw syscl  usr sys  wt idl
  0    0   0  317   303  183  367  163   28   63    0  1110   94   6   0   0
  1    0   0    4   371  100  340  148   27   86    0 56271   43  57   0   0
```

USING THE AUTOMOUNTER

The automounter is an rpc daemon that services requests from clients to mount and unmount remote volumes using NFS. During installation, a set of server-side maps is created that lists the file system to be automatically mounted. Typically, these file systems include shared-user home directories (under /home), and network-wide mail directories (/var/mail). The automount daemon is typically started from /etc/init.d/autofs during the multiuser startup (init state 2); thus, the automount daemon can be started and stopped manually by using the respective commands:

```
bash-2.03# /etc/init.d/autofs start
bash-2.03# /etc/init.d/autofs stop
```

Enabling the Automounter

automount is a command that installs autofs mount points and associates an automount map with each mount point. This requires that the automount daemon (automountd) be running. When the automount daemon is initialized on the server, no exported directories are mounted by the clients: these are only mounted when a remote user attempts to access a file on the directory from a client. The connection eventually times out; in that case, the exported directory is unmounted by the client.

Automounter maps usually use a network information service like NIS+ to manage shared volumes, meaning that a single home directory for individual users can be provided on request from a single server, no matter which client machine they log in to. Connection and reconnection is handled by the automount daemon. If automount starts up and has nothing to mount or unmount, this is reported and is quite normal:

```
london# automount
automount: no mounts
automount: no unmounts
```

The /etc/auto_master file contains the central map that names all automounted volumes. By default, this file contains four entries:

```
server# cat /etc/auto_master
# Master map for automounter
#
+auto_master
/net            -hosts          -nosuid
/home           auto_home
/xfn            -xfn
```

The automounter handles the network and auto_home shares, the latter providing a shared home directory for all NIS+ users in a domain. The auto_home entry corresponds to /etc/auto_home:

```
# Home directory map for automounter
#
+auto_home
```

If you didn't want to use NIS+, your auto_home file might look like this:

```
brad            london:/export/home/brad
karleen         london:/export/home/karleen
```

Of course, for the automounter to work using files, the following entry must appear in the name switch service configuration file (/etc/nsswitch.conf):

```
automount:   files nisplus
```

This instructs the automounter to use configuration files first before consulting NIS+ (for more information on nsswitch.conf, see Chapter 19).

A common problem with auto_home is that systems in an NIS+ environment may create user accounts on a file system mounted as /home. This means that if auto_home is active, as defined by /etc/auto_master, then after rebooting, the shared home directories are mounted on /home; and when the local /home attempts to mount the same point, it fails. This is one of the most frequently asked questions about Solaris 8, as the convention was different for earlier Solaris systems, which used local /home directories.

For Solaris 8, the recommended practice is to create home directories under /export/home, on the local file system if required, or to use auto_home in an NIS+ environment. However, if you wish to disable this feature altogether and stick with a local /home, simply remove "+auto_master" from the master map (/etc/auto_master).

Other entries can also be made in the master map. For example, to share a common directory for mail between a number of clients and a mail server, we enter the definition:

```
/-              /etc/auto_mail
```

This creates a share called "auto_mail," which makes mail on a single server accessible to all client machines upon request.

Automounter permits two kinds of shares that can be defined by direct and indirect maps: a direct map is a set of arbitrary mount points that are listed together, while an indirect map mounts everything under a specific directory. For example, auto_home mounts user directories, and all subdirectories beneath them. If an auto- mounted share is available on the server, you should see its details displayed in the /etc/mnttab file:

```
london:/var/mail    /var/mail     nfs      nosuid,dev=2bc0012      951071258
```

Continuing with the example of auto_mail, as defined in the master map, a file /etc/auto_mail would have to contain the following entry:

```
clacton# cat /etc/auto_mail
  /var/mail    london:/var/mail
```

This ensures that the london server knows where to physically find the /var/mail directory and that automount can mount the shared volume at will.

Sometimes, the network load caused by mounting and unmounting home directories can lead to an increase in I/O load and reduce the effective bandwidth of a network. For this reason, only volumes that need to be shared should be shared. Alternatively, the timeout parameter for automount can be modified to extend its latency for mounting and unmounting directories.

SUMMARY

In this chapter, we have examined Sun's NFS as a method of sharing volumes across local area networks. In particular, NFS is suited to sharing volumes among servers and clients that form part of an NIS domain, as changes to configuration are dynamically modified without the need for editing files manually.

NFS is widely used to share mail folders, CD-ROMs, and home directories, although it can quickly exceed the capacity of many 10MB networks when mounting and un-mounting volumes. Although many heterogeneous networks will use Samba to serve PC clients, NFS has historically played an important part in sharing file systems across networks.

The following books are excellent references for learning more about NFS and the automounter:

▼ *TCP/IP and ONC/NFS: Internetworking in a UNIX Environment* by Michael Santifaller (Addison-Wesley, 1994)

■ *Managing NFS and NIS* by Hal Stern (O'Reilly & Associates, 1991)

▲ *Sun Performance and Tuning: Java and the Internet* by Adrian Cockcroft, and others (Prentice-Hall, 1998)

CHAPTER 19

Network Information Service (NIS+)

Until recently, Microsoft Windows did not have a hierarchical domain service that could be used to manage individual groups of users who were located within an organizational hierarchy. Instead, a flat namespace was used to identify individual workgroups by their domain names. In large organizations with many different domains and workgroups, it was impossible to tell whether or not the SUPPORT domain belonged to the Information Technology (IT) group from one division or another. So, flat domain names were sometimes created to reflect the hierarchical nature of the organizational structures that the domains were attempting to model.

Thus, the SUPPORT domain for Atlanta might have been named GASUPPORT, while the SUPPORT domain for Raleigh may have been named NCSUPPORT. Such a system becomes unwieldy very quickly. Fortunately, with the introduction of Active Directory (AD), Windows 2000 users now have access to a hierarchical domain name system.

In contrast, Solaris has had a hierarchical domain name system for many years that is supported by NIS, which uses a series of maps to create hierarchical namespace structures. Sometimes administrators ask why NIS is required, since the Domain Name Service (DNS) (covered in Chapter 11) already provides name resolution for Internet hosts by converting computer-friendly Internet Protocol (IP) addresses of human-friendly names. However, NIS does not just provide naming services: an NIS server also acts as a central repository of all information about users, hosts, Ethernet addresses, mail aliases, and supported Remote Procedure Call (RPC) services within a network.

This information is physically stored in a set of maps that are intended to replace the network configuration files usually stored in a server's /etc directory, ensuring that configuration data within the local area network is always synchronized. Many large organizations use NIS alongside DNS to manage both their Internet and local area network (LAN) spaces effectively. Linux also supports NIS.

In recent years, Sun has introduced an enhanced version of NIS known as NIS+. Instead of a simple mapping system, NIS+ uses a complex series of tables to store configuration information and hierarchical naming data for all networks within an organization. Individual namespaces may contain up to 10,000 hosts, with individual NIS+ servers working together to support a completely distributed service. NIS+ also includes greater capabilities in the area of authentication, security (using DES encryption), and resource access control.

In this chapter, we will examine how to install and configure the new NIS+ system. We will walk through the configuration of key NIS+ entities, such as the primary and slave servers, as well as higher-level conceptual issues, such as how to plan an NIS+ network.

PLANNING AN NIS+ NETWORK

An NIS+ namespace is most easily constructed by mirroring the domains that are created for use with DNS. This makes it easy to match internal network domain information with the external DNS information used by Internet users. However, while DNS can be used to advertise host information about an organization's servers, NIS+ hides this information from the public.

Although some organizations will not have Internet connectivity, most will at least use Transmission Control Protocol/Internet Protocol (TCP/IP) networking, and so it makes sense to keep all DNS network mapping consistent with NIS+ host tables. Some organizations that use DNS alone have avoided NIS+ because of its reputation as a complex, time-consuming system that imposes a heavy administrative burden on system administrators.

This is certainly true for small networks that have less than five hosts—configuration files can be easily copied between hosts on a regular basis to keep data consistent. However, any reasonably sized network will soon require up to 15 key system configuration files that will need to be updated between hosts. Increasing the number of hosts by one in a network will then increase the administrative overhead well beyond the centralized maintenance of an NIS+ server.

In addition, the possibility for inconsistent data being entered into the configuration files of different servers makes it impossible to ensure that correct user, group, and network data is always available. For this reason alone, NIS+ provides a solution to key data-management issues for system administrators. The script-based installation and management method also makes it easier to create the necessary infrastructure to support and maintain NIS+.

In this section, we examine the elements that go into planning and setting up an NIS+ network. The first step is to register a DNS domain name, obtain a license to use a particular type of network (Class A, B, or C), and determine the range of IP addresses and subnets that will be supported within the NIS+ network.

For example, the company Cassowary Computing decided to set up an internal network based on NIS+. The administrator's first two tasks were to register the DNS domain name (cassowary.net) and then set up three Class C networks: one for the company (10.12.1.0), one for the sales division (10.12.2.0), and one for the development division (10.12.3.0).

These are mapped to the DNS domains cassowary.net, sales.cassowary.net, and develop.cassowary.net, respectively. To support DNS, the first hosts to be set up are the DNS servers for three DNS domains: ns.cassowary.net (10.12.1.16), ns.sales.cassowary.net (10.12.1.16), and ns.develop.cassowary.net (10.12.2.16).

Each primary DNS server will be authoritative for its domain, as well as act as a secondary server for the other two domains. For example, ns.cassowary.net will be the primary DNS server for the cassowary.net domain, but it will also act as a secondary server for the develop.cassowary.net and sales.cassowary.net networks. A total of 255×3 Class C network addresses, for a total of 765 IP addresses, are now available for the company. Figure 19-1 shows the DNS configuration for the company.

Once the DNS naming has been decided, it is then very easy to create the NIS+ namespace, as the same names may be used for the network and domain names, as well as the hosts. Thus, the DNS domain name cassowary.net is written in NIS+ terms as "Cassowary.Net." Notice the terminating period on the NIS+ domain name.

The NIS+ domains for Cassowary Computing can exactly mirror the DNS configuration, as shown in Figure 19-2. However, some differences in naming are immediately apparent: while DNS convention uses lowercase names that do not terminate in a period, the NIS+ convention uses capital letters and terminates with a period.

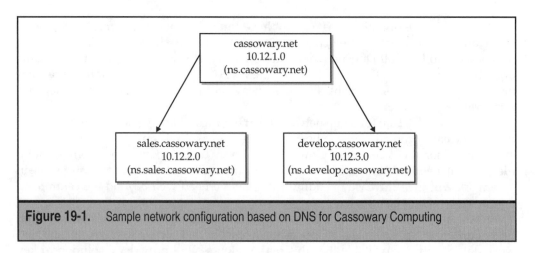

Figure 19-1.   Sample network configuration based on DNS for Cassowary Computing

The root domain of an NIS+ network is usually equivalent to a second- or third- level DNS domain; thus, in our cassowary.net DNS example, the NIS+ root domain is Cassowary.Net. Each of the DNS subdomains (develop.cassowary.net and sales.cassowary.net) are, therefore, nonroot domains in NIS+, even though they have their own DNS servers. However, nonroot NIS+ domains can also have their own NIS+ servers.

Indeed, a sensible NIS+ planning policy sees domains having at least two servers: a master server and a replica server. The master server is authoritative under normal operation; however, if the master server is not available for some reason, the replica server is able to service NIS+ clients. Figure 19-3 shows the envisaged scenario for the Cassowary.Net. domain in terms of planned DNS servers, and master and replica NIS+ servers.

The overall purpose of NIS+ is to provide services to clients. Unsurprisingly, NIS+ client notations follow the standards set out for DNS; thus, a DNS client like brad.sales.cassowary.net has the NIS+ name Brad.Sales.Cassowary.Net. This client would be serviced by the NIS+ server Master.Sales.Cassowary.Net, with Replica.Sales.Cassowary.Net acting as a backup.

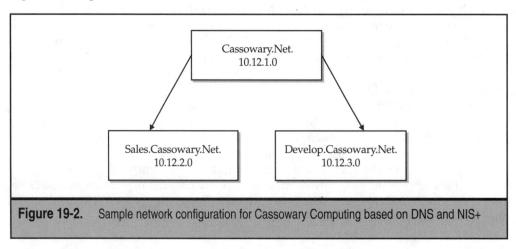

Figure 19-2.   Sample network configuration for Cassowary Computing based on DNS and NIS+

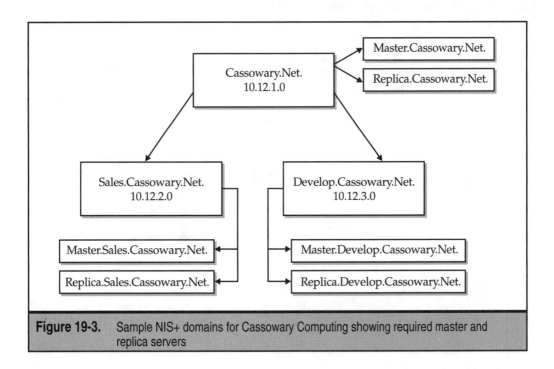

Figure 19-3.   Sample NIS+ domains for Cassowary Computing showing required master and replica servers

All NIS+ clients need to be manually installed and registered by using a script, during which time a directory cache is initialized that allows for local network directory lookups for supported services. This configuration is shown in Figure 19-4.

In these examples, we've equated NIS+ namespaces with DNS namespaces, so you may be wondering why we would be bothered using NIS+ if it is so similar to DNS. In fact, the host-oriented namespace we've examined so far is only one aspect of NIS+ operation: many objects other than hosts, such as groups, directories, and tables, can be managed within NIS+ domains.

Centralizing storage of these objects allows greater security than if these objects could be modified directly. In addition, authentication of client credentials uses the DES encryption algorithm, while DNS has little, if any, security features built in. Although the similarity of NIS+ naming to DNS is useful for learning about NIS+, there are some important differences that we will examine in the next section.

CONFIGURING NIS+

Now that we have examined how a network based on NIS+ can be created, we will focus on how to configure NIS+ services on the network. Typically, an NIS+ administrator will begin by setting up the NIS+ domains, as reviewed in the previous section, followed by the configuration of master and replica servers for both root and nonroot domains. Finally, clients and users are configured and added to the domain.

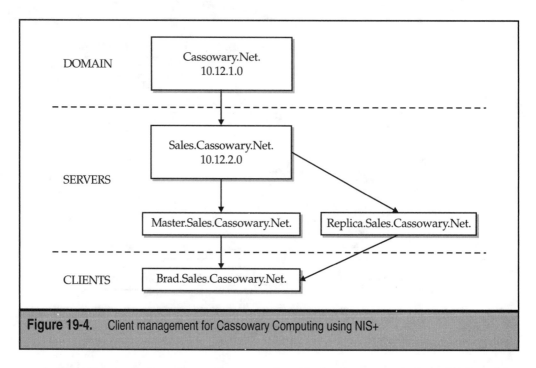

Figure 19-4.   Client management for Cassowary Computing using NIS+

At least the master server must be operational before any population of NIS+ tables can take place: a replica server can wait if time is precious. A number of administrative groups should also be created prior to client configuration. Root domains must always be set up before nonroot domains. In the following sections, we will review the steps required to get your NIS+ network up and running quickly.

Name Service Switch Setup

The name service switch (/etc/nsswitch.conf) governs how name lookups are performed under Solaris 8. We saw in Chapter 11 how the DNS service uses the name service switch to determine how host lookups are performed: the order in which different name resolution strategies are used can also be modified.

For example, the following line specifies that IP address lookups on hostnames should be performed by first examining the /etc/hosts file; if the name is not resolved, then it is passed to the DNS server. If the DNS server cannot resolve the name, or does not respond, then NIS maps are consulted. Failing NIS, the final link in the resolution chain is a query to NIS+ tables:

```
hosts: files dns nis nisplus
```

Of course, if you didn't use NIS maps or NIS+ tables on your network, you could simply use the following entry for host lookups in /etc/nsswitch.conf:

```
hosts: files dns
```

If your system is not connected to the Internet and you use NIS+ as your sole network information service, you can use the following entry instead:

```
hosts: files nisplus
```

The order in which the entries are made clearly affects how the name resolution will be performed. Specifying multiple services for hostname resolutions ensures that if one of the methods attempted early in the resolution chain does not respond or provide the information required, an alternative source of information can be consulted.

The name service switch does not just dictate how hostnames are looked up: in fact, some 13 other services use /etc/nsswitch.conf to determine how various services are resolved by the various information services available on a Solaris system. The following is a typical name-service switch file that is targeted at DNS name resolution:

```
passwd:       files
group:        files
hosts:        dns [NOTFOUND=return] files
networks:     files
protocols:    files
rpc:          files
ethers:       files
netmasks:     files
bootparams:   files
publickey:    files
netgroup:     files
automount:    files
aliases:      files
services:     files
sendmailvars:   files
```

Alternatively, for a system that mainly uses NIS+, we would set up a name service switch file as follows:

```
passwd:       files nisplus
group:        files nisplus
hosts:        nisplus dns [NOTFOUND=return] files
services:     nisplus [NOTFOUND=return] files
networks:     nisplus [NOTFOUND=return] files
protocols:    nisplus [NOTFOUND=return] files
rpc:          nisplus [NOTFOUND=return] files
ethers:       nisplus [NOTFOUND=return] files
netmasks:     nisplus [NOTFOUND=return] files
bootparams:   nisplus [NOTFOUND=return] files
publickey:    nisplus
netgroup:     nisplus
```

```
automount: nisplus files
aliases: nisplus files
sendmailvars: nisplus files
```

This scenario favors NIS+ over files in most situations, and it doesn't even consult DNS for name resolution. The contents of your /etc/nsswitch.conf file will depend largely on the way in which your network is configured, and whether or not DNS, NIS+, NIS, or some other naming service is operating.

Root Domain Installation

Before any other services may be installed, NIS+ requires that the master server for the root domain be created. The master server will primarily be responsible for the management of the NIS+ namespace. For example, for the Cassowary.Net. domain, the DNS server (ns.cassowary.net) will also be used for NIS+. This means that the nisserver script can be executed on the DNS server system (ns.cassowary.net) in order to initialize the master server for the root domain:

```
ns.cassowary.net# nisserver -r -d Cassowary.Net.
```

That's all that's required for NIS+ support. However, in order to enable support for NIS clients within the domain, you would need to use the following command instead:

```
ns.cassowary.net# nisserver -Y -r -d Cassowary.Net.
```

Creating Tables

As we mentioned earlier, NIS+ operates by creating a centralized set of tables, which act as replacements for the localized configuration files in the /etc directory. In order to begin the process of creating these tables on the master server for the root domain, we need to use the nispopulate command to insert initial values into the tables:

```
ns.cassowary.net# nispopulate -F -p /nis+files -d Cassowary.Net.
```

The nispopulate command is responsible for storing all of the appropriate information in the NIS+ tables.

If your master server or the root domain needs to support NIS clients, then you would need to use the following command instead:

```
ns.cassowary.net# nispopulate -Y -F -p /nis+files -d Cassowary.Net.
```

Next, we need to determine which users on the master server for the root domain should have administrative access to the NIS+ namespace. This gives the users named as administrators the ability to modify all of the data that NIS+ clients can look up; thus, it is a role of considerable responsibility.

Changes made to the NIS+ tables do not just affect the local machine—they are reflected network wide. If we had two network administrators—brad and karleen—they could be added to the administrator's group by using the nisgrpadm command:

```
ns.cassowary.net# nisgrpadm -a Cassowary.Net. brad.Cassowary.Net. karleen.Cassowary.Net.
```

In order to check the configuration and create a checkpoint, you can use the nisping command on the domain:

```
ns.cassowary.net# nisping -C Cassowary.Net.
```

This concludes the configuration required to install the root domain. In the next section, we will examine how to set up master and replica servers for the two nonroot domains that lie underneath the Cassowary.Net. domain: Develop.Cassowary.Net. and Sales.Cassowary.Net.

Nonroot Domain Installation

The first step in installing the nonroot domains Develop.Cassowary.Net. and Sales.Cassowary.Net. is to configure a master server for each nonroot domain by using the nisclient command. These master servers are effectively clients of the Cassowary.Net. root domain, which is why the nisclient command is used to initialize their settings.

In this case, the server moorea.cassowary.net is assigned to be the root server of the nonroot domain Sales.Cassowary.Net., while the host borabora.cassowary.net is assigned to be the root server of the nonroot domain Develop.Cassowary.Net. To create the master servers, we would execute the following commands on each of these hosts, respectively:

```
moorea.cassowary.net# nisclient -i -d Cassowary.Net. -h Ns.Cassowary.Net
borabora.cassowary.net# nisclient -i -d Cassowary.Net. -h Ns.Cassowary.Net
```

After the master servers have been initialized, clients for that domain can actually set up from individual user accounts. For example, for the user maya in the domain Sales.Cassowary.Net, we would use the following command to allow client access to the local namespace:

```
maya@moorea.cassowary.net$ nisclient -u
```

Alternatively, for the user natashia in the domain Develop.Cassowary.Net, we would use the following to initialize client access:

```
natashia@borabora.cassowary.net$ nisclient -u
```

Now that the servers that will act as master servers for the nonroot domains have been set up as clients of the server that manages the root domain, these systems must themselves be set up as master servers for their own domains. In addition, replica servers may be installed at this time. In the previous example, we allocated moorea.cassowary.net the role of being master server for the nonroot domain Sales.Cassowary.Net.

Imagine that we now allocate tahiti.cassowary.net the role of replica server for the nonroot domain Sales.Cassowary.Net. The first step is to ensure that the NIS+ service is running via RPC:

```
moorea.cassowary.net# rpc.nisd
```

Next, we use a command similar to that used for setting up the master server for the root domain:

```
ns.cassowary.net# nisserver -R -d Cassowary.Net. -h moorea.cassowary.net
```

Authority to begin serving is then set by using the following command:

```
ns.cassowary.net# nisserver -M -d Sales.Cassowary.Net. -h moorea.cassowary.net
```

The tables for the domain Sales.Cassowary.Net must then be populated by using the same procedure as for the master server:

```
moorea.cassowary.net# nispopulate -F -p /nis+files -d Sales.Cassowary.Net.
```

The final step is assigning the role of replica server to the host tahiti.cassowary.net by using the nisclient command:

```
moorea.cassowary.net# nisclient -R -d Sales.Cassowary.Net. -h tahiti.cassowary.net
```

We now repeat these commands for the nonroot domain Develop.Cassowary.Net., which has been assigned the server orana.cassowary.net as a replica server:

```
borabora.cassowary.net# rpc.nisd
orana.cassowary.net# rpc.nisd
ns.cassowary.net# nisserver -R -d Cassowary.Net. -h borabora.cassowary.net
ns.cassowary.net# nisserver -M -d Develop.Cassowary.Net. -h borabora.cassowary.net
borabora.cassowary.net# nispopulate -F -p /nis+files -d Develop.Cassowary.Net.
borabora.cassowary.net# nisclient -R -d Develop.Cassowary.Net. -h orana.cassowary.net
```

NIS+ TABLES

All data within NIS+ is stored in tables, which are loosely based on several configuration files that are located in the /etc directory on a standard host. The major difference between file-centric and NIS+ administration is security and centralization of administration: on a network with 100 hosts, around 1500 individual configuration files need to be managed using a files approach, while an NIS+ approach requires maintenance of only 15 files. Any modifications to the NIS+ tables are automatically distributed to clients requesting namespace data—this applies equally to hostname resolution as it does to access authorization credentials, such as usernames and passwords.

Trying to update a password file on 100 hosts takes a long time, if that user needs access to any particular host on the network. For example, students may work on any workstation within a computer lab, or stock traders may be rotated regularly throughout an office for security reasons. Access to any workstation at any time, using a single set of credentials, is required. NIS+ is particularly suited to this environment.

If you are worried about redundancy and backups, the master/replica server model used by NIS+ ensures that even if the master server for a root or nonroot domain goes down, its replica server will be able to serve authoritative data until normal service is resumed.

Auto_Home

The Auto_Home table enables all users within a domain to access a single home directory, irrespective of which system they log in to. The ability to centrally support this kind of distributed filesystem is one of the best features of NIS+. One of the main issues that arises when using the automounter is that local partitions called "/home" cannot be mounted by the local system—this mount point is reserved for the automounter. This can cause some consternation for administrators who are unfamiliar with the automounter.

There are two columns in the Auto_Home table: the username, which identifies the user on a network; the hostname; and the path to the home directory for that user's home directory. Once an entry is created in the Auto_Home table, the home directory for that user will be available for mounting on any host within the network that is part of the NIS+ domain. Let's look at an example:

```
julian      avarua:/users/export/julian
```

In the previous code, the user julian's home directory is always mounted from the host avarua with the mount point /users/export/julian.

Auto_Master

The Auto_Master is used in conjunction with the Network File System (NFS) to create maps that relate specific mount points to use the automounter. For example, if we wanted to map home directories from /staff and /students using Auto_Home, we'd need to insert the following entries into the Auto_Master table:

```
/staff      auto_home
/students   auto_home
```

Bootparams

Solaris supports the booting of diskless clients, such as X-terminals, by using the Bootparams table. Every diskless client within the domain will have an entry in the Bootparams table, which defines the root directory, swap, and dump partitions for the client. For example, the diskless client cardiff has its root directory on the server macquarie, but actually accesses its swap and dump partitions from the server tuggerah. The following entry would need to be inserted into the Bootparams table to support this functionality:

```
cardiff    root=macquarie:/export/root/cardiff\
               swap=tuggerah:/export/swap/cardiff\
               dump=tuggerah:/export/dump/cardiff
```

Ethers

All network interface cards have a low-level hardware address associated with them called an Ethernet (MAC) address. NIS+ associates each host's Ethernet address with a specific hostname within the domain. For example, if the host charlestown had a single network interface with the Ethernet address 01:ab:b1:c3:d2:c3, the following entry would be inserted into the Ethers table:

```
01:ab:b1:c3:d2:c3   charlestown
```

All entries in the ethers table are statically stored as ARP entries and are typically used by diskless X-terminals or for jumpstart configurations.

Group

The Group table stores information about user groups that have been defined within the domain. We cover the definition and planning of groups within Solaris in Chapter 7. The NIS+ Group table stores details of the group name, a group password (if applicable), the group ID (GID), and a list of all users who are members of the group. For example, the group staff may have the members paul, maya, brad, and karleen, as shown in the following entry:

```
staff::10:paul,maya,brad,karleen
```

Hosts

The Hosts table associates an IP address with a specific hostname, and/or a number of optional hostname aliases. For example, if the host speers had an IP address of 10.36.12.54 and an alias of cockle, then the following entry would be inserted into the Hosts table:

```
192.34.54.3    speers    cockle
```

Mail Aliases

Mail Transport Agents (MTAs) under Solaris typically make use of the mail aliases database (/etc/aliases) to define mailing lists or aliases for specific users. In an NIS+ domain, the /etc/aliases file is replaced by the Mail Aliases table, which can map a specific username to an alias name or a single alias to a list of valid usernames, like a mailing list. For example, the alias postmaster is typically used to identify the mail administrator within a domain. To associate this alias with a specific user account (such as maya), we would insert the following alias into the Mail Aliases table:

```
postmaster:maya
```

Aliases can also be matched with other aliases that have already been defined. For example, many sites forward all e-mail to the root user to the alias postmaster. In combination with our existing rule that forwards all e-mail for postmaster to maya, the following entry would have the net result of forwarding all e-mail to root to the user maya:

```
root:postmaster
```

Finally, imagine that a restaurant chain had an e-mail distribution list to managers at all local restaurants. A mail alias called "managers" could be set up so that the managers at the different restaurants would all receive a copy of e-mails sent to the user managers. In this example, the accounts hamilton, swansea, barbeach, and belmont would all receive a copy of any messages sent to the alias managers:

```
managers: hamilton,swansea,barbeach,belmont
```

Netgroups

Netgroups are authorization lists that can be used to govern access to resources within a network and to determine which groups of users can perform specific operations. For example, a group called "admins" within the Cassowary.Net. domain might be authorized to add or delete clients to the domain. A netgroups entry that defines the admins Netgroup would look like this:

```
admins      cassowary.net
```

Netmasks

The Netmasks table defines all of the netmasks required for the local network. For a Class A network, the netmask is 255.0.0.0, while the netmask for a Class B network is 255.255.0.0. The most common netmask is 255.255.255.0, which is for a Class C network (for example, 204.128.64.0), as shown in the following line of code:

```
204.128.64.0      255.255.255.0
```

Networks

Individual networks can be defined within an NIS+ domain by inserting entries into the Networks table. In addition, aliases for entire networks can also be entered into the Networks table. For example, if the network broadmeadow (203.48.16.0) acted as a backup network for a primary network, it may have the alias backup:

```
broadmeadow   203.48.16.0   backup
```

Passwd

The Passwd table replaces the /etc/passwd file that is typically used by non-NIS+ systems for user identification and authentication. The Passwd table contains one row for each user; each row contains a number of fields. These fields include the username, an encrypted password, a user ID (UID), the primary GID, and the user's real name and home directory default login shell.

In addition, there are extra fields shown, including the number of days before which a password must be changed and/or how often a password must be changed. A sample row inserted into the Passwd table for the user pwatters would look like this:

```
pwatters:x:1024:20:Paul Watters:/home/pwatters:/bin/csh:10923:-1:-1:-1:-1::0
```

Protocols

The Protocols table lists all protocols that are supported on the network. For example, to support the Transmission Control Protocol (TCP) and User Datagram Protocol (UDP) transport layers, the IP must be supported, which is typically listed as protocol zero:

```
ip     0
```

RPC

The RPC table lists all of the available RPC services on the local network. The first program that must be supported is the rpcbind program, also known as the portmap program, which runs on port 100000:

```
rpcbind     100000     portmap
```

In addition, to support services like NFS, the rquotad and mountd services will need to be supported:

```
rquotad 100011  quotad
mountd 100005
```

For more information on NFS services, see Chapter 18.

Services

The Services table contains entries that define all of the services that are available on the NIS+ network under both UDP and TCP. For example, the sendmail service typically runs on TCP port 25; thus, the following entry would have to be inserted into the Services table to be supported in the network:

```
sendmail    25/tcp
```

Timezone

The Timezone table sets the appropriate time zone for hosts within the NIS+ domain. For example, the following entry sets the time zone for the host borabora to be Australia/NSW:

```
borabora Australia/NSW
```

However, the server tahiti might well be located in a different time zone, particularly if the NIS+ extends beyond the local area:

```
tahiti Australia/QLD
```

The Timezone entries affect all applications that need to process dates and times, such as mail transport agents and the cron process scheduling application.

USING NIS+

Having reviewed the configuration of NIS+ and the main tables that are used to define a NIS+ domain, we will now examine how to use NIS+ effectively to manage hosts and resources within a domain.

As we have seen, many different objects can be managed and identified within an NIS+ domain, and there are several commands that are used to access them. In this section, we will examine commands such as nisdefault, which displays the NIS+ settings for the local client system, as well as nischmod, which is used to set access rights on NIS+ objects. In addition, the nisls command, which can be used for object lookups and queries, is reviewed.

Finally, we will examine the niscat command, which displays the contents of table entries and can be used to examine NIS+ objects in detail.

Displaying Default Settings

The current settings for a local client system and the active user can be displayed by using the nisdefaults command. The nisdefaults command is commonly used when attempting to troubleshoot an error, such as a user's credentials not being correctly authenticated from the Passwd table.

As an example, let's examine the nisdefaults for the host comorin when executed by the user sukhdev:

```
comorin$ nisdefaults
Principal Name : sukhdev.develop.cassowary.net.
Domain Name    : develop.cassowary.net.
Host Name      : comorin.develop.cassowary.net.
Group Name     : develop
Access Rights  : ----rmcdr---r---
Time to live   : 11:00:00
Search Path    : develop.cassowary.net. cassowary.net.
```

The output of the nisdefaults command can be interpreted in the following way:

▼ The principal user is sukhdev, who belongs to the NIS+ domain develop.cassowary.net.

■ The primary domain name is develop.cassowary.net.

■ The hostname of the local system is comorin.develop.cassowary.net.

■ The user sukhdev's primary group is develop.

■ The client's access rights within the domain are stated.

■ The time-to-live setting is 11 hours.

▲ The search path starts with the current nonroot domain (develop.cassowary.net), followed by the root domain (cassowary.net).

The access rights stated for the user in this example are outlined in more detail in the next section.

Understanding Object Permissions

Every user has a set of access rights for accessing objects within the network. The notation for setting and accessing object permissions is very similar to that used for Solaris filesystems (see Chapter 6). The following permissions may be set on any object or may be defined as the default settings for a particular client:

▼ c Sets create permission

■ d Sets delete permission

■ m Sets modify permission

▲ r Sets read permission

The nischmod command is used to set permissions on objects within the domain. The following operands are used to specify access rights for specific classes of users:

▼ a All (all authenticated and unauthenticated users)

■ g Group

■ n Nobody (all unauthenticated users)

■ o Object owner

▲ w World (all authenticated users)

There are two operators that can be used to set and remove permissions.

▼ + Sets a permission

▲ – Removes a permission

Some examples of how permissions strings are constructed will clarify how these operators and operands are combined for use with the nichmod command. The following command removes all modify (m) and create (c) access rights on the password table for all unauthenticated (n) users:

```
moorea# nischmod n-cm passwd.org_dir
```

Even unauthenticated users require read (r) access to the password table for authentication, which can be granted with the following command:

```
moorea# nischmod n+r passwd.org_dir
```

To grant modify and create access rights to the current user (in this case root) and his/her primary group on the same table, we would use the following command:

```
moorea# nischmod og+cm passwd.org_dir
```

NIS+ permission strings are easy to remember but hard to combine into single commands where some permissions are granted while others are removed, unlike the octal codes used to specify absolute permissions on Solaris file systems; however, it is possible to combine permissions strings by using a comma to separate individual strings.

The following complex string is an example of how it is possible to set permissions within a single string, and it shows how challenging it is to interpret:

```
moorea# nischmod o=rmcd,g=rmc,w=rm,n=r hosts.org_dir
```

The previous command grants the following permissions to four different categories of users:

▼   **owner**   Read, modify, create, and delete
■   **group**   Read, modify, and create
■   **world**   Read and modify
▲   **nobody**   Read only

Listing Objects

The nisls command is used as a lookup and query command that can provide views on NIS+ directories and tables. For example, to view all of the NIS+ directories that have been populated within the local namespace, we can use the nisls command:

```
moorea# nisls
develop.cassowary.net.:
org_dir
groups_dir
```

There are two directory object types listed in the preceding code: the org_dir, which lists all of the tables that have been set up within the namespace, while the groups_dir stores details of all NIS+ groups.

We can view a list of tables by using the nisls command once again on the org_dir directory:

```
moorea# nisls org_dir
org_dir.sales.cassowary.net.:
auto_home
auto_master
bootparams
client_info
cred
ethers
group
hosts
mail_aliases
netgroup
netmasks
networks
passwd
protocols
rpc
sendmailvars
services
timezone
```

A large number of tables have, therefore, been populated for sales.cassowary.net.

The groups directory contains the admin group we created earlier, which lists all of the administrators, as well as several other groups that are based on distinct organizational units within the current domain:

```
moorea# nisls groups_dir
groups_dir.sales.cassowary.net.:
admin
adverts
legal
media
```

Displaying Objects

The niscat command is used to retrieve the contents of objects within the domain, primarily the data contained within NIS+ tables. For example, all hosts listed within the domain can be listed by using the following command:

```
moorea$ niscat -h hosts.org_dir
moorea.cassowary.net moorea 10.58.64.16
borabora.cassowary.net borabora 10.58.64.17
tahiti.cassowary.net tahiti 10.58.64.18
orana.cassowary.net orana 10.58.64.19
```

Alternatively, we can use the niscat command to examine the contents of the Password table:

```
moorea$ niscat passwd.org_dir
brad:*LK*:1001:1:brad:/staff/brad:/bin/tcsh:10910:-1:-1:-1:-1::0
karleen:*LK*:1002:1:karleen:/staff/karleen:/bin/bash:10920:-1:-1:-1:-1::0
maya:*LK*:1003:1:maya:/staff/maya:/bin/sh:10930:-1:-1:-1:-1::0
paul:*LK*:1004:1:paul:/staff/paul:/bin/csh:10940:-1:-1:-1:-1::0
```

We can examine which groups these users belong to by using the niscat command once again:

```
moorea$ niscat group.org_dir
root::0:root
staff::1:brad,karleen,maya,paul
bin::2:root,bin,daemon
sys:*:3:root,bin,sys,adm
adm::4:root,adm,daemon
uucp::5:root,uucp
mail::6:root
```

All of the hosts that form part of the local domain can be examined based on their Ethernet addresses, which are extracted from the ethers table, as shown in the following example:

```
moorea$ niscat ethers.org_dir
1:4a:16:2f:13:b2 moorea.cassowary.net.
1:02:1e:f4:61:2e borabora.cassowary.net.
f4:61:2e:1:4a:16 tahiti.cassowary.net.
2f:13:b2:1:02:1e orana.cassowary.net.
```

To get an idea of the services that are offered to these hosts, we can examine the services table:

```
moorea$ niscat services.org_dir
tcpmux tcpmux tcp 1
echo echo tcp 7
echo echo udp 7
discard discard tcp 9
discard sink tcp 9
discard null tcp 9
```

```
discard discard udp 9
discard sink udp 9
discard null udp 9
systat systat tcp 11
systat users tcp 11
daytime daytime tcp 13
daytime daytime udp 13
```

Every other table that is defined within the domain may be viewed by using the niscat command in this way.

SUMMARY

In this chapter, we have examined the hierarchical naming and network object management service known as NIS+. Administrators of Windows 2000 will find some similarities to AD, while Linux Administrators will find the newer features of NIS+, compared to standard NIS, of great benefit. NIS+ works best along with the DNS, which is used to map IP addresses to domain names; however, NIS+ domains can operate independent of DNS if desired.

CHAPTER 20

Printing

Managing print services is an important function of Solaris services. In addition to supporting both Berkeley Software Distribution (BSD) and System V–style print services, Solaris provides a wide variety of text-processing tools that can be used to render material suitable for printing. In this chapter, readers will learn to install and configure printing services and use Solaris word processing tools like the StarOffice word processor.

SUPPORTED PRINTERS

Solaris supports a wide variety of printers, and their details are stored in the terminfo database (/usr/share/lib/terminfo). Most plain text and PostScript printers are supported; however, some older, Scalable Processor Architecture (SPARC)–specific printing hardware, which relied on the proprietary NeWSPrint software, is no longer supported in Solaris 8. In order to correctly install a printer for Solaris, it is necessary to verify that a driver exists in the terminfo database, as this defines printer interface data.

The terminfo database is just a set of hierarchical directories that contain files that define communication settings for each printer type. Printers from different vendors are defined in files that sit in a subdirectory in which the name is defined by the first letter of the vendor's name; thus, the directory /usr/share/lib/terminfo contains the following entries:

```
bash-2.03# ls /usr/share/lib/terminfo
1   3   5   7   9   a   b   d   f   g   h   j   l   m   o   p   r   s   u   w   y
2   4   6   8   A   B   c   e   G   H   i   k   M   n   P   q   S   t   v   x   z
```

For example, if we wanted to see which Epson printers are supported under Solaris 8, we would change to the root directory of the terminfo database and then to the subdirectory in which Epson drivers are found (/usr/share/lib/terminfo/e). This directory contains drivers for the following printers:

```
bash-2.03# ls -l
total 80
-rw-r--r--   2 bin      bin          1424 Sep   1   1998 emots
-rw-r--r--   2 bin      bin          1505 Sep   1   1998 env230
-rw-r--r--   2 bin      bin          1505 Sep   1   1998 envision230
-rw-r--r--   1 bin      bin          1717 Sep   1   1998 ep2500+basic
-rw-r--r--   1 bin      bin          1221 Sep   1   1998 ep2500+color
-rw-r--r--   1 bin      bin          1093 Sep   1   1998 ep2500+high
-rw-r--r--   1 bin      bin          1040 Sep   1   1998 ep2500+low
-rw-r--r--   2 bin      bin           971 Sep   1   1998 ep40
-rw-r--r--   2 bin      bin           971 Sep   1   1998 ep4000
-rw-r--r--   2 bin      bin           971 Sep   1   1998 ep4080
-rw-r--r--   2 bin      bin           971 Sep   1   1998 ep48
```

```
-rw-r--r--   1 bin      bin        2179 Sep  1  1998 epson2500
-rw-r--r--   1 bin      bin        2200 Sep  1  1998 epson2500-80
-rw-r--r--   1 bin      bin        2237 Sep  1  1998 epson2500-hi
-rw-r--r--   1 bin      bin        2257 Sep  1  1998 epson2500-hi80
-rw-r--r--   2 bin      bin        1209 Sep  1  1998 ergo4000
-rw-r--r--   1 bin      bin        1095 Sep  1  1998 esprit
-rw-r--r--   1 bin      bin         929 Sep  1  1998 ethernet
-rw-r--r--   1 bin      bin         927 Sep  1  1998 ex3000
-rw-r--r--   2 bin      bin        1053 Sep  1  1998 exidy
-rw-r--r--   2 bin      bin        1053 Sep  1  1998 exidy2500
```

In the preceding code, we can see that the Epson 2500, for example, has its settings contained within the file ep2500+basic. However, several other versions of the printer driver are available, including ep2500+color, ep2500+high, and ep2500+low.

There are several important system configuration issues to keep in mind when planning to set up printing services on a Solaris system. First, you must ensure that there is plenty of disk space in the /var partition so that print jobs may be spooled in /var/spool. This is particularly important when spooling PostScript print jobs that may be several megabytes in size.

When several PostScript jobs are submitted concurrently, the system will require 10–20MB of disk space. In addition, you need to ensure that sufficient physical RAM is available: otherwise, spooling will be slowed down by the use of virtual RAM.

If you must use virtual RAM for spooling, ensure that enough virtual RAM is available (more can be added by using the swap command). Second, when spooling print jobs, it pays to invest in fast SCSI disks for the /var partition: 10,000 RPM disks are now available as standard in all new UltraSPARC systems, and these offer excellent print-spooling performance.

CONFIGURING PRINT SERVICES

The first place to start is the configuration of the printers entry in the /etc/nsswitch.conf file, where your local naming service is used to resolve printer names. For example, if you only use file-based naming resolution, then the printers entry in /etc/nsswitch.conf would look like this:

```
printers: files
```

Alternatively, if you use NIS, then the entry would look like this:

```
printers: files nis
```

Finally, if you use NIS+, then the entry would contain the following:

```
printers: nisplus files xfn
```

It is also possible that individual users will define printers in the file ~/.printers. In this case, the entry user can also be added to the /etc/nsswitch.conf printer configuration entry in the order in which the ~/.printers file should be consulted.

In addition, the environment variables LPDEST and PRINTER can be set to indicate which printer should be used as the default. For example, the following command will set the default printer for the current user to be the local hp1 printer:

```
bash-2.03$ PRINTER=hp1; export PRINTER
```

The LPDEST environment variable can be set in the same manner:

```
bash-2.03$ LPDEST=hp1; export LPDEST
```

Next, we need to examine entries within the /etc/printers.conf file, which determines, for file-based name resolution, which printers are available for use by users of the local system. The printers concerned may be connected locally, through the parallel port, or they could be mounted remotely, by using NFS or Samba. A typical /etc/printers.conf file looks like this:

```
bash-2.03$ cat /etc/printers.conf
hp1:\
        :bsdaddr=pserver,hp1,Solaris:\
        :description=HP Primary:
hp2:\
        :bsdaddr=pserver,hp2,Solaris:\
        :description=HP Secondary:
_default:\
        :use=hp1:
```

ADMINTOOL

The easiest way to add printers to a Solaris system is by using the admintool, as shown in Figure 20-1. Here, there are several fields that can be used to define a printer entry:

▼ A Printer Name, such as hp1, must be set. This should uniquely identify a printer with respect to the local host, so that there is no confusion about which printer a job should be sent to.

■ The name of the server on which the printer is attached, such as "admin" or "finance"

■ A Description of the printer, which could refer to its physical location, such as "Building C Level 2 Room 143"

■ A Printer Port, such as /dev/term/a, which identifies the parallel port

■ The Printer Type, such as a Hewlett-Packard (HP) Printer

■ The File Contents that will be accepted for printing, usually both PostScript and ASCII for supported printers

■ Fault Notification, or who should be notified in case of faults, such as sending an e-mail message to the superuser

■ Several Options settings, such as whether the current printer is the default printer and whether or not to always print a banner

▲ User Access List, or the list of users who can submit jobs to the printer queue. Many printers have no user restrictions on printing, so **all** can be entered in the user list.

The admintool can also be used to modify all current settings for installed printers.

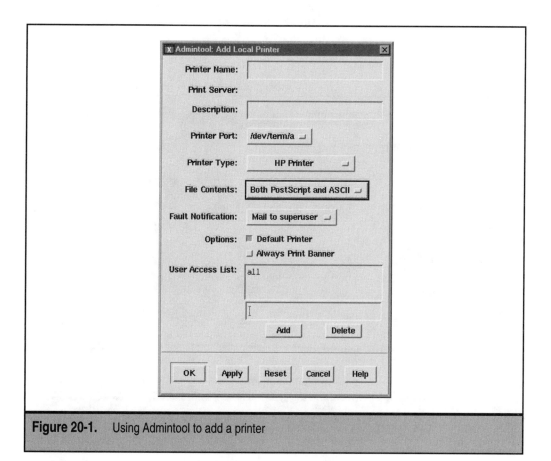

Figure 20-1. Using Admintool to add a printer

SOLARIS PRINT MANAGER

The Solaris Print Manager provides a more sophisticated view of current printer settings by displaying a list of all printers that are known to the local system, as well as their configuration settings. In addition, it is possible to set display options for the Print Manager, which makes it easy to customize views based on local site preferences.

In Figure 20-2, for example, we show the default view on a network that has three printers available: yasimov, henryov, and prova. The entry [Empty] appears next to the icon for each printer, because no jobs are currently being processed by any of the printers. The details of print jobs can be minimized for each printer by clicking the – symbol next to the appropriate icon.

The printer properties window can be raised for each printer defined on the system. For the printer yasimov, the current properties are shown in Figure 20.3. There are several key characteristics noted:

▼   The Icon Label, which is usually the name of the printer

■   The Icons set to be used for the printer

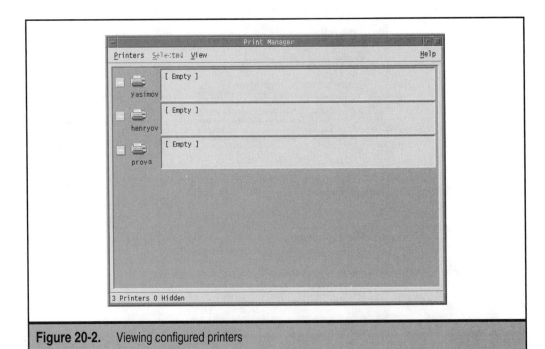

Figure 20-2.   Viewing configured printers

- A Description of the printer
- The Printer Queue name of the printer
- The Status of the printer queue
- The Device Name of the printer device
- ▲ The Status of the printer device

It is possible to further modify the display of printer sets (see Figure 20-4), by selecting the Set Options item from the View menu:

- ▼ Representation: representation of printers by using Large or Small Icons, Name Only, or full Details
- Jobs to Show: whether or not to show only the jobs of the current user (Only Mine) or all jobs on the printer (Everyone's)
- Status: whether to display various flags when errors are encountered
- ▲ Updates: how often to update the display of printers on the system

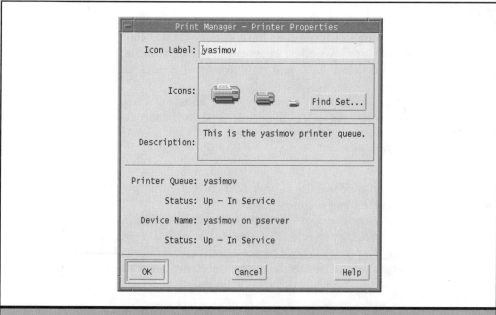

Figure 20-3. Viewing Printer Properties for individual printers

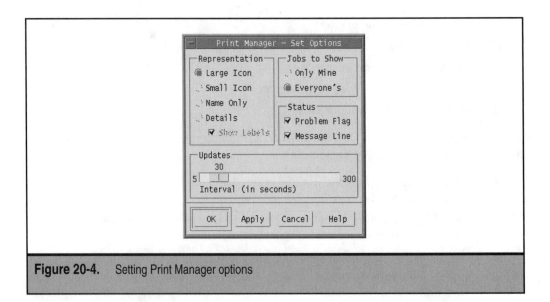

Figure 20-4.   Setting Print Manager options

COMMAND-LINE TOOLS

The line printer (lp) commands pre-date the admintool and Solaris Print Manager inter-faces and are most likely to be used by experienced Solaris administrators. They are typi-cally used to add and delete local and remote printer entries and a number of other administrative tasks.

Once a printer is configured, it's then very easy to submit jobs. Let's look at some ex-amples. To submit a PostScript job to the printer hp1 on the server admin, we would use the following command:

```
bash-2.03$ lp -d hp1 file.ps
```

Once the job has been spooled, the printer will correctly interpret the PostScript com-mands embedded in the file.

If your printer does not support PostScript, then you will be printing the embedded PostScript codes and not the rendered document. The -d flag is used to specify the name of the printer (hp1). If a printer is not specified, the job will be sent to the default printer (in this case, hp1 is the default printer, so it's not necessary to use the -d option). A similar command can be used to spool a text file to the same printer:

```
bash-2.03$ lp file.txt
```

Alternatively, the Portable Operating System Interface for Computer Environments (POSIX) style of printing can be used to submit jobs. This involves specifying both the print server name and the printer name, rather than just the printer name. This ensures that there is no conflict between printers with the same names that are attached to differ-ent hosts.

For example, the server admin could have a printer called "hp1," as could the server finance: if we just passed "-d hp1" on the command line with lp, it's not clear which printer would be selected for our job. The solution is to specify both the server and printer on the command line. Let's revisit our PostScript example, using a POSIX-compliant format:

```
bash-2.03$ lpr -P admin:hp1 file.ps
```

If you wanted to print to the hp1 server attached to the server finance, you could use the following command instead:

```
bash-2.03$ lpr -P finance:hp1 file.ps
```

You can check the status of a particular printer by using the lpstat command. To check the status of the printer hp1, you could use the following command:

```
bash-2.03$ lpstat -D -p hp1
printer hp1 is idle. enabled since Nov 06 16:13 1999. available.
```

WORD PROCESSING (STAROFFICE)

Solaris has earned a well-deserved reputation as an operating environment that supports precision text processing and layout in preparation for printing. Consider the TeX, LaTeX, and troff packages and the support for the PostScript language, which have been used for many years to prepare text for printing.

However, if you're a Windows administrator, then you probably don't want to learn how to use TeX just to do simple word processing for creating memos. You're probably much more comfortable with Microsoft Word, Word Perfect, and similar products that provide WYSIWYG layout of text, as opposed to a manual marking-up procedure undertaken using the vi editor.

Fortunately, Solaris now provides the ability to use a fully featured productivity package in the form of StarOffice 5.1, which is supplied with the Solaris 8 distribution. Because many administrative duties are based on the preparation of memos and the creation of simple databases for bug tracking and fault resolution, gaining access to StarOffice is an important boost to the breadth of tools that are supported on Solaris.

StarOffice was originally developed by Star Division, a German company that aimed to build a complete productivity suite that was cross-platform and based on Java. Thus, in order to support some features of StarOffice, you will need to install a Java Virtual Machine (JVM) if you didn't install one during the Solaris installation process.

Sun bought StarOffice, and now supplies it free of charge to users of Microsoft Windows, Linux, and Solaris. Given that Microsoft Word is not available for Linux or Solaris, StarOffice is now the productivity suite of choice in heterogeneous network environments.

Being able to run StarOffice on all of the major computing platforms, and releasing the source code to the entire package, has broadened the appeal of Solaris to administrators and developers who might otherwise have decided to use Linux or Microsoft Windows for reasons of improving cost efficiency (Linux is free) or support of productivity applications (the reason often given for using Microsoft Windows).

In the remainder of this chapter, we will cover the user configuration of a StarOffice installation, as well as review the major components of the package. Finally, we will walk through the use of the word processing component of the package, which features advanced template-driven document creation, powered by AutoPilot wizards, that will convince you to never use LaTeX again!

Introducing StarOffice

The StarOffice productivity suite resembles similar packages since it features several independent applications that have the ability to work together. For example, the word processing package can use database tables for mail merge, and it can form letters in the word processing package that can extract their data from the address book.

These features are designed to save time, but, more important, to ensure data integrity. The main applications within the StarOffice suite are

- ▼ **StarOffice Base**   Relational database system
- ■ **StarOffice Calc**   Spreadsheet with graphics
- ■ **StarOffice Discussion**   Threaded discussion board access through Usenet
- ■ **StarOffice Draw**   Graphics editing and development
- ■ **StarOffice Impress**   Presentation development and deployment tool
- ■ **StarOffice Mail**   E-mail client that supports the Post Office Protocol (POP) retrieval protocol
- ■ **StarOffice Math**   Mathematical equation solver
- ■ **StarOffice Schedule**   Diary and scheduling application for single users
- ■ **StarOffice Workplace**   Integrated desktop environment from which all applications are launched
- ▲ **StarOffice Writer**   Fully featured word processing application

Although StarOffice uses English by default, support is provided for several other European languages, including Dutch, French, German, Italian, Portuguese, Spanish, and Swedish. As mentioned above, it runs on Solaris (including SPARC and Intel platforms), Linux (many distributions), Microsoft Windows, and IBM OS/2.

Configuring StarOffice

One of the striking features of StarOffice is its complete integration with the Internet—it features an e-mail client, a Usenet client, and native development of Web pages. To support this functionality, you will first be asked to set up your Internet settings before launching the StarOffice application for the first time.

One of the first options you will need to set is the Internet proxy server for your local area network. A proxy is a shield between your system and the external Internet. Usually operating in conjunction with a firewall, a proxy server might also cache Internet content on the local hard drive to reduce network traffic.

One popular proxy server is the socks server, although other applications, such as the Apache Web server at http://www.apache.org, may also operate as proxy servers. If your network uses a proxy, then you will need to enter the hostname and port number into the fields shown in the following illustration before using the Internet features of StarOffice.

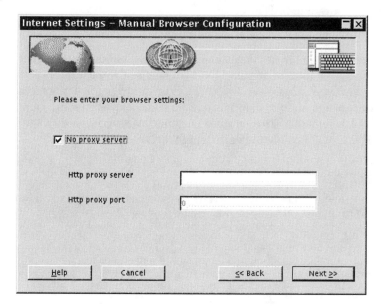

Next, you will need to personalize StarOffice for use with the current user.

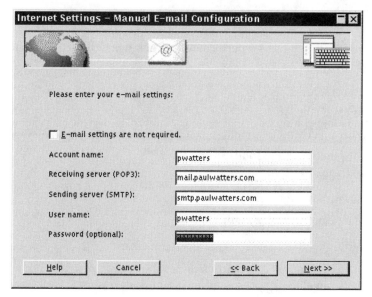

This involves entering the following information:

▼ E-mail address, which is either linked to a POP account or an address on the local system

■ User details for remote mail account

■ Name of POP e-mail server

■ Name of outgoing SMTP server

▲ Password

A connection profile for the local Usenet news server will then need to be inserted. The news server must use the Network News Transfer Protocol (NNTP), and your local firewall must not block access on the NNTP port in order for news messages to be retrieved. Usenet groups, such as comp.unix.solaris, can be very useful sources of information about Solaris and related operating systems. After completing the NNTP server configuration, you will be able to begin using StarOffice.

Word Processing

The main panel in StarOffice is designed to give users easy access to all of the major services provided by the productivity suite, including word processing.

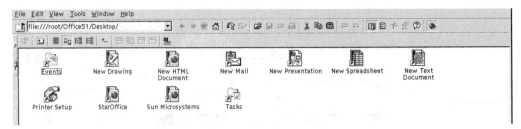

The following actions can be performed by clicking on the appropriate icon on the main panel:

▼ Insert new Events

■ Create New Drawing

■ Begin New HTML Document

■ E-mail someone (New Mail)

■ Develop New Presentation

■ Build New Spreadsheet

■ Install a printer (Printer Setup)

▲ Start new Tasks

As you can see from this list, StarOffice has the ability to perform a wide variety of tasks, including developing presentations, building sophisticated images by using state-of-the-art design tools, mailing messages to mailing lists extracted from a customer database, and performing modeling and simulation using the spreadsheet. These capabilities easily match any of the competitive productivity packages that are available for Microsoft Windows. In addition, because StarOffice is truly cross-platform, sharing data with other users is not affected by platform differences.

The StarOffice word processor supports all of the standard features that you would expect to find in a word processing package. These include the following:

▼ A selection of built-in paragraph styles, with up to ten different heading and subheading styles. These styles are managed by a floating style manager window, as shown in Figure 20-5.

■ Automated proofing tools, including a comprehensive dictionary and thesaurus, which both work in combination with an AutoFormat/AutoCorrect facility to reduce error correction times

■ Insert data directly from multiple database tables into your word processing document

▲ Support for complex data objects, such as applets, Object Linking and Embedding (OLE) objects, and mathematical formulas, which can be edited inline or through a customizable equation editor application

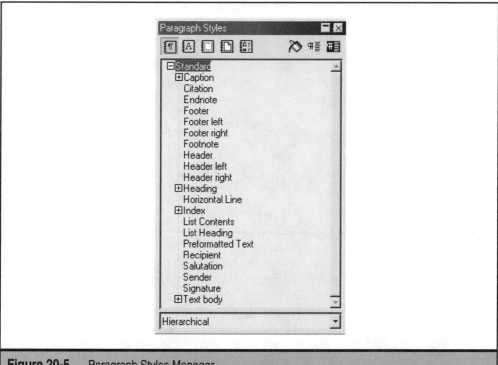

Figure 20-5.   Paragraph Styles Manager

The function that truly distinguishes StarOffice from other word processing packages is the inclusion of a wizard-based AutoPilot system for creating documents and Web pages. The AutoPilot system is able to generate a document skeleton from a large set of templates. The wizards walk the user through the process of planning and developing documents. The wizards take care of complex tasks like matching database tables to word processing fields and extracting spreadsheet data into a format suitable for display.

Form letters are easy to create using the wizards, and the letters can be combined with the Mail Merge program to generate template-based but individualized letters for clients, customers, suppliers, and others. This is particularly useful when generating accounts, invitations, press releases, and so on. The AutoPilot wizards give you the opportunity to preview all choices made about the document design at any stage, and previous decisions can easily be reversed by navigating through the menus.

The AutoPilot wizard for letter writing offers templates for personal and business letters, conforming to several predefined layout styles, including decorative, classic, or modern. A preview of the letter always appears in the left-hand side of the wizard screen. This makes is easy to determine whether or not your letter will appear as you wish after printing (true WYSIWYG capability).

A corporate or personal logo can also be inserted into the letter. This logo can be eithera graphic image or a text logo, where the text might contain your company's Web site address, contact details, or quote of the day. The location of the logo on your page may also be customized: whereas a business letter might position the logo at the top or bottom of a page, a personal logo could be placed anywhere on the page. The specification can be made in inches from any margin on the page. The displayed width and height of the logo can also be customized, as shown in the illustration.

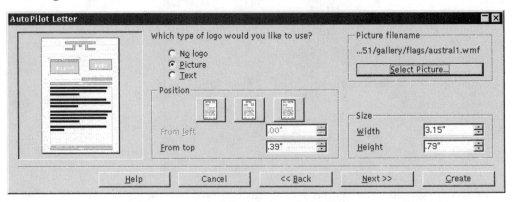

The AutoPilot will guide you through the process of specifying address elements on the page for both the sender and the recipient. Starting with the sender's address, you can specify its location on any part of the page, just like the logo. In addition, the sender's address does not need to be retyped at each stage: it can be extracted from the address book using a simple code, which the wizard will generate for you depending on your selection.

The recipient's address can also be entered directly or retrieved from the address book. The recipient's address can contain a company name, contact person, and street and city details, as well as phone and fax numbers. Again, it's completely your decision about what information will be printed on the letter. The interface from the wizard to the address book is shown in the illustration.

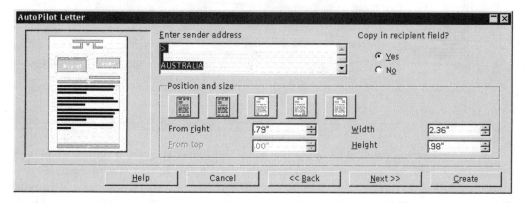

The next stage of the document creation process involves the insertion of standard display elements into the page. These can include elements such as today's date, page numbers, reference numbers, and carbon copy (CC:) lines. The final display elements that need to be inserted are the header and footer of the document. These may can contain several lines of text, such as a company address or slogan, and their location may be specified in inches from the margin of the page edges.

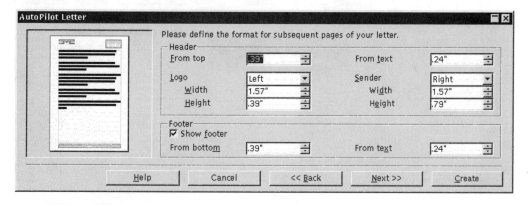

After completing your letter, you must determine several file properties, including the document title, and you must also decide whether or not to create a customized file template for generating future letters based on the layout developed for the current letter. A filename will be generated automatically for you, based on the document title; however, you are free to choose your own filename if you wish. A number of printing options can also be set from this page, including which trays your documents are printed from, and whether or not preprinted letterhead stationery is available. This process is shown in the illustration on the next page.

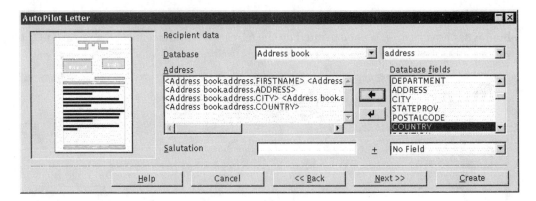

After developing your letter using the AutoPilot Letter Wizard, it will be displayed within the word processing work area, and you will be able to edit, delete, or create display elements at will. A completed letter is shown in Figure 20-6. For example, if you did not like the footer or header that you specified during document creation, you may now update these fields as you wish.

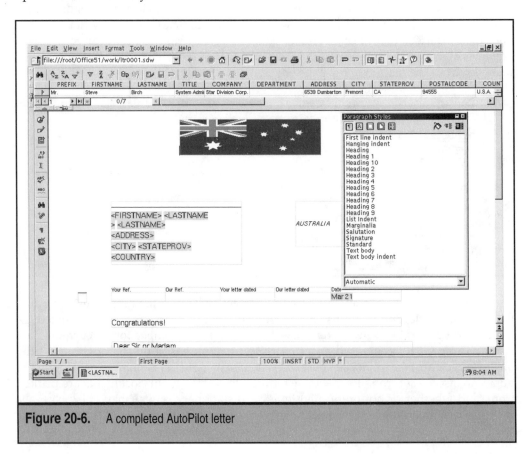

Figure 20-6. A completed AutoPilot letter

SUMMARY

In this chapter, we have examined how to install and configure printers with Solaris, as well as how to use the StarOffice word processing package for document preparation. As we have seen in this chapter, Solaris is not just a command-line operating environment; although command-line tools can be used for printing and text layout, there are also many advanced tools that make full use of the Common Desktop Environment (CDE).

Index

▼ H

hard drive, formatting, 35–36
Hardware Compatibility List (HCL), 44
hardware devices, 44–48. *See also* Scalable
   Processor Architecture (SPARC)
      device configuration assistant, 49–51
      displaying configuration details,
         10–12
      mice, 46
      monitors, 46
      motherboards, 44–45
      network adapters, 47
      PCMCIA devices, 48
      SCSI host adapters, 46–47
      selecting and installing, 47–48
      Symmetric Multi Processing
         (SMP), 46
      understanding device names
         (references), 31–33
      video cards, 45–46
      Zip/Jaz devices, 47
HCL (Hardware Compatibility List), 44
head command
      Bash, 90
      UNIX, 108
headers, e-mail, 193–194
Help facility, 78
Hewlett Packard (HP), Solaris
   compatibility, 14
hostname lookups. *See also* Domain Name
   Service (DNS)
      Apache, 259
      /etc/hosts and, 352
      name resolution and, 205–208
Hosts table, NIS+, 358
HOSTS.TXT. *See* /etc/hosts
HotJava, Web browsing, 71–72
htdocs directory, Apache, 257
HTML (Hypertext Markup Language), 252
HTTP. *See* Hypertext Transfer Protocol
   (HTTP)
httpd.conf, Apache
      global environment configuration,
         254–255
      main server configuration, 255–261

Hypertext Markup Language (HTML), 252
Hypertext Transfer Protocol (HTTP)
      Apache and, 252
      Apache response codes, 260–261
      HotJava as HTTP client, 71
      WebNFS as potential replacement
        for, 330

▼ I

IBM, Solaris compatibility, 14
icon editor, 76–77
Image Convertor program, 76
image viewer, 75–76
IMAP. *See* Internet Message Access
   Protocol (IMAP)
include, /etc/name.conf file, 214
in.dhcpd, 322
inetd (Internet daemon), 204–218
      configuration files, /etc/inetd.conf
        file, 222–223
      configuration files, /etc/services file,
        223–225
      configuration files, overview,
        220–222
      configuring, 204–209
      disabling IP ports, 289
      drawbacks of, 220
      FTP, 209–217
      FTP, anonymous FTP, 230–231
      FTP, commands, 228–229
      FTP, example session, 226–228
      FTP, telnet utility, 231–233
      other services, 234
init process, run levels and, 16
installation, hardware, 44–48
      mice, 46
      monitors, 46
      motherboards, 44–45
      network adapters, 47
      PCMCIA devices, 48
      SCSI host adapters, 46–47
      Symmetric Multi Processing
         (SMP), 46
      video cards, 45–46

O

P

R

S